STAR WARS
THE HIGH REPUBLIC

JEDI'S END

D1379640

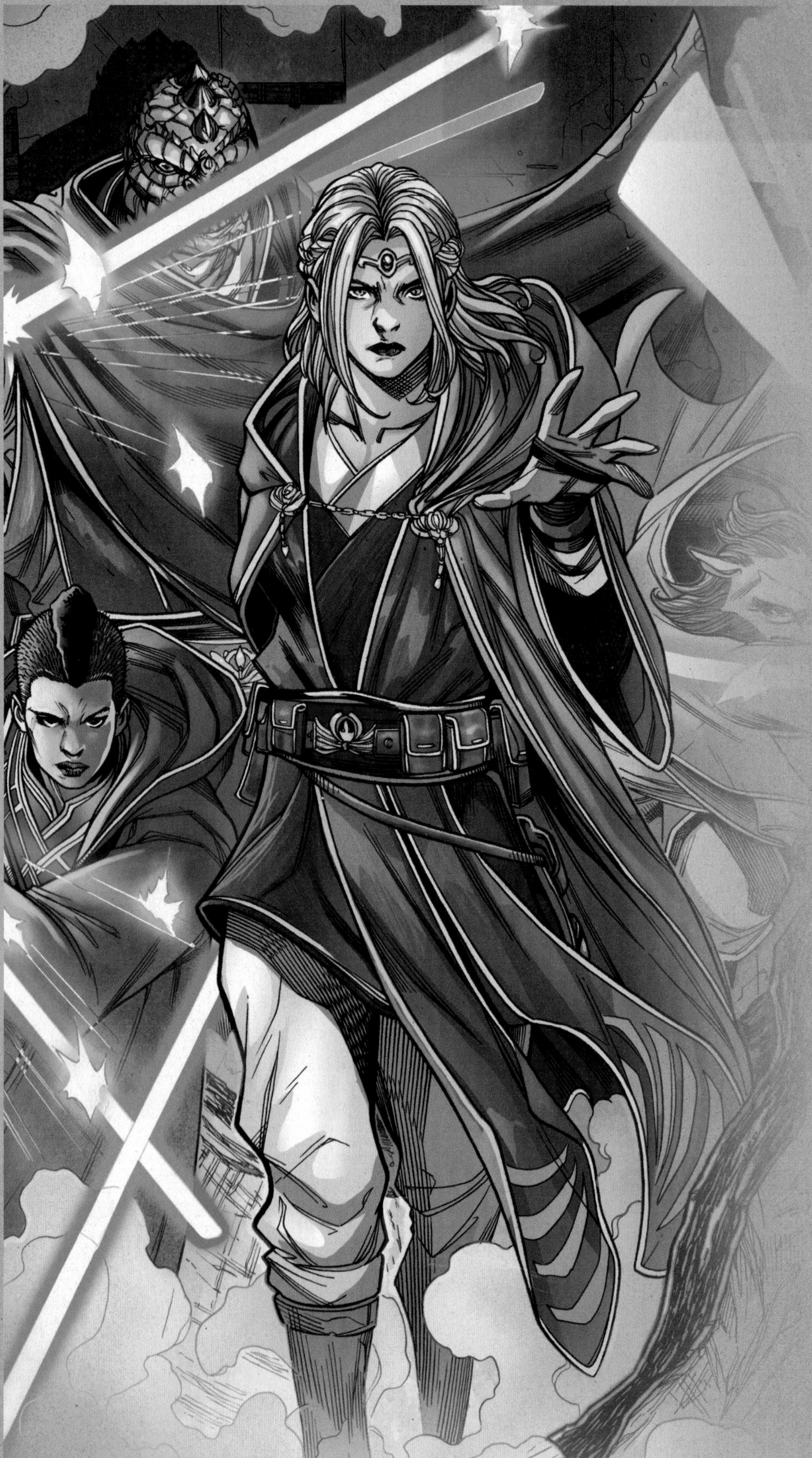

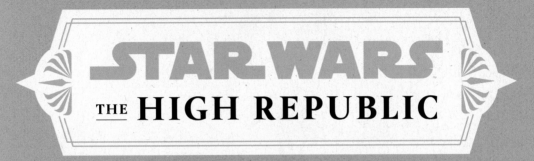

STAR WARS
THE HIGH REPUBLIC

JEDI'S END

HIGH REPUBLIC #11-15

Writer
CAVAN SCOTT

Pencilers
GEORGES JEANTY (#11-12) & **ARIO ANINDITO** (#13-15)

Inkers
KARL STORY (#11-12), **VICTOR OLAZABA** (#11, #15) & **MARK MORALES** (#11, #13-15)

Color Artists
CARLOS LOPEZ with **JESUS ABURTOV** (#10)

Letterers
VC's **TRAVIS LANHAM** (#11) & **ARIANA MAHER** (#12-15)

Cover Art
PHIL NOTO

Timeline Design
CARLOS LAO

Assistant Editor
DANNY KHAZEM

Editor
MARK PANICCIA

HIGH REPUBLIC: EYE OF THE STORM #1-2

Writer
CHARLES SOULE

Artist
GUILLERMO SANNA

Color Artists
JIM CAMPBELL (#1-2) & **ANTONIO FABELA** (#2)

Letterer
VC's **ARIANA MAHER**

Cover Art
RYAN BROWN

Editor
DANNY KHAZEM

Supervising Editor
MARK PANICCIA

Collection Editor **JENNIFER GRÜNWALD**
Assistant Editor **DANIEL KIRCHHOFFER**
Assistant Managing Editor **MAIA LOY**
Associate Manager, Talent Relations **LISA MONTALBANO**
VP Production & Special Projects **JEFF YOUNGQUIST**
Book Designer **ADAM DEL RE**
SVP Print, Sales & Marketing **DAVID GABRIEL**
Editor in Chief **C.B. CEBULSKI**

For Lucasfilm:

Senior Editor **ROBERT SIMPSON**
Creative Director **MICHAEL SIGLAIN**
Art Director **TROY ALDERS**
Lucasfilm Story Group **MATT MARTIN**
PABLO HIDALGO
EMILY SHKOUKANI
JASON D. STEIN
Creative Art Manager **PHIL SZOSTAK**

STAR WARS: THE HIGH REPUBLIC VOL. 3 — JEDI'S END. Contains material originally published in magazine form as STAR WARS: THE HIGH REPUBLIC (2021) #11-15 and STAR WARS: THE HIGH REPUBLIC — EYE OF THE STORM (2022) #1-2. First printing 2022. ISBN 978-1-302-93277-0. Published by MARVEL WORLDWIDE, INC., a subsidiary of MARVEL ENTERTAINMENT, LLC. OFFICE OF PUBLICATION: 1290 Avenue of the Americas, New York, NY 10104.

Manufactured between 2/18/2022 and 3/22/2022 by SOLISCO PRINTERS, SCOTT, QC, CANADA.

10 9 8 7 6 5 4 3 2 1

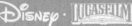

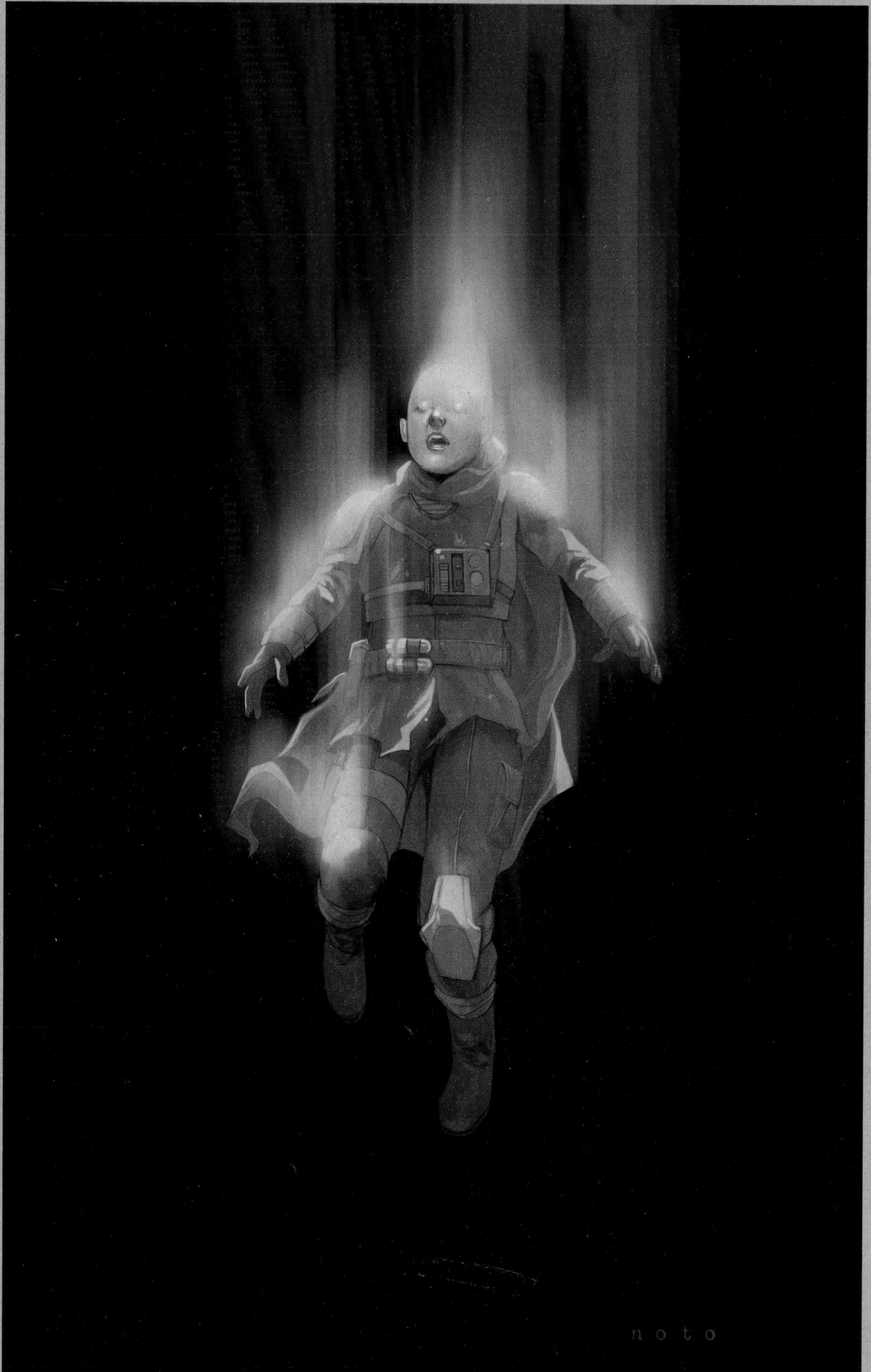
noto

11 | ONLY FEAR

**THE HIGH
REPUBLIC**

THE
PHANTOM
MENACE

ATTACK OF
THE CLONES

THE CLONE
WARS

REVENGE OF
THE SITH

**FALL OF
THE JEDI**

**REIGN OF
THE EMPIRE**

THE
BAD BATCH

SOLO:
A STAR WARS
STORY

REBELS

ROGUE ONE:
A STAR WARS
STORY

A NEW HOPE

THE EMPIRE
STRIKES BACK

RETURN OF
THE JEDI

**AGE OF
REBELLION**

**THE NEW
REPUBLIC**

THE
MANDALORIAN

RESISTANCE

THE FORCE
AWAKENS

THE LAST JEDI

THE RISE OF
SKYWALKER

**RISE OF THE
FIRST ORDER**

THE HIGH REPUBLIC
JEDI'S END
CHAPTER 1: ONLY FEAR

Sent undercover by Marshal Avar Kriss, the true identities of Jedi Keeve Trennis and Terec have been discovered by brutal Nihil leader, Lourna Dee.

Dee has unleashed a terrible horror that is attacking the young Jedi--Terec's bond-twin Ceret feeling the effects far away on board the Jedi cruiser, Ataraxia.

As Kriss and Master Sskeer--still battling his own demons--watch in horror, Ceret's body begins to calcify....

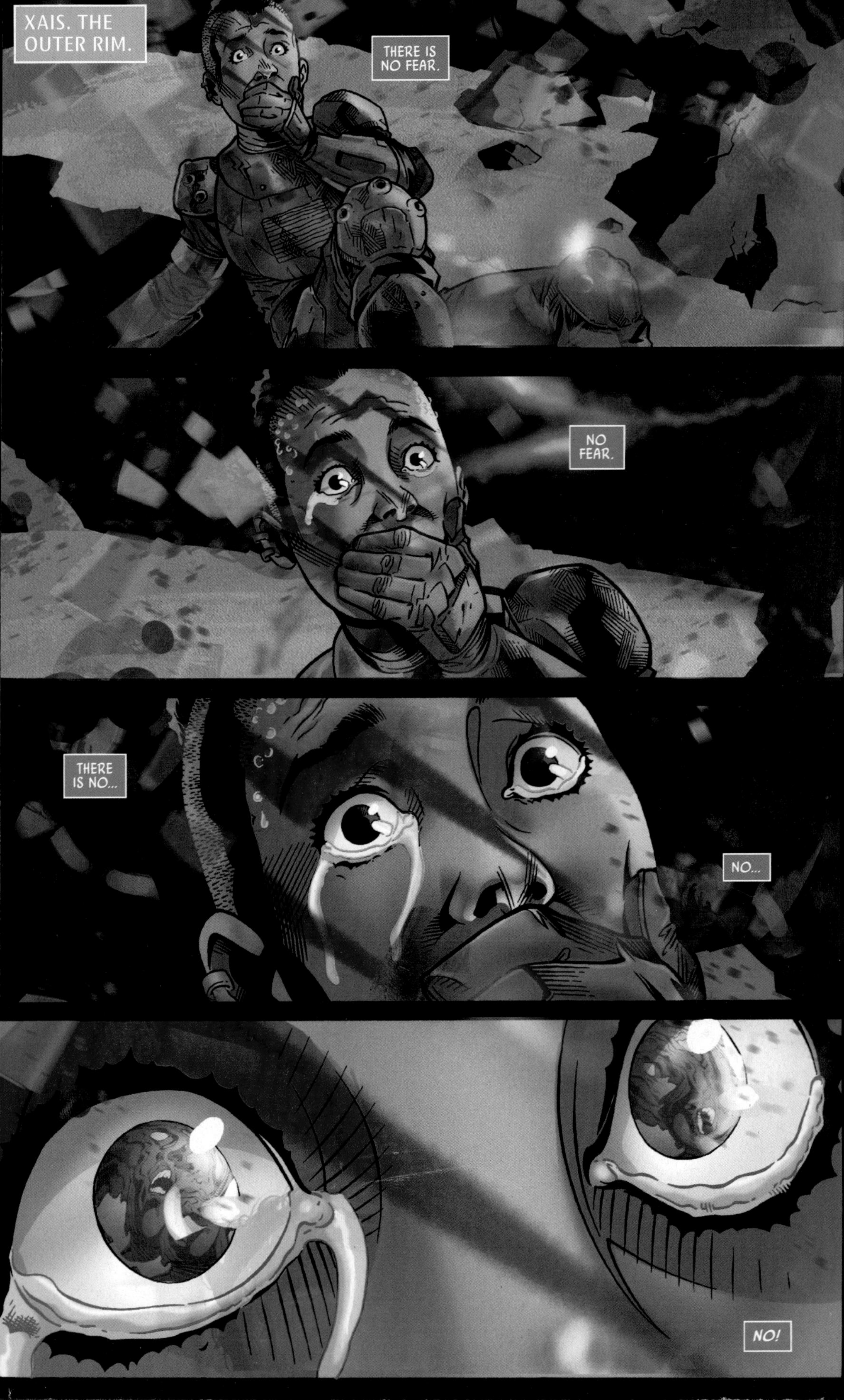
XAIS. THE OUTER RIM.
THERE IS NO FEAR.
NO FEAR.
THERE IS NO...
NO...
NO!

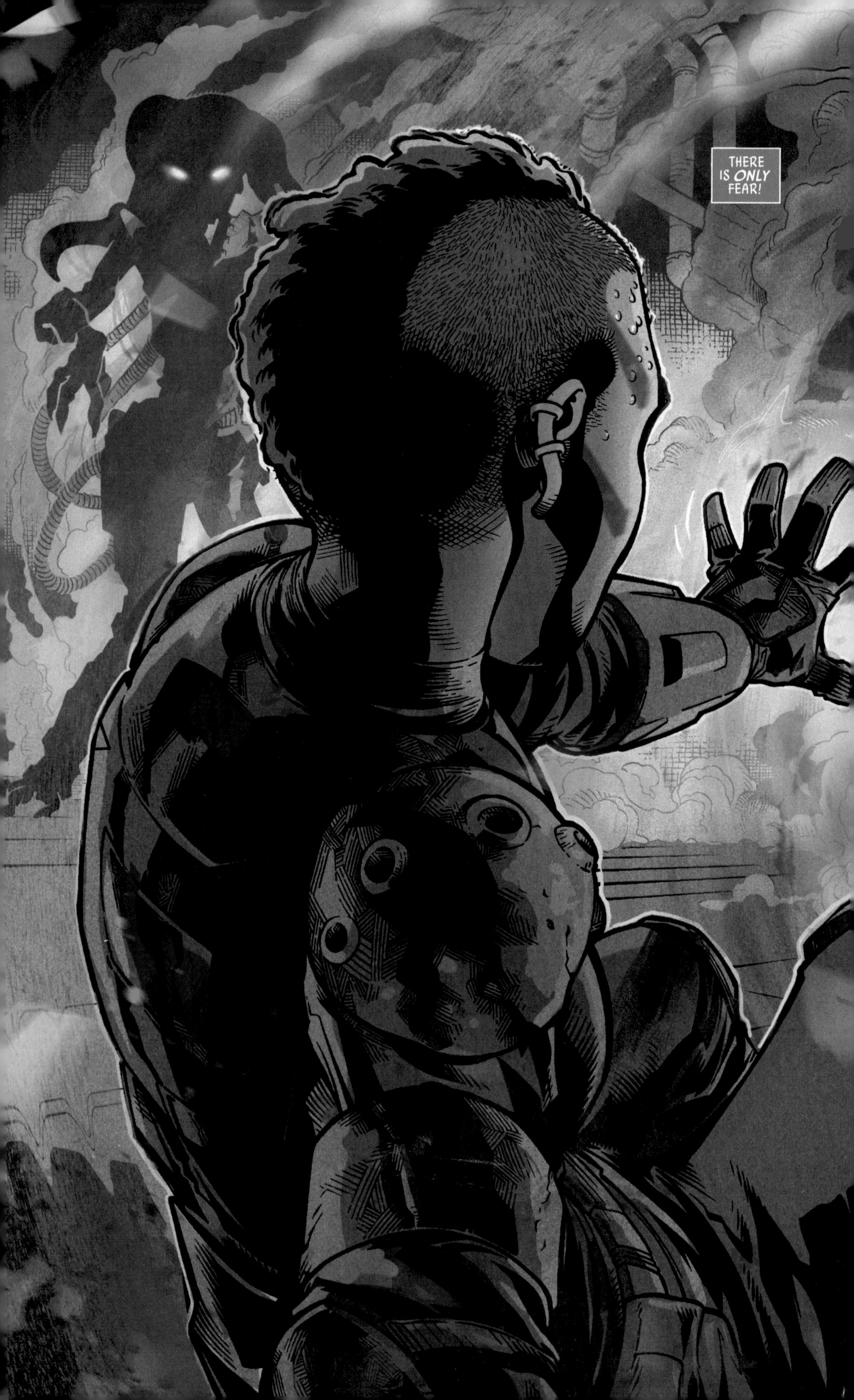
THERE IS ONLY FEAR!

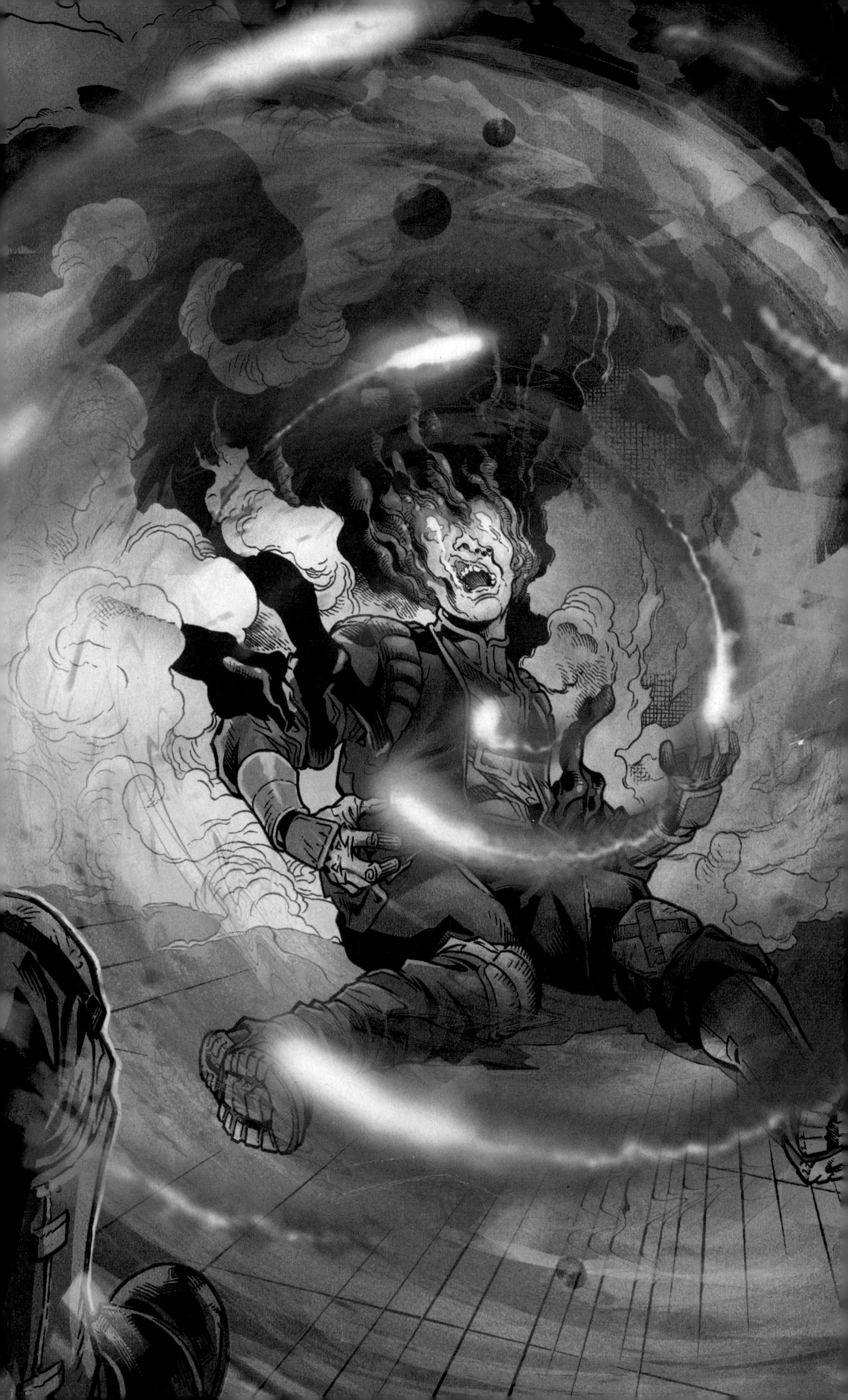

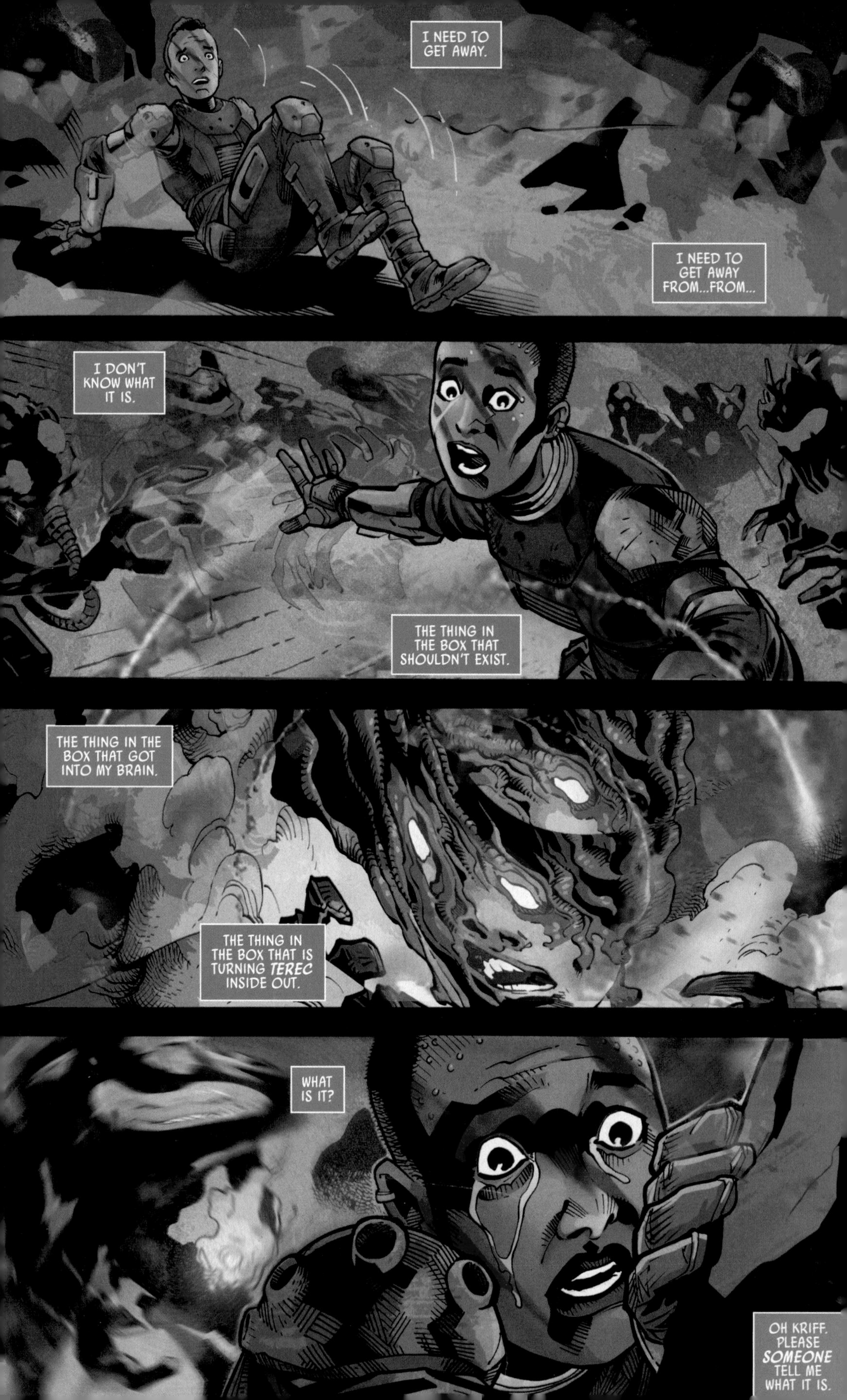
I NEED TO GET AWAY.
I NEED TO GET AWAY FROM...FROM...
I DON'T KNOW WHAT IT IS.
THE THING IN THE BOX THAT SHOULDN'T EXIST.
THE THING IN THE BOX THAT GOT INTO MY BRAIN.
THE THING IN THE BOX THAT IS TURNING *TEREC* INSIDE OUT.
WHAT IS IT?
OH KRIFF. PLEASE *SOMEONE* TELL ME WHAT IT IS.

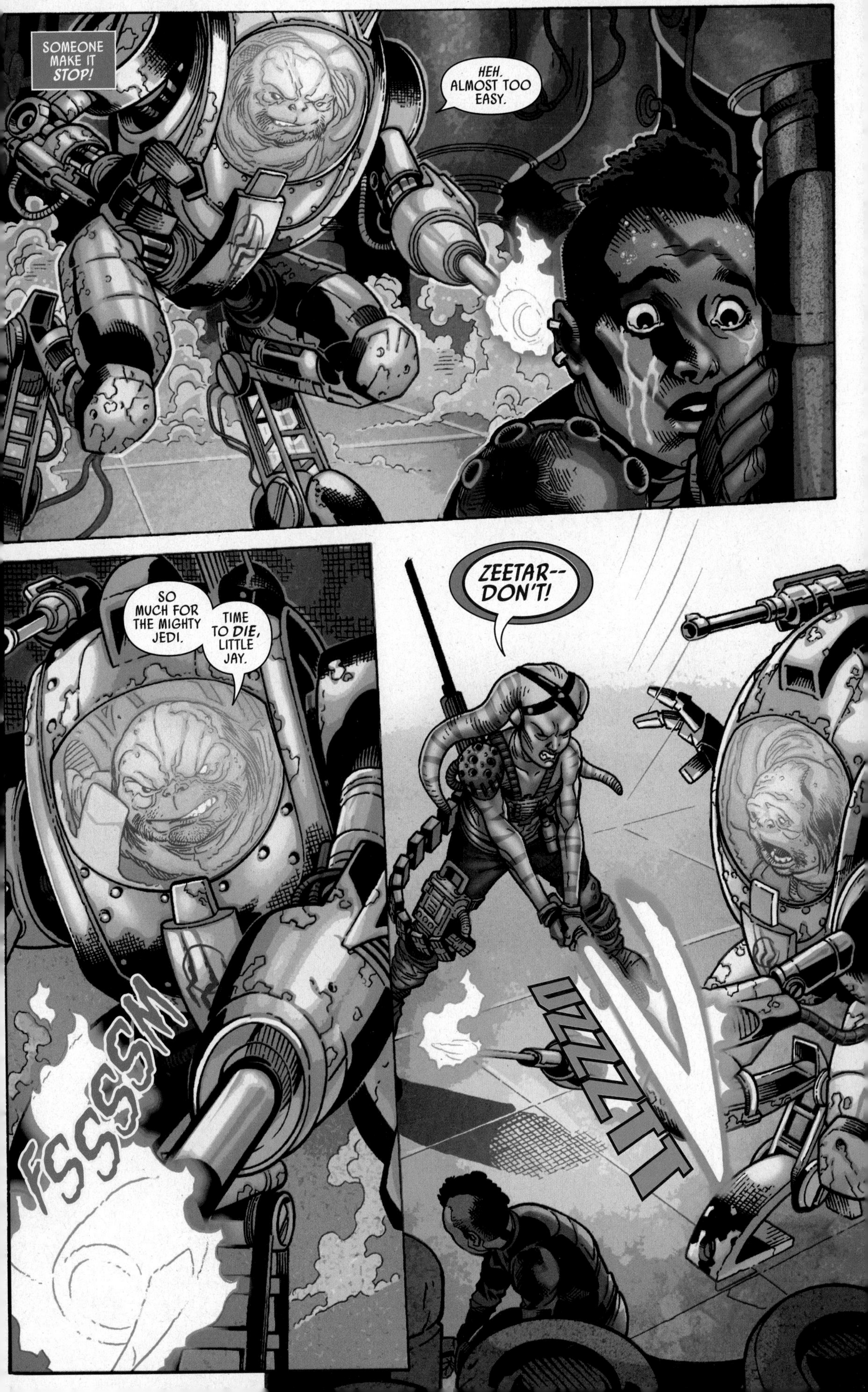
SOMEONE MAKE IT STOP!
HEH. ALMOST TOO EASY.
SO MUCH FOR THE MIGHTY JEDI.
TIME TO DIE, LITTLE JAY.
ZEETAR-- DON'T!
FSSSSM
VZZZZT

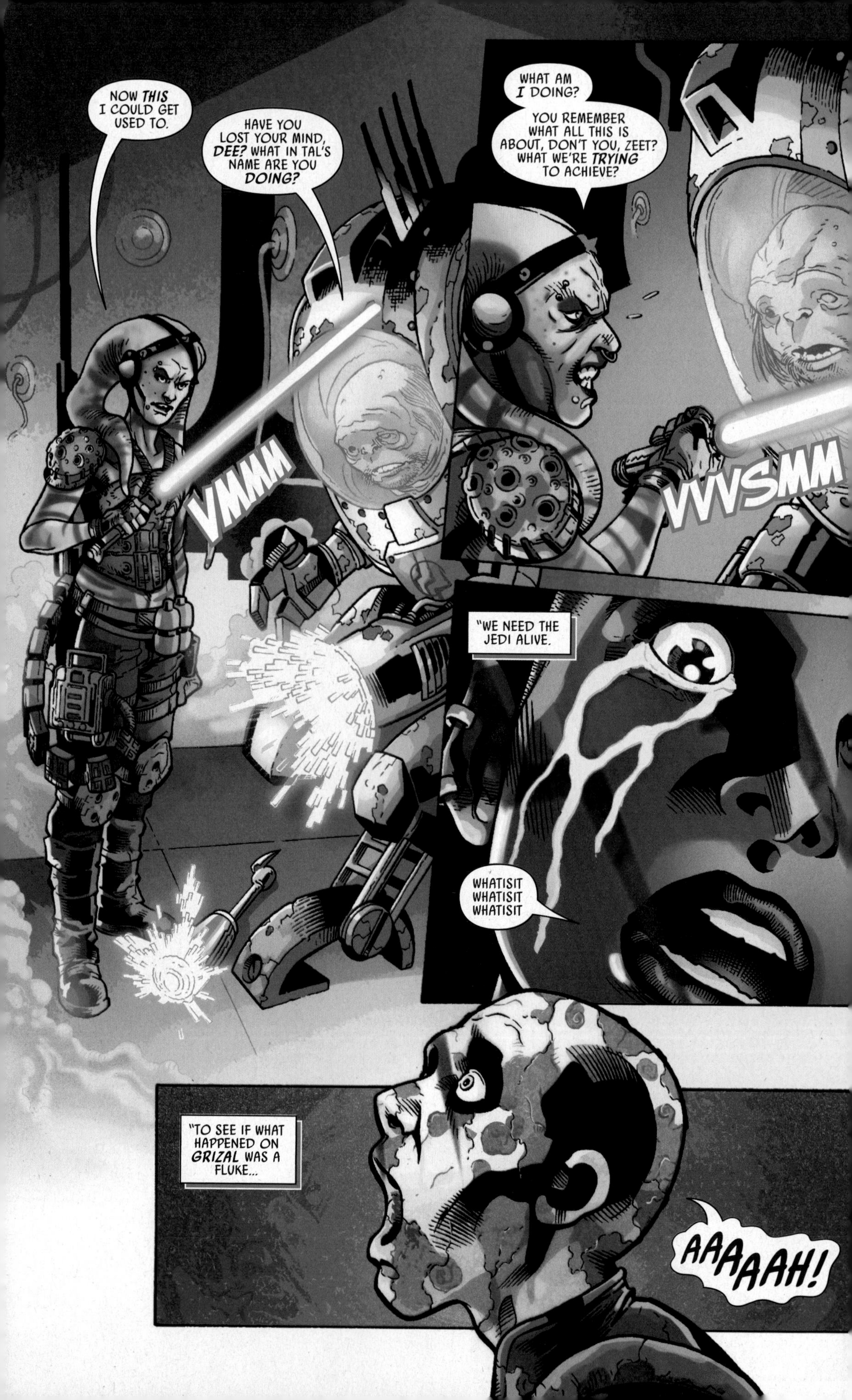
NOW THIS I COULD GET USED TO.
HAVE YOU LOST YOUR MIND, DEE? WHAT IN TAL'S NAME ARE YOU DOING?
WHAT AM I DOING?
YOU REMEMBER WHAT ALL THIS IS ABOUT, DON'T YOU, ZEET? WHAT WE'RE TRYING TO ACHIEVE?
VMMM
VVVSMM
"WE NEED THE JEDI ALIVE.
WHATISIT WHATISIT WHATISIT
"TO SEE IF WHAT HAPPENED ON GRIZAL WAS A FLUKE...
AAAAAH!

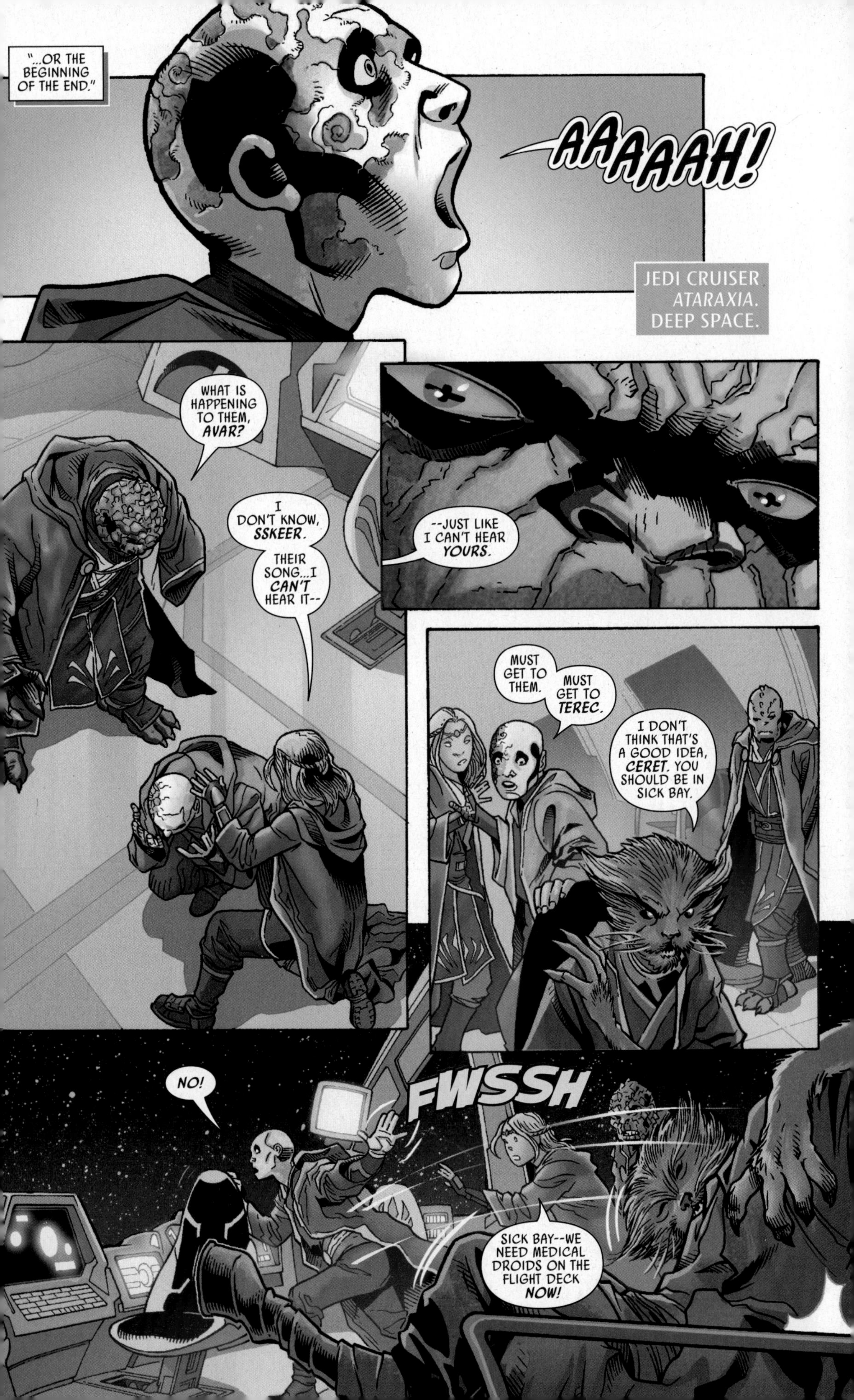
"...OR THE BEGINNING OF THE END."
AAAAAH!
JEDI CRUISER ATARAXIA. DEEP SPACE.
WHAT IS HAPPENING TO THEM, AVAR?
I DON'T KNOW, SSKEER.
THEIR SONG...I CAN'T HEAR IT--
--JUST LIKE I CAN'T HEAR YOURS.
MUST GET TO THEM.
MUST GET TO TEREC.
I DON'T THINK THAT'S A GOOD IDEA, CERET. YOU SHOULD BE IN SICK BAY.
NO!
FWSSH
SICK BAY--WE NEED MEDICAL DROIDS ON THE FLIGHT DECK NOW!

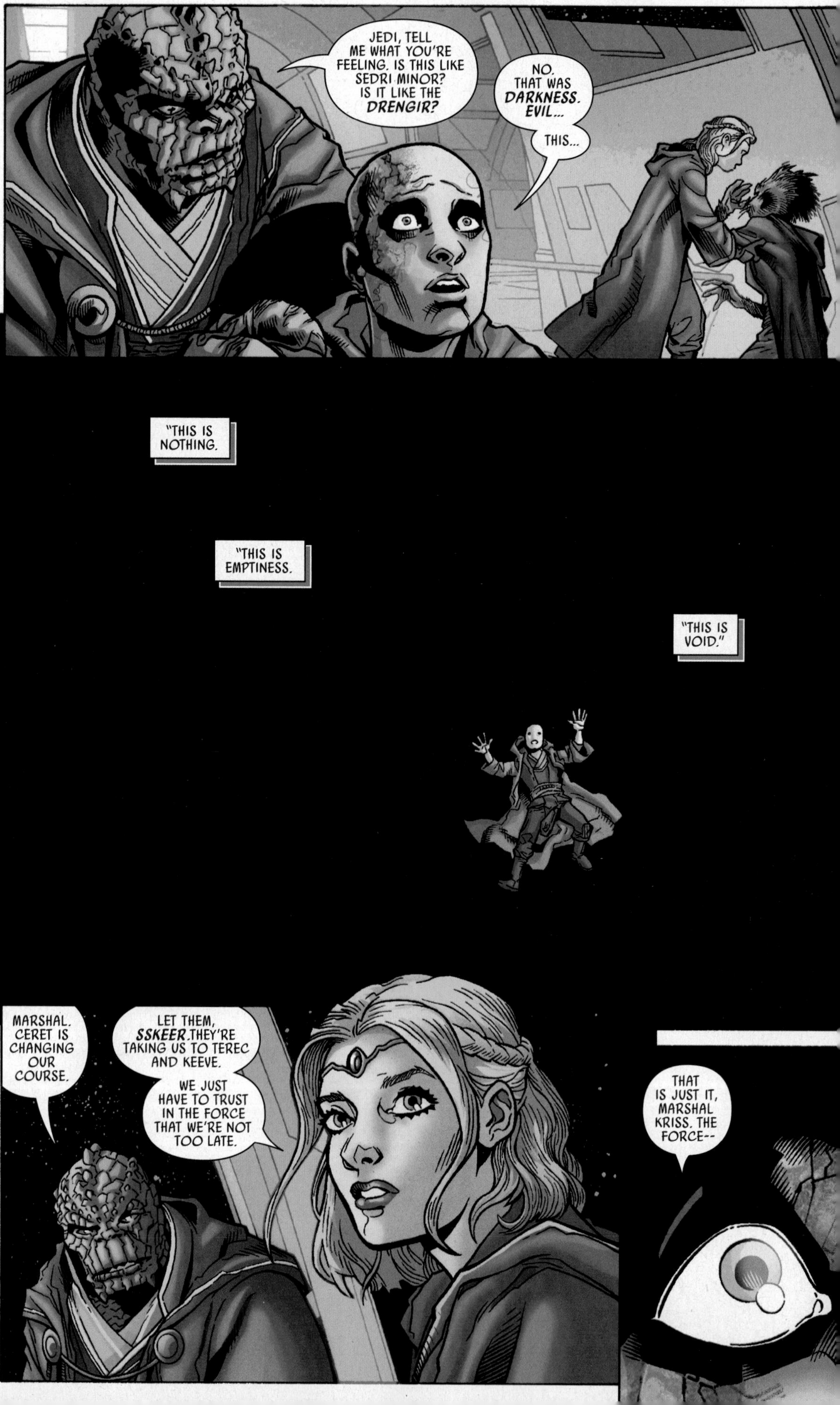
JEDI, TELL ME WHAT YOU'RE FEELING. IS THIS LIKE SEDRI MINOR? IS IT LIKE THE *DRENGIR?*
NO. THAT WAS *DARKNESS. EVIL...*
THIS...
"THIS IS NOTHING.
"THIS IS EMPTINESS.
"THIS IS VOID."
MARSHAL. CERET IS CHANGING OUR COURSE.
LET THEM, ***SSKEER.*** THEY'RE TAKING US TO TEREC AND KEEVE.
WE JUST HAVE TO TRUST IN THE FORCE THAT WE'RE NOT TOO LATE.
THAT IS JUST IT, MARSHAL KRISS. THE FORCE--

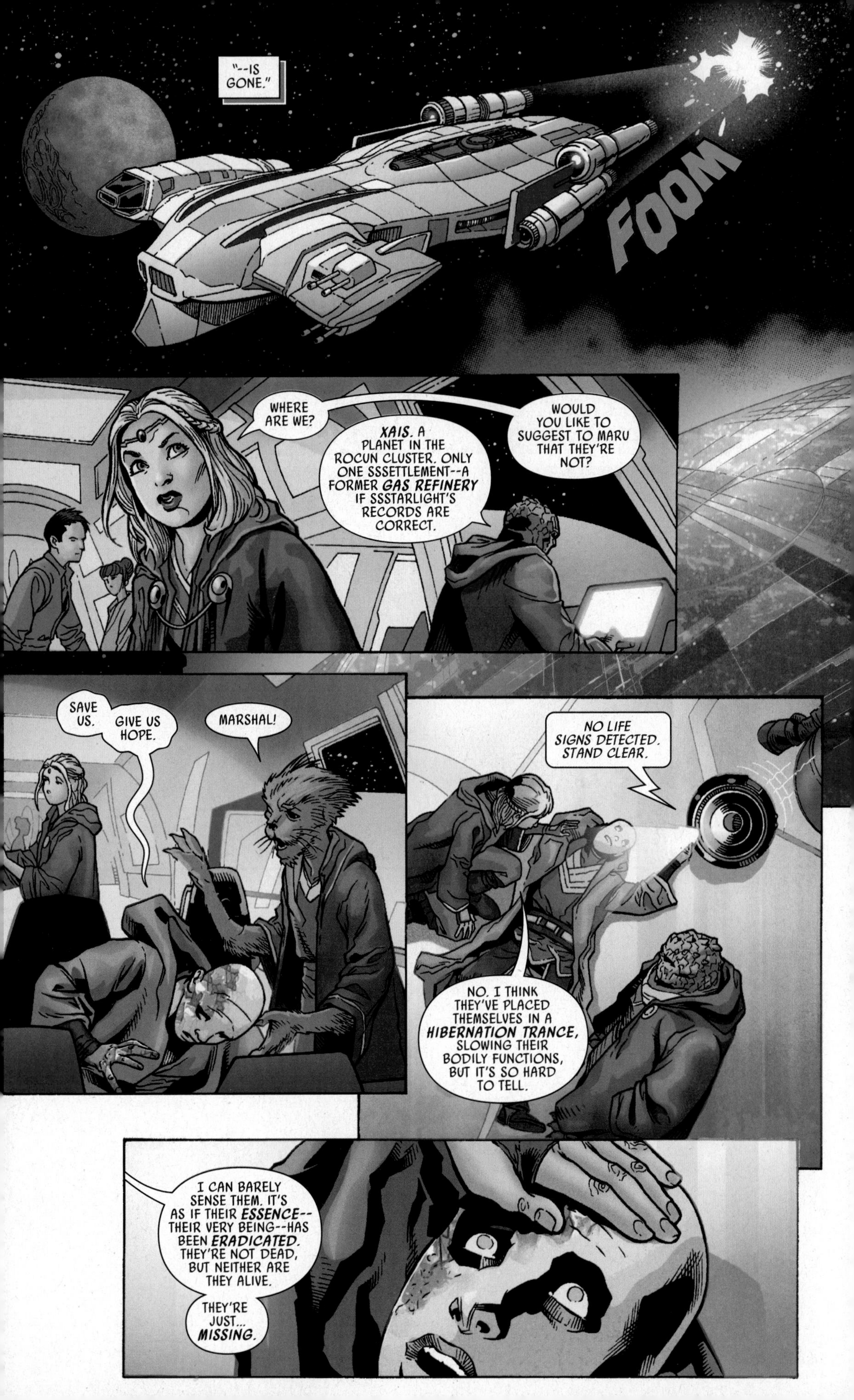
"--IS GONE."
FOOM
WHERE ARE WE?
XAIS. A PLANET IN THE ROCUN CLUSTER. ONLY ONE SSSETTLEMENT--A FORMER GAS REFINERY IF SSSTARLIGHT'S RECORDS ARE CORRECT.
WOULD YOU LIKE TO SUGGEST TO MARU THAT THEY'RE NOT?
SAVE US.
GIVE US HOPE.
MARSHAL!
NO LIFE SIGNS DETECTED. STAND CLEAR.
NO. I THINK THEY'VE PLACED THEMSELVES IN A HIBERNATION TRANCE, SLOWING THEIR BODILY FUNCTIONS, BUT IT'S SO HARD TO TELL.
I CAN BARELY SENSE THEM. IT'S AS IF THEIR ESSENCE--THEIR VERY BEING--HAS BEEN ERADICATED. THEY'RE NOT DEAD, BUT NEITHER ARE THEY ALIVE.
THEY'RE JUST... MISSING.

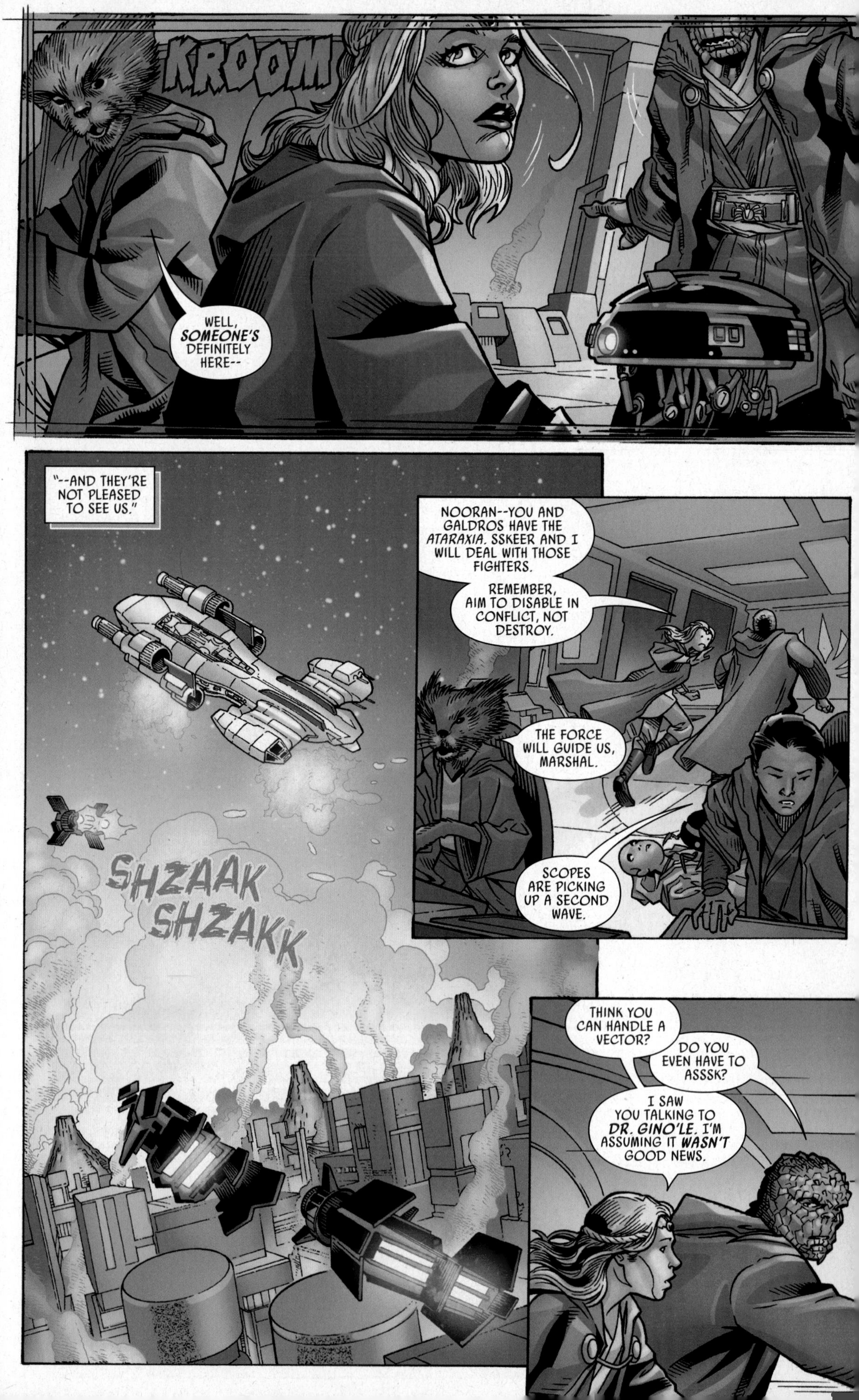

KROOM
WELL, SOMEONE'S DEFINITELY HERE--
"--AND THEY'RE NOT PLEASED TO SEE US."
SHZAAK
SHZAKK
NOORAN--YOU AND GALDROS HAVE THE ATARAXIA. SSKEER AND I WILL DEAL WITH THOSE FIGHTERS.
REMEMBER, AIM TO DISABLE IN CONFLICT, NOT DESTROY.
THE FORCE WILL GUIDE US, MARSHAL.
SCOPES ARE PICKING UP A SECOND WAVE.
THINK YOU CAN HANDLE A VECTOR?
DO YOU EVEN HAVE TO ASSSK?
I SAW YOU TALKING TO DR. GINO'LE. I'M ASSUMING IT WASN'T GOOD NEWS.

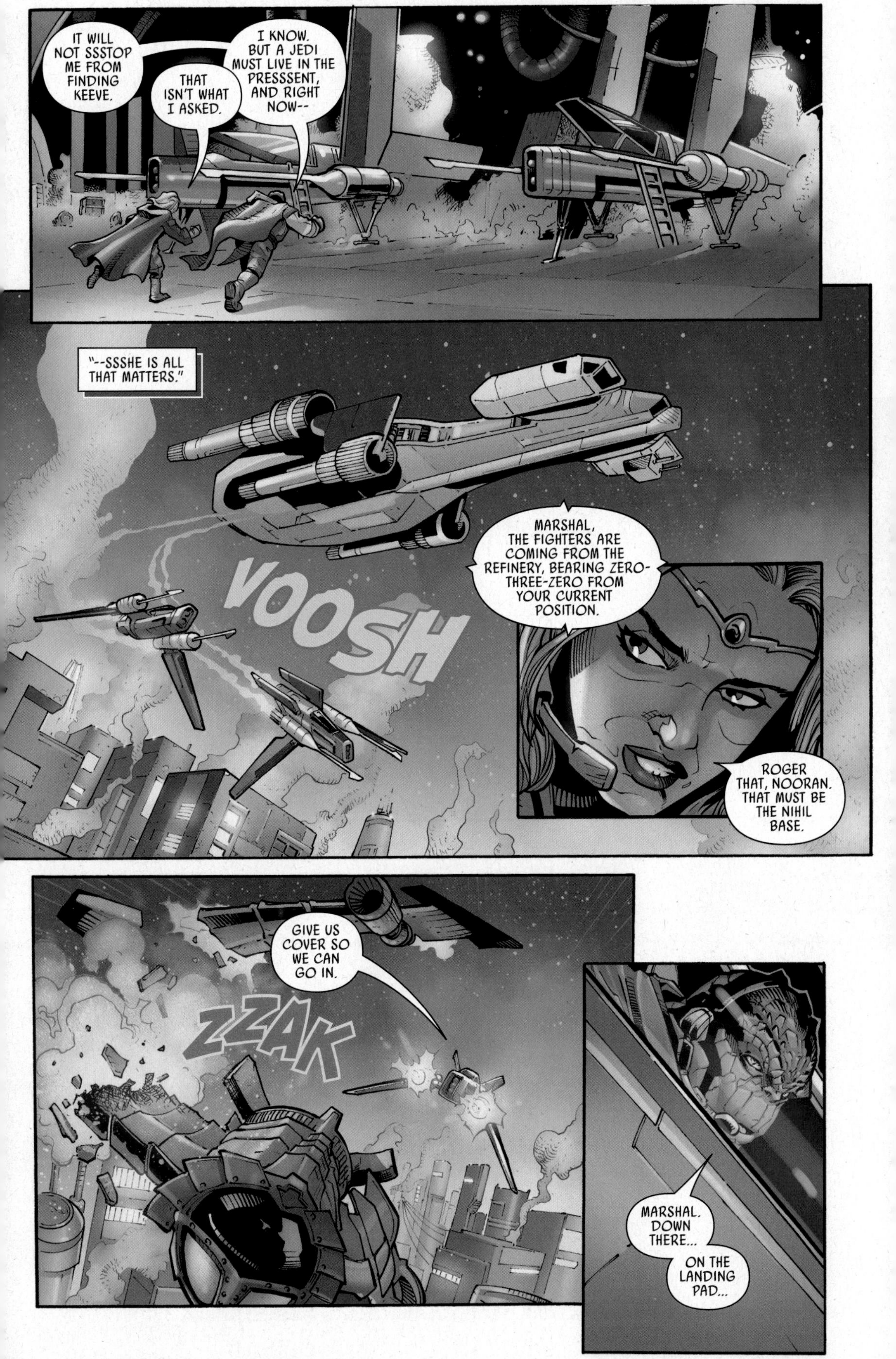
IT WILL NOT SSSTOP ME FROM FINDING KEEVE.
THAT ISN'T WHAT I ASKED.
I KNOW. BUT A JEDI MUST LIVE IN THE PRESSSENT, AND RIGHT NOW--
"--SSSHE IS ALL THAT MATTERS."
VOOSH
MARSHAL, THE FIGHTERS ARE COMING FROM THE REFINERY, BEARING ZERO-THREE-ZERO FROM YOUR CURRENT POSITION.
ROGER THAT, NOORAN. THAT MUST BE THE NIHIL BASE.
GIVE US COVER SO WE CAN GO IN.
ZZAK
MARSHAL. DOWN THERE...
ON THE LANDING PAD...

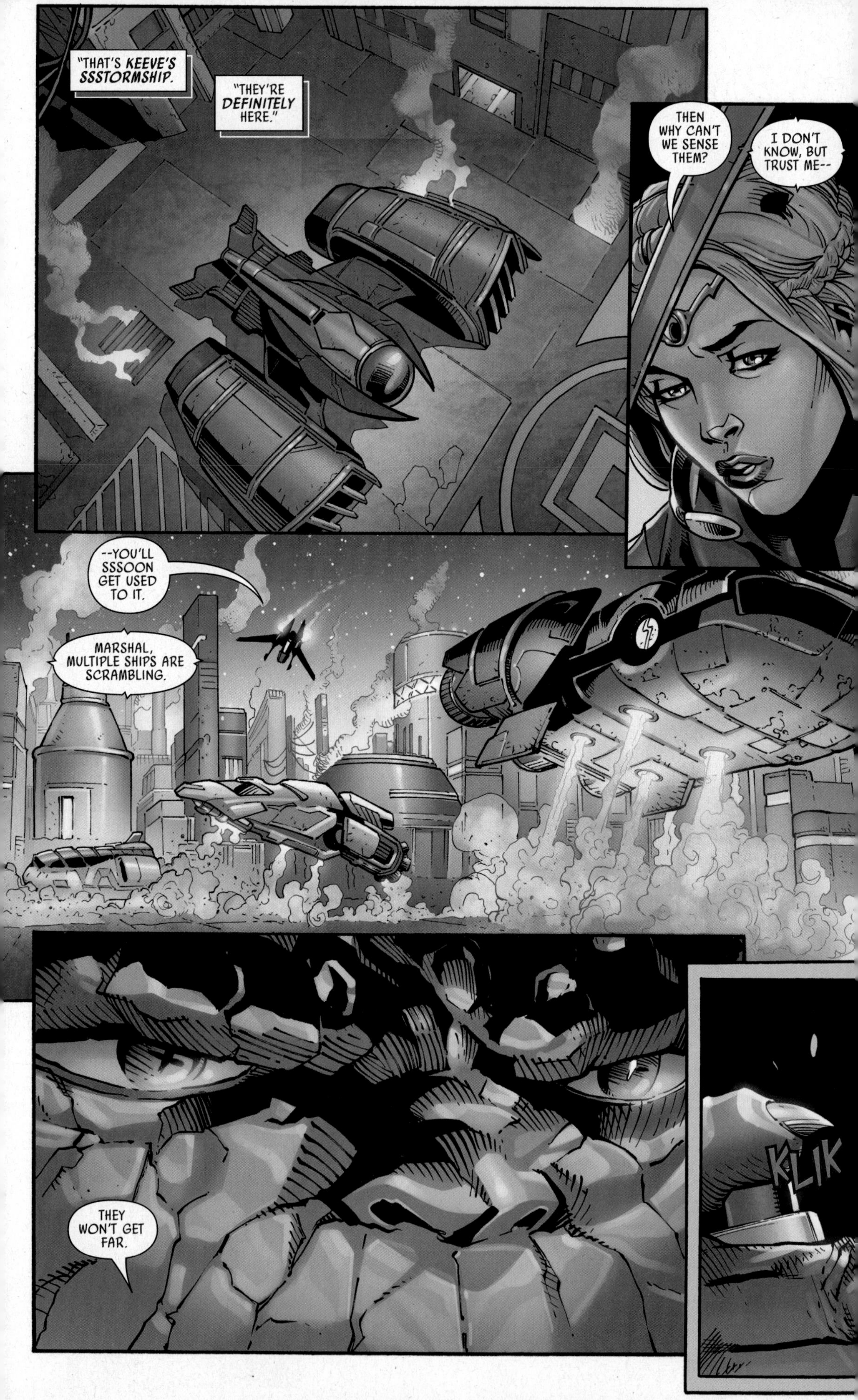
"THAT'S KEEVE'S SSSTORMSHIP.
"THEY'RE DEFINITELY HERE."
THEN WHY CAN'T WE SENSE THEM?
I DON'T KNOW, BUT TRUST ME--
--YOU'LL SSSOON GET USED TO IT.
MARSHAL, MULTIPLE SHIPS ARE SCRAMBLING.
THEY WON'T GET FAR.
KLIK

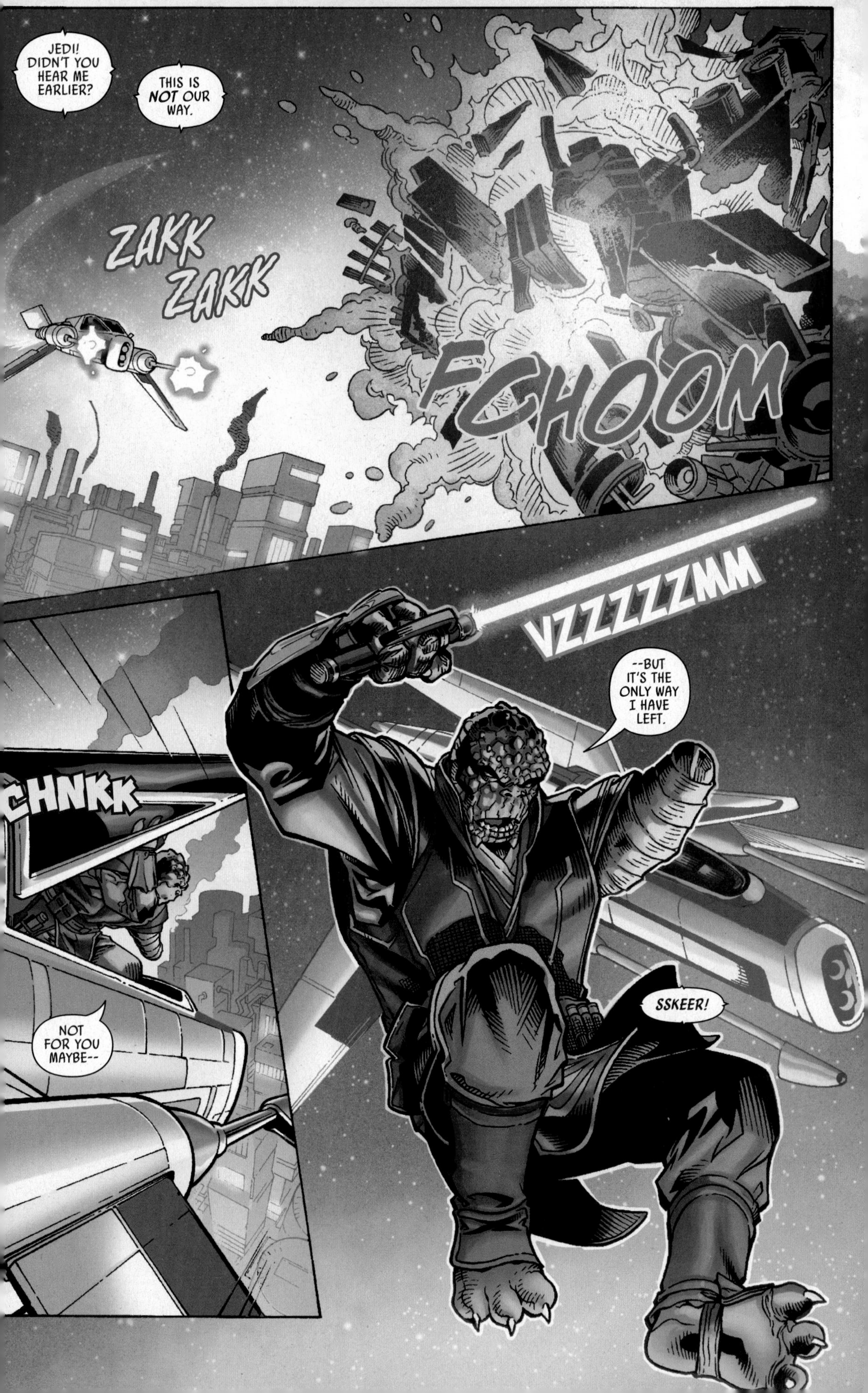
JEDI! DIDN'T YOU HEAR ME EARLIER?
THIS IS NOT OUR WAY.
ZAKK ZAKK
FCHOOM
VZZZZZMM
CHNKK
NOT FOR YOU MAYBE--
--BUT IT'S THE ONLY WAY I HAVE LEFT.
SSKEER!

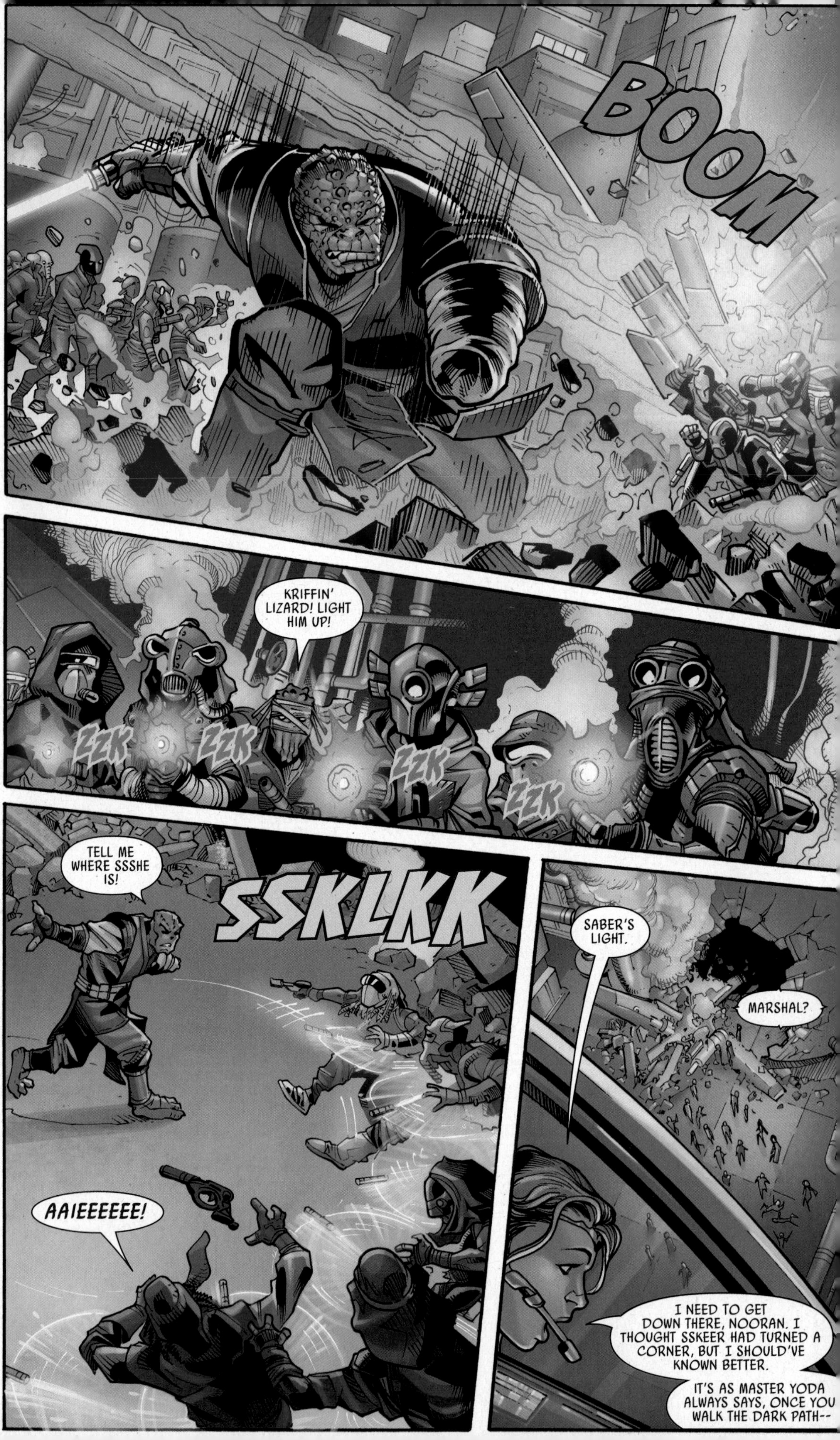
BOOM
KRIFFIN' LIZARD! LIGHT HIM UP!
ZZK
ZZK
ZZK
ZZK
TELL ME WHERE SSSHE IS!
SSKLKK
AAIEEEEEE!
SABER'S LIGHT.
MARSHAL?
I NEED TO GET DOWN THERE, NOORAN. I THOUGHT SSKEER HAD TURNED A CORNER, BUT I SHOULD'VE KNOWN BETTER.
IT'S AS MASTER YODA ALWAYS SAYS, ONCE YOU WALK THE DARK PATH--

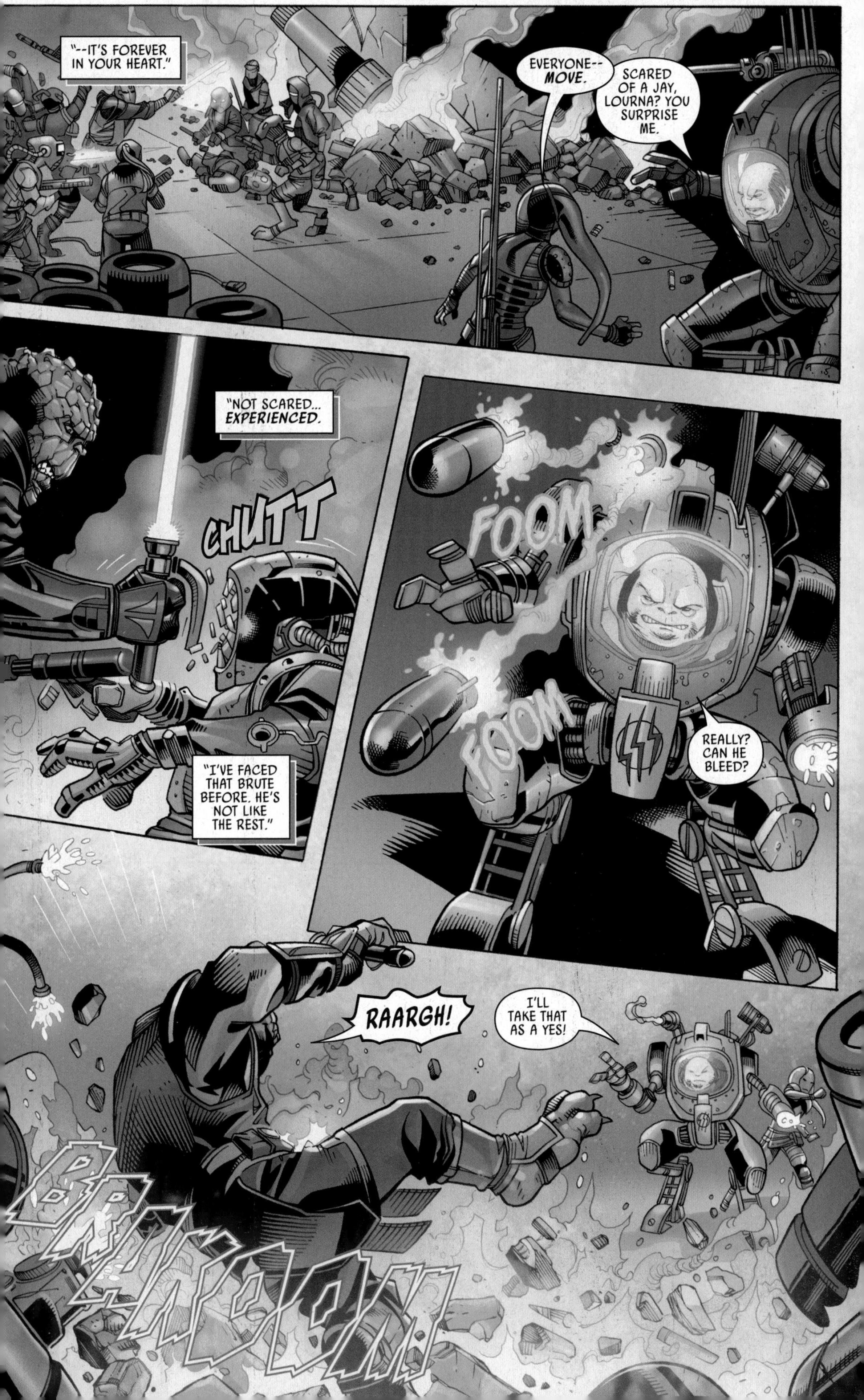
"--IT'S FOREVER IN YOUR HEART."
EVERYONE-- MOVE.
SCARED OF A JAY, LOURNA? YOU SURPRISE ME.
"NOT SCARED... EXPERIENCED.
CHUTT
"I'VE FACED THAT BRUTE BEFORE. HE'S NOT LIKE THE REST."
FOOM
FOOM
REALLY? CAN HE BLEED?
RAARGH!
I'LL TAKE THAT AS A YES!

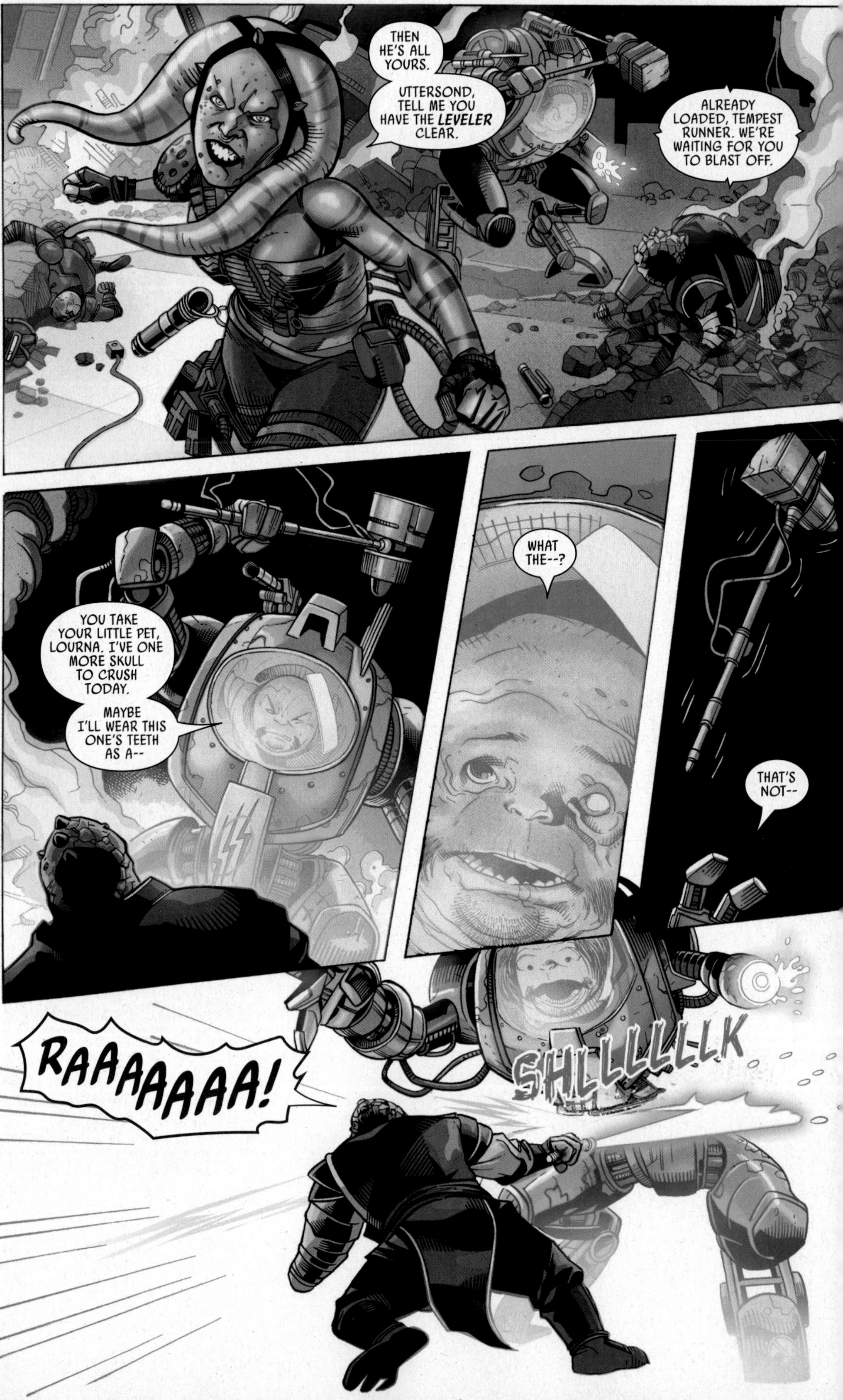
THEN HE'S ALL YOURS.
UTTERSOND, TELL ME YOU HAVE THE LEVELER CLEAR.
ALREADY LOADED, TEMPEST RUNNER. WE'RE WAITING FOR YOU TO BLAST OFF.
YOU TAKE YOUR LITTLE PET, LOURNA. I'VE ONE MORE SKULL TO CRUSH TODAY.
MAYBE I'LL WEAR THIS ONE'S TEETH AS A--
WHAT THE--?
THAT'S NOT--
RAAAAAAAA!
SHLLLLLLK

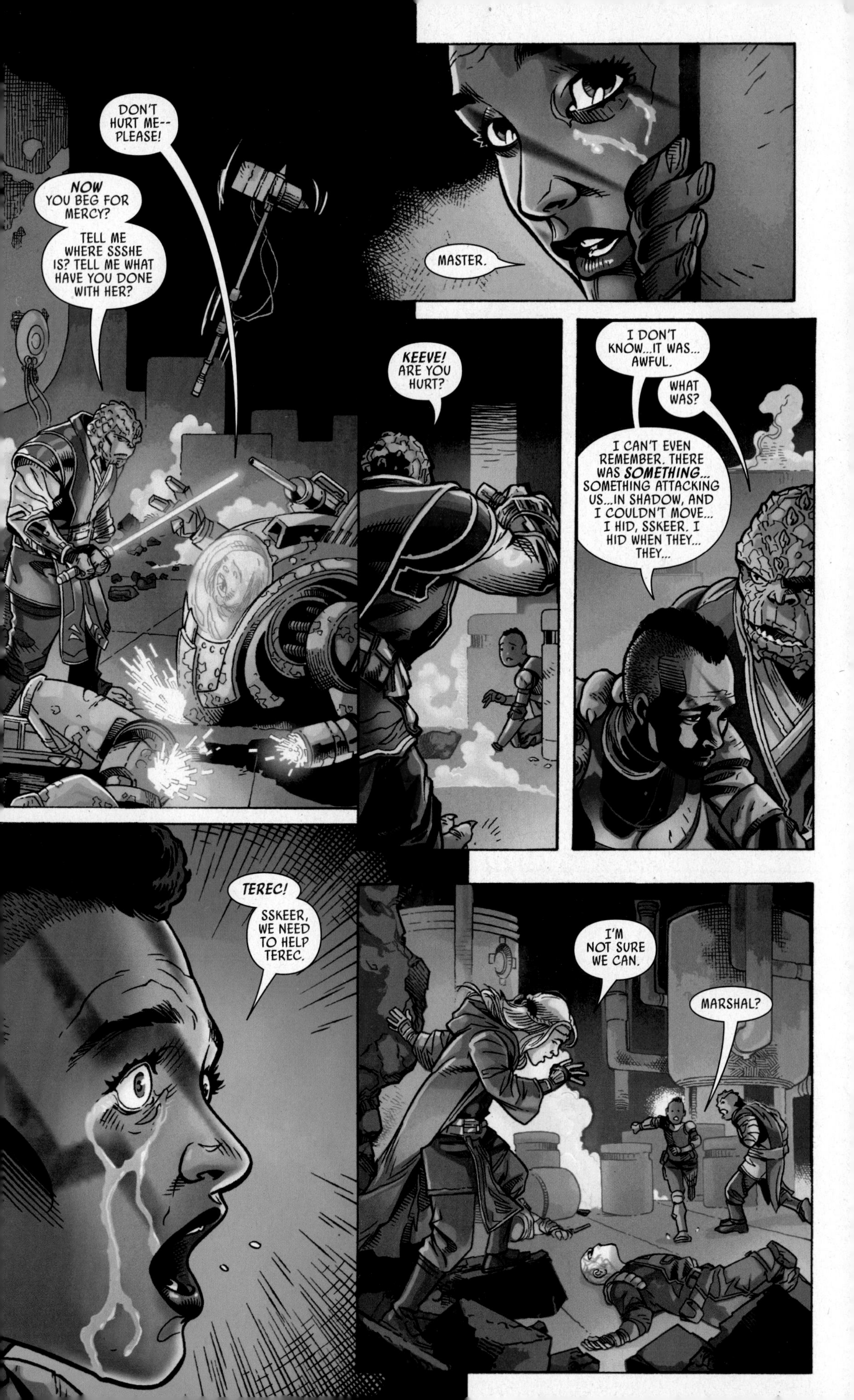
DON'T HURT ME-- PLEASE!
MASTER.
NOW YOU BEG FOR MERCY?
TELL ME WHERE SSSHE IS? TELL ME WHAT HAVE YOU DONE WITH HER?
KEEVE! ARE YOU HURT?
I DON'T KNOW...IT WAS... AWFUL.
WHAT WAS?
I CAN'T EVEN REMEMBER. THERE WAS SOMETHING... SOMETHING ATTACKING US...IN SHADOW, AND I COULDN'T MOVE... I HID, SSKEER. I HID WHEN THEY... THEY...
TEREC!
SSKEER, WE NEED TO HELP TEREC.
I'M NOT SURE WE CAN.
MARSHAL?

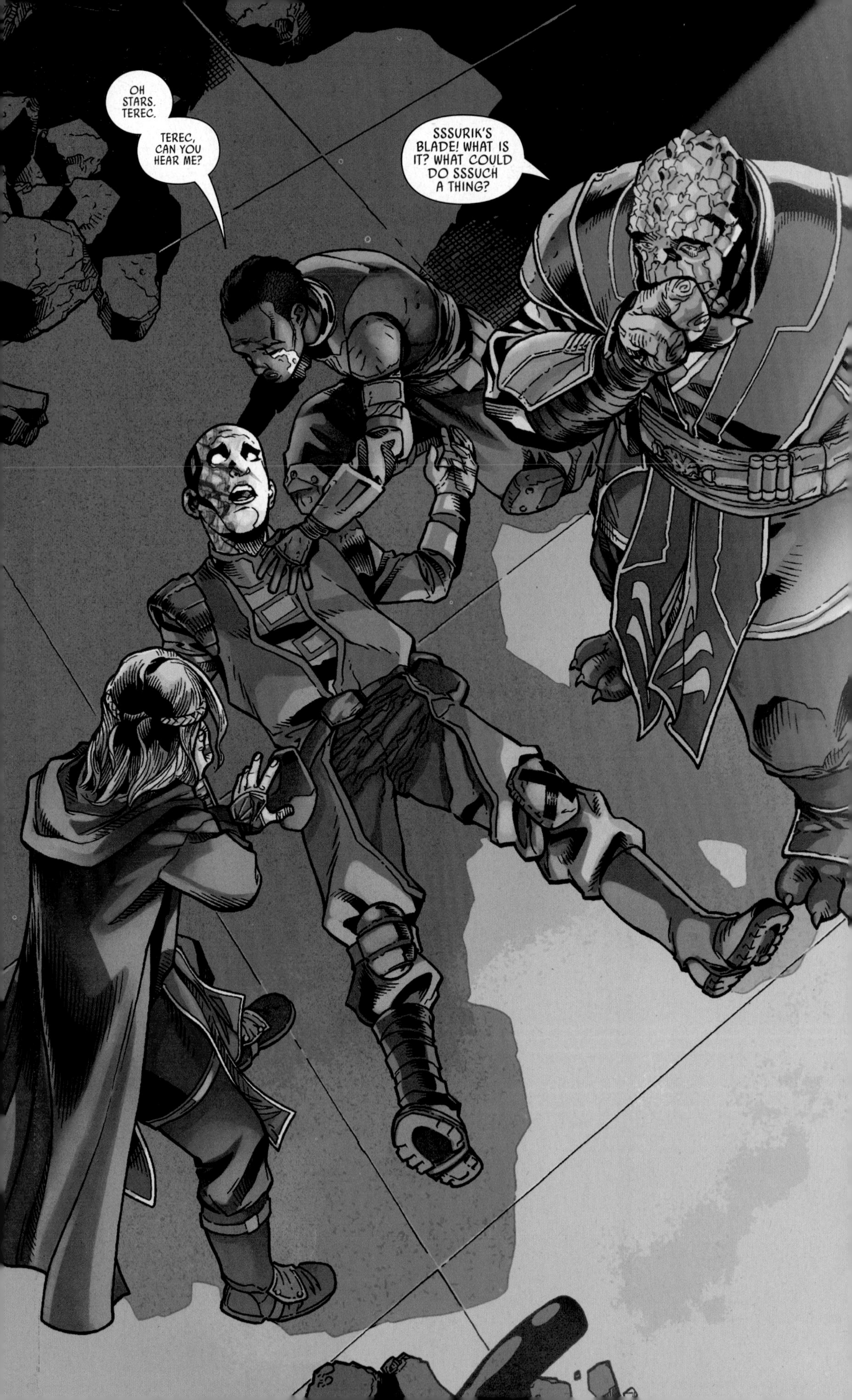
OH STARS. TEREC.
TEREC, CAN YOU HEAR ME?
SSSURIK'S BLADE! WHAT IS IT? WHAT COULD DO SSSUCH A THING?

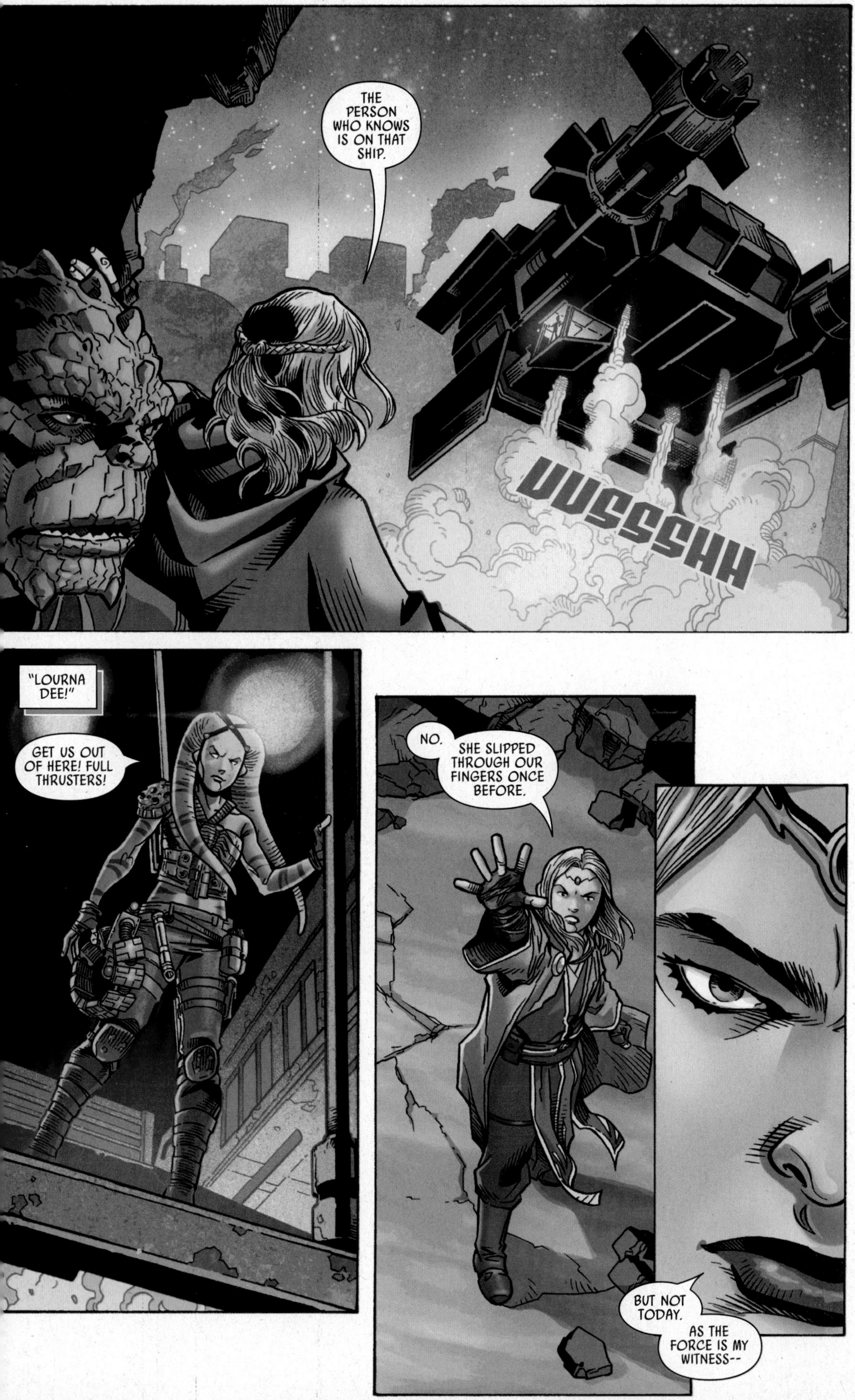
THE PERSON WHO KNOWS IS ON THAT SHIP.
"LOURNA DEE!"
GET US OUT OF HERE! FULL THRUSTERS!
NO.
SHE SLIPPED THROUGH OUR FINGERS ONCE BEFORE.
BUT NOT TODAY.
AS THE FORCE IS MY WITNESS--

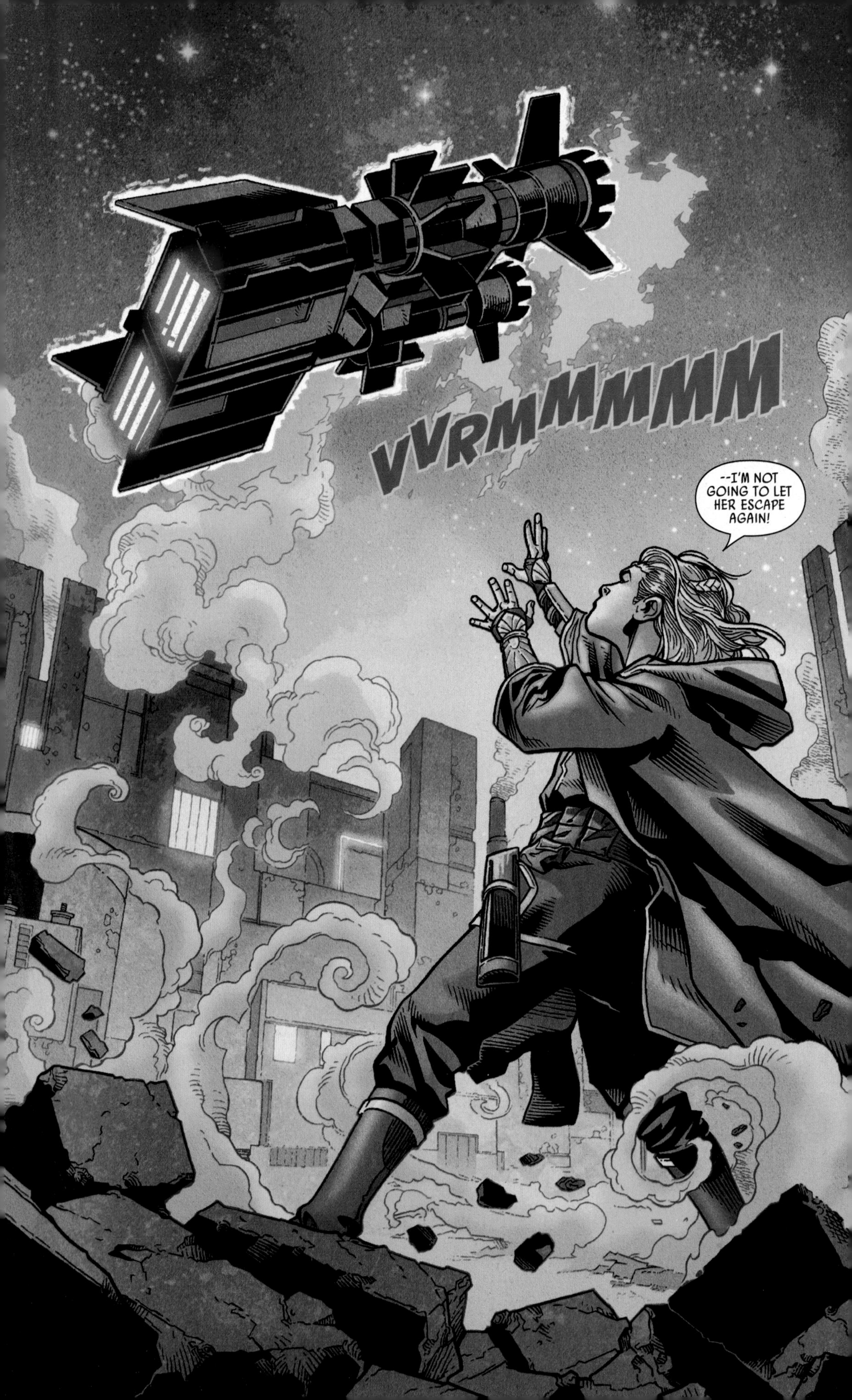
VVRMMMMMM
--I'M NOT GOING TO LET HER ESCAPE AGAIN!

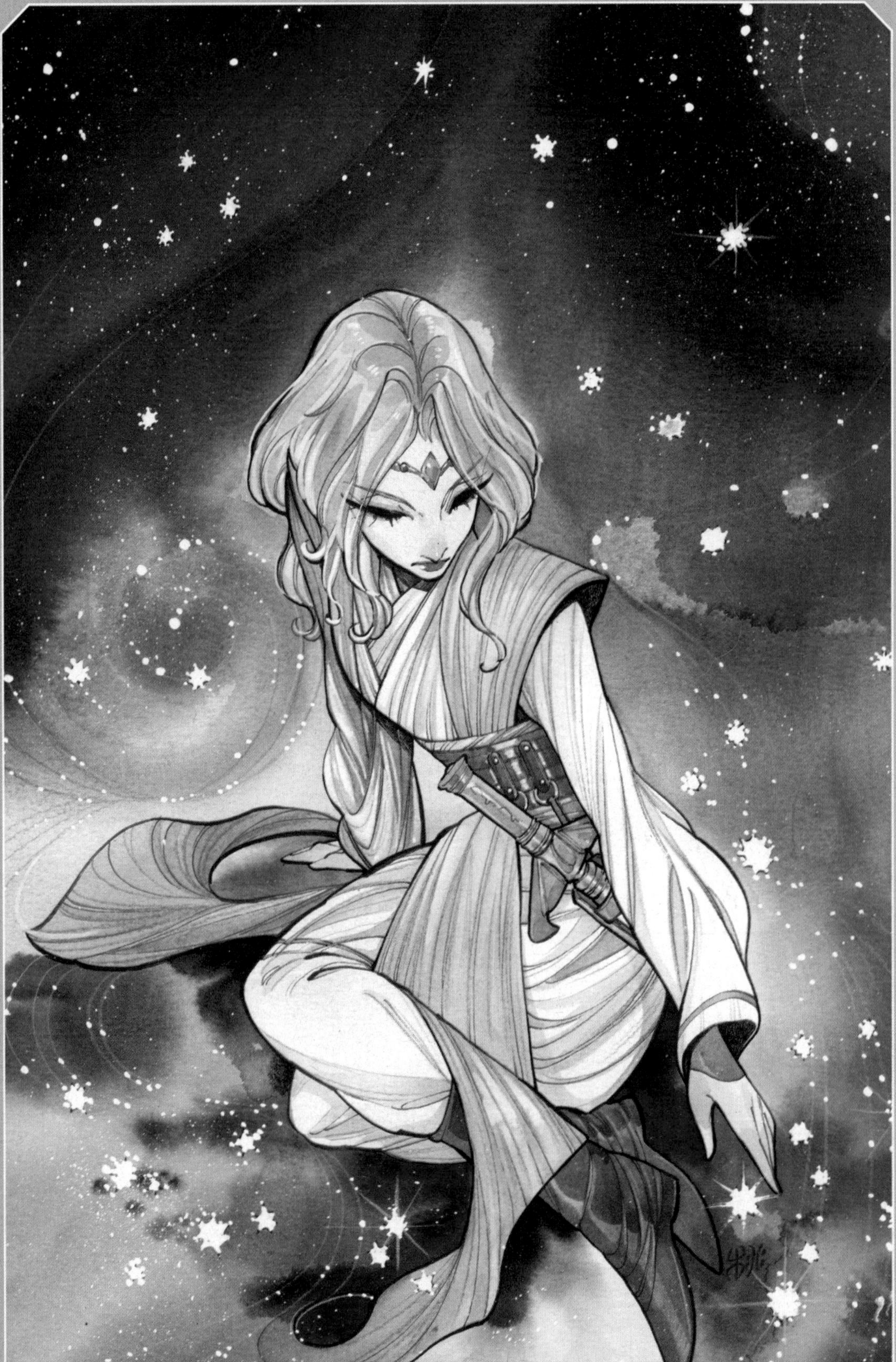

#11 Variant by
PEACH MOMOKO

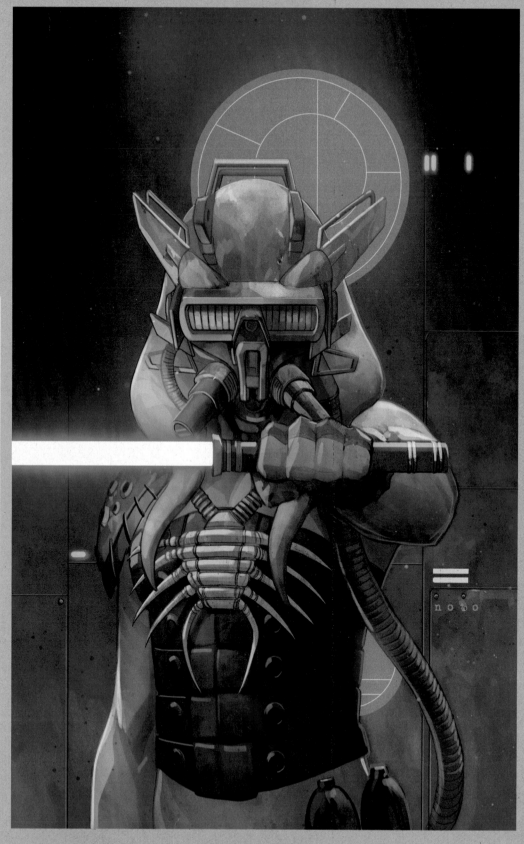

12 | THE SPIRIT OF DISUNITY

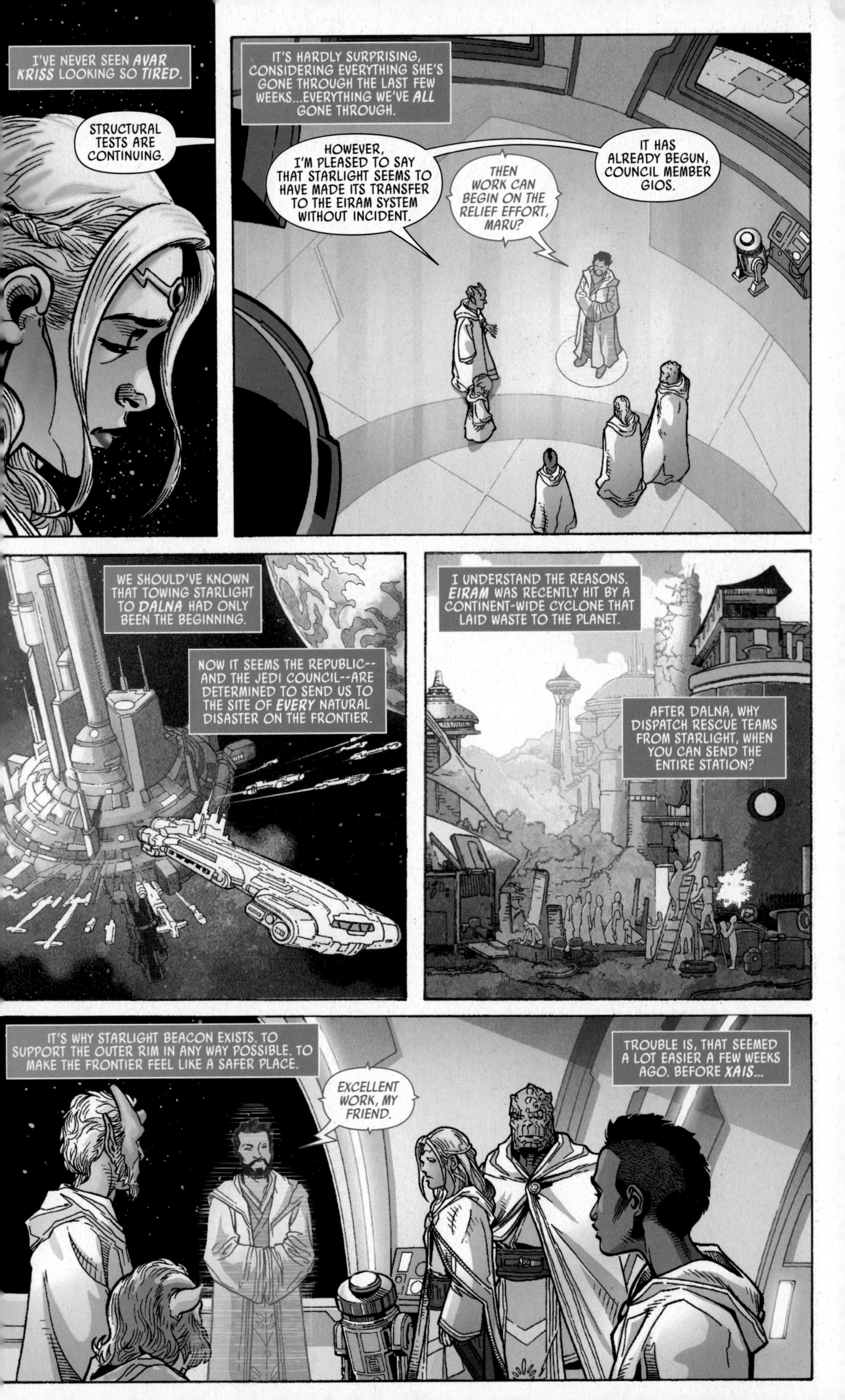
I'VE NEVER SEEN AVAR KRISS LOOKING SO TIRED.
STRUCTURAL TESTS ARE CONTINUING.
IT'S HARDLY SURPRISING, CONSIDERING EVERYTHING SHE'S GONE THROUGH THE LAST FEW WEEKS...EVERYTHING WE'VE ALL GONE THROUGH.
HOWEVER, I'M PLEASED TO SAY THAT STARLIGHT SEEMS TO HAVE MADE ITS TRANSFER TO THE EIRAM SYSTEM WITHOUT INCIDENT.
THEN WORK CAN BEGIN ON THE RELIEF EFFORT, MARU?
IT HAS ALREADY BEGUN, COUNCIL MEMBER GIOS.
WE SHOULD'VE KNOWN THAT TOWING STARLIGHT TO DALNA HAD ONLY BEEN THE BEGINNING.
NOW IT SEEMS THE REPUBLIC--AND THE JEDI COUNCIL--ARE DETERMINED TO SEND US TO THE SITE OF EVERY NATURAL DISASTER ON THE FRONTIER.
I UNDERSTAND THE REASONS. EIRAM WAS RECENTLY HIT BY A CONTINENT-WIDE CYCLONE THAT LAID WASTE TO THE PLANET.
AFTER DALNA, WHY DISPATCH RESCUE TEAMS FROM STARLIGHT, WHEN YOU CAN SEND THE ENTIRE STATION?
IT'S WHY STARLIGHT BEACON EXISTS. TO SUPPORT THE OUTER RIM IN ANY WAY POSSIBLE. TO MAKE THE FRONTIER FEEL LIKE A SAFER PLACE.
EXCELLENT WORK, MY FRIEND.
TROUBLE IS, THAT SEEMED A LOT EASIER A FEW WEEKS AGO. BEFORE XAIS...

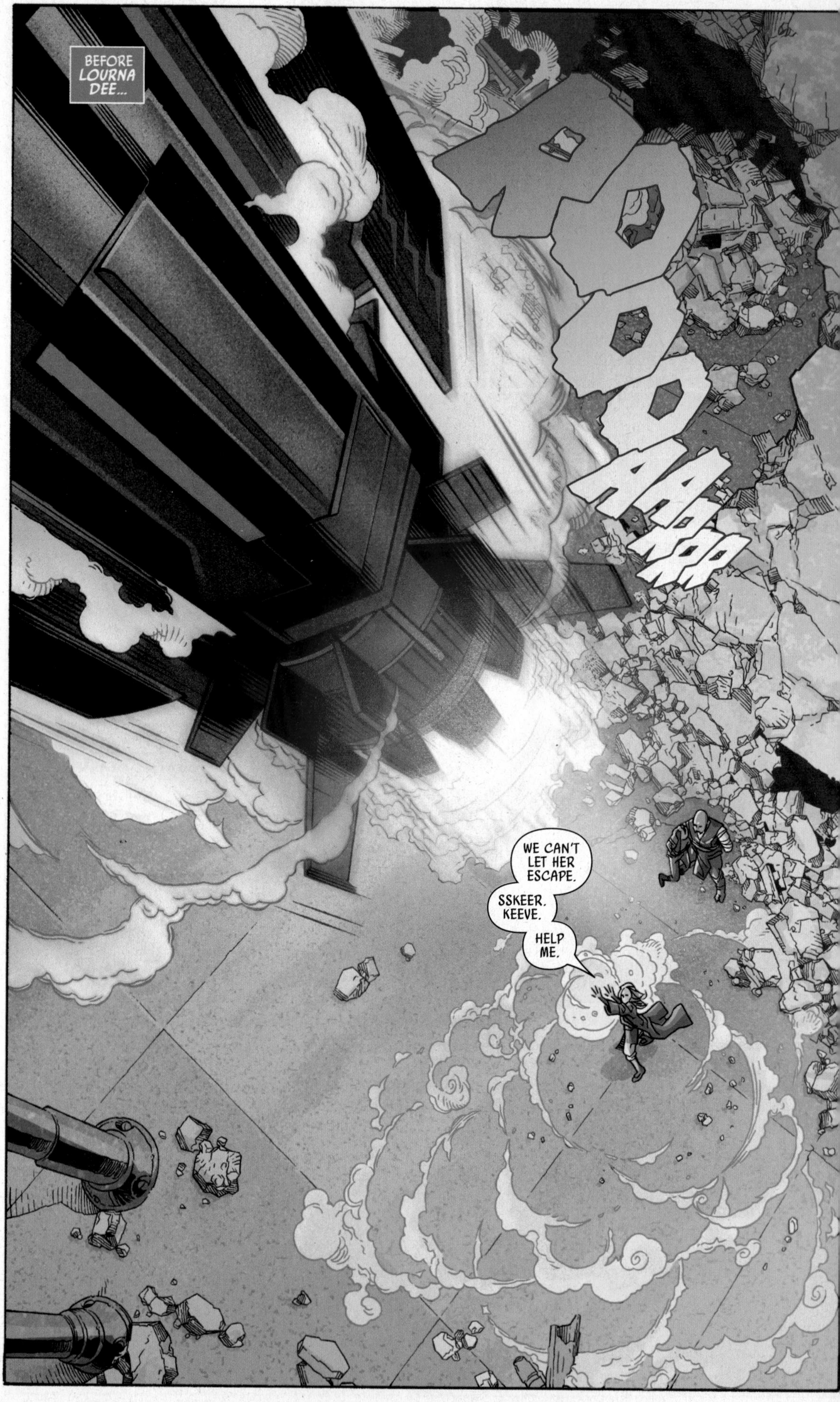
BEFORE LOURNA DEE...
ROOOAARR
WE CAN'T LET HER ESCAPE.
SSKEER. KEEVE.
HELP ME.

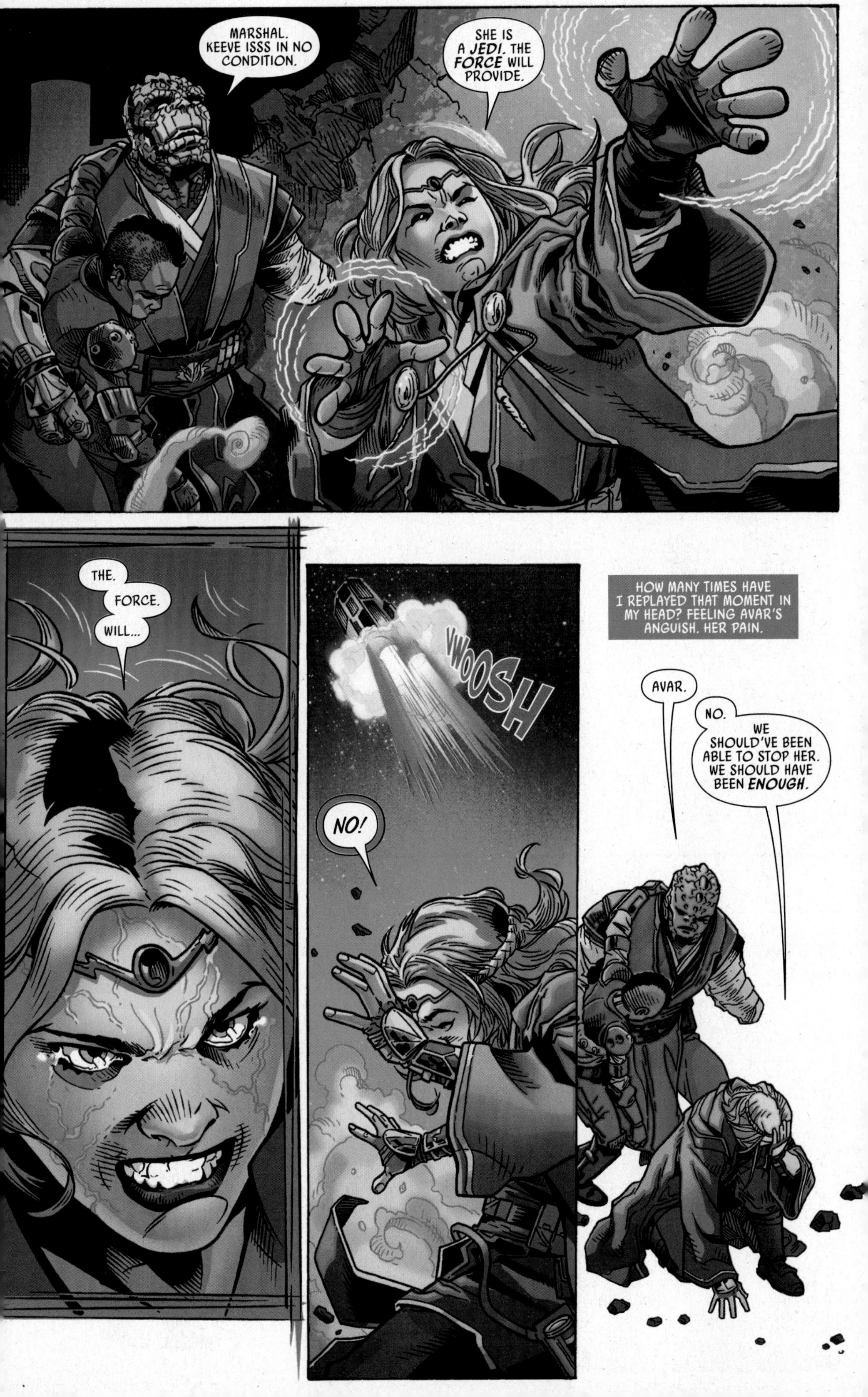
MARSHAL. KEEVE ISSS IN NO CONDITION.
SHE IS A *JEDI*. THE *FORCE* WILL PROVIDE.
THE.
FORCE.
WILL...
VWOOSH
NO!
HOW MANY TIMES HAVE I REPLAYED THAT MOMENT IN MY HEAD? FEELING AVAR'S ANGUISH. HER PAIN.
AVAR.
NO.
WE SHOULD'VE BEEN ABLE TO STOP HER. WE SHOULD HAVE BEEN *ENOUGH*.

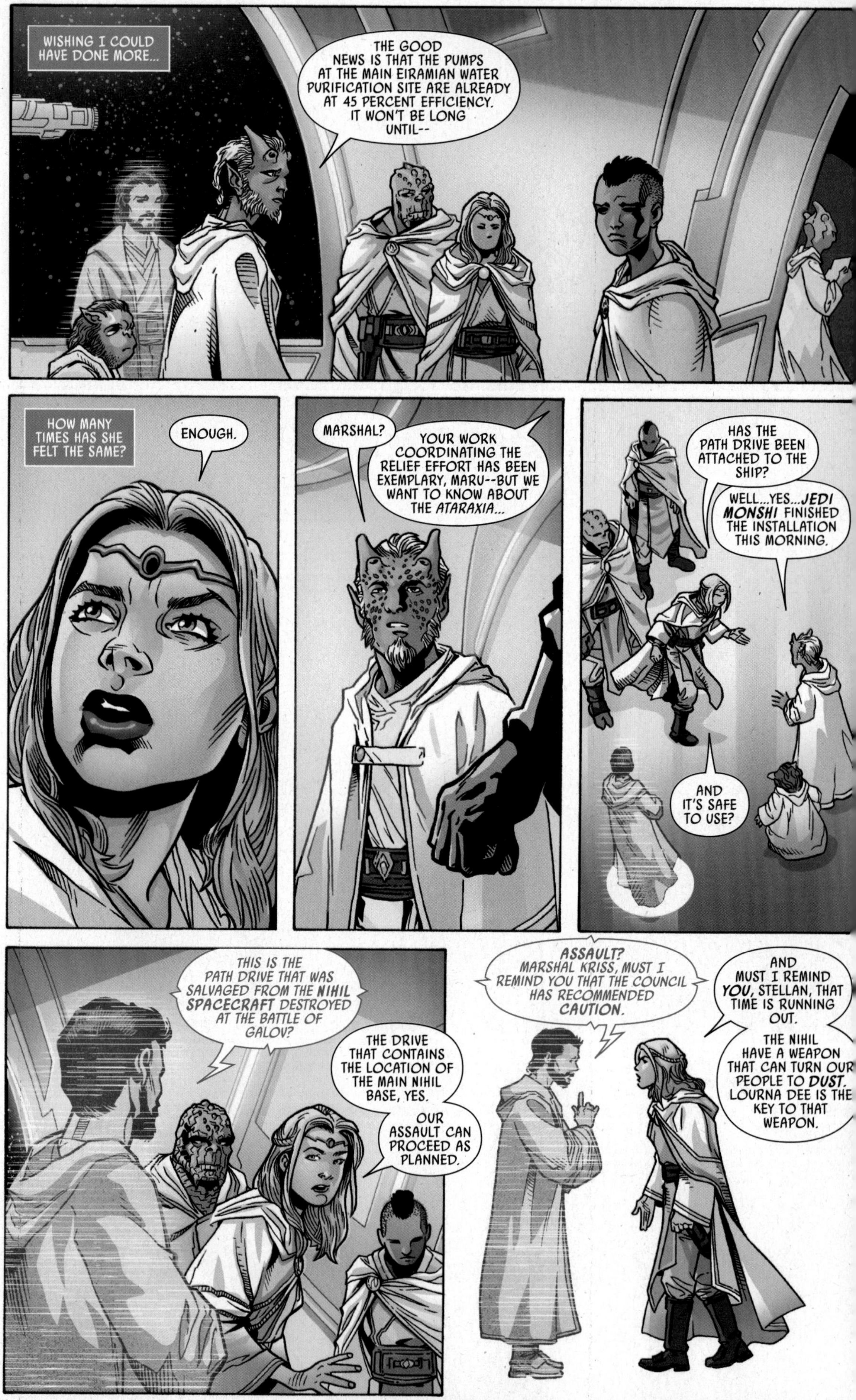
WISHING I COULD HAVE DONE MORE...
THE GOOD NEWS IS THAT THE PUMPS AT THE MAIN EIRAMIAN WATER PURIFICATION SITE ARE ALREADY AT 45 PERCENT EFFICIENCY. IT WON'T BE LONG UNTIL--
HOW MANY TIMES HAS SHE FELT THE SAME?
ENOUGH.
MARSHAL?
YOUR WORK COORDINATING THE RELIEF EFFORT HAS BEEN EXEMPLARY, MARU--BUT WE WANT TO KNOW ABOUT THE ATARAXIA...
HAS THE PATH DRIVE BEEN ATTACHED TO THE SHIP?
WELL...YES...JEDI MONSHI FINISHED THE INSTALLATION THIS MORNING.
AND IT'S SAFE TO USE?
THIS IS THE PATH DRIVE THAT WAS SALVAGED FROM THE NIHIL SPACECRAFT DESTROYED AT THE BATTLE OF GALOV?
THE DRIVE THAT CONTAINS THE LOCATION OF THE MAIN NIHIL BASE, YES.
OUR ASSAULT CAN PROCEED AS PLANNED.
ASSAULT? MARSHAL KRISS, MUST I REMIND YOU THAT THE COUNCIL HAS RECOMMENDED CAUTION.
AND MUST I REMIND YOU, STELLAN, THAT TIME IS RUNNING OUT.
THE NIHIL HAVE A WEAPON THAT CAN TURN OUR PEOPLE TO DUST. LOURNA DEE IS THE KEY TO THAT WEAPON.

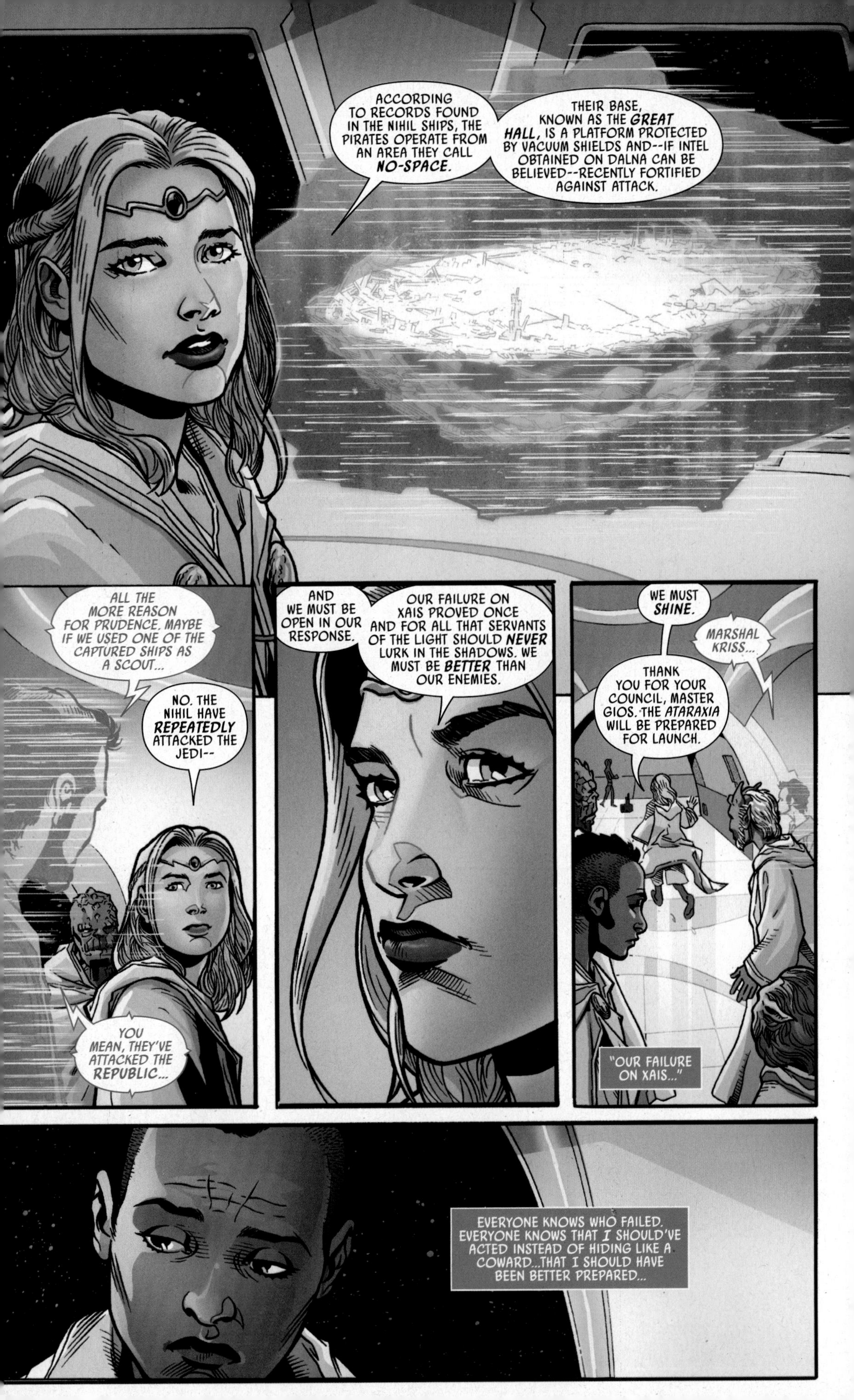
ACCORDING TO RECORDS FOUND IN THE NIHIL SHIPS, THE PIRATES OPERATE FROM AN AREA THEY CALL NO-SPACE.
THEIR BASE, KNOWN AS THE GREAT HALL, IS A PLATFORM PROTECTED BY VACUUM SHIELDS AND--IF INTEL OBTAINED ON DALNA CAN BE BELIEVED--RECENTLY FORTIFIED AGAINST ATTACK.
ALL THE MORE REASON FOR PRUDENCE. MAYBE IF WE USED ONE OF THE CAPTURED SHIPS AS A SCOUT...
NO. THE NIHIL HAVE REPEATEDLY ATTACKED THE JEDI--
YOU MEAN, THEY'VE ATTACKED THE REPUBLIC...
AND WE MUST BE OPEN IN OUR RESPONSE.
OUR FAILURE ON XAIS PROVED ONCE AND FOR ALL THAT SERVANTS OF THE LIGHT SHOULD NEVER LURK IN THE SHADOWS. WE MUST BE BETTER THAN OUR ENEMIES.
WE MUST SHINE.
MARSHAL KRISS...
THANK YOU FOR YOUR COUNCIL, MASTER GIOS. THE ATARAXIA WILL BE PREPARED FOR LAUNCH.
"OUR FAILURE ON XAIS..."
EVERYONE KNOWS WHO FAILED, EVERYONE KNOWS THAT I SHOULD'VE ACTED INSTEAD OF HIDING LIKE A COWARD...THAT I SHOULD HAVE BEEN BETTER PREPARED...

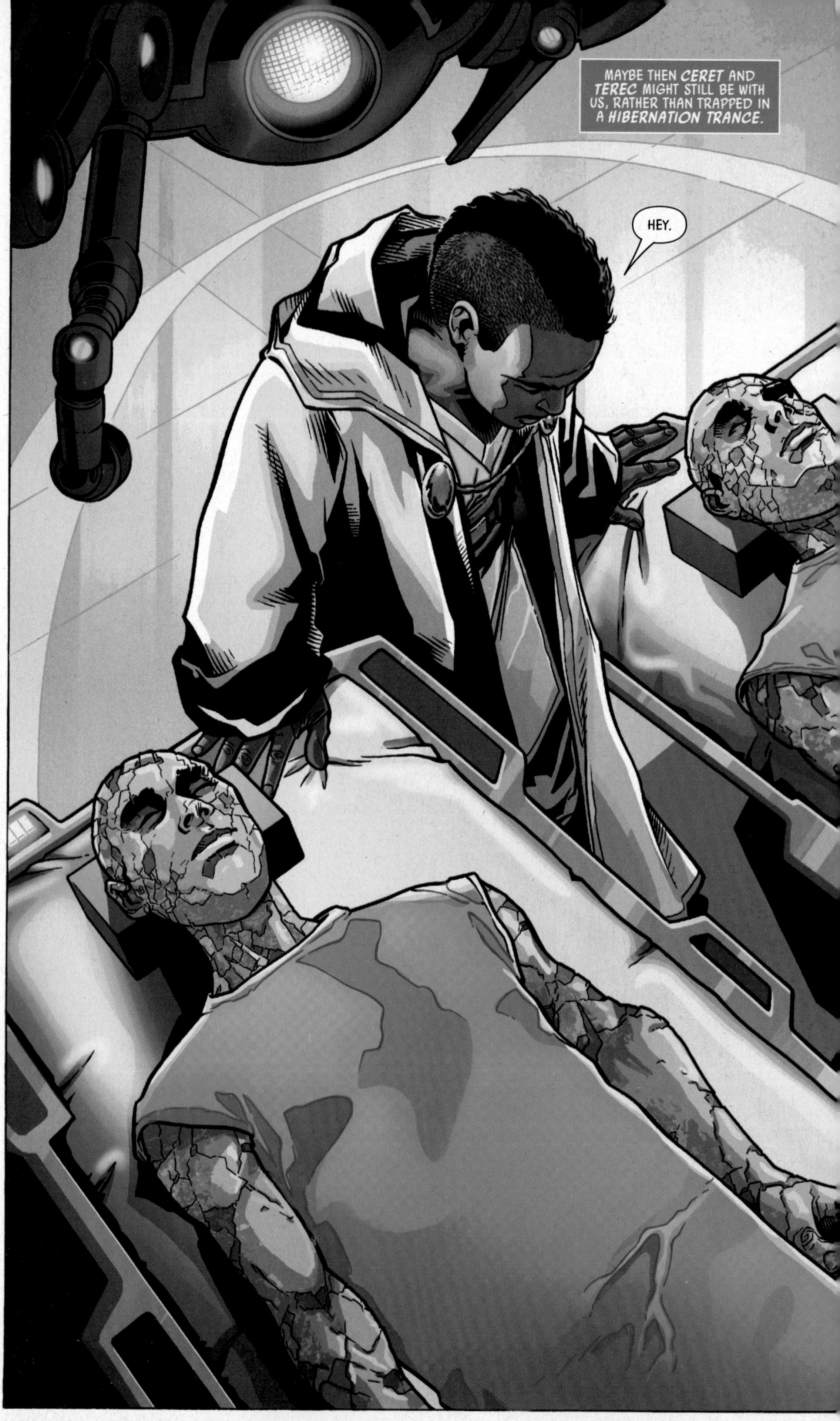
MAYBE THEN CERET AND TEREC MIGHT STILL BE WITH US, RATHER THAN TRAPPED IN A HIBERNATION TRANCE.
HEY.

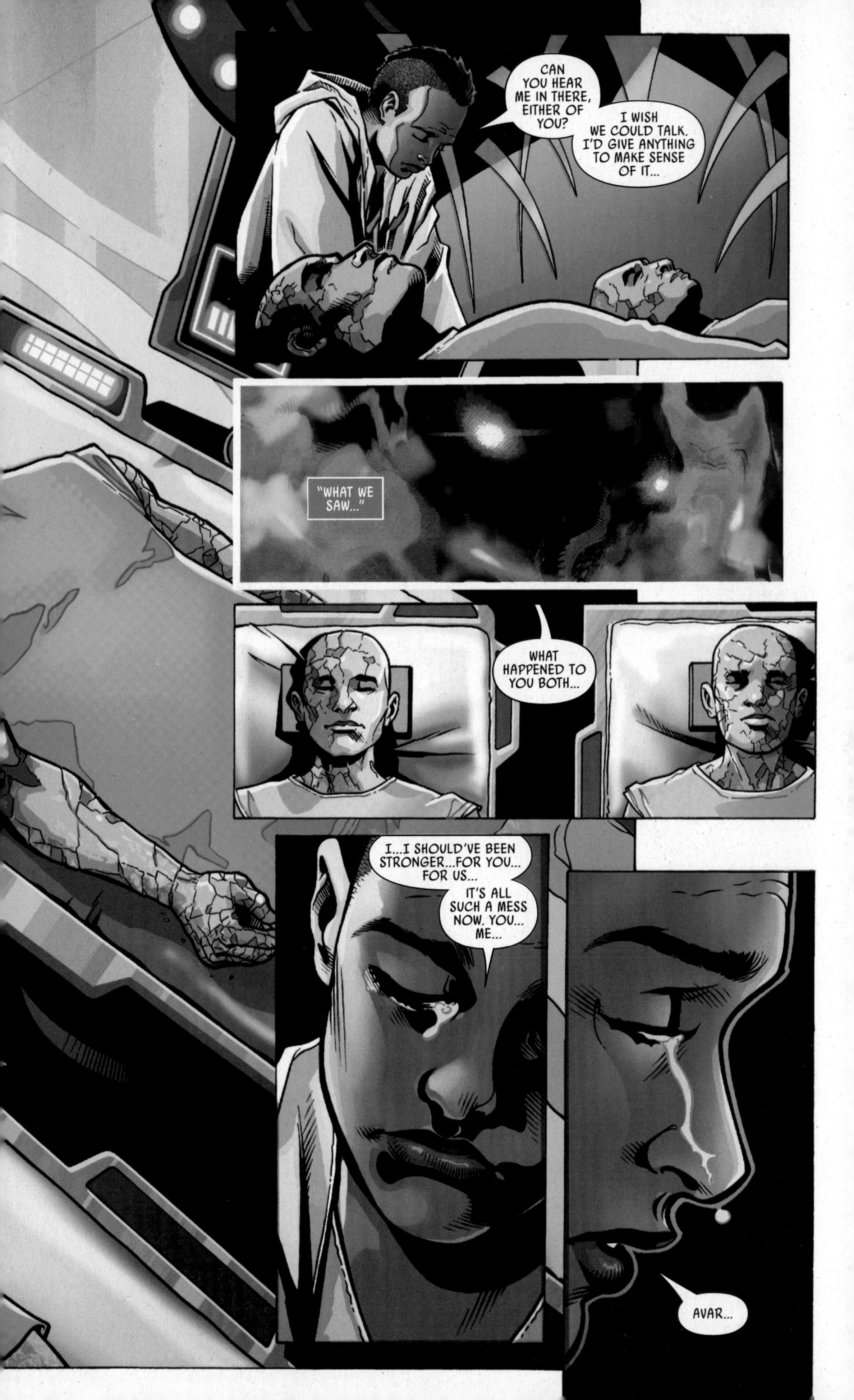

CAN YOU HEAR ME IN THERE, EITHER OF YOU?
I WISH WE COULD TALK. I'D GIVE ANYTHING TO MAKE SENSE OF IT...
"WHAT WE SAW..."
WHAT HAPPENED TO YOU BOTH...
I...I SHOULD'VE BEEN STRONGER...FOR YOU... FOR US...
IT'S ALL SUCH A MESS NOW. YOU... ME...
AVAR...

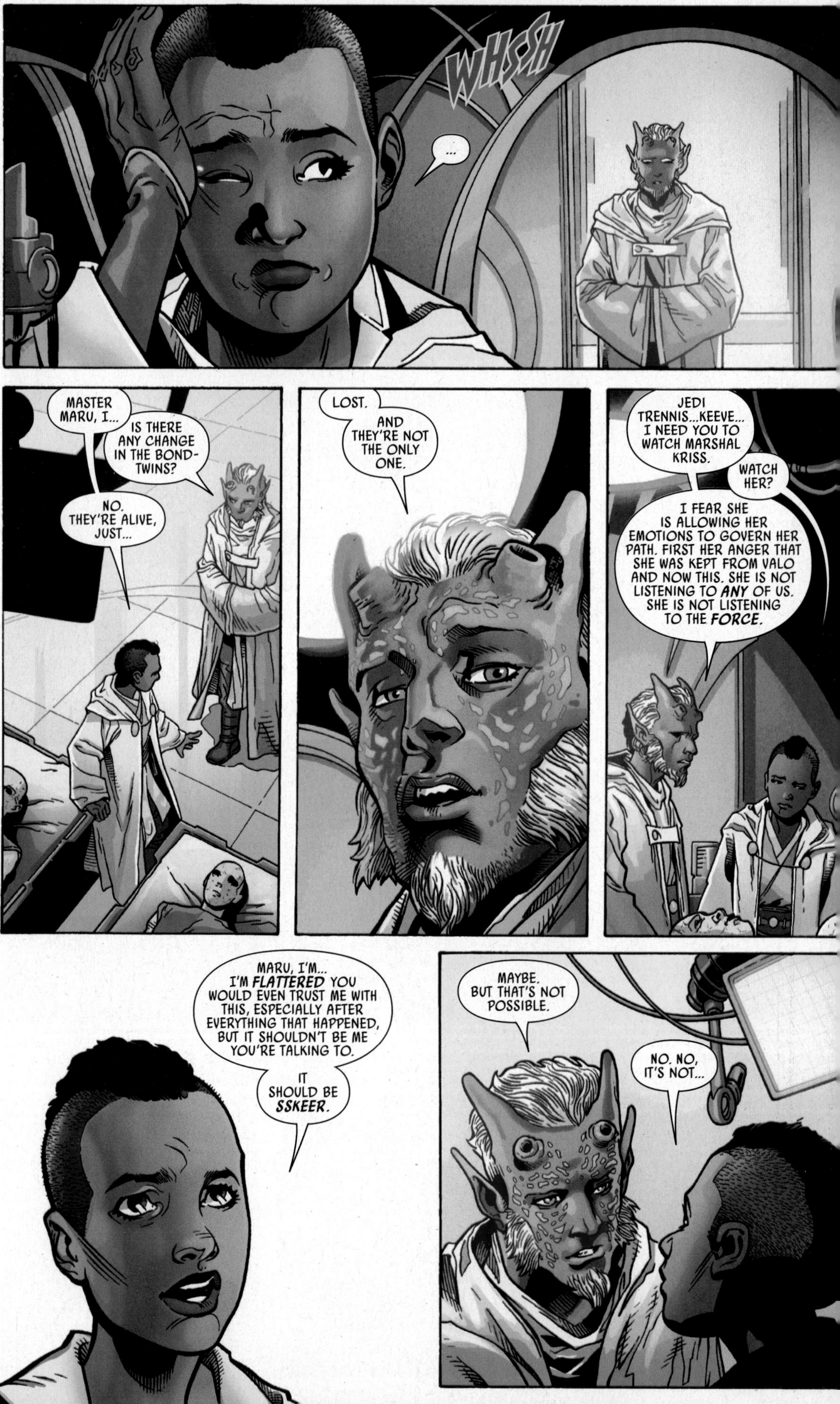
WHSSH
...
MASTER MARU, I...
IS THERE ANY CHANGE IN THE BOND-TWINS?
NO. THEY'RE ALIVE, JUST...
LOST.
AND THEY'RE NOT THE ONLY ONE.
JEDI TRENNIS...KEEVE... I NEED YOU TO WATCH MARSHAL KRISS.
WATCH HER?
I FEAR SHE IS ALLOWING HER EMOTIONS TO GOVERN HER PATH. FIRST HER ANGER THAT SHE WAS KEPT FROM VALO AND NOW THIS. SHE IS NOT LISTENING TO ANY OF US. SHE IS NOT LISTENING TO THE FORCE.
MARU, I'M... I'M FLATTERED YOU WOULD EVEN TRUST ME WITH THIS, ESPECIALLY AFTER EVERYTHING THAT HAPPENED, BUT IT SHOULDN'T BE ME YOU'RE TALKING TO.
IT SHOULD BE SSKEER.
MAYBE. BUT THAT'S NOT POSSIBLE.
NO. NO, IT'S NOT...

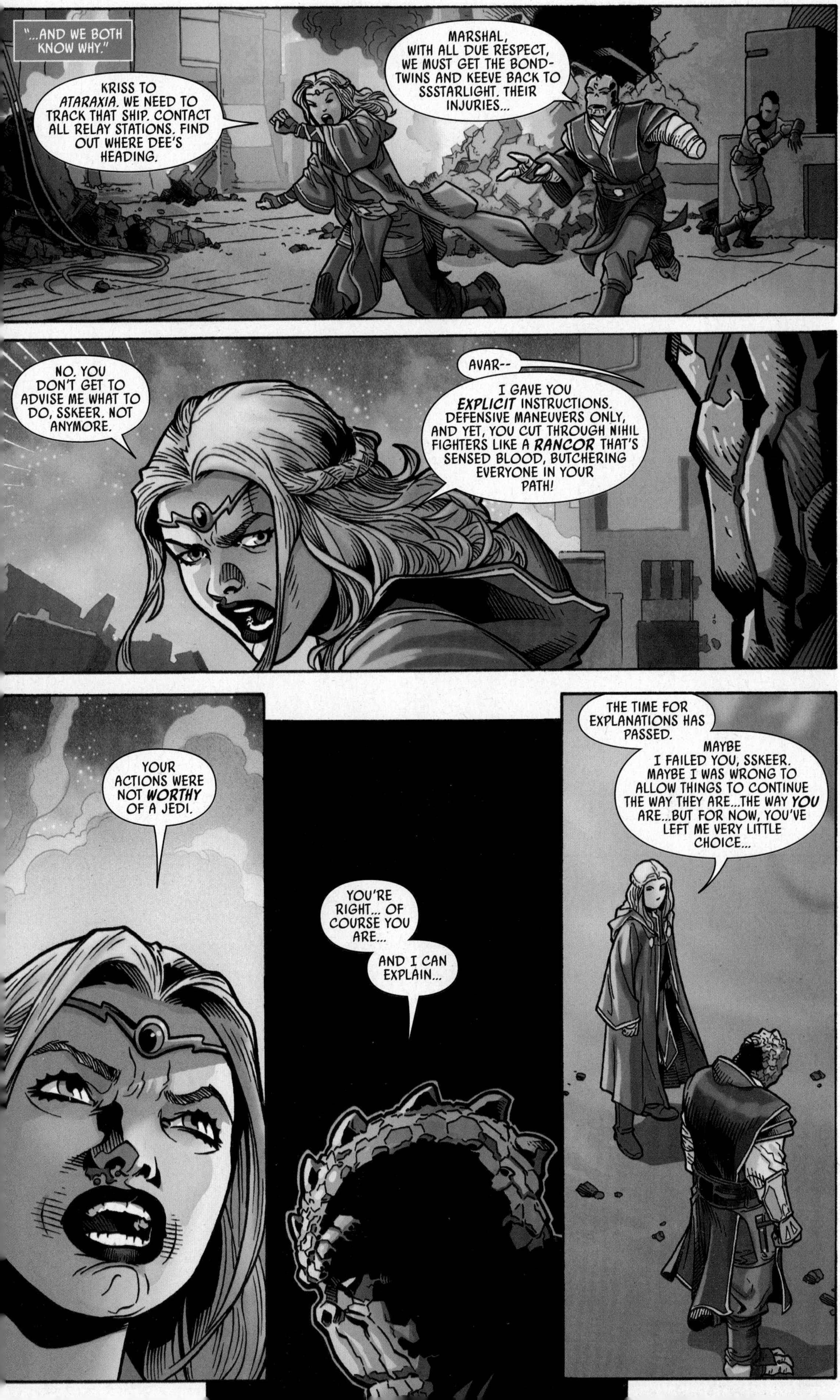
"...AND WE BOTH KNOW WHY."
KRISS TO ATARAXIA. WE NEED TO TRACK THAT SHIP. CONTACT ALL RELAY STATIONS. FIND OUT WHERE DEE'S HEADING.
MARSHAL, WITH ALL DUE RESPECT, WE MUST GET THE BOND-TWINS AND KEEVE BACK TO SSSTARLIGHT. THEIR INJURIES...
NO. YOU DON'T GET TO ADVISE ME WHAT TO DO, SSKEER. NOT ANYMORE.
AVAR--
I GAVE YOU EXPLICIT INSTRUCTIONS. DEFENSIVE MANEUVERS ONLY, AND YET, YOU CUT THROUGH NIHIL FIGHTERS LIKE A RANCOR THAT'S SENSED BLOOD, BUTCHERING EVERYONE IN YOUR PATH!
YOUR ACTIONS WERE NOT WORTHY OF A JEDI.
YOU'RE RIGHT... OF COURSE YOU ARE...
AND I CAN EXPLAIN...
THE TIME FOR EXPLANATIONS HAS PASSED.
MAYBE I FAILED YOU, SSKEER. MAYBE I WAS WRONG TO ALLOW THINGS TO CONTINUE THE WAY THEY ARE...THE WAY YOU ARE...BUT FOR NOW, YOU'VE LEFT ME VERY LITTLE CHOICE...

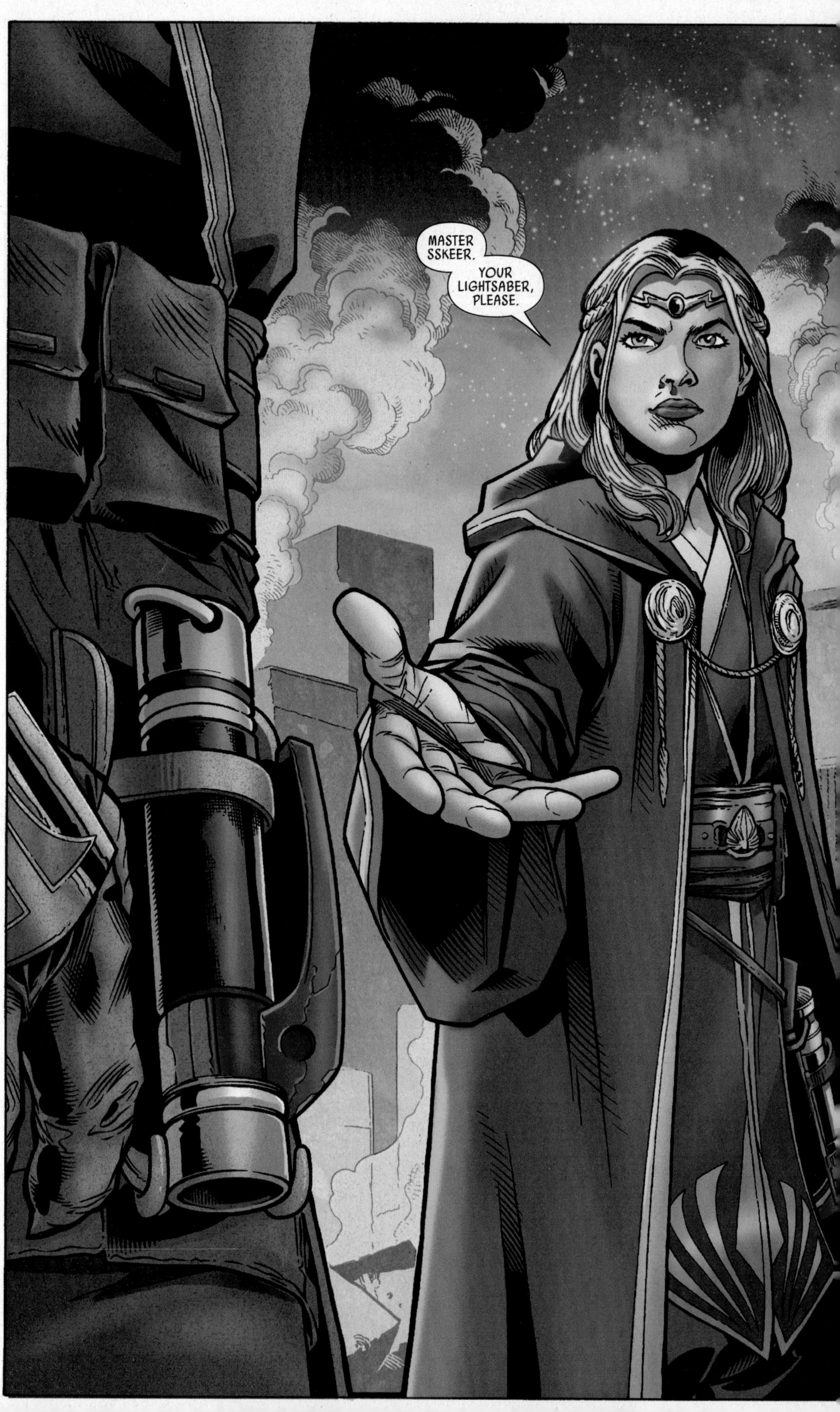
MASTER SSKEER.
YOUR LIGHTSABER, PLEASE.

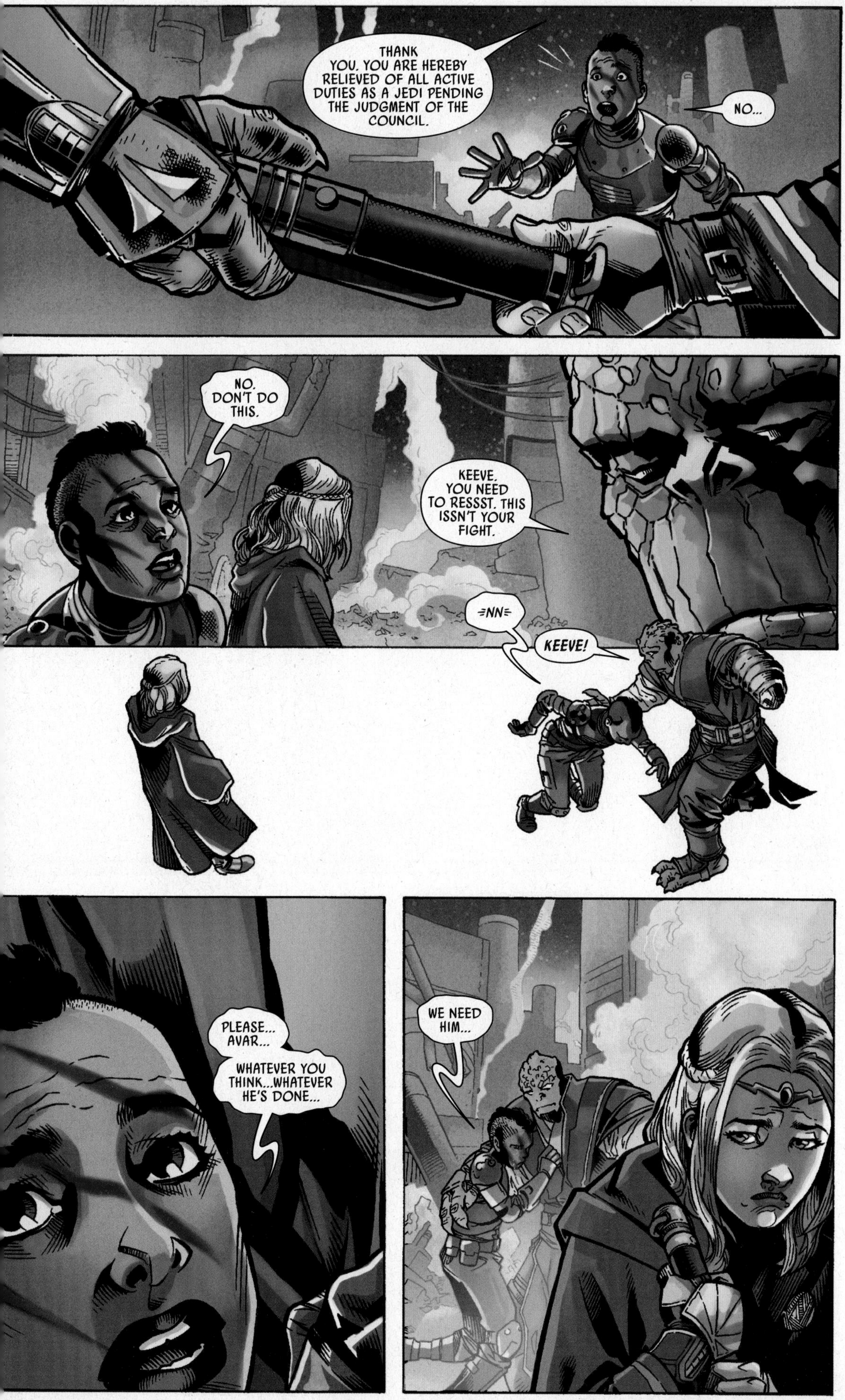
THANK YOU. YOU ARE HEREBY RELIEVED OF ALL ACTIVE DUTIES AS A JEDI PENDING THE JUDGMENT OF THE COUNCIL.
NO...
NO. DON'T DO THIS.
KEEVE. YOU NEED TO RESSST. THIS ISSN'T YOUR FIGHT.
=NN=
KEEVE!
PLEASE... AVAR...
WHATEVER YOU THINK...WHATEVER HE'S DONE...
WE NEED HIM...

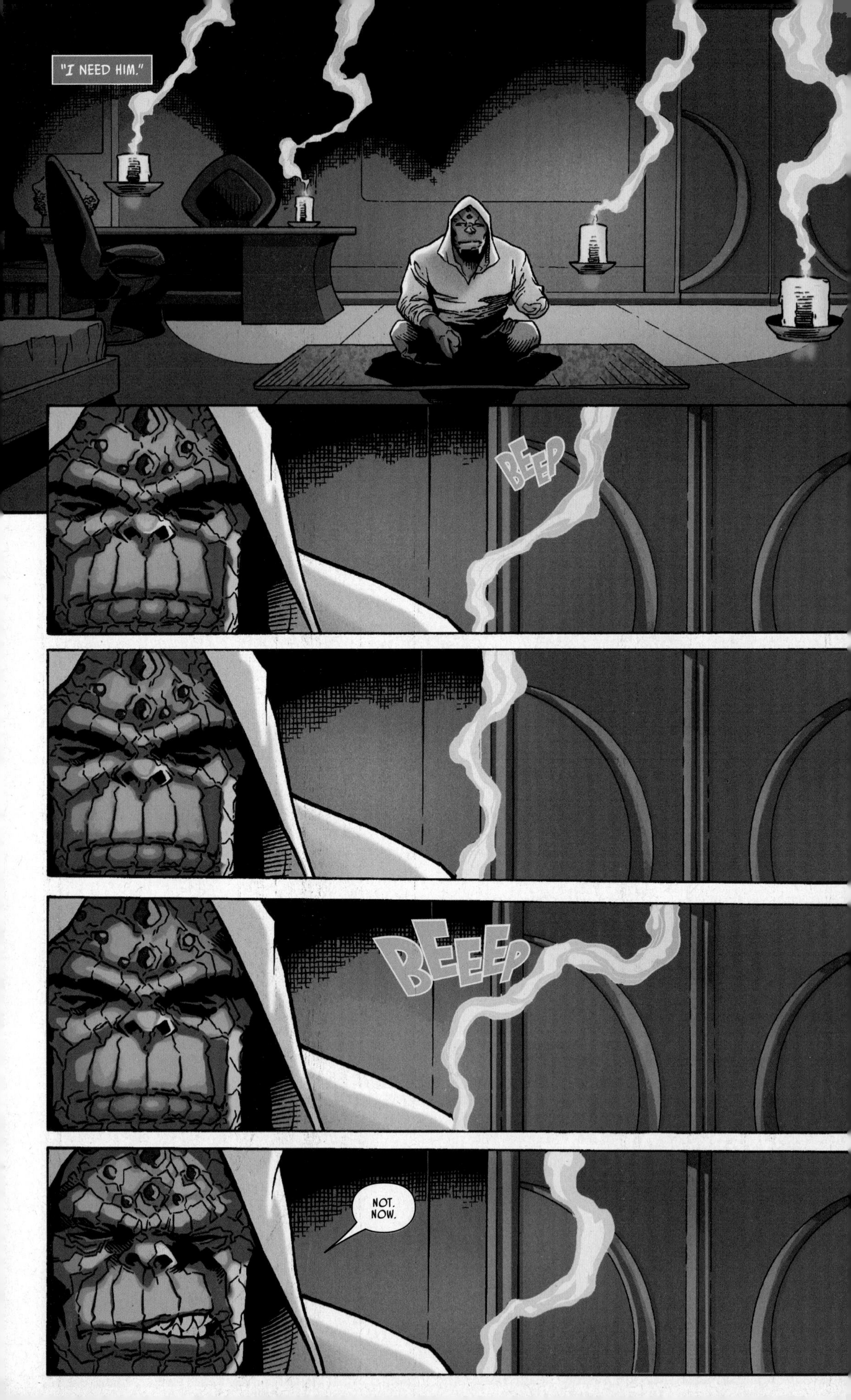
"I NEED HIM."
BEEP
BEEEP
NOT. NOW.

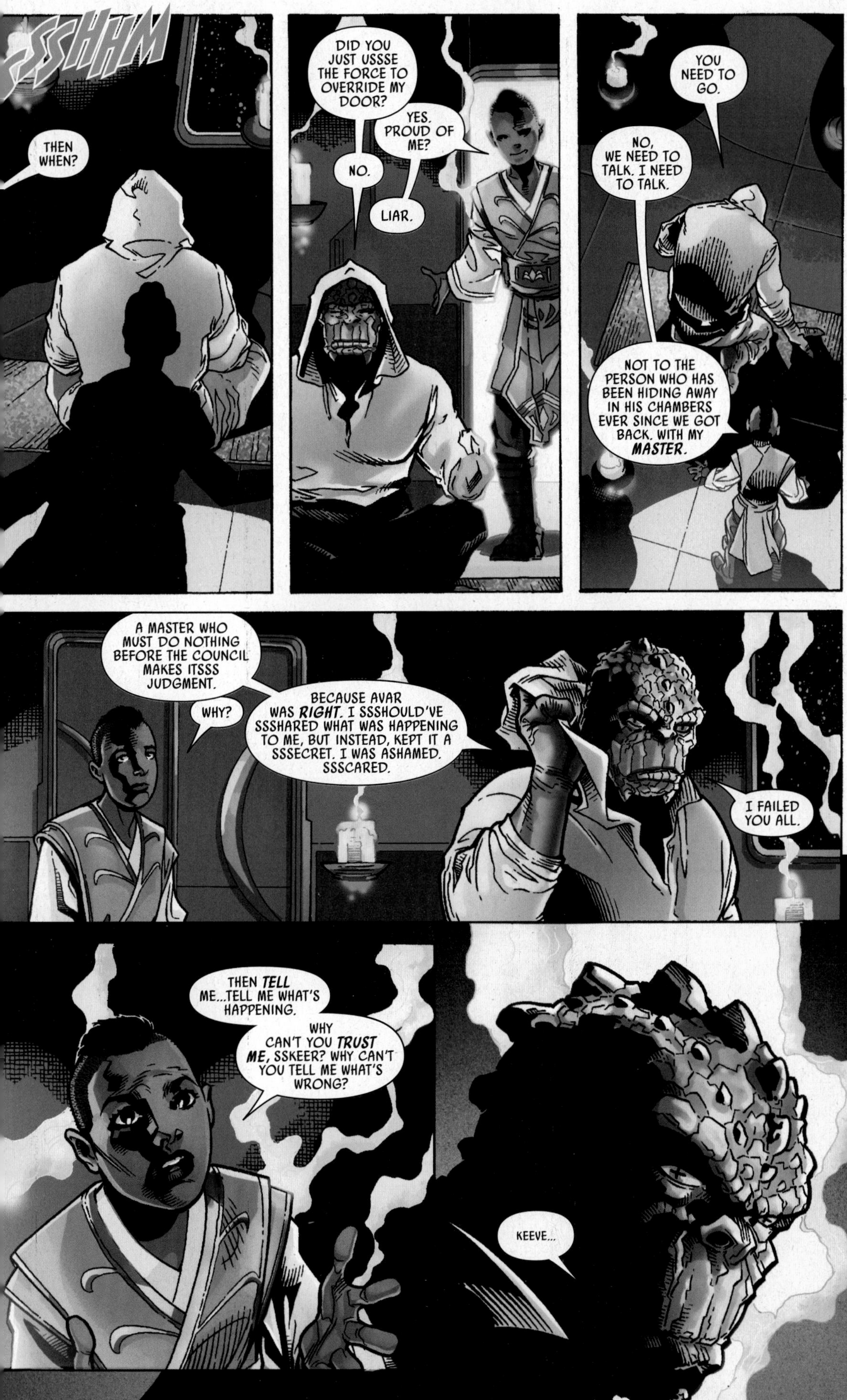
SSHHM
THEN WHEN?
DID YOU JUST USSSE THE FORCE TO OVERRIDE MY DOOR?
YES. PROUD OF ME?
NO.
LIAR.
YOU NEED TO GO.
NO, WE NEED TO TALK. I NEED TO TALK.
NOT TO THE PERSON WHO HAS BEEN HIDING AWAY IN HIS CHAMBERS EVER SINCE WE GOT BACK. WITH MY MASTER.
A MASTER WHO MUST DO NOTHING BEFORE THE COUNCIL MAKES ITSSS JUDGMENT.
WHY?
BECAUSE AVAR WAS RIGHT. I SSSHOULD'VE SSSHARED WHAT WAS HAPPENING TO ME, BUT INSTEAD, KEPT IT A SSSECRET. I WAS ASHAMED. SSSCARED.
I FAILED YOU ALL.
THEN TELL ME...TELL ME WHAT'S HAPPENING.
WHY CAN'T YOU TRUST ME, SSKEER? WHY CAN'T YOU TELL ME WHAT'S WRONG?
KEEVE...

KEEVE, I'VE NEVER TRUSTED ANYONE MORE.

IT'S *ME* I CAN'T TRUST.

WHAT'S THIS?

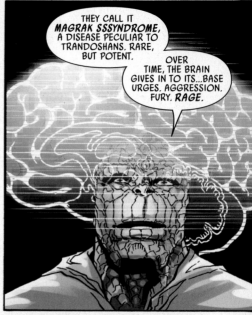

THEY CALL IT *MAGRAK SSSYNDROME,* A DISEASE PECULIAR TO TRANDOSHANS. RARE, BUT POTENT.

OVER TIME, THE BRAIN GIVES IN TO ITS...BASE URGES. AGGRESSION. FURY. *RAGE.*

MY MIND HAS BEEN SSSUBCONSCIOUSLY DEALING WITH THE CONDITION...BUT THE EFFORT REQUIRED...

HAS LEFT YOU UNABLE TO CONNECT TO THE FORCE.

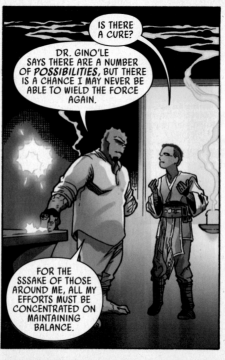

IS THERE A CURE?

DR. GINO'LE SAYS THERE ARE A NUMBER OF *POSSIBILITIES,* BUT THERE IS A CHANCE I MAY NEVER BE ABLE TO WIELD THE FORCE AGAIN.

FOR THE SSSAKE OF THOSE AROUND ME, ALL MY EFFORTS MUST BE CONCENTRATED ON MAINTAINING BALANCE.

UNTIL THEN...I AM A *DANGER.*

NO. I CAN'T BELIEVE THAT. I *WON'T.*

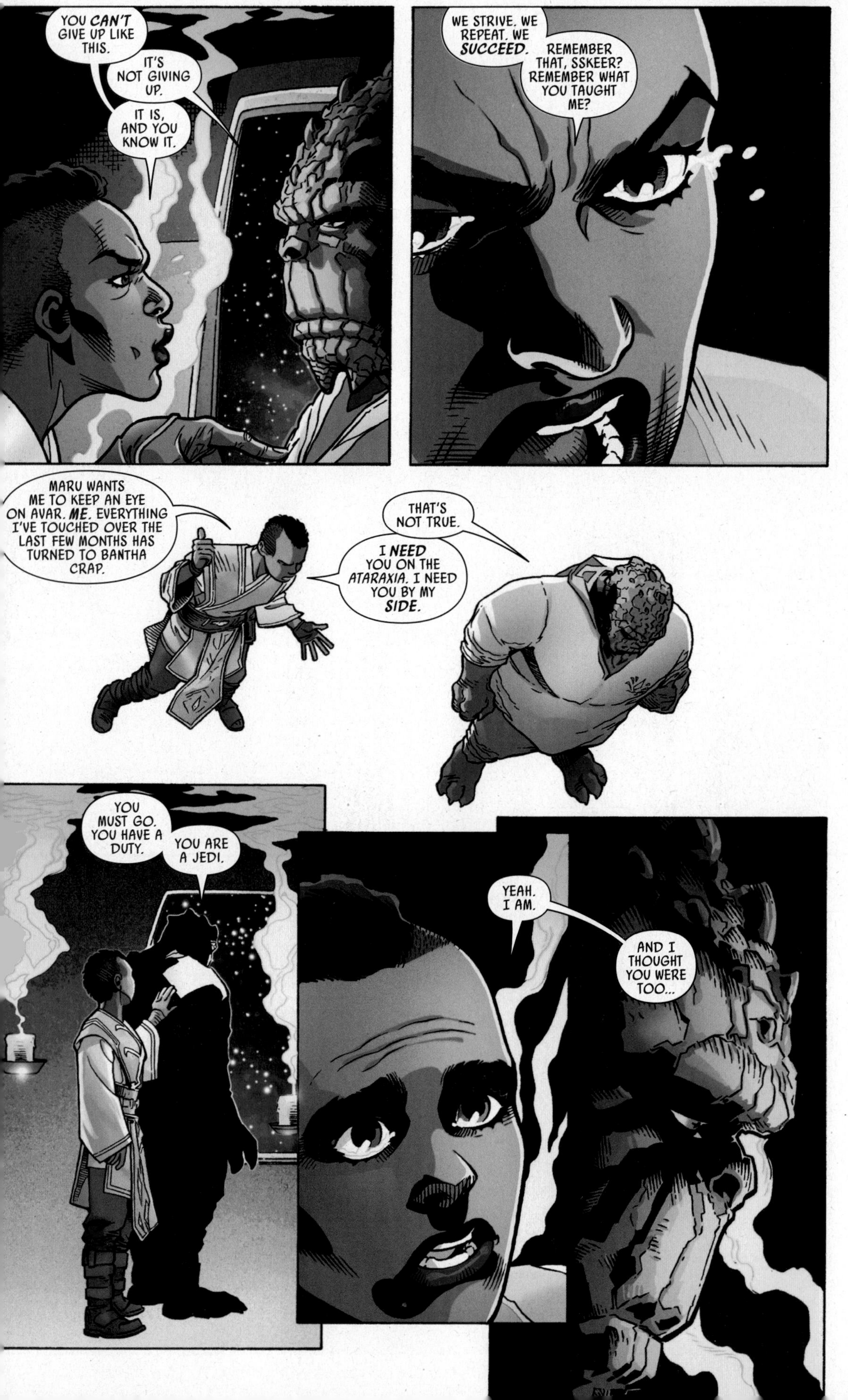
YOU CAN'T GIVE UP LIKE THIS.
IT'S NOT GIVING UP.
IT IS, AND YOU KNOW IT.
WE STRIVE. WE REPEAT. WE SUCCEED.
REMEMBER THAT, SSKEER? REMEMBER WHAT YOU TAUGHT ME?
MARU WANTS ME TO KEEP AN EYE ON AVAR. ME. EVERYTHING I'VE TOUCHED OVER THE LAST FEW MONTHS HAS TURNED TO BANTHA CRAP.
THAT'S NOT TRUE.
I NEED YOU ON THE ATARAXIA. I NEED YOU BY MY SIDE.
YOU MUST GO. YOU HAVE A DUTY.
YOU ARE A JEDI.
YEAH. I AM.
AND I THOUGHT YOU WERE TOO...

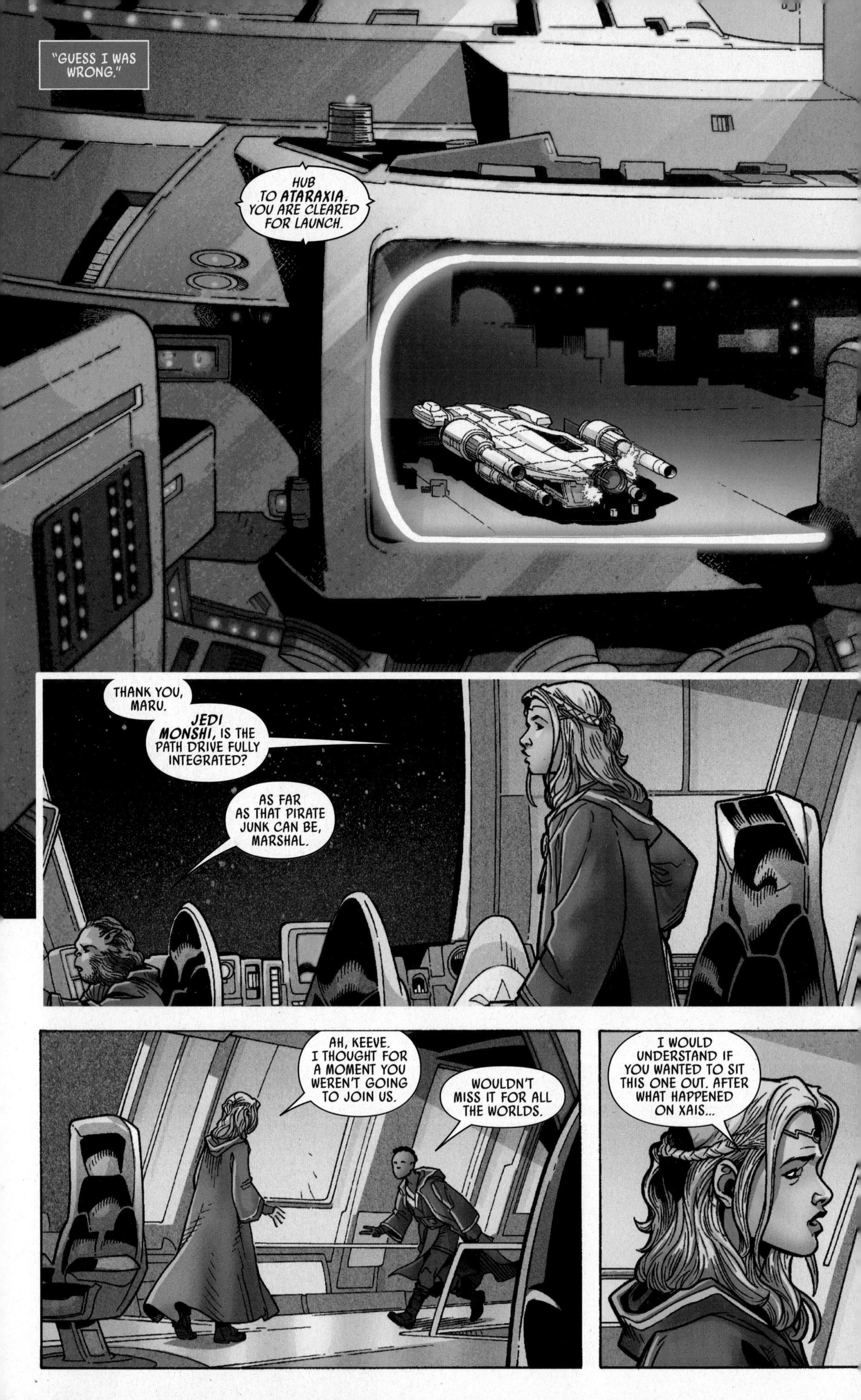
"GUESS I WAS WRONG."
HUB TO ATARAXIA. YOU ARE CLEARED FOR LAUNCH.
THANK YOU, MARU.
JEDI MONSHI, IS THE PATH DRIVE FULLY INTEGRATED?
AS FAR AS THAT PIRATE JUNK CAN BE, MARSHAL.
AH, KEEVE. I THOUGHT FOR A MOMENT YOU WEREN'T GOING TO JOIN US.
WOULDN'T MISS IT FOR ALL THE WORLDS.
I WOULD UNDERSTAND IF YOU WANTED TO SIT THIS ONE OUT. AFTER WHAT HAPPENED ON XAIS...

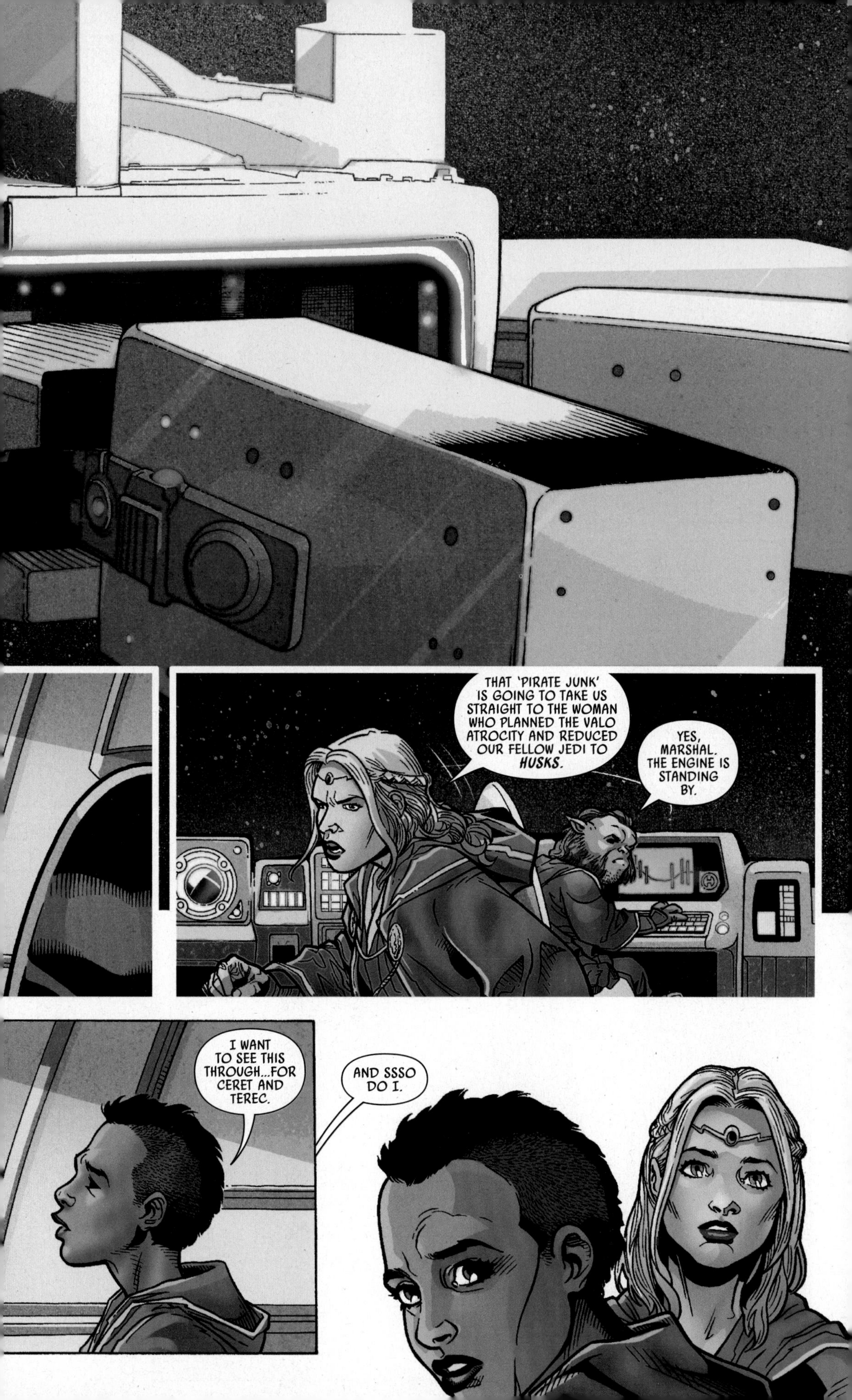
THAT 'PIRATE JUNK' IS GOING TO TAKE US STRAIGHT TO THE WOMAN WHO PLANNED THE VALO ATROCITY AND REDUCED OUR FELLOW JEDI TO *HUSKS.*
YES, MARSHAL. THE ENGINE IS STANDING BY.
I WANT TO SEE THIS THROUGH...FOR CERET AND TEREC.
AND SSSO DO I.

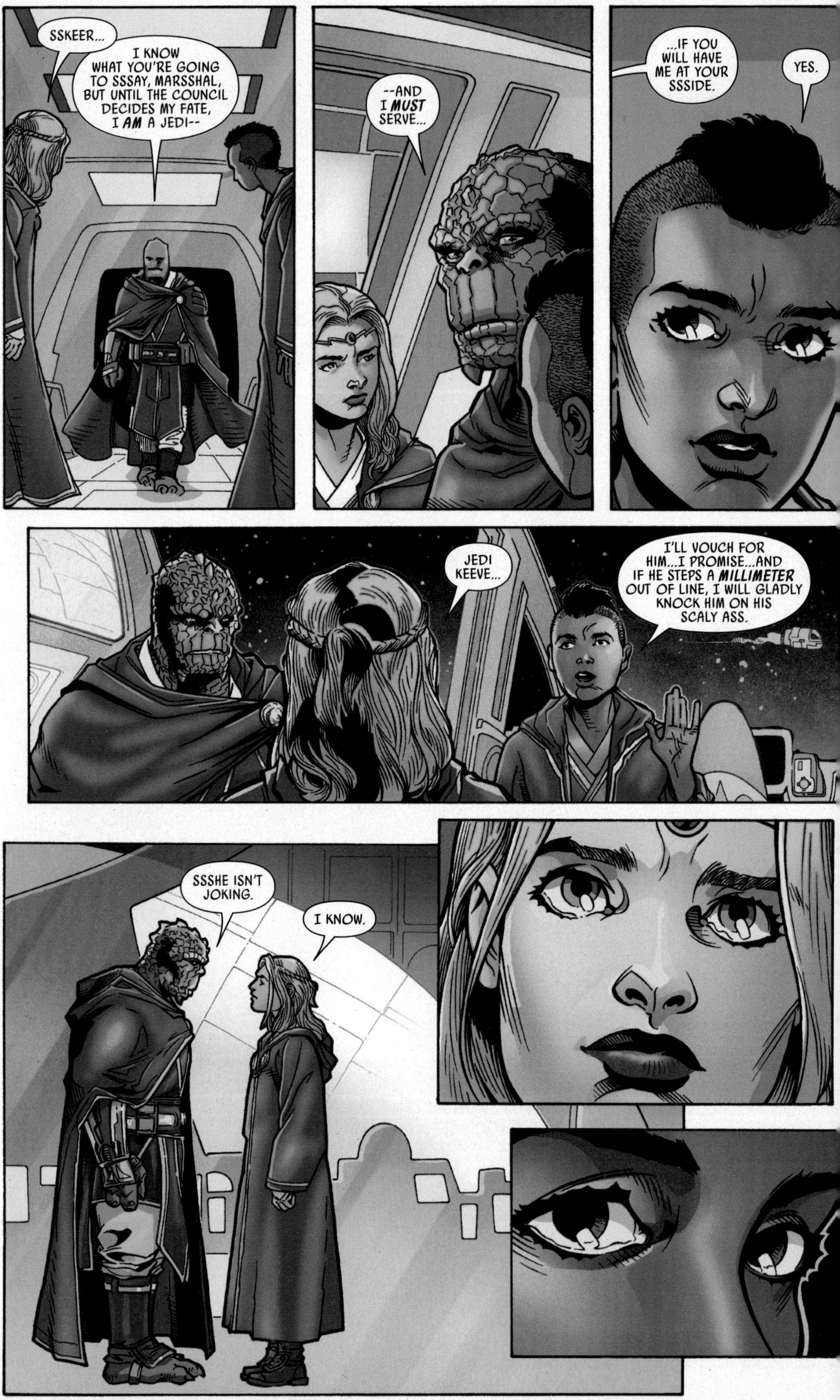
SSKEER...
I KNOW WHAT YOU'RE GOING TO SSSAY, MARSSHAL, BUT UNTIL THE COUNCIL DECIDES MY FATE, I *AM* A JEDI--
--AND I *MUST* SERVE...
...IF YOU WILL HAVE ME AT YOUR SSSIDE.
YES.
JEDI KEEVE...
I'LL VOUCH FOR HIM...I PROMISE...AND IF HE STEPS A *MILLIMETER* OUT OF LINE, I WILL GLADLY KNOCK HIM ON HIS SCALY ASS.
SSSHE ISN'T JOKING.
I KNOW.

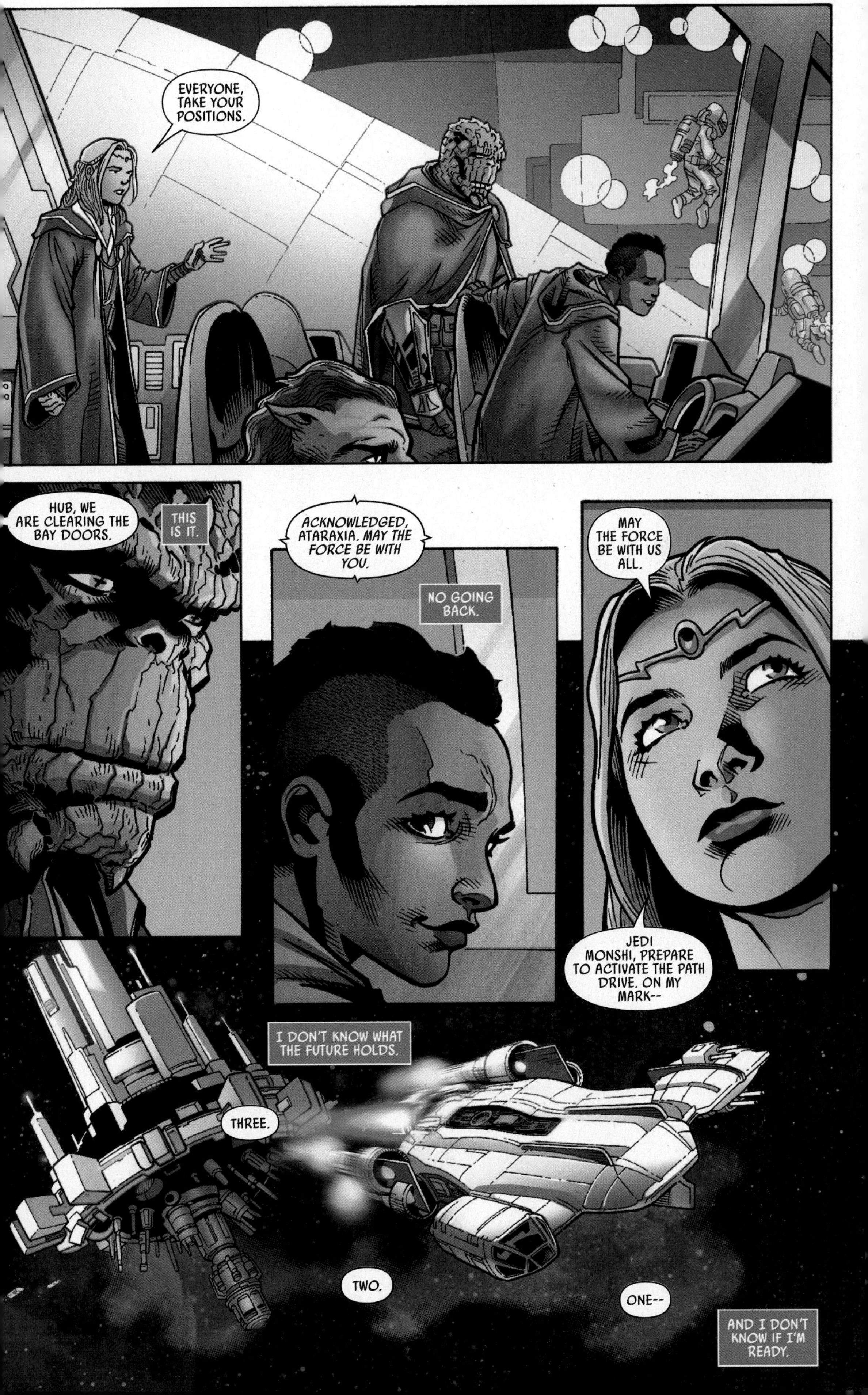
EVERYONE, TAKE YOUR POSITIONS.
HUB, WE ARE CLEARING THE BAY DOORS.
THIS IS IT.
ACKNOWLEDGED, ATARAXIA. MAY THE FORCE BE WITH YOU.
NO GOING BACK.
MAY THE FORCE BE WITH US ALL.
JEDI MONSHI, PREPARE TO ACTIVATE THE PATH DRIVE. ON MY MARK--
I DON'T KNOW WHAT THE FUTURE HOLDS.
THREE.
TWO.
ONE--
AND I DON'T KNOW IF I'M READY.

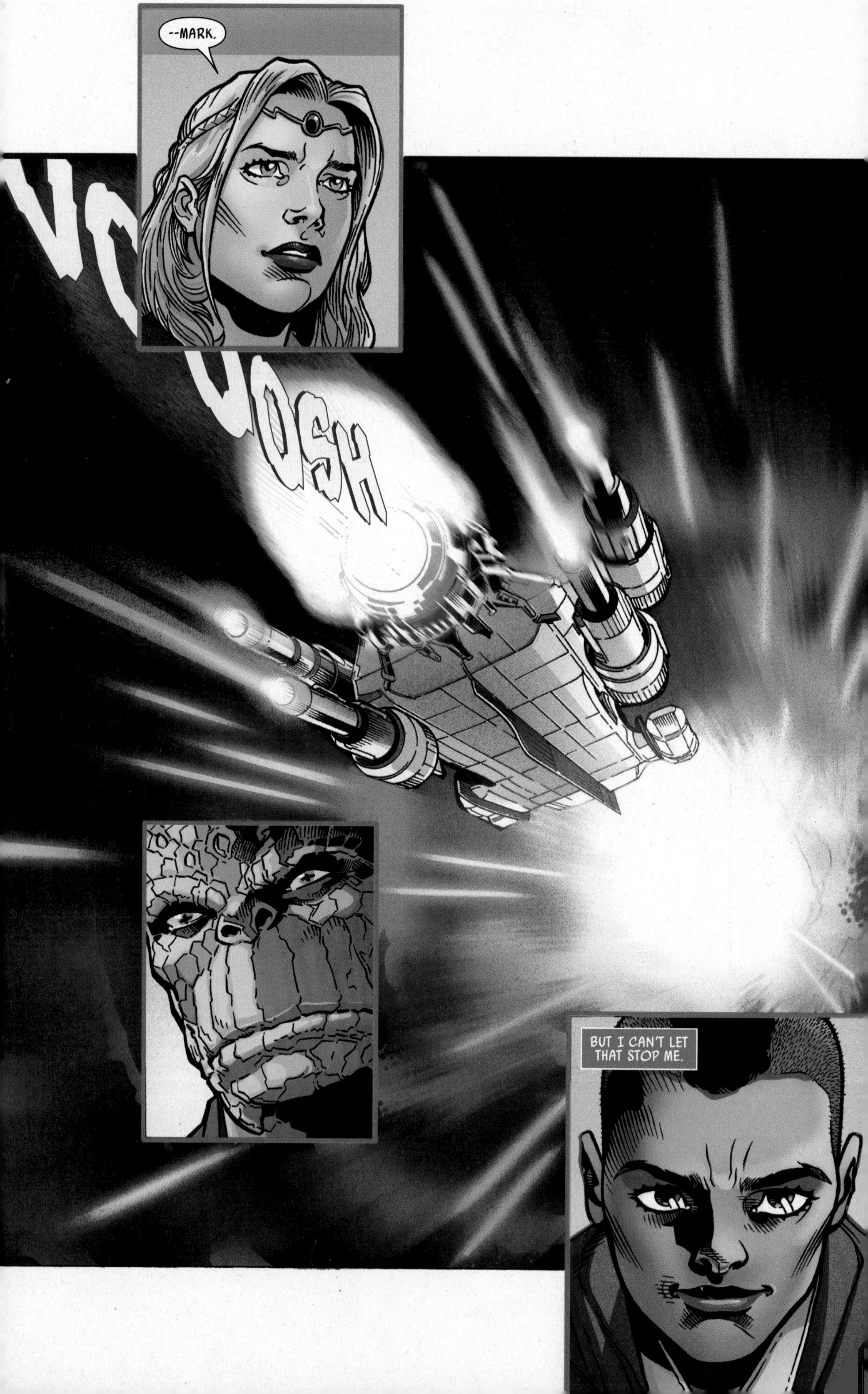
--MARK.
VOOOSH
BUT I CAN'T LET THAT STOP ME.

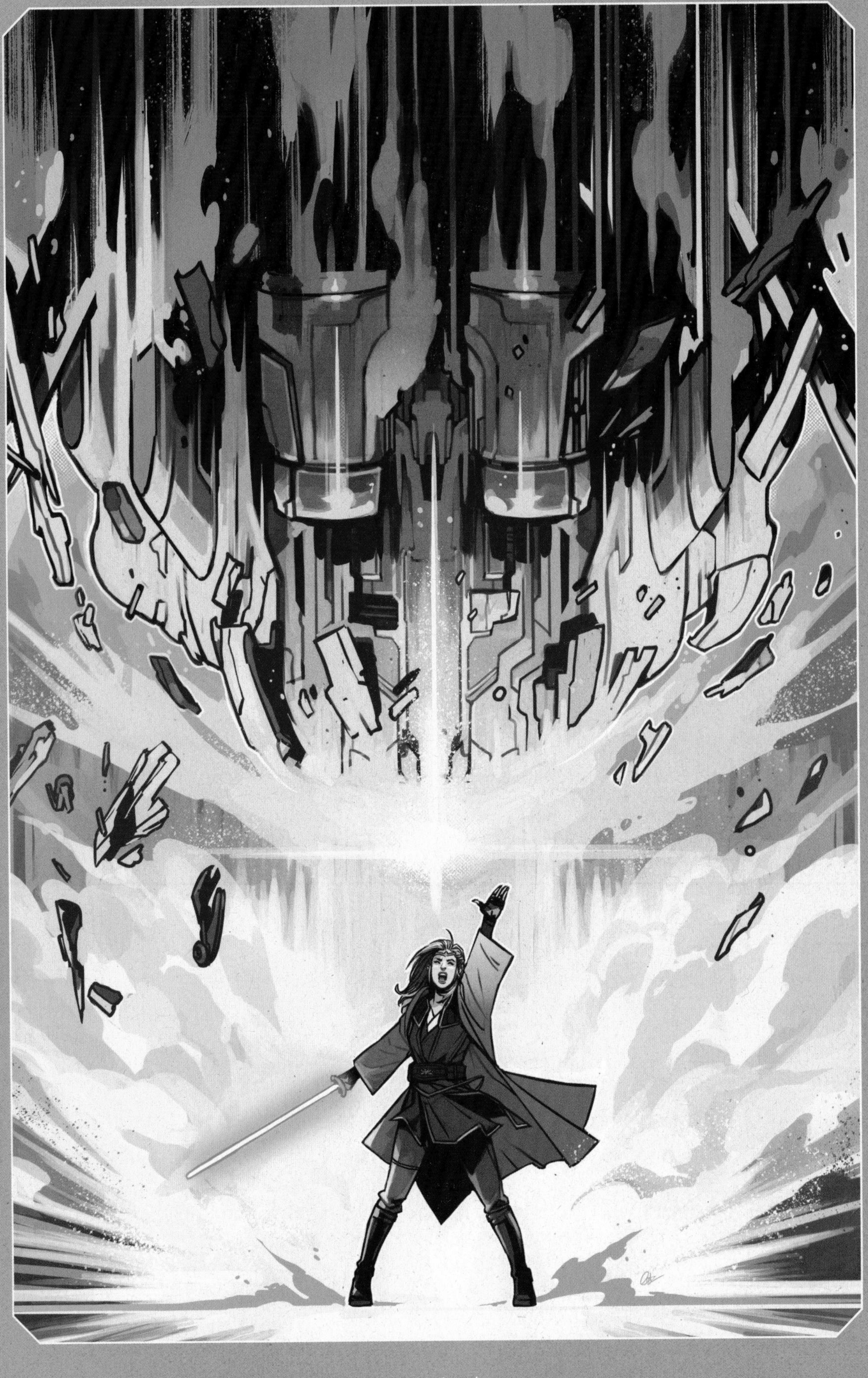

#12 Variant by
CASPAR WIJNGAARD

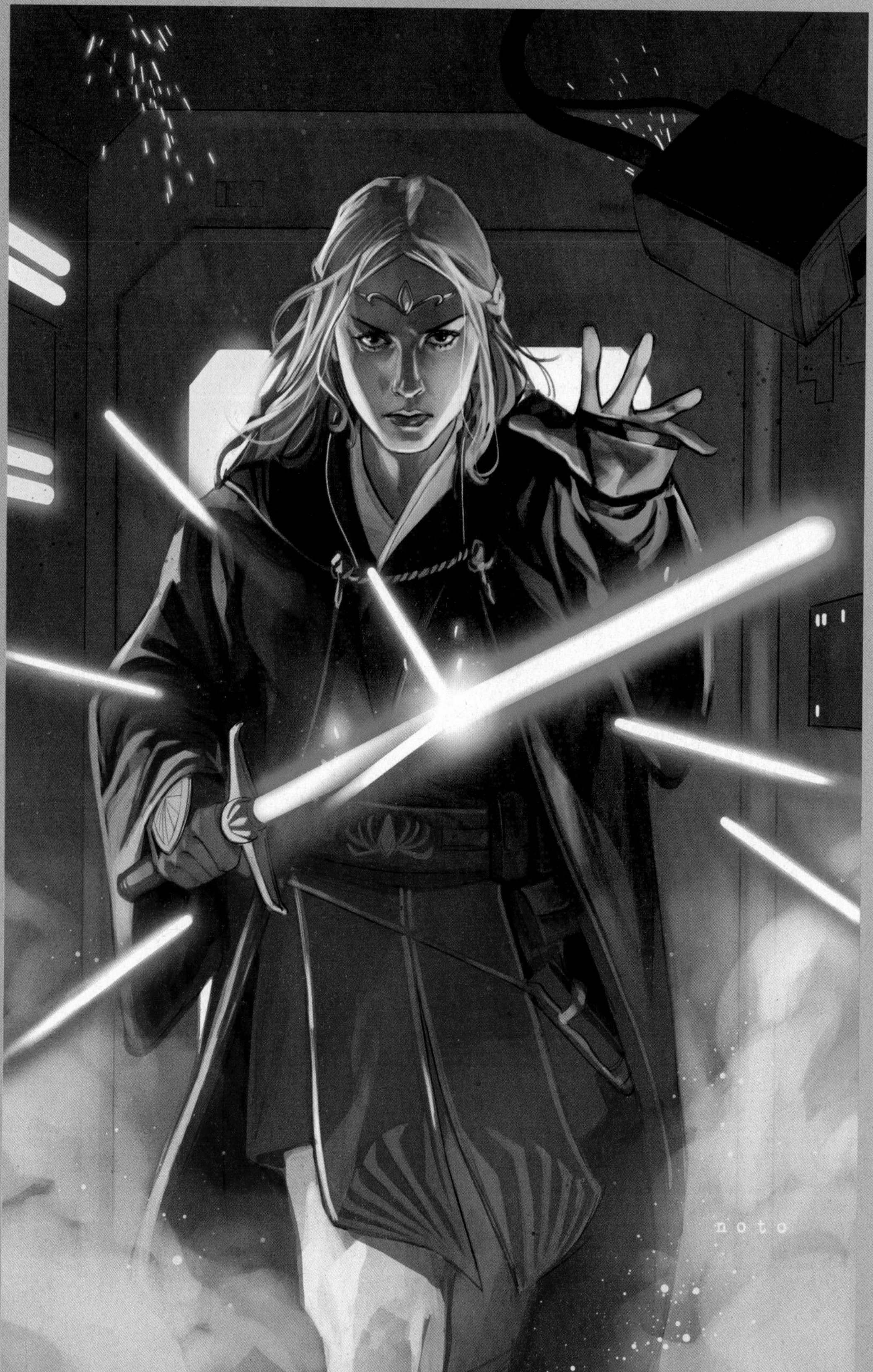
noto

13 | THE BATTLE OF NO-SPACE

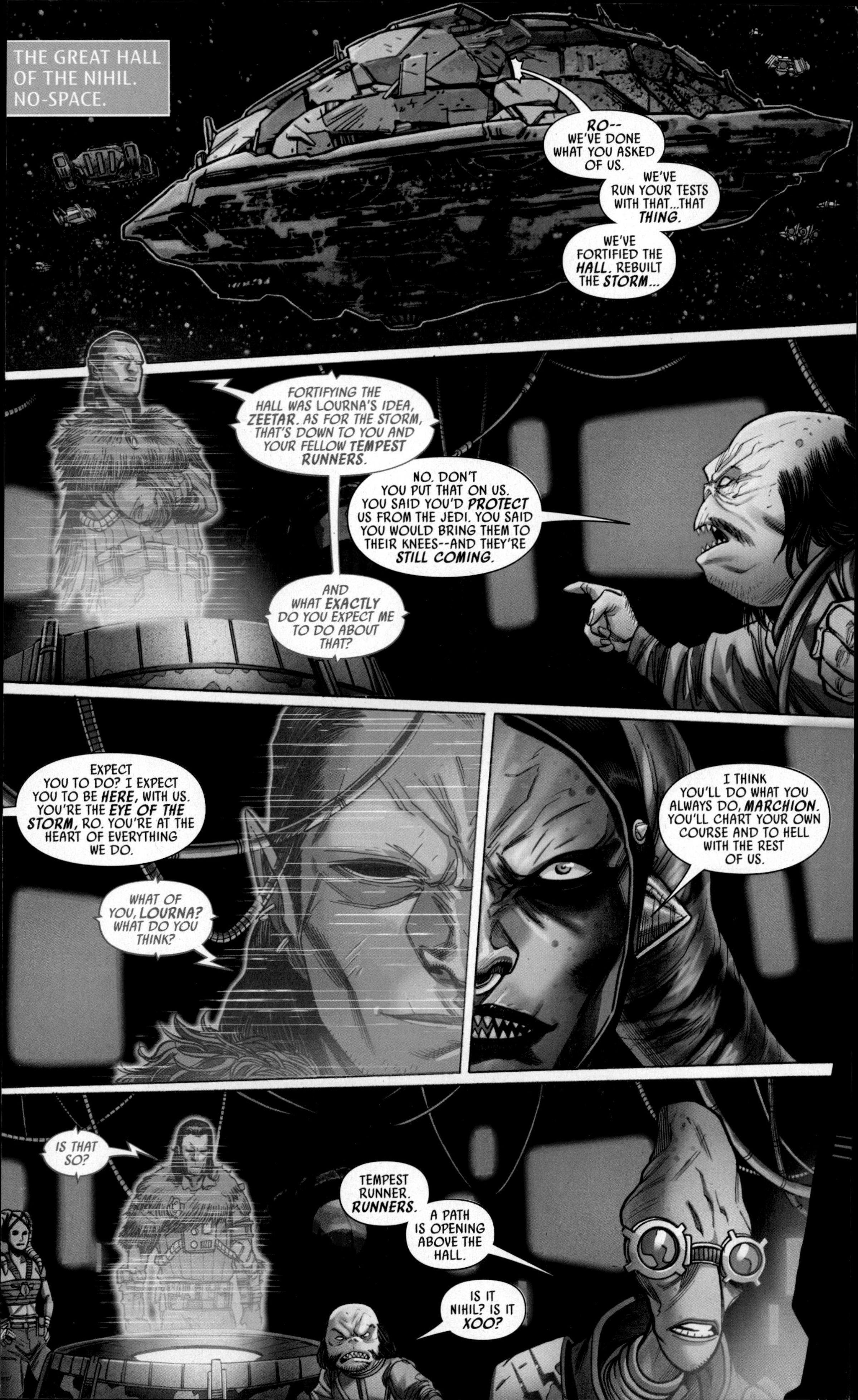
THE GREAT HALL OF THE NIHIL. NO-SPACE.
RO-- WE'VE DONE WHAT YOU ASKED OF US.
WE'VE RUN YOUR TESTS WITH THAT...THAT THING.
WE'VE FORTIFIED THE HALL. REBUILT THE STORM...
FORTIFYING THE HALL WAS LOURNA'S IDEA, ZEETAR. AS FOR THE STORM, THAT'S DOWN TO YOU AND YOUR FELLOW TEMPEST RUNNERS.
NO. DON'T YOU PUT THAT ON US. YOU SAID YOU'D PROTECT US FROM THE JEDI. YOU SAID YOU WOULD BRING THEM TO THEIR KNEES--AND THEY'RE STILL COMING.
AND WHAT EXACTLY DO YOU EXPECT ME TO DO ABOUT THAT?
EXPECT YOU TO DO? I EXPECT YOU TO BE HERE, WITH US. YOU'RE THE EYE OF THE STORM, RO. YOU'RE AT THE HEART OF EVERYTHING WE DO.
WHAT OF YOU, LOURNA? WHAT DO YOU THINK?
I THINK YOU'LL DO WHAT YOU ALWAYS DO, MARCHION. YOU'LL CHART YOUR OWN COURSE AND TO HELL WITH THE REST OF US.
IS THAT SO?
TEMPEST RUNNER. RUNNERS.
A PATH IS OPENING ABOVE THE HALL.
IS IT NIHIL? IS IT XOO?

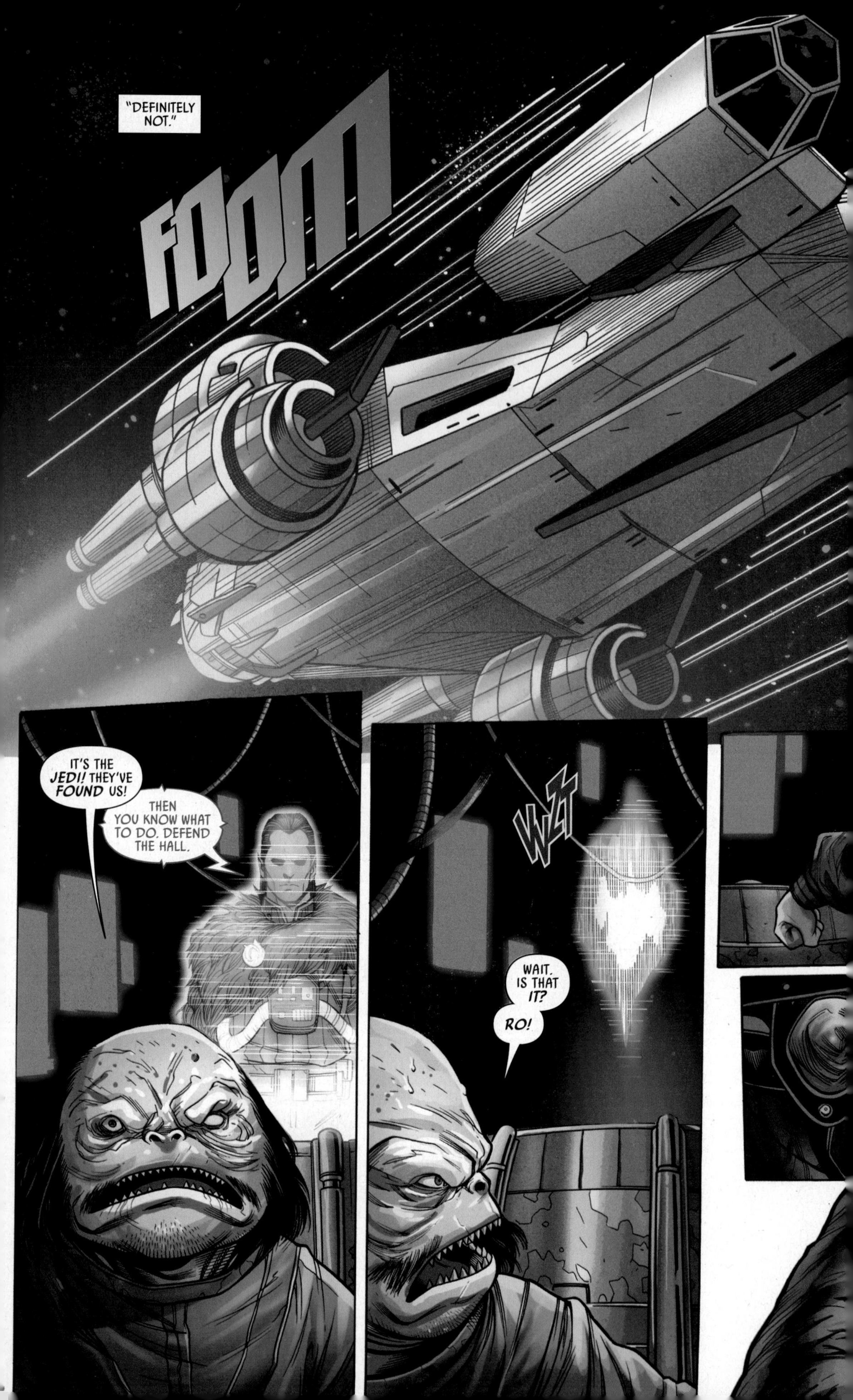
"DEFINITELY NOT."
FOOM
IT'S THE JEDI! THEY'VE FOUND US!
THEN YOU KNOW WHAT TO DO. DEFEND THE HALL.
WZZT
WAIT. IS THAT IT?
RO!

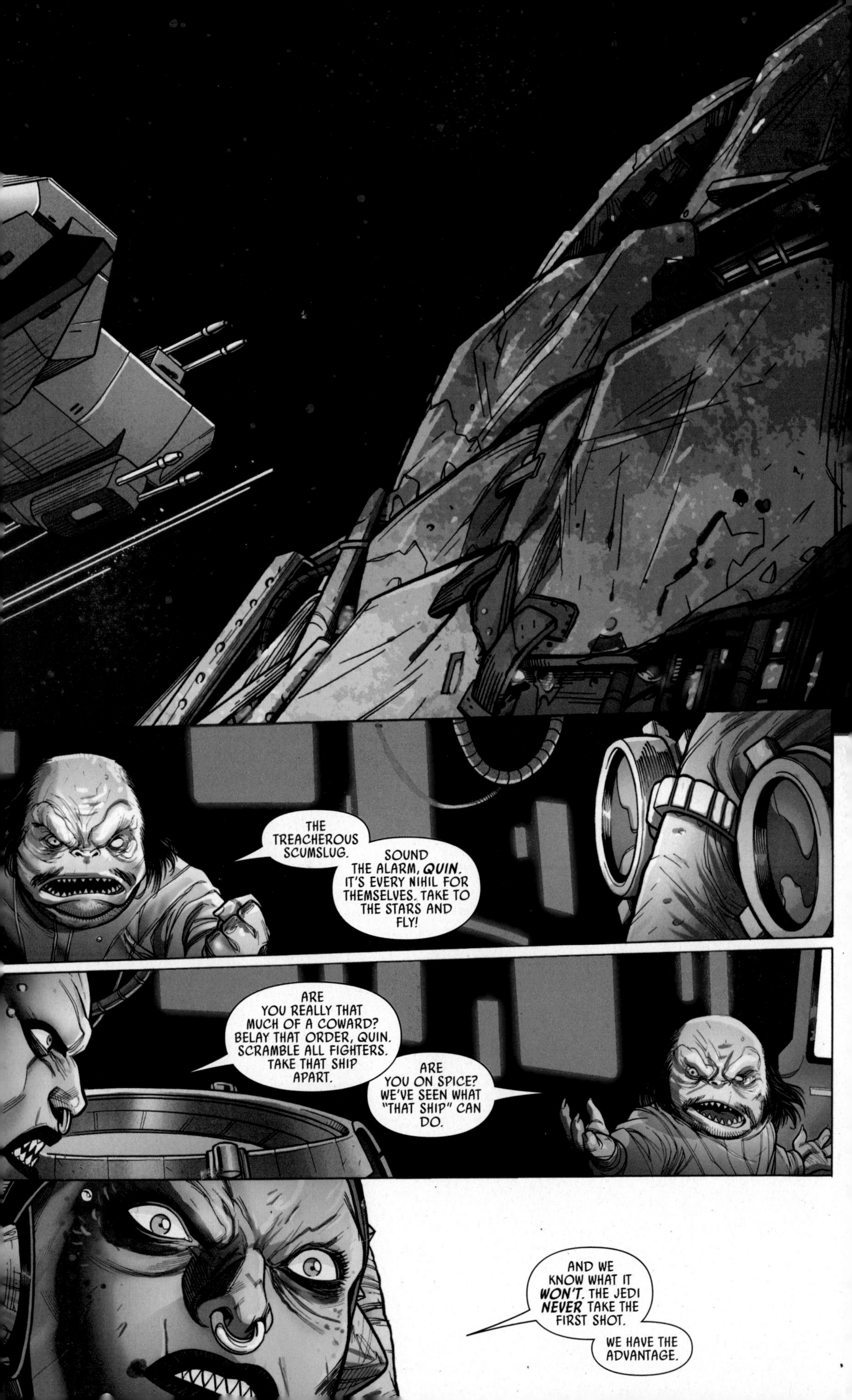
THE TREACHEROUS SCUMSLUG.
SOUND THE ALARM, ***QUIN***. IT'S EVERY NIHIL FOR THEMSELVES. TAKE TO THE STARS AND FLY!
ARE YOU REALLY THAT MUCH OF A COWARD? BELAY THAT ORDER, QUIN. SCRAMBLE ALL FIGHTERS. TAKE THAT SHIP APART.
ARE YOU ON SPICE? WE'VE SEEN WHAT "THAT SHIP" CAN DO.
AND WE KNOW WHAT IT ***WON'T***. THE JEDI ***NEVER*** TAKE THE FIRST SHOT.
WE HAVE THE ADVANTAGE.

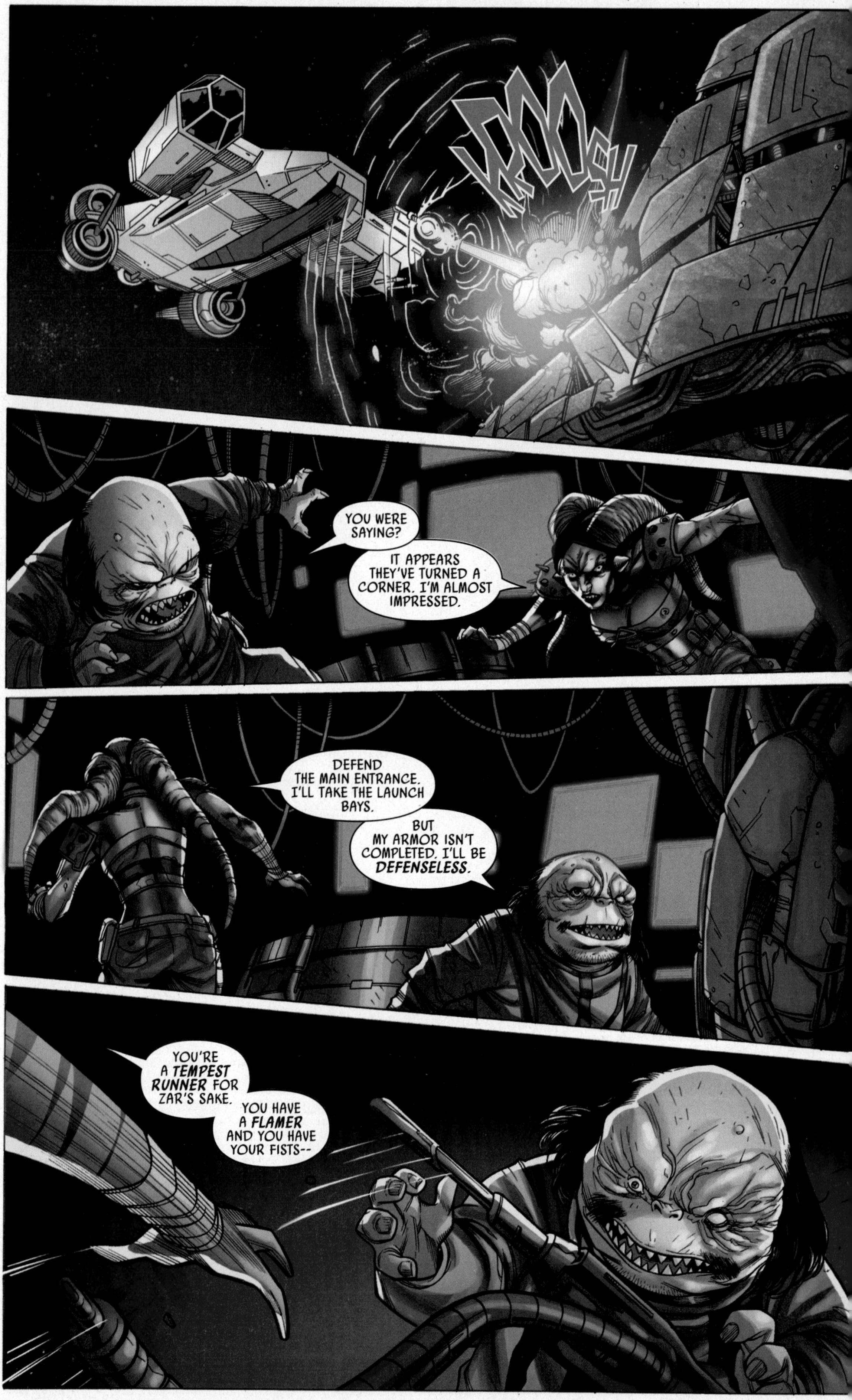
YOU WERE SAYING?
IT APPEARS THEY'VE TURNED A CORNER. I'M ALMOST IMPRESSED.
DEFEND THE MAIN ENTRANCE. I'LL TAKE THE LAUNCH BAYS.
BUT MY ARMOR ISN'T COMPLETED. I'LL BE *DEFENSELESS.*
YOU'RE A *TEMPEST RUNNER* FOR ZAR'S SAKE.
YOU HAVE A *FLAMER* AND YOU HAVE YOUR FISTS--

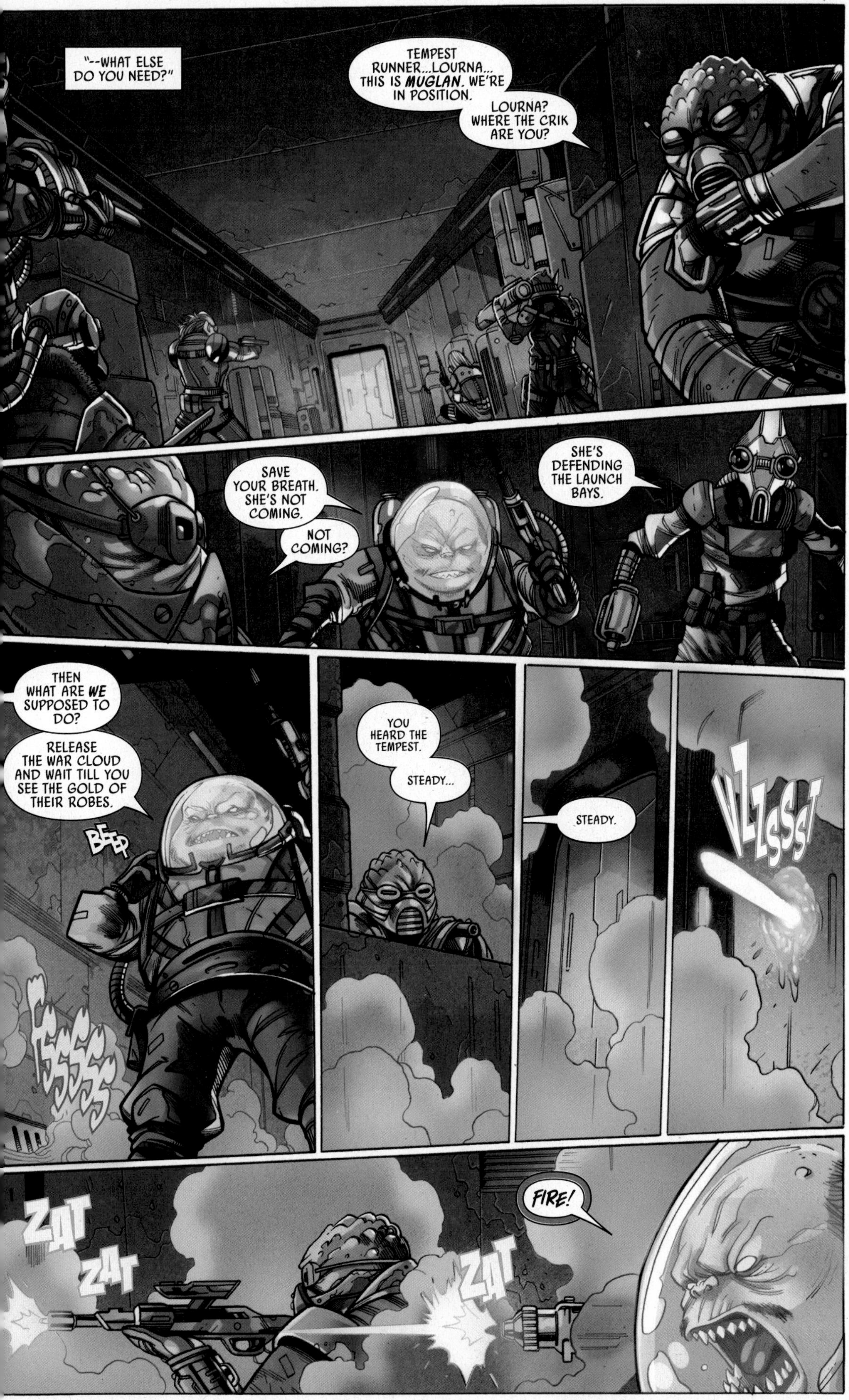
"--WHAT ELSE DO YOU NEED?"
TEMPEST RUNNER...LOURNA... THIS IS MUGLAN. WE'RE IN POSITION.
LOURNA? WHERE THE CRIK ARE YOU?
SAVE YOUR BREATH. SHE'S NOT COMING.
NOT COMING?
SHE'S DEFENDING THE LAUNCH BAYS.
THEN WHAT ARE WE SUPPOSED TO DO?
RELEASE THE WAR CLOUD AND WAIT TILL YOU SEE THE GOLD OF THEIR ROBES.
BEEP
FSSSSS
YOU HEARD THE TEMPEST.
STEADY...
STEADY.
VZZSSST
FIRE!
ZAT
ZAT
ZAT

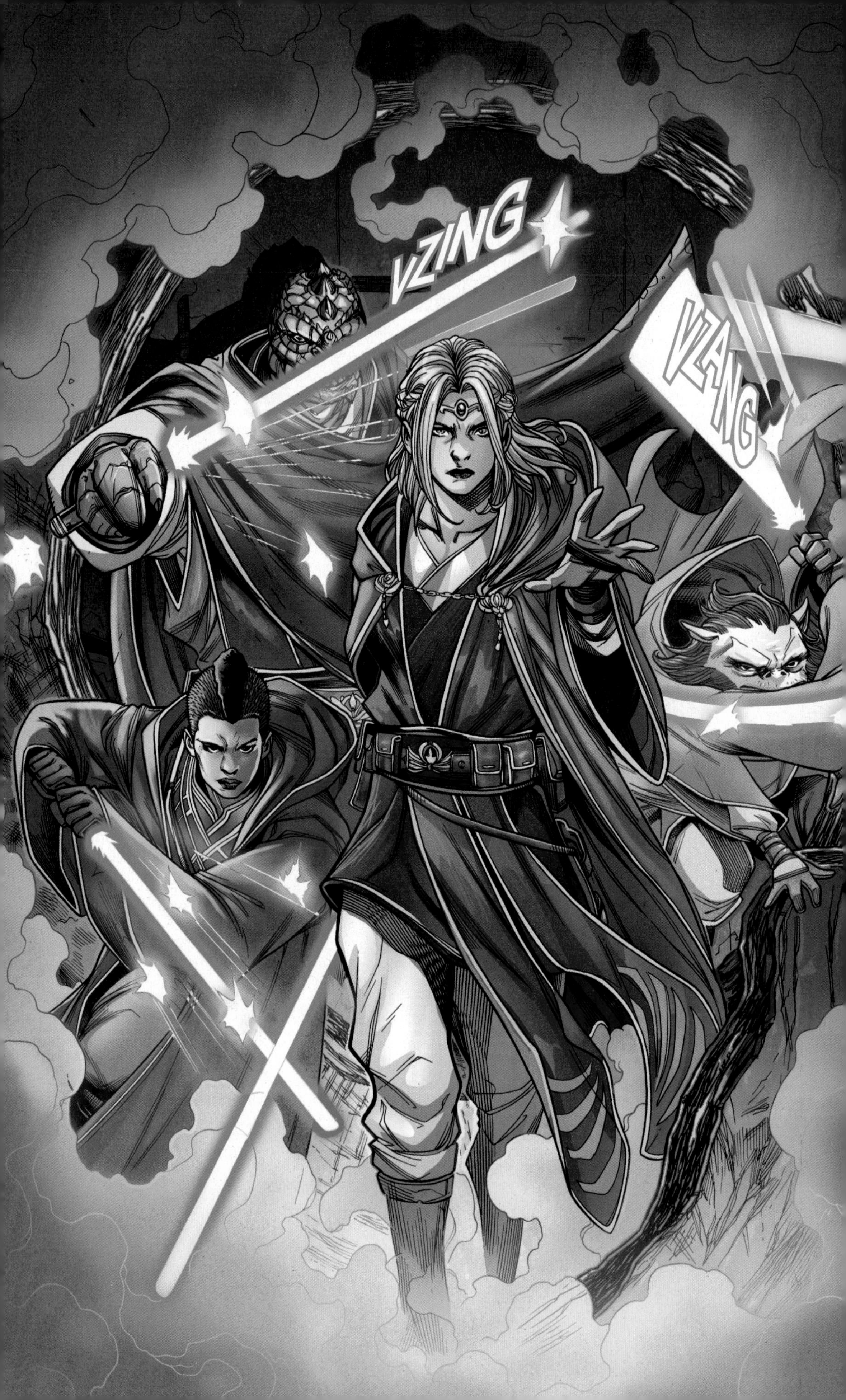
VZING
VZANG

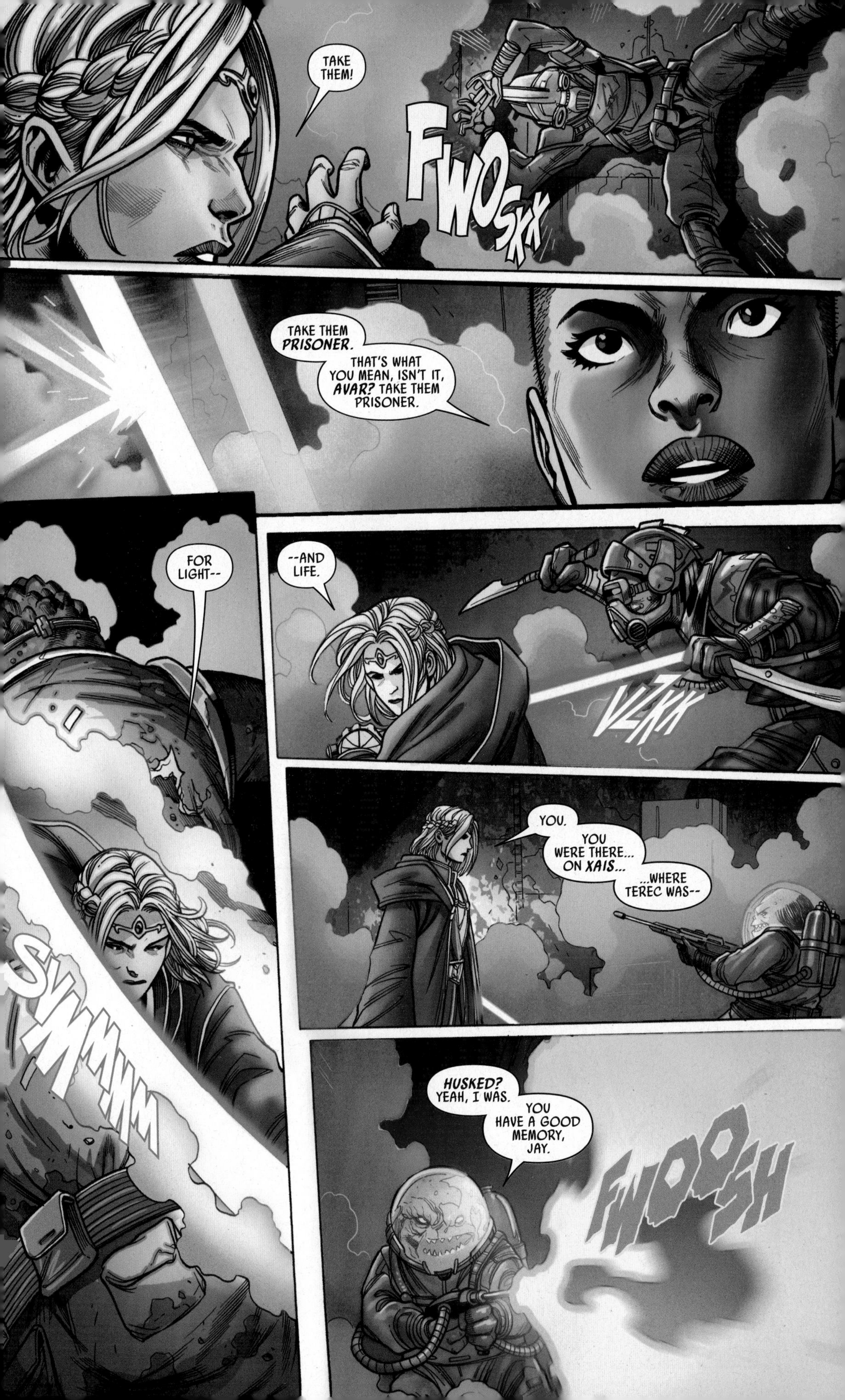

TAKE THEM!
FWOSKK
TAKE THEM PRISONER.
THAT'S WHAT YOU MEAN, ISN'T IT, AVAR? TAKE THEM PRISONER.
FOR LIGHT--
--AND LIFE.
VLZKK
SWMMMM
YOU.
YOU WERE THERE... ON XAIS...
...WHERE TEREC WAS--
HUSKED? YEAH, I WAS.
YOU HAVE A GOOD MEMORY, JAY.
FWOOSH

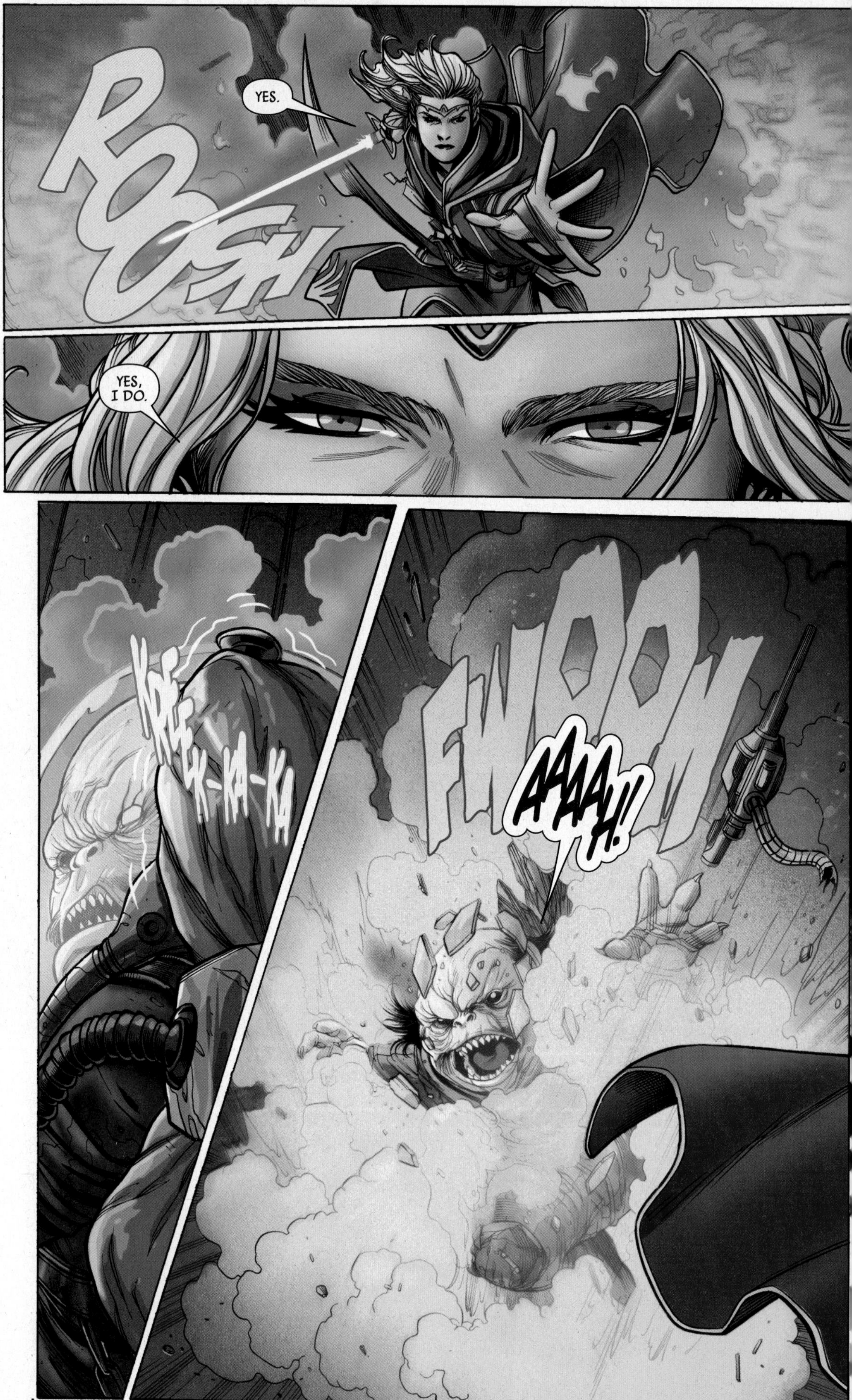
ROOSH
YES.
YES, I DO.
KREEEK-KA-KA
FWOOM
AAAAAH!!

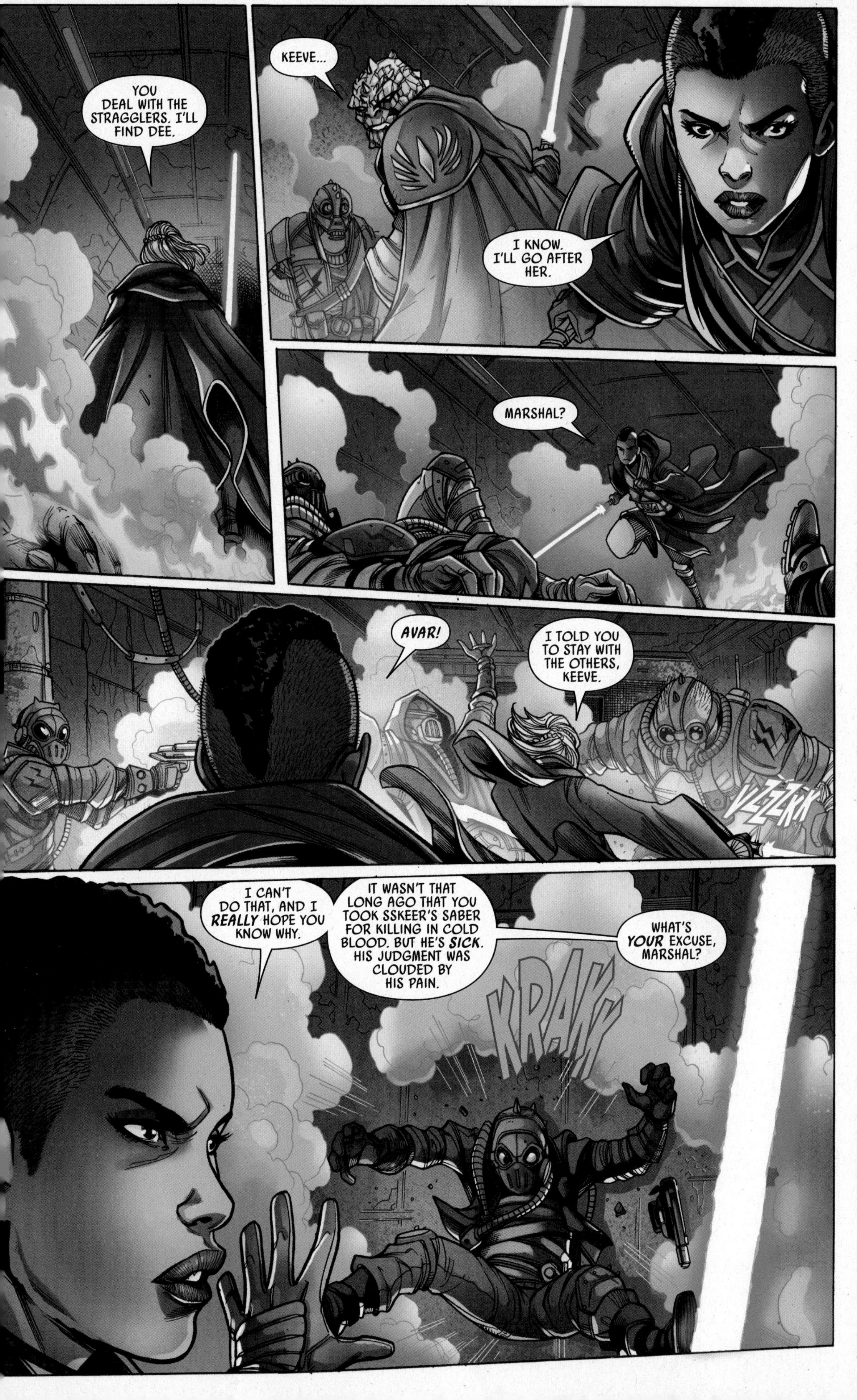
YOU DEAL WITH THE STRAGGLERS. I'LL FIND DEE.
KEEVE...
I KNOW. I'LL GO AFTER HER.
MARSHAL?
AVAR!
I TOLD YOU TO STAY WITH THE OTHERS, KEEVE.
VZZZRK
I CAN'T DO THAT, AND I *REALLY* HOPE YOU KNOW WHY.
IT WASN'T THAT LONG AGO THAT YOU TOOK SSKEER'S SABER FOR KILLING IN COLD BLOOD. BUT HE'S *SICK*. HIS JUDGMENT WAS CLOUDED BY HIS PAIN.
WHAT'S *YOUR* EXCUSE, MARSHAL?
KRAKK

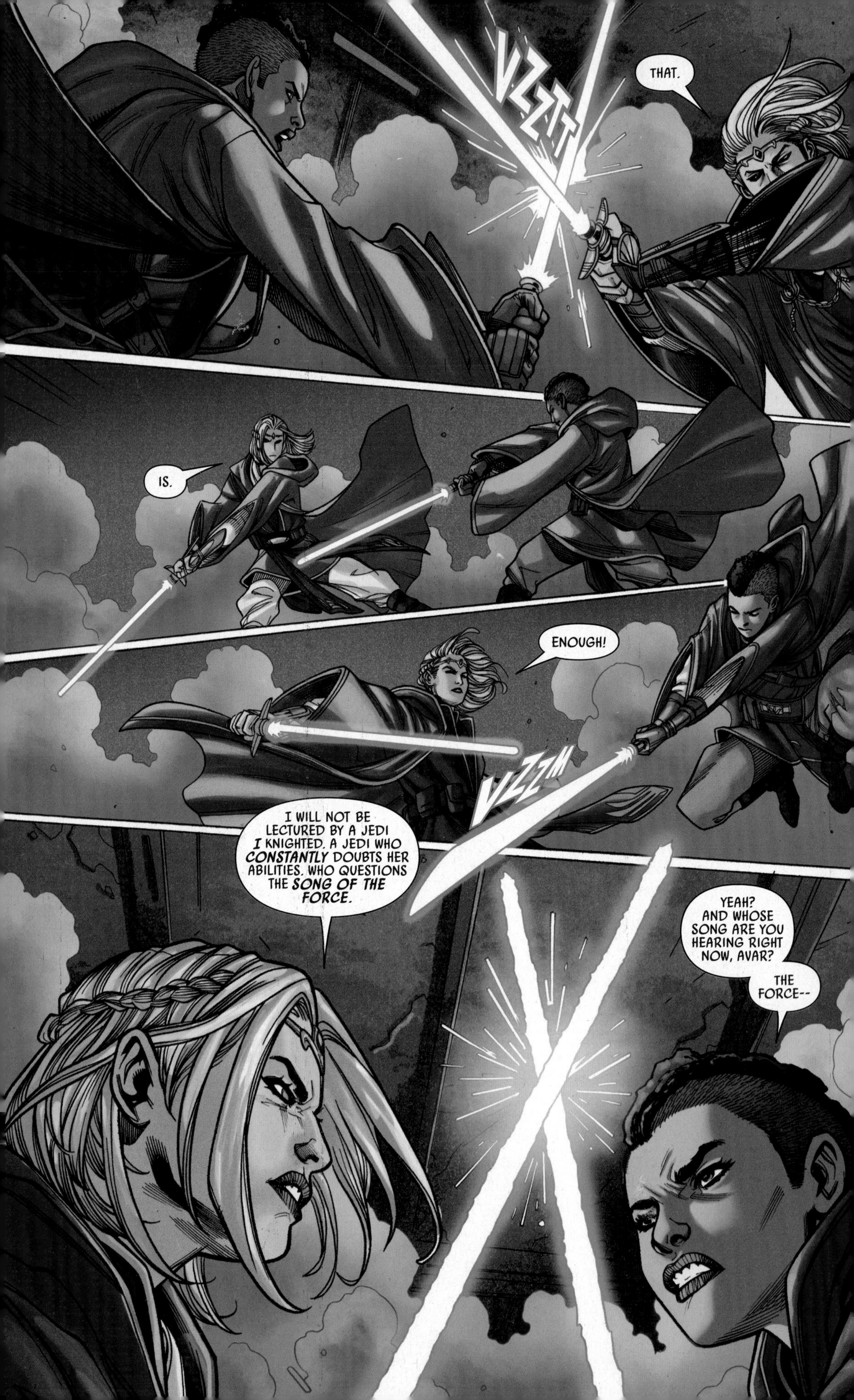
VZZT
THAT.
IS.
ENOUGH!
VZZM
I WILL NOT BE LECTURED BY A JEDI *I* KNIGHTED. A JEDI WHO *CONSTANTLY* DOUBTS HER ABILITIES. WHO QUESTIONS THE *SONG OF THE FORCE*.
YEAH? AND WHOSE SONG ARE YOU HEARING RIGHT NOW, AVAR?
THE FORCE--

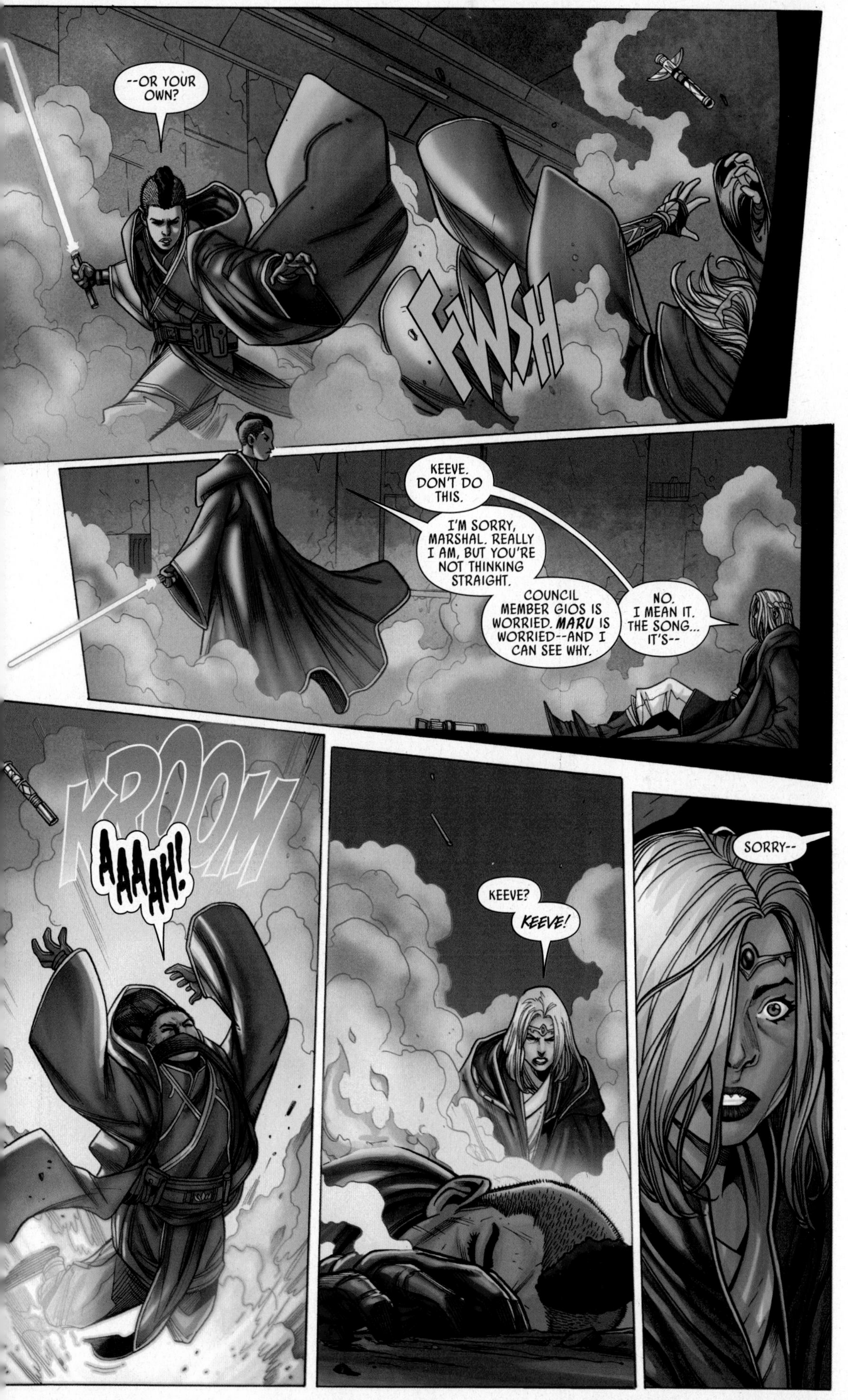
--OR YOUR OWN?
FWSH
KEEVE. DON'T DO THIS.
I'M SORRY, MARSHAL. REALLY I AM, BUT YOU'RE NOT THINKING STRAIGHT.
COUNCIL MEMBER GIOS IS WORRIED. MARU IS WORRIED--AND I CAN SEE WHY.
NO. I MEAN IT. THE SONG... IT'S--
KROOM
AAAAH!
KEEVE? KEEVE!
SORRY--

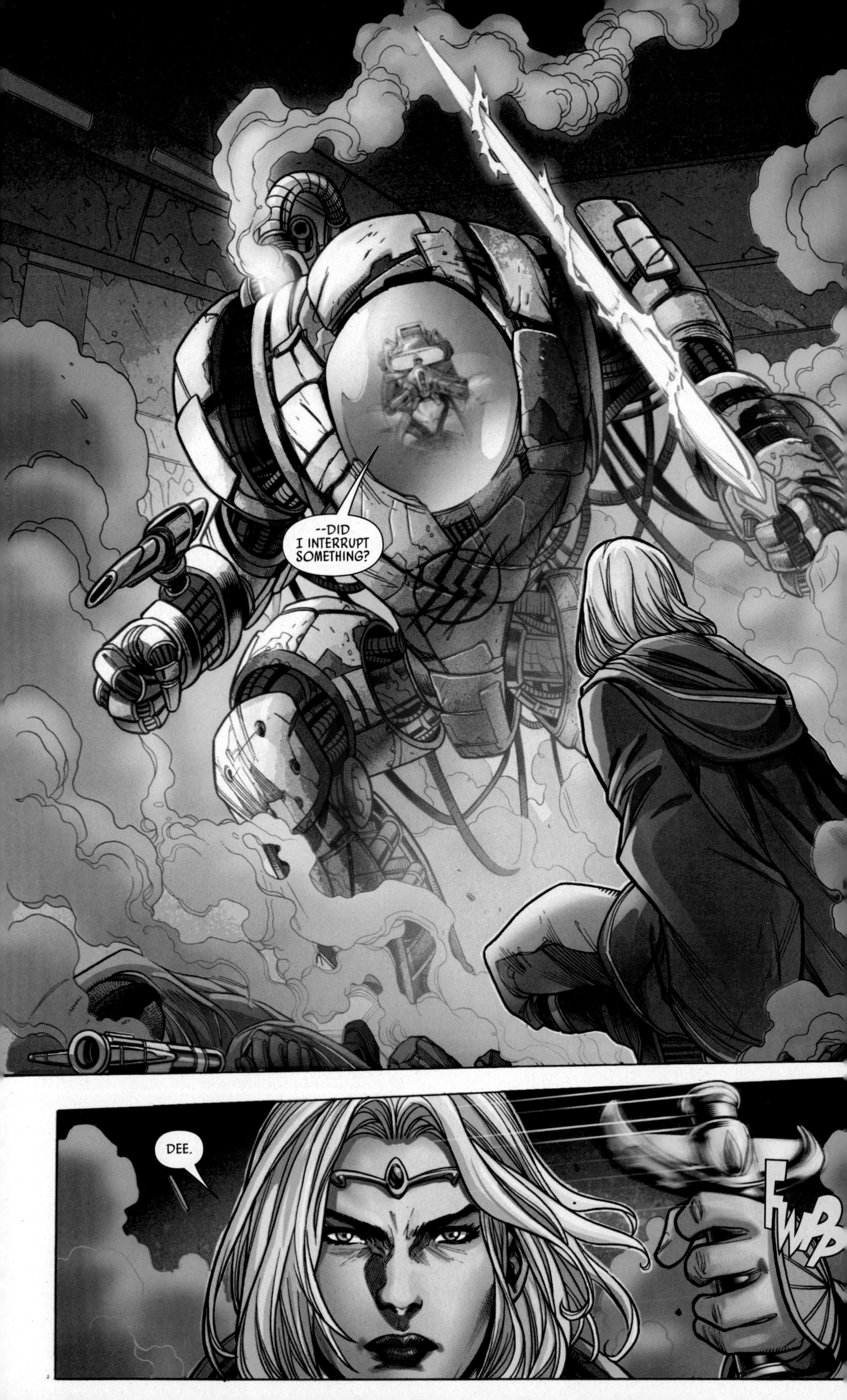
--DID
I INTERRUPT
SOMETHING?
DEE.
FWPP

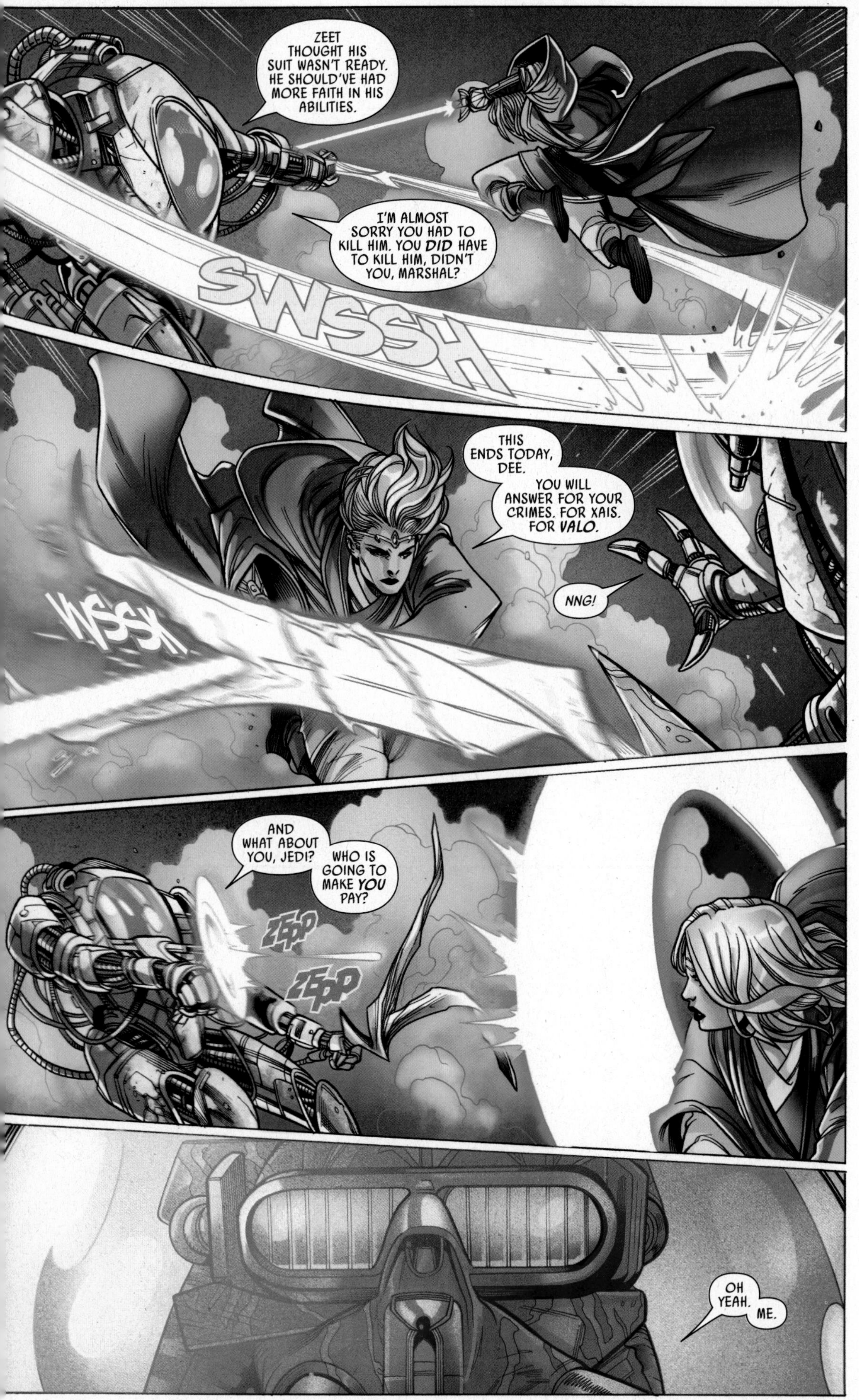
ZEET THOUGHT HIS SUIT WASN'T READY. HE SHOULD'VE HAD MORE FAITH IN HIS ABILITIES.
I'M ALMOST SORRY YOU HAD TO KILL HIM. YOU DID HAVE TO KILL HIM, DIDN'T YOU, MARSHAL?
SWSSH
THIS ENDS TODAY, DEE.
YOU WILL ANSWER FOR YOUR CRIMES. FOR XAIS. FOR VALO.
NNG!
WSSH
AND WHAT ABOUT YOU, JEDI?
WHO IS GOING TO MAKE YOU PAY?
ZEPP
ZEPP
OH YEAH.
ME.

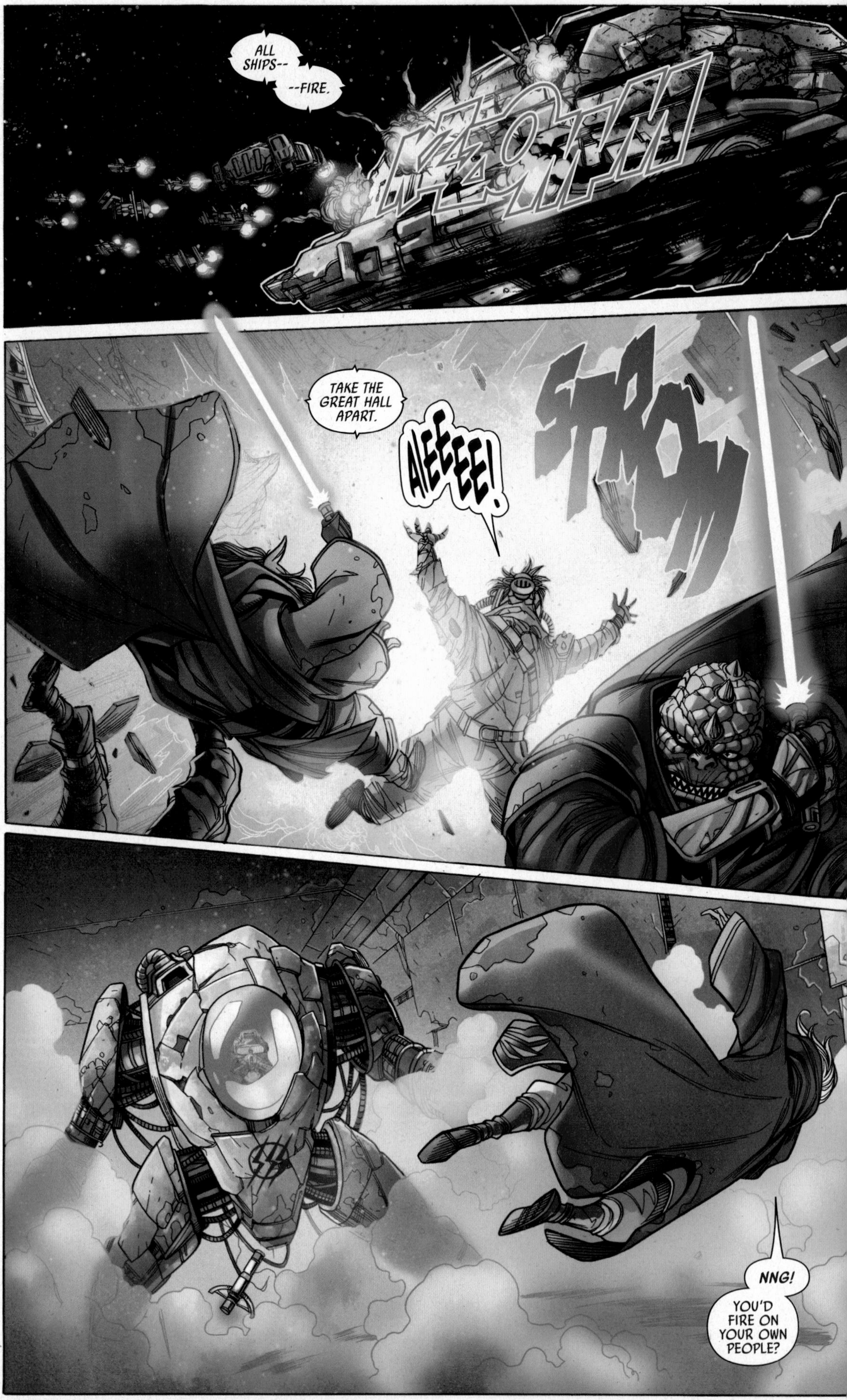
ALL SHIPS--
--FIRE.
TAKE THE GREAT HALL APART.
AIEEEEE!
NNG!
YOU'D FIRE ON YOUR OWN PEOPLE?

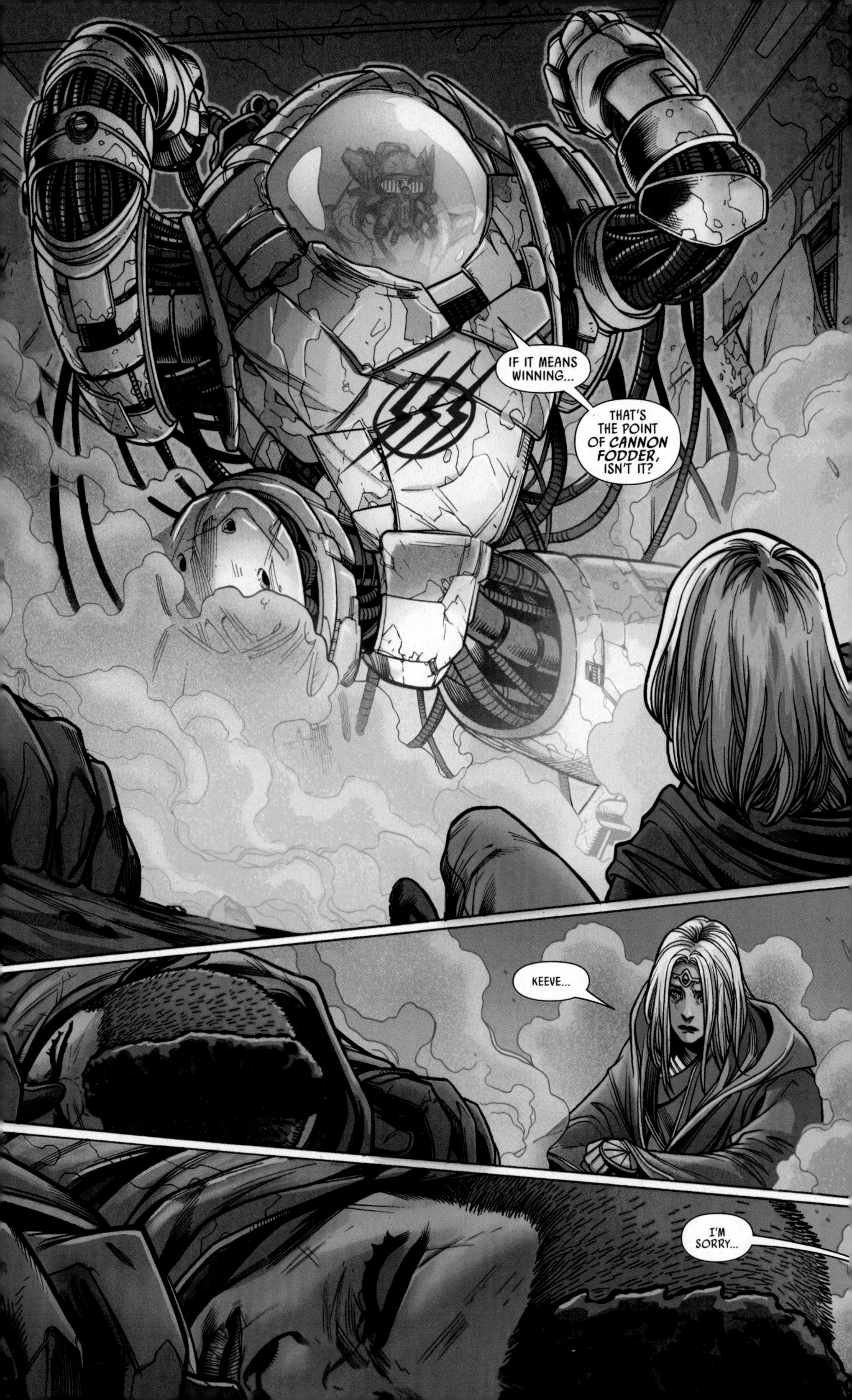
IF IT MEANS WINNING...
THAT'S THE POINT OF CANNON FODDER, ISN'T IT?
KEEVE...
I'M SORRY...

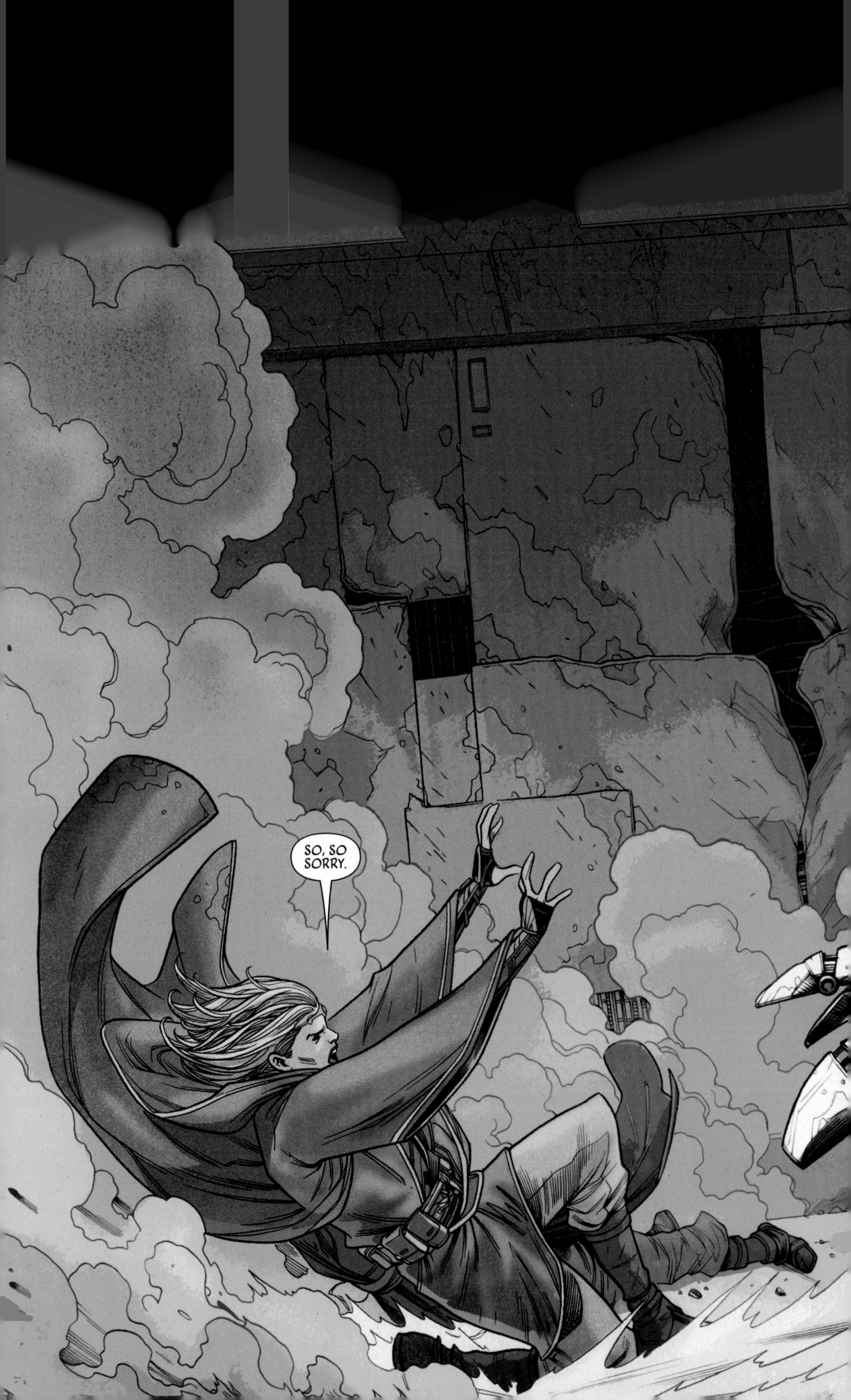
SO, SO SORRY.

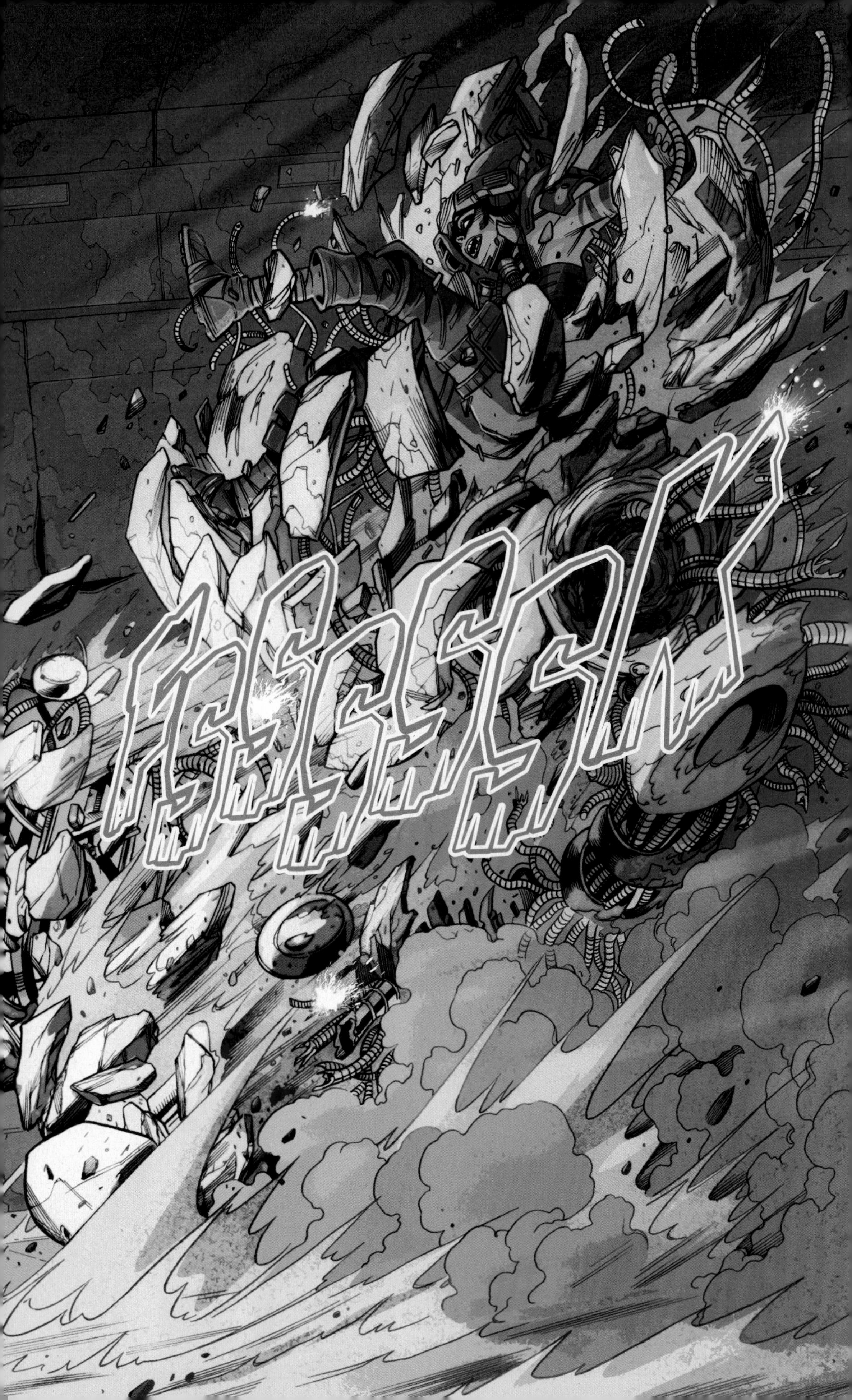

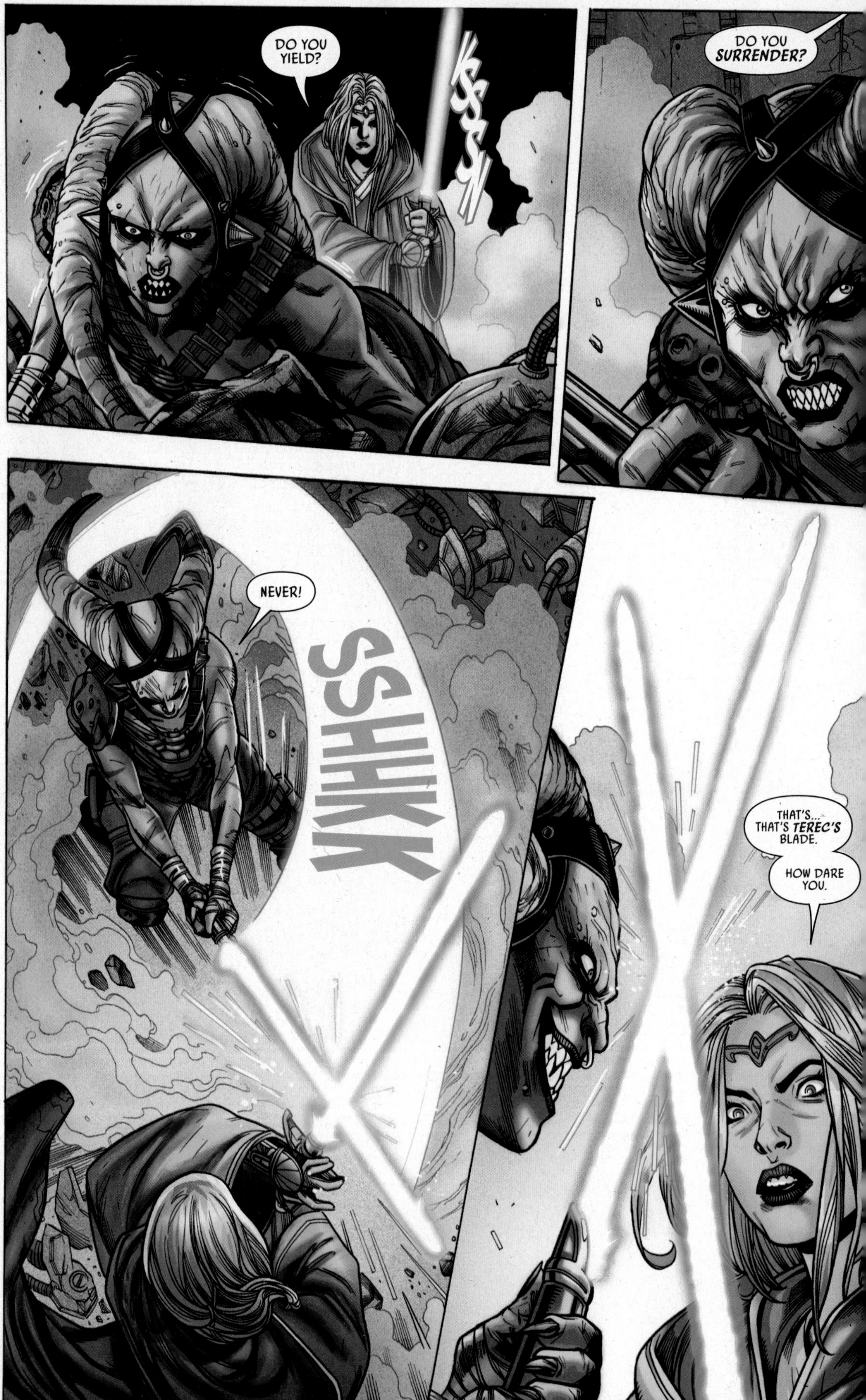
DO YOU YIELD?
VSSSN
DO YOU SURRENDER?
NEVER!
SSHHKK
THAT'S... THAT'S TEREC'S BLADE.
HOW DARE YOU.

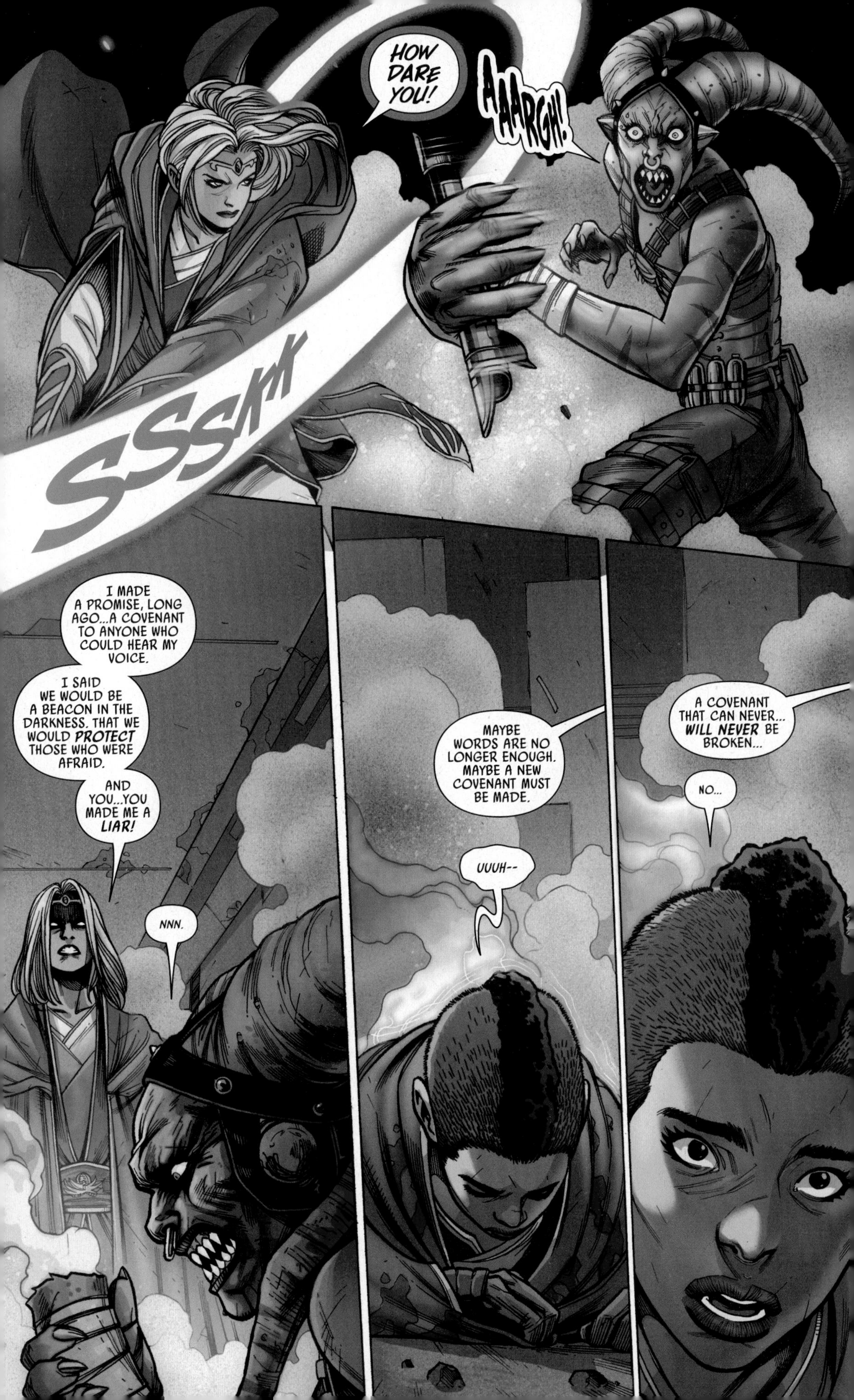
HOW DARE YOU!
AAARGH!
SSSKK
I MADE A PROMISE, LONG AGO...A COVENANT TO ANYONE WHO COULD HEAR MY VOICE.
I SAID WE WOULD BE A BEACON IN THE DARKNESS. THAT WE WOULD PROTECT THOSE WHO WERE AFRAID.
AND YOU...YOU MADE ME A LIAR!
NNN.
MAYBE WORDS ARE NO LONGER ENOUGH. MAYBE A NEW COVENANT MUST BE MADE.
UUUH--
A COVENANT THAT CAN NEVER... WILL NEVER BE BROKEN...
NO...

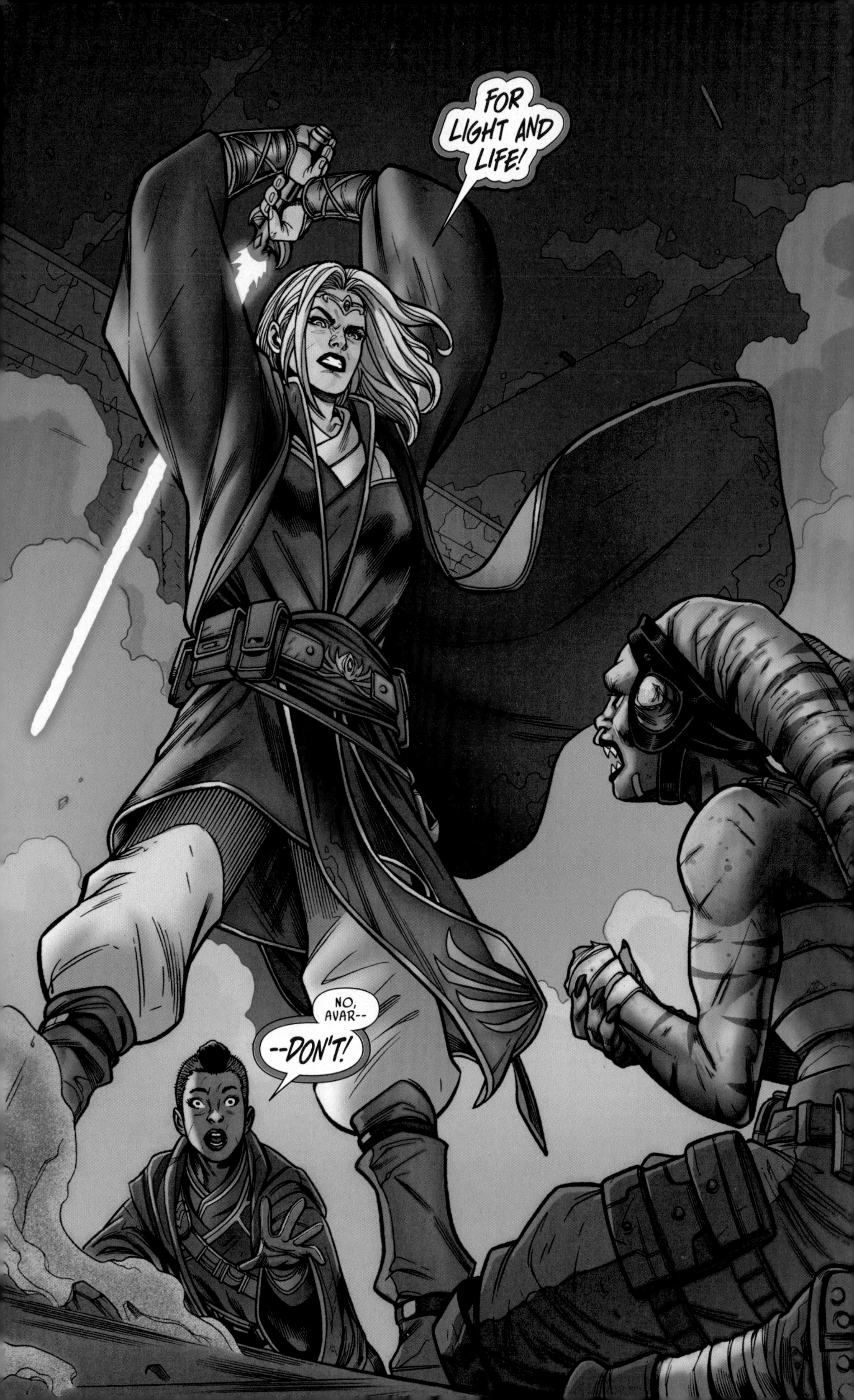
FOR LIGHT AND LIFE!
NO, AVAR--
--DON'T!

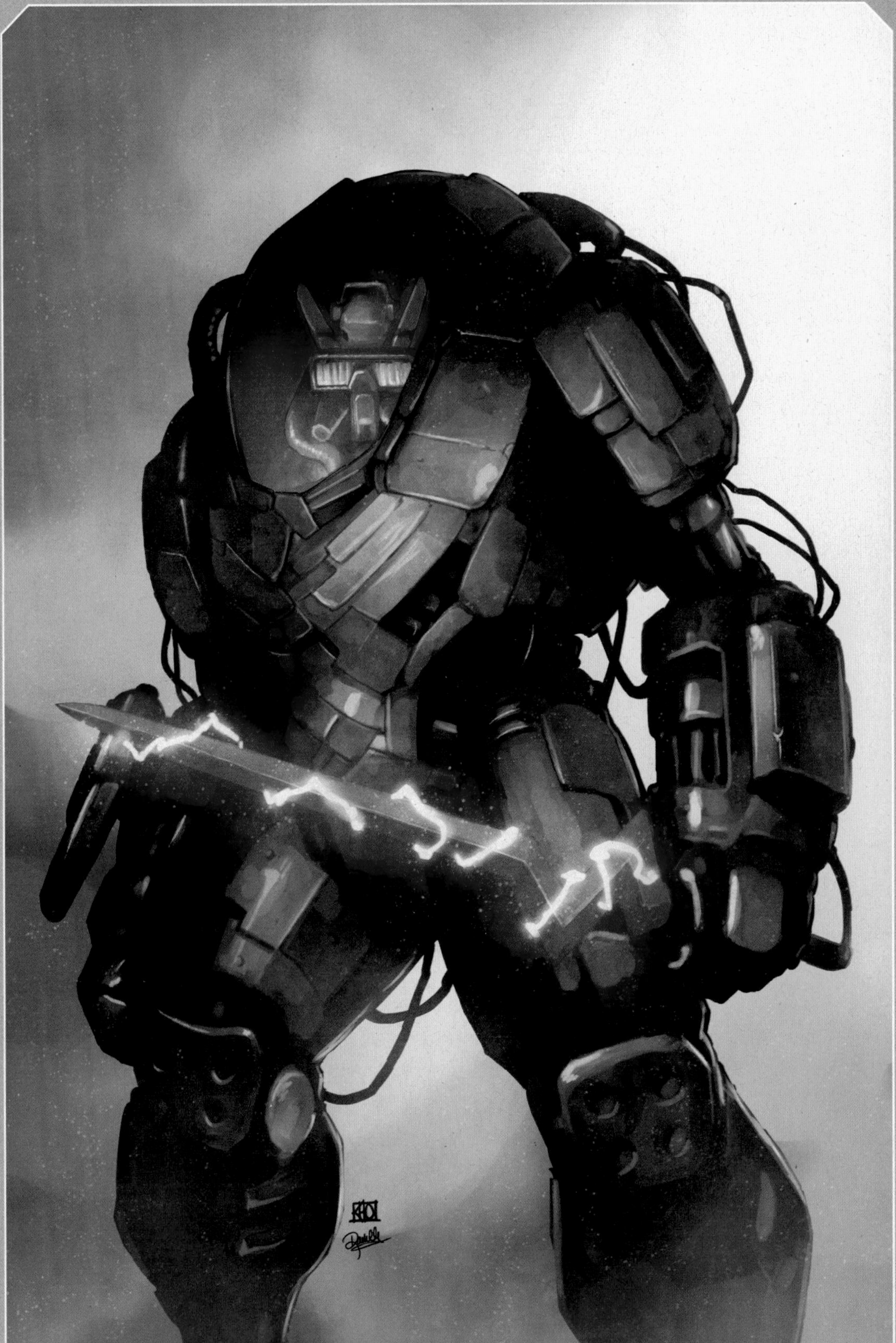

#13 Variant by
KHOI PHAM & RACHELLE ROSENBERG

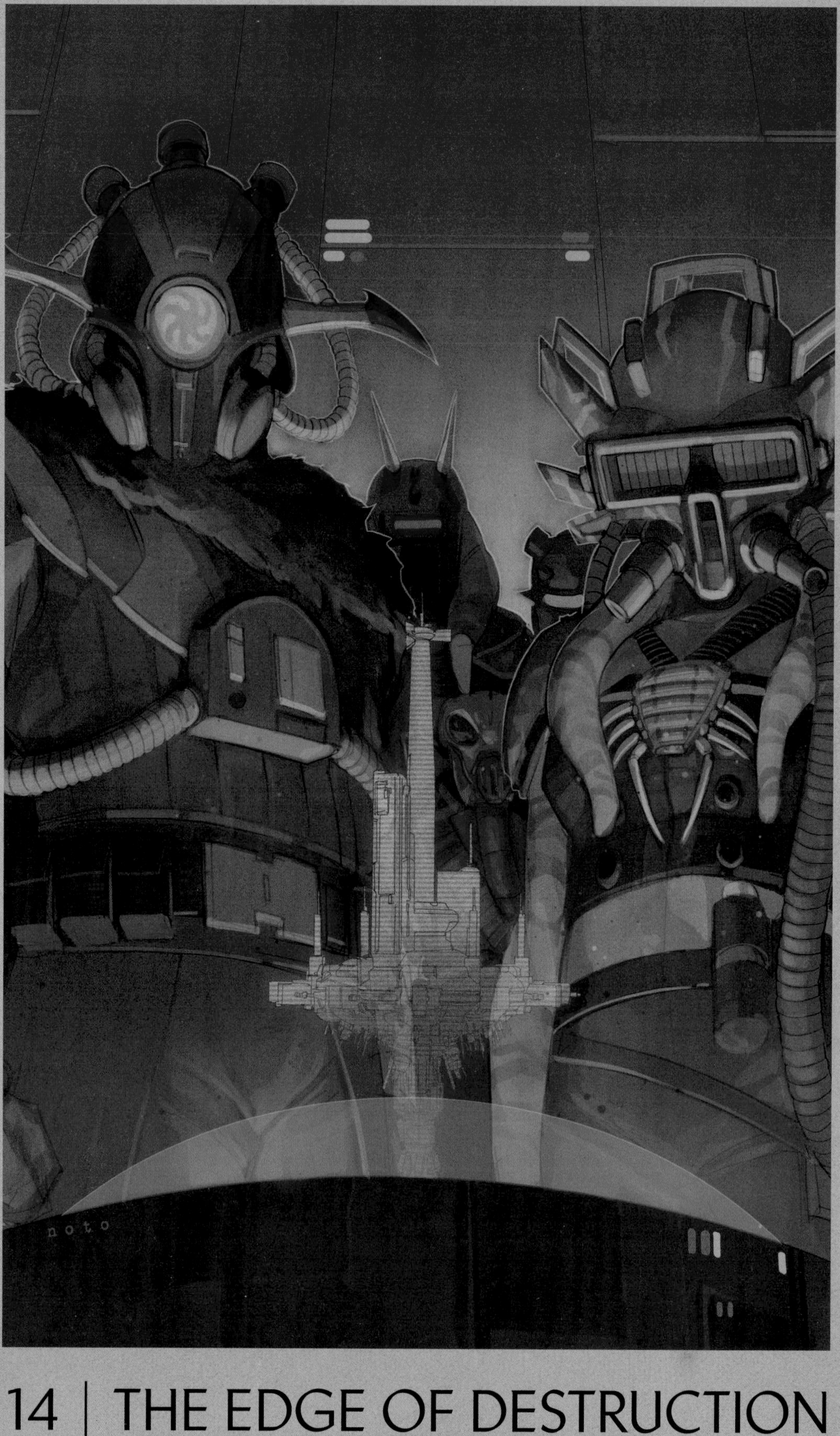
noto

14 | THE EDGE OF DESTRUCTION

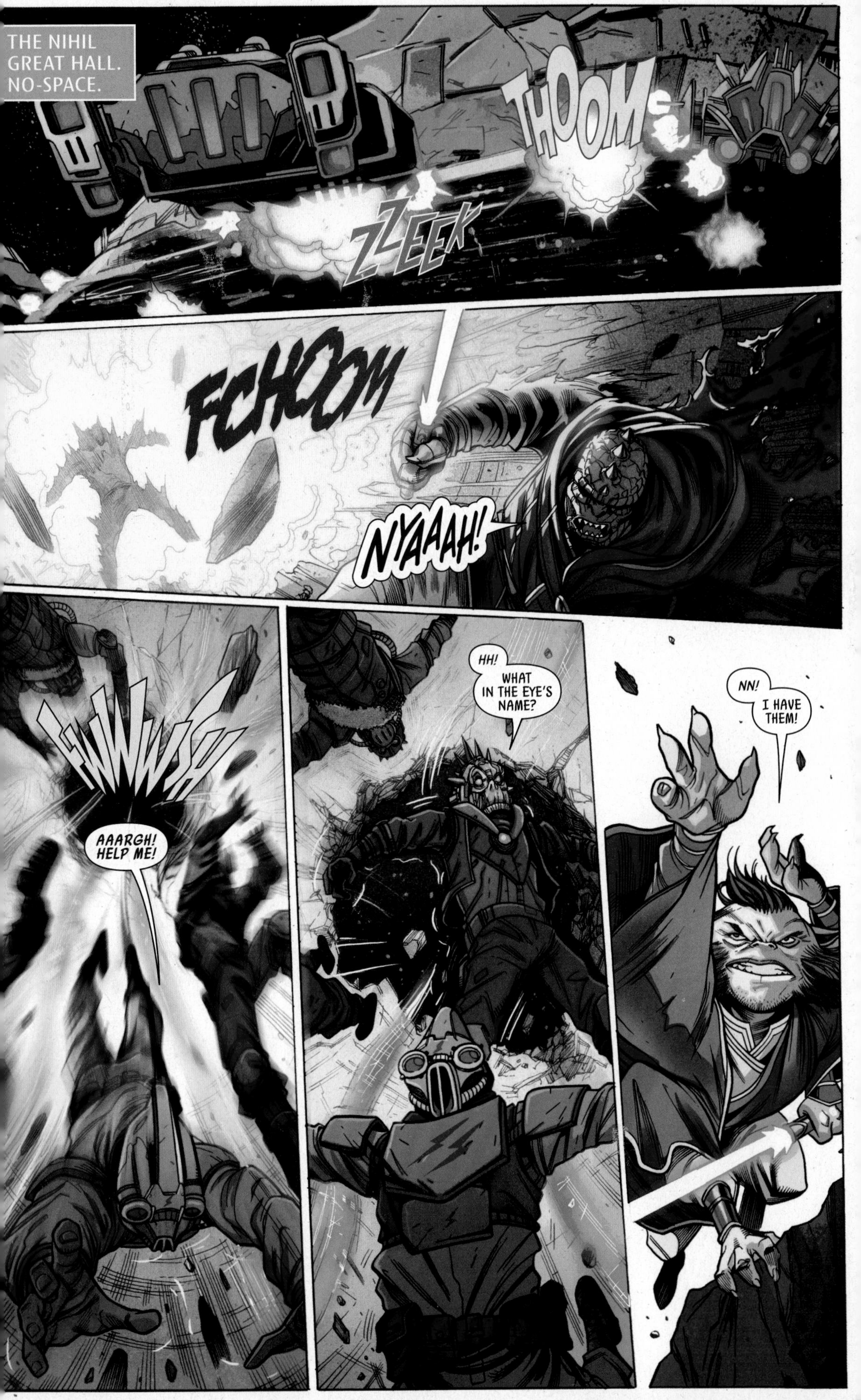
THE NIHIL GREAT HALL. NO-SPACE.
THOOM
ZZEEK
FCHOOM
NYAAAH!
FWWWSH
AAARGH! HELP ME!
HH! WHAT IN THE EYE'S NAME?
NN! I HAVE THEM!

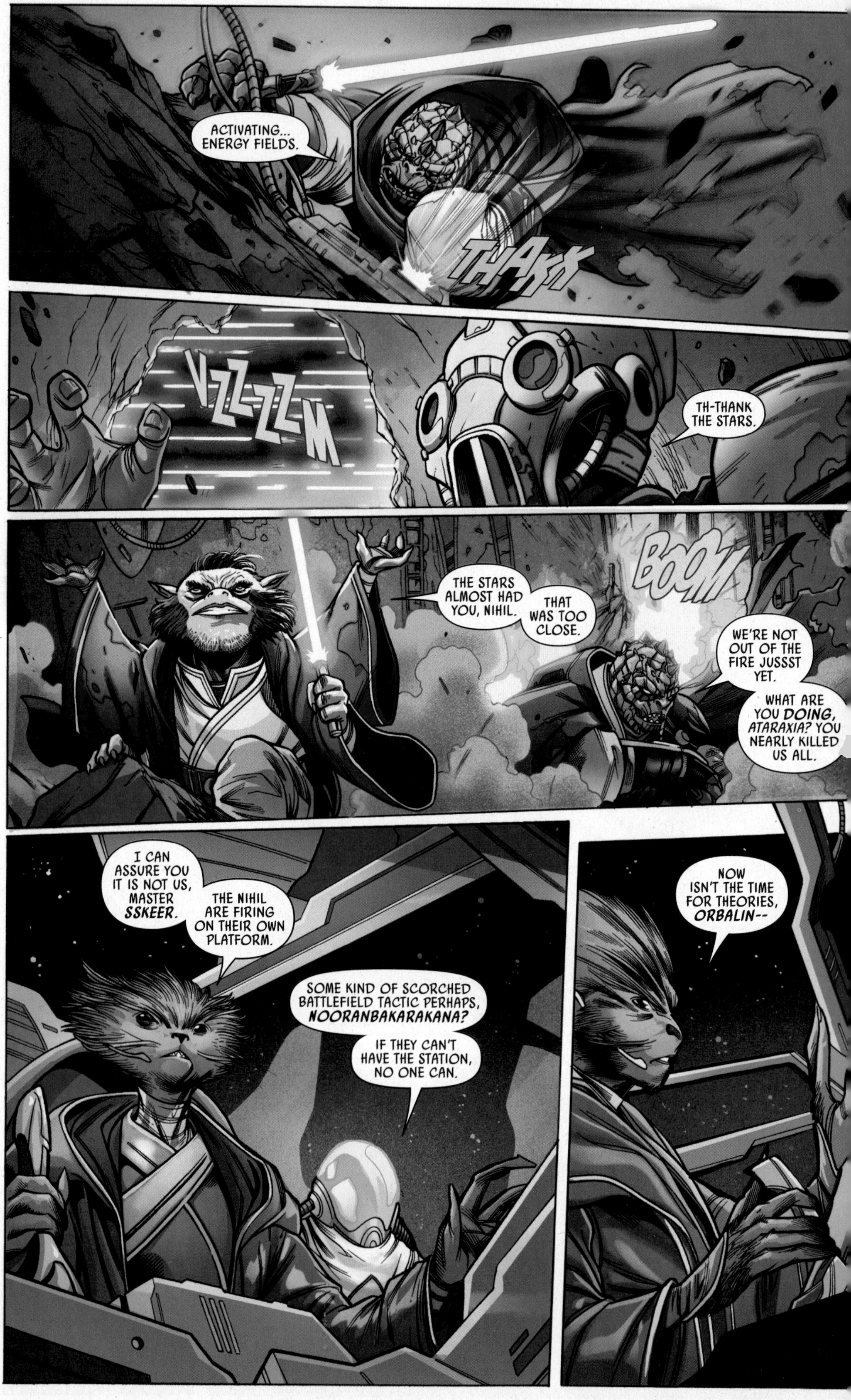
ACTIVATING... ENERGY FIELDS.
THAKK
VZZZZZM
TH-THANK THE STARS.
BOOM
THE STARS ALMOST HAD YOU, NIHIL.
THAT WAS TOO CLOSE.
WE'RE NOT OUT OF THE FIRE JUSSST YET.
WHAT ARE YOU *DOING*, *ATARAXIA?* YOU NEARLY KILLED US ALL.
I CAN ASSURE YOU IT IS NOT US, MASTER *SSKEER.*
THE NIHIL ARE FIRING ON THEIR OWN PLATFORM.
SOME KIND OF SCORCHED BATTLEFIELD TACTIC PERHAPS, *NOORANBAKARAKANA?*
IF THEY CAN'T HAVE THE STATION, NO ONE CAN.
NOW ISN'T THE TIME FOR THEORIES, *ORBALIN--*

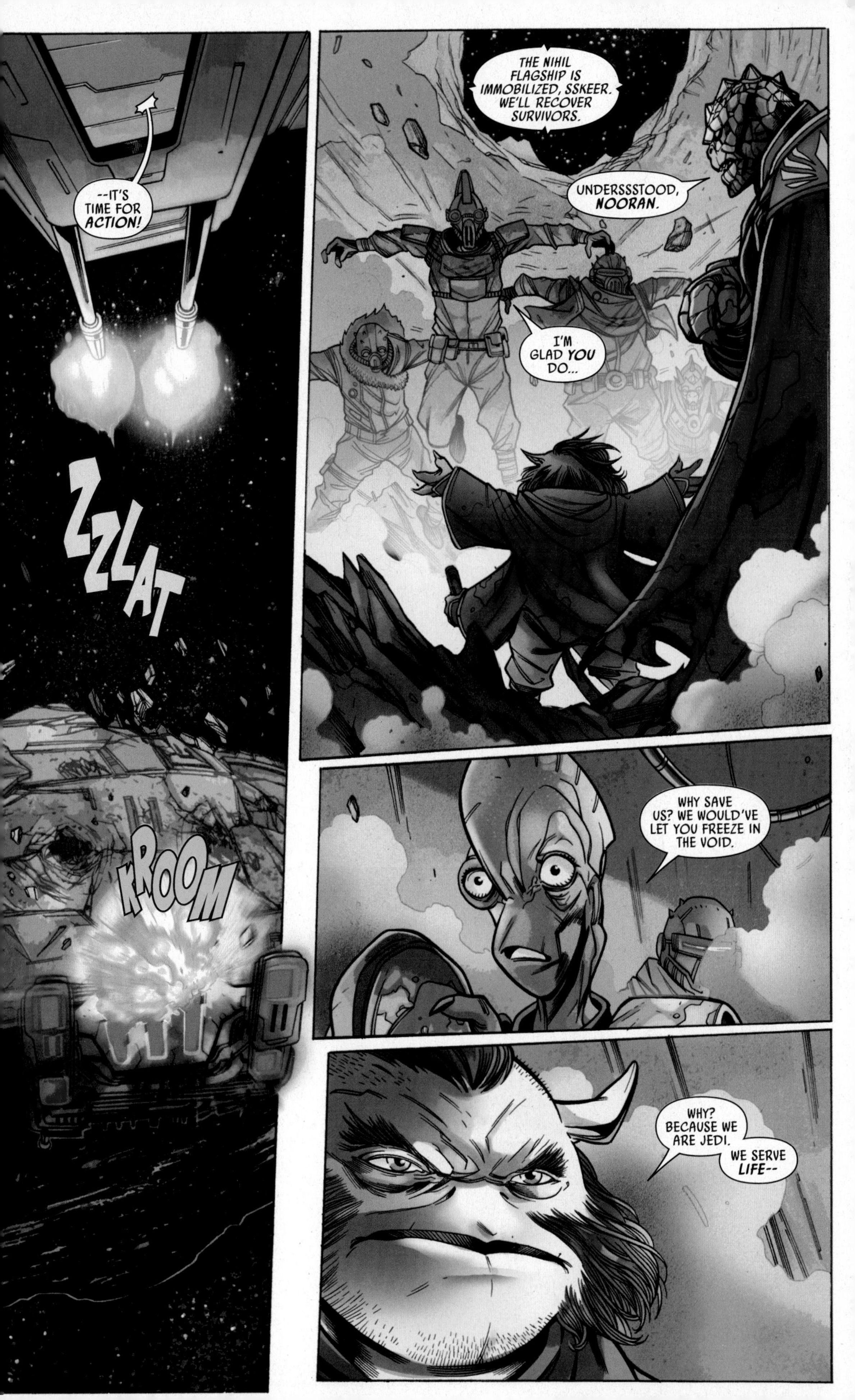
--IT'S TIME FOR ACTION!
ZZLAT
KROOM
THE NIHIL FLAGSHIP IS IMMOBILIZED, SSKEER. WE'LL RECOVER SURVIVORS.
UNDERSSSTOOD, NOORAN.
I'M GLAD YOU DO...
WHY SAVE US? WE WOULD'VE LET YOU FREEZE IN THE VOID.
WHY? BECAUSE WE ARE JEDI.
WE SERVE LIFE--

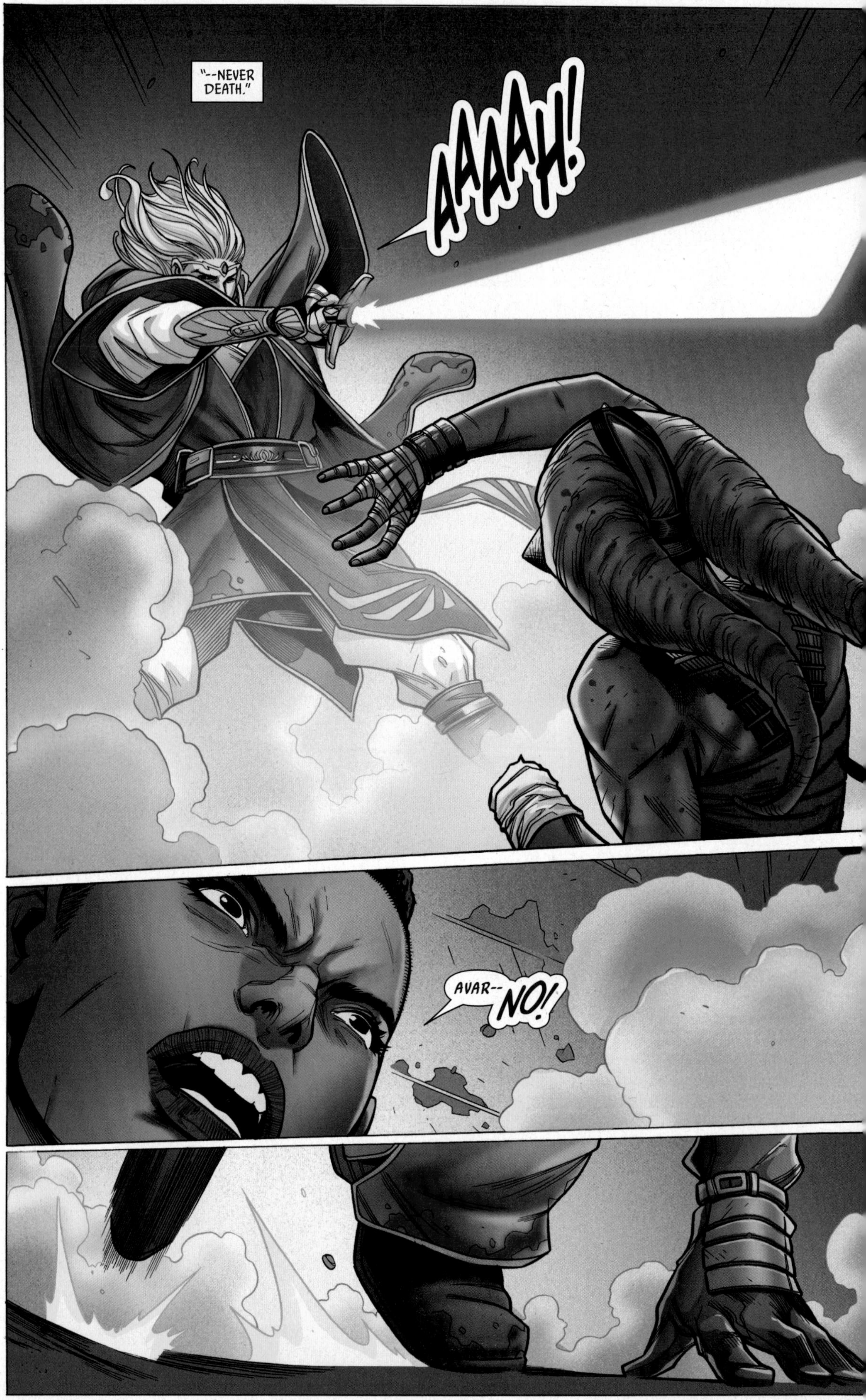
"--NEVER DEATH."
AAAAH!
AVAR--NO!

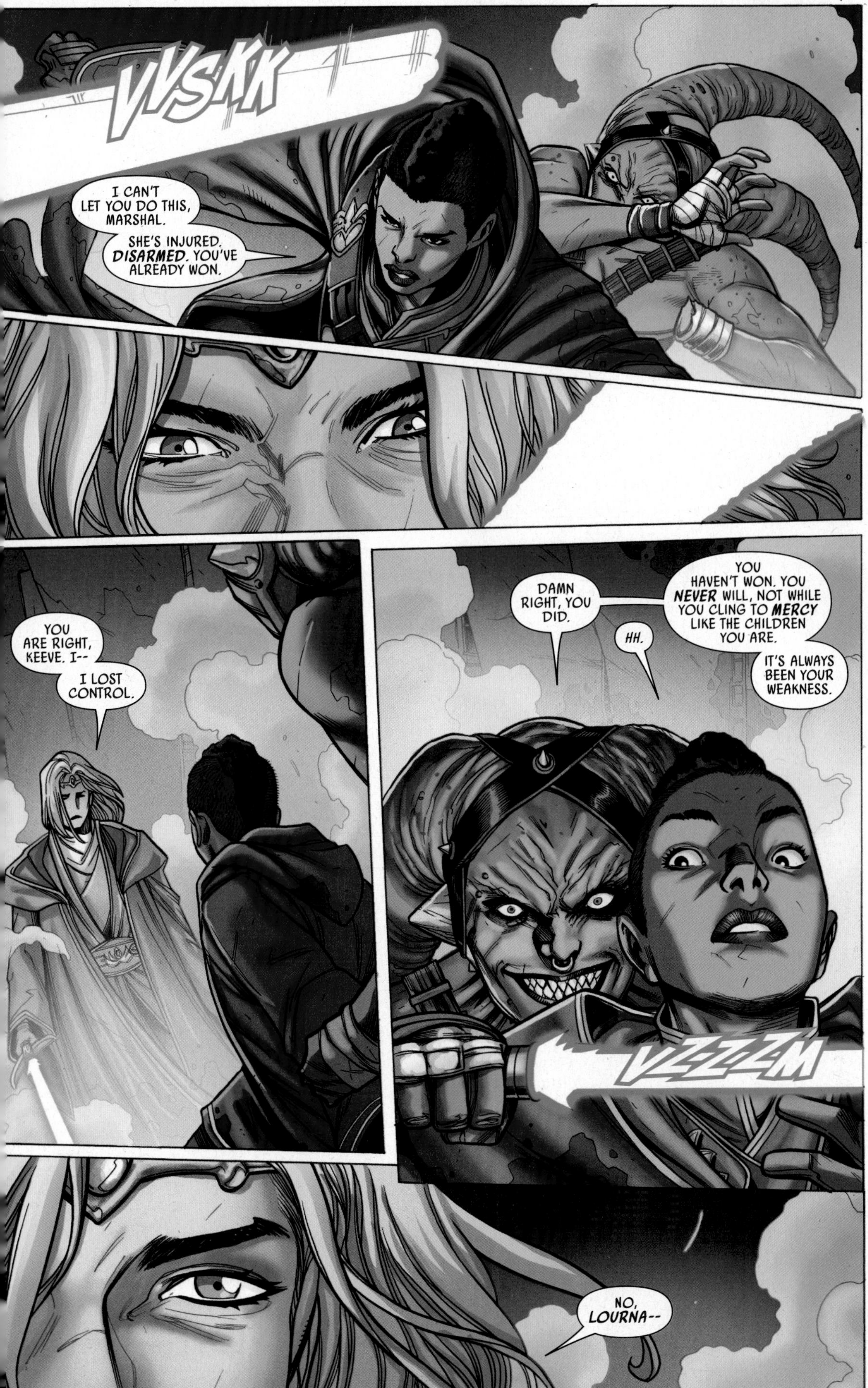
VVSKK
I CAN'T LET YOU DO THIS, MARSHAL.
SHE'S INJURED. **DISARMED.** YOU'VE ALREADY WON.
YOU ARE RIGHT, KEEVE. I--
I LOST CONTROL.
DAMN RIGHT, YOU DID.
HH.
YOU HAVEN'T WON. YOU **NEVER** WILL, NOT WHILE YOU CLING TO **MERCY** LIKE THE CHILDREN YOU ARE.
IT'S ALWAYS BEEN YOUR WEAKNESS.
VZZZM
NO, **LOURNA**--

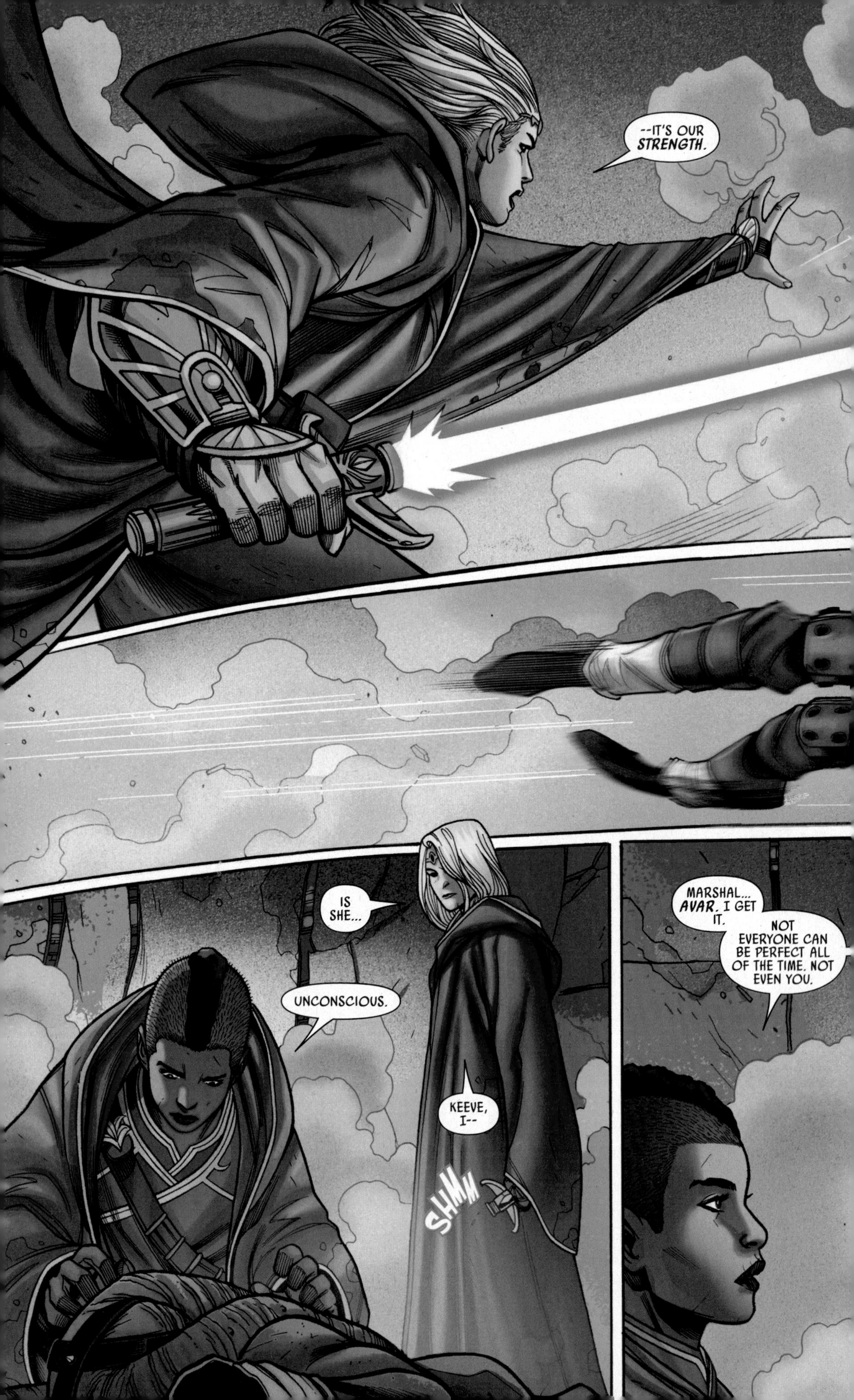
--IT'S OUR STRENGTH.
IS SHE...
UNCONSCIOUS.
KEEVE, I--
SHMM
MARSHAL... AVAR. I GET IT.
NOT EVERYONE CAN BE PERFECT ALL OF THE TIME. NOT EVEN YOU.

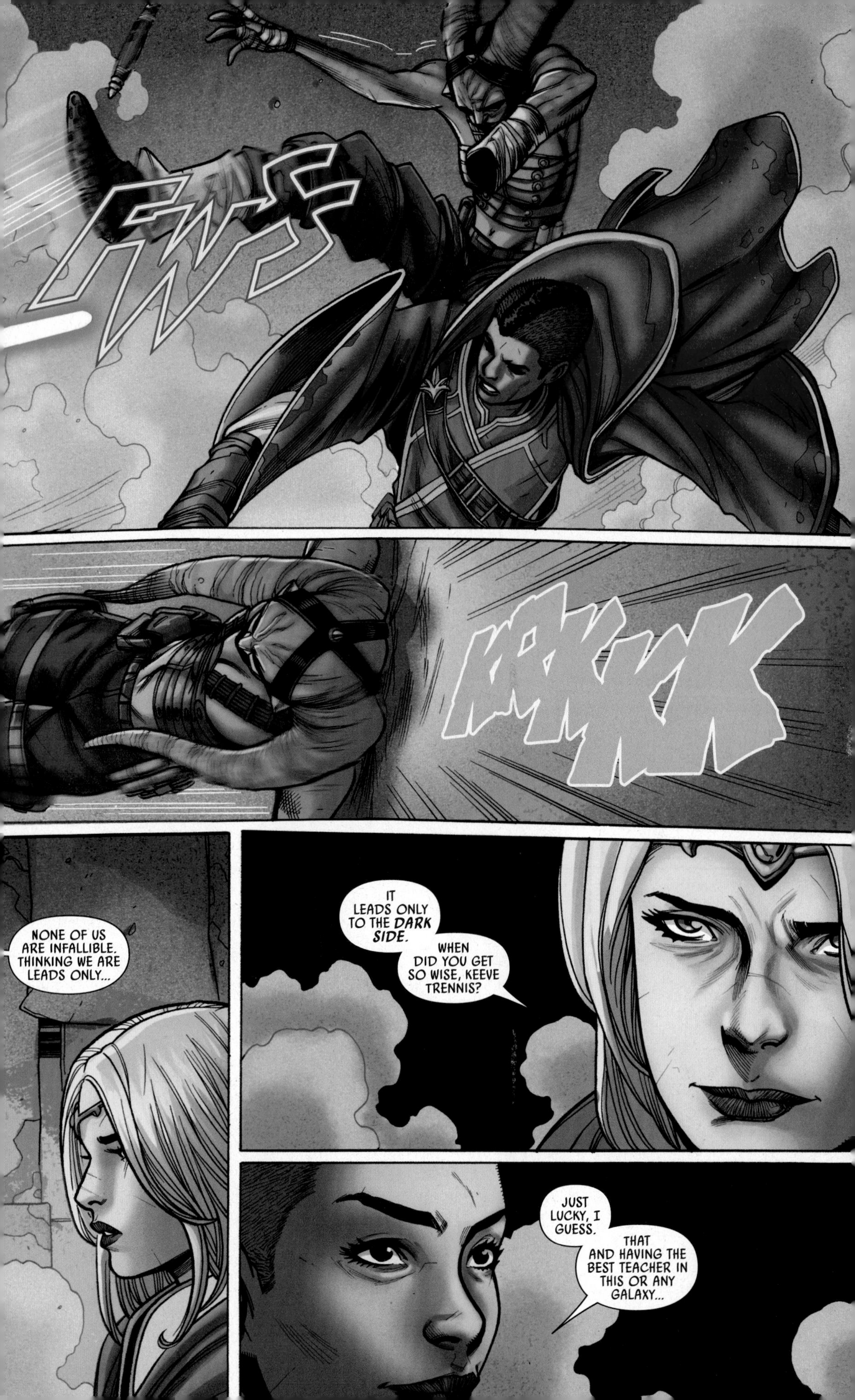
NONE OF US ARE INFALLIBLE. THINKING WE ARE LEADS ONLY...
IT LEADS ONLY TO THE DARK SIDE.
WHEN DID YOU GET SO WISE, KEEVE TRENNIS?
JUST LUCKY, I GUESS.
THAT AND HAVING THE BEST TEACHER IN THIS OR ANY GALAXY...

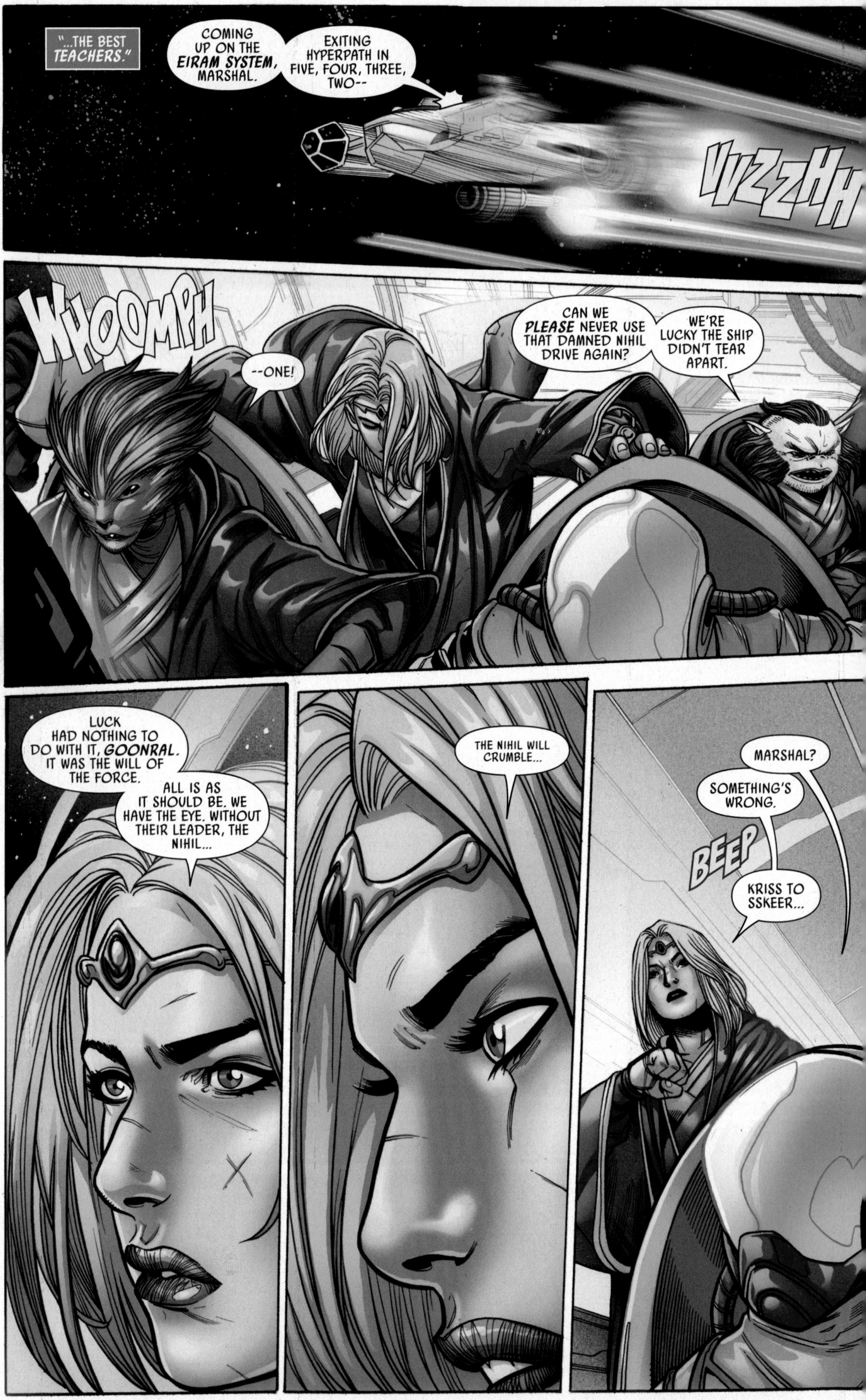
"...THE BEST TEACHERS."
COMING UP ON THE EIRAM SYSTEM, MARSHAL.
EXITING HYPERPATH IN FIVE, FOUR, THREE, TWO--
VVZZHH
WHOOMPH
--ONE!
CAN WE PLEASE NEVER USE THAT DAMNED NIHIL DRIVE AGAIN?
WE'RE LUCKY THE SHIP DIDN'T TEAR APART.
LUCK HAD NOTHING TO DO WITH IT, GOONRAL. IT WAS THE WILL OF THE FORCE.
ALL IS AS IT SHOULD BE. WE HAVE THE EYE. WITHOUT THEIR LEADER, THE NIHIL...
THE NIHIL WILL CRUMBLE...
MARSHAL?
SOMETHING'S WRONG.
BEEP
KRISS TO SSKEER...

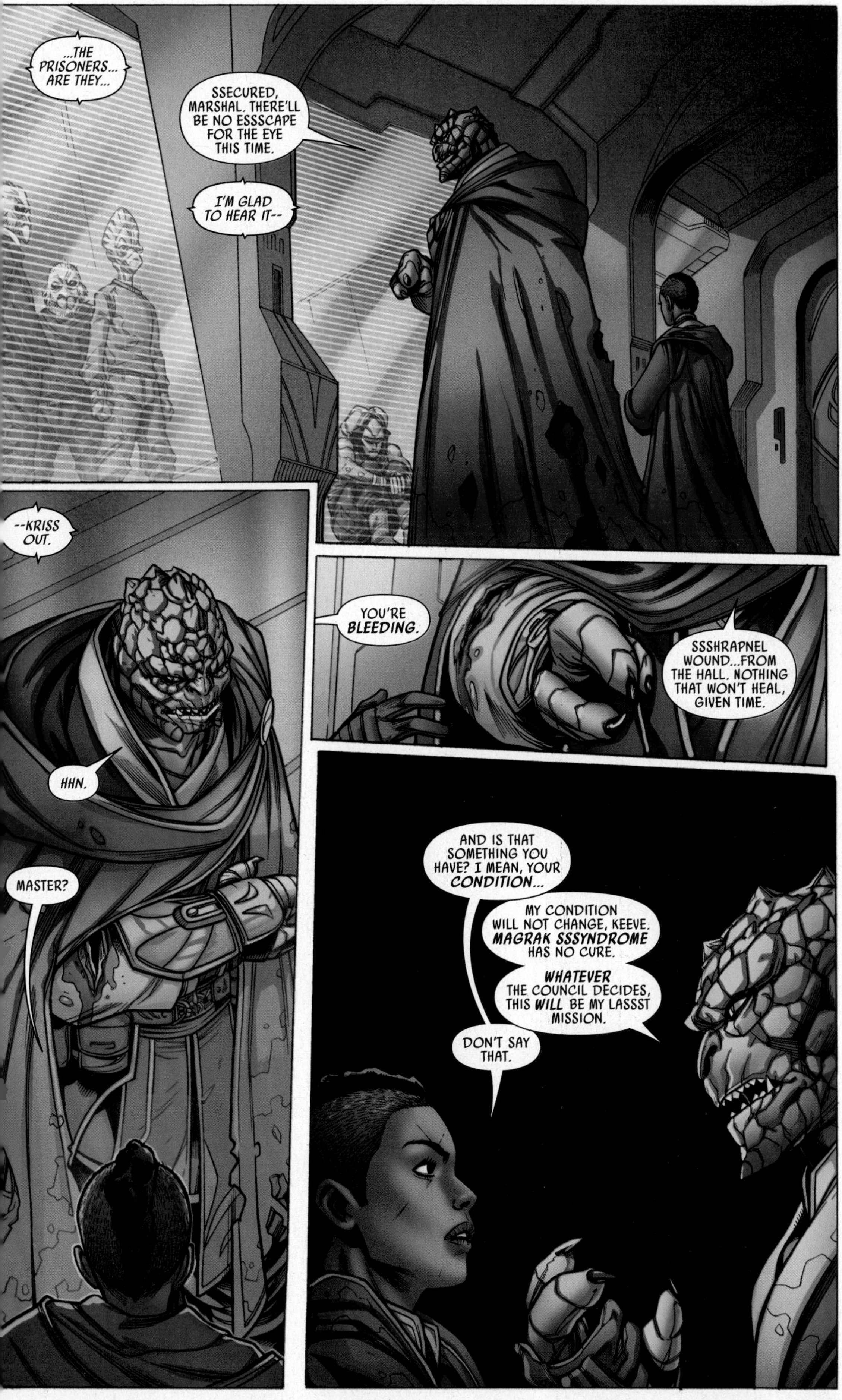
...THE PRISONERS... ARE THEY...
SSECURED, MARSHAL. THERE'LL BE NO ESSSCAPE FOR THE EYE THIS TIME.
I'M GLAD TO HEAR IT--
--KRISS OUT.
HHN.
MASTER?
YOU'RE BLEEDING.
SSSHRAPNEL WOUND...FROM THE HALL. NOTHING THAT WON'T HEAL, GIVEN TIME.
AND IS THAT SOMETHING YOU HAVE? I MEAN, YOUR CONDITION...
MY CONDITION WILL NOT CHANGE, KEEVE. MAGRAK SSSYNDROME HAS NO CURE.
WHATEVER THE COUNCIL DECIDES, THIS WILL BE MY LASSST MISSION.
DON'T SAY THAT.

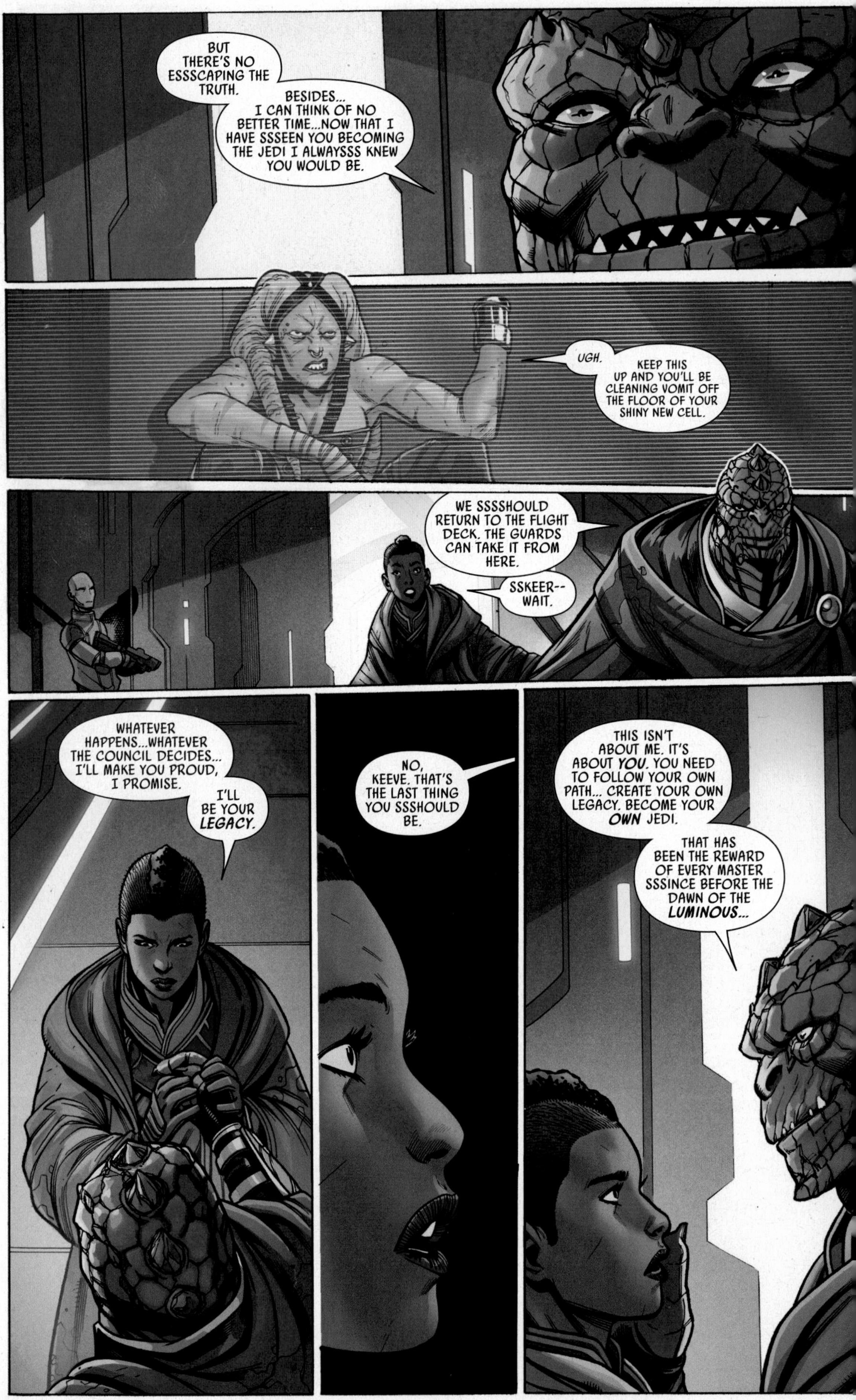
BUT THERE'S NO ESSSCAPING THE TRUTH.
BESIDES... I CAN THINK OF NO BETTER TIME...NOW THAT I HAVE SSSEEN YOU BECOMING THE JEDI I ALWAYSSS KNEW YOU WOULD BE.
UGH.
KEEP THIS UP AND YOU'LL BE CLEANING VOMIT OFF THE FLOOR OF YOUR SHINY NEW CELL.
WE SSSSHOULD RETURN TO THE FLIGHT DECK. THE GUARDS CAN TAKE IT FROM HERE.
SSKEER-- WAIT.
WHATEVER HAPPENS...WHATEVER THE COUNCIL DECIDES... I'LL MAKE YOU PROUD, I PROMISE.
I'LL BE YOUR LEGACY.
NO, KEEVE. THAT'S THE LAST THING YOU SSSHOULD BE.
THIS ISN'T ABOUT ME. IT'S ABOUT YOU. YOU NEED TO FOLLOW YOUR OWN PATH... CREATE YOUR OWN LEGACY. BECOME YOUR OWN JEDI.
THAT HAS BEEN THE REWARD OF EVERY MASTER SSSINCE BEFORE THE DAWN OF THE LUMINOUS...

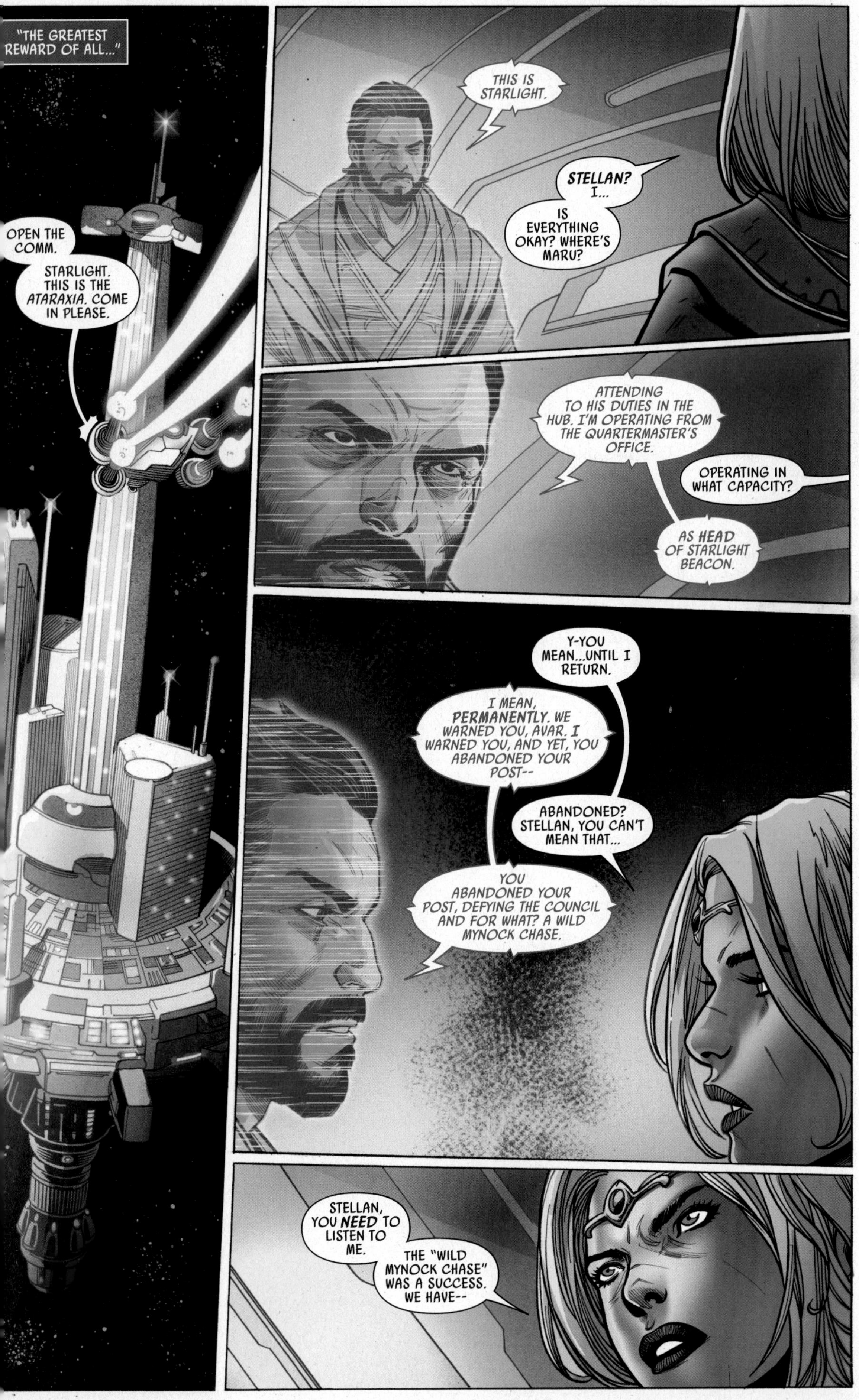
"THE GREATEST REWARD OF ALL..."
OPEN THE COMM.
STARLIGHT. THIS IS THE ATARAXIA. COME IN PLEASE.
THIS IS STARLIGHT.
STELLAN? I...
IS EVERYTHING OKAY? WHERE'S MARU?
ATTENDING TO HIS DUTIES IN THE HUB. I'M OPERATING FROM THE QUARTERMASTER'S OFFICE.
OPERATING IN WHAT CAPACITY?
AS HEAD OF STARLIGHT BEACON.
Y-YOU MEAN...UNTIL I RETURN.
I MEAN, PERMANENTLY. WE WARNED YOU, AVAR. I WARNED YOU, AND YET, YOU ABANDONED YOUR POST--
ABANDONED? STELLAN, YOU CAN'T MEAN THAT...
YOU ABANDONED YOUR POST, DEFYING THE COUNCIL AND FOR WHAT? A WILD MYNOCK CHASE.
STELLAN, YOU NEED TO LISTEN TO ME.
THE "WILD MYNOCK CHASE" WAS A SUCCESS. WE HAVE--

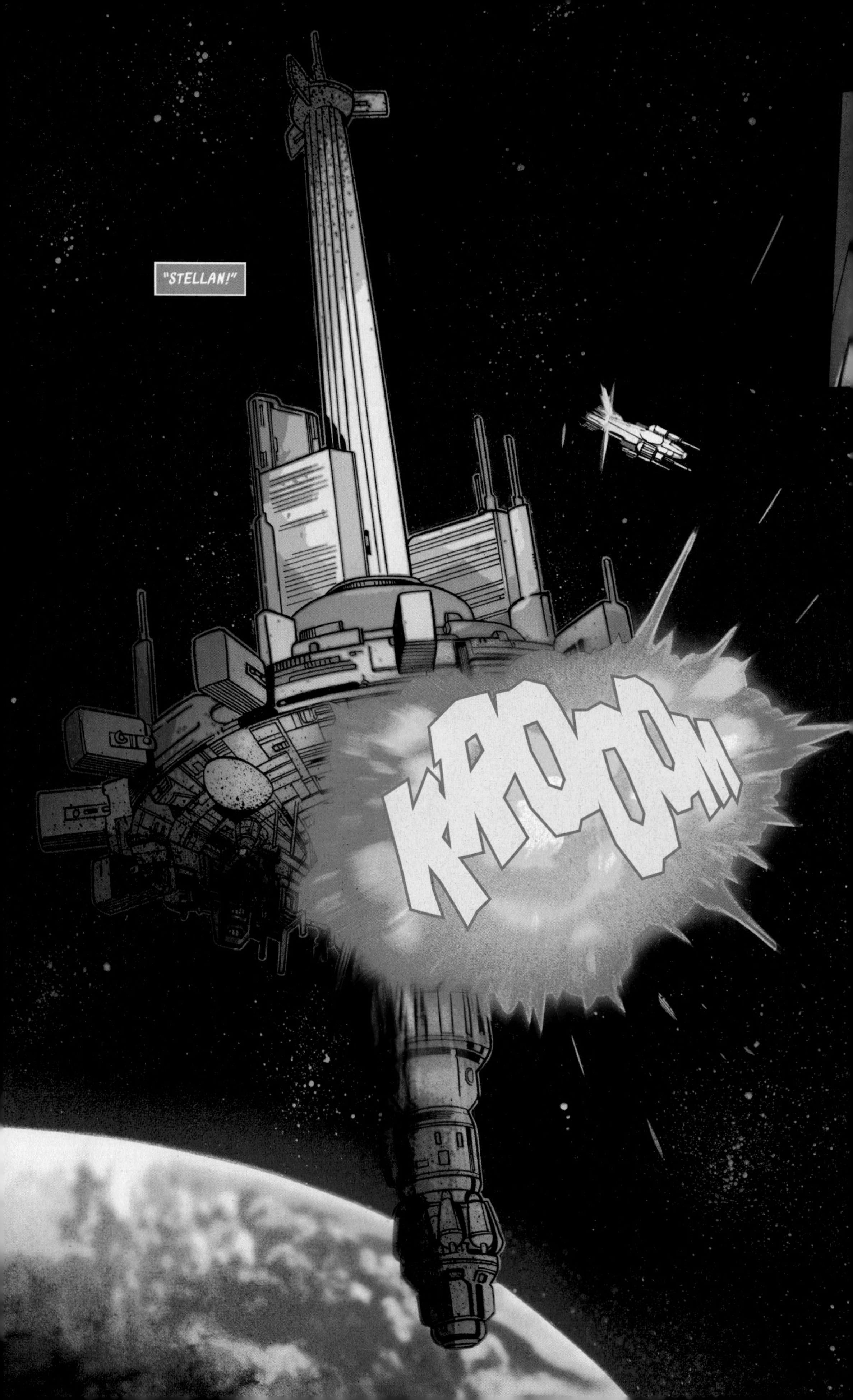
"STELLAN!"
KROOOOM

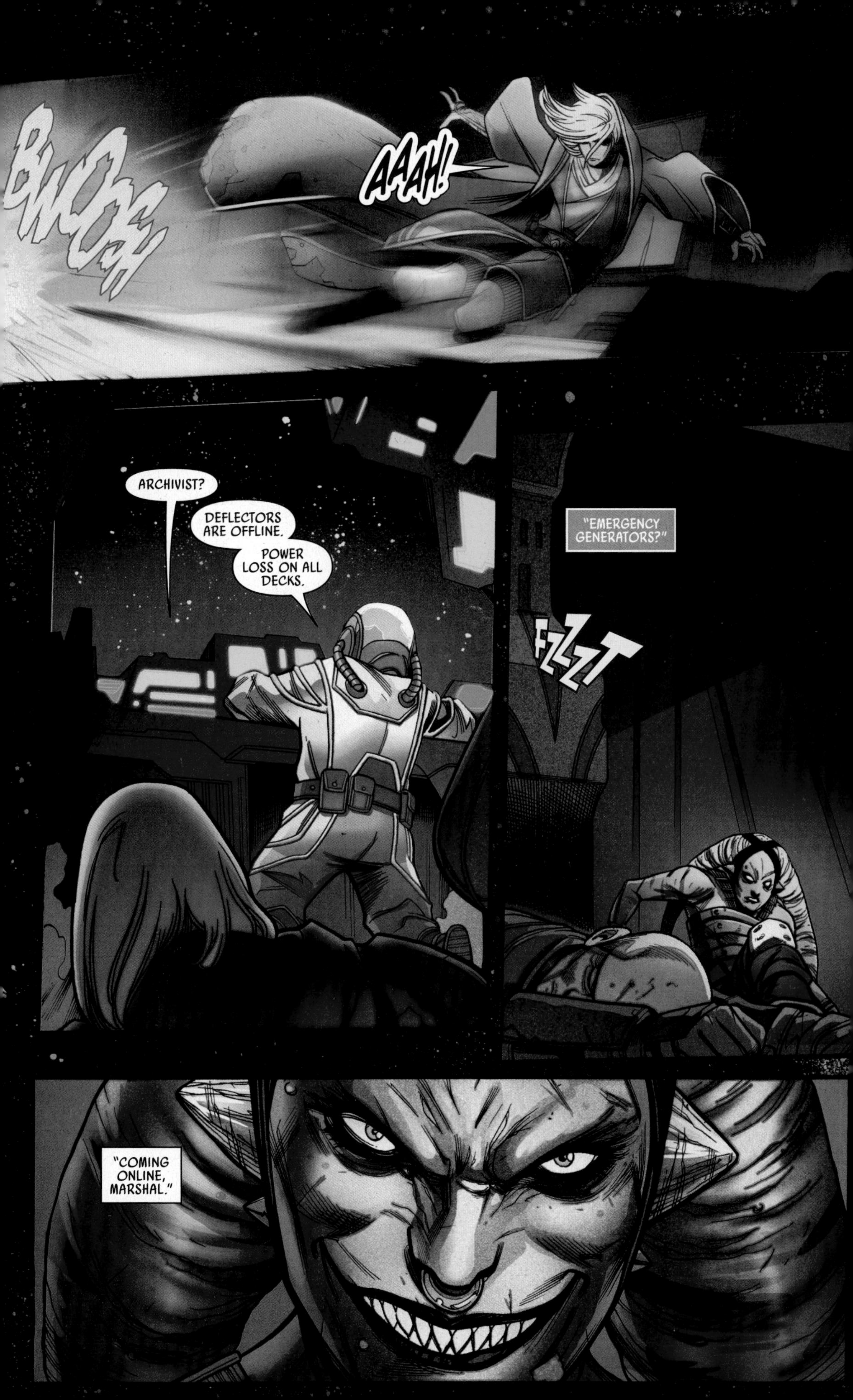
BWOOSH
AAAH!
ARCHIVIST?
DEFLECTORS ARE OFFLINE.
POWER LOSS ON ALL DECKS.
"EMERGENCY GENERATORS?"
FZZZT
"COMING ONLINE, MARSHAL."

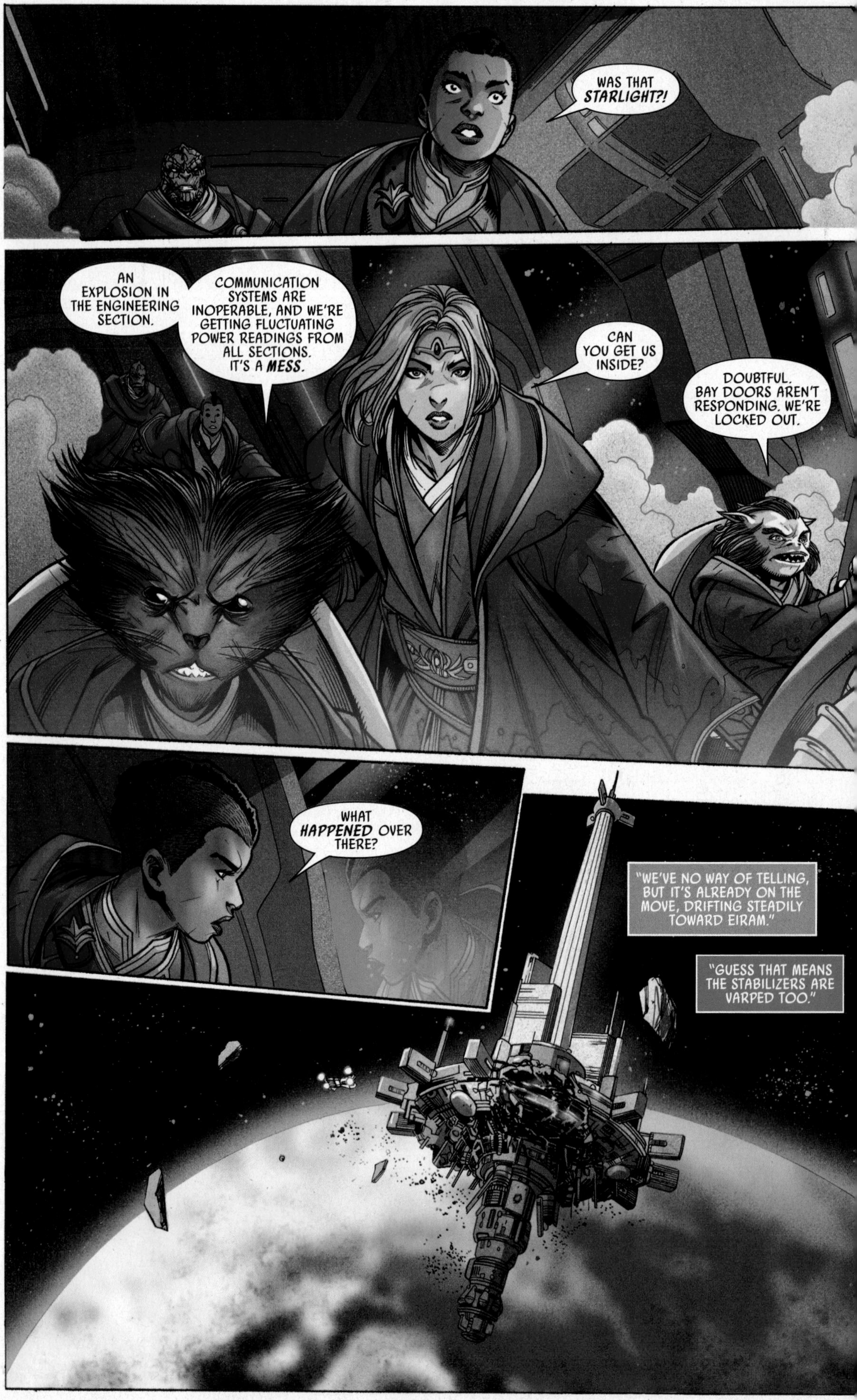
WAS THAT STARLIGHT?!
AN EXPLOSION IN THE ENGINEERING SECTION.
COMMUNICATION SYSTEMS ARE INOPERABLE, AND WE'RE GETTING FLUCTUATING POWER READINGS FROM ALL SECTIONS. IT'S A MESS.
CAN YOU GET US INSIDE?
DOUBTFUL. BAY DOORS AREN'T RESPONDING. WE'RE LOCKED OUT.
WHAT HAPPENED OVER THERE?
"WE'VE NO WAY OF TELLING, BUT IT'S ALREADY ON THE MOVE, DRIFTING STEADILY TOWARD EIRAM."
"GUESS THAT MEANS THE STABILIZERS ARE VARPED TOO."

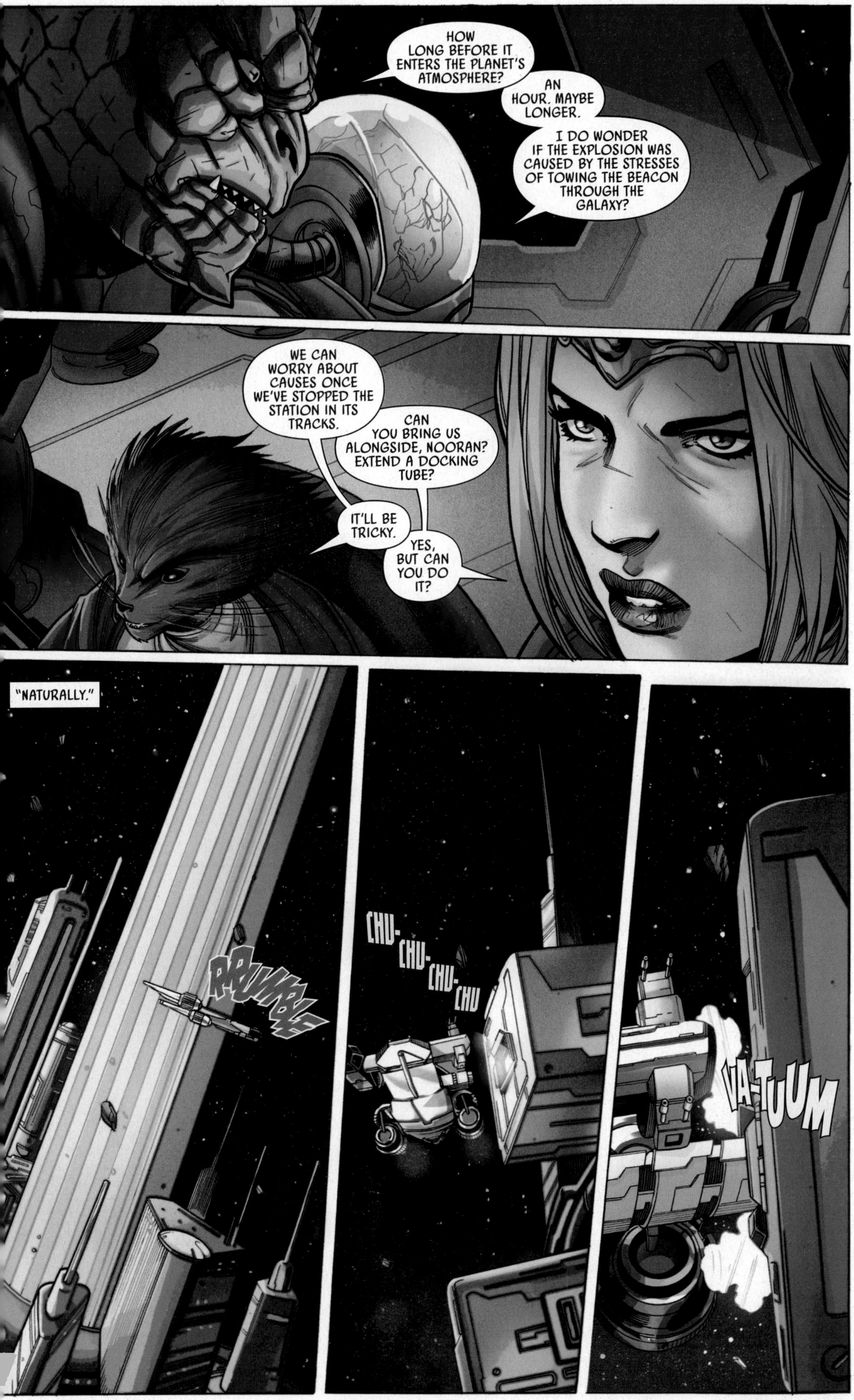
HOW LONG BEFORE IT ENTERS THE PLANET'S ATMOSPHERE?
AN HOUR. MAYBE LONGER.
I DO WONDER IF THE EXPLOSION WAS CAUSED BY THE STRESSES OF TOWING THE BEACON THROUGH THE GALAXY?
WE CAN WORRY ABOUT CAUSES ONCE WE'VE STOPPED THE STATION IN ITS TRACKS.
CAN YOU BRING US ALONGSIDE, NOORAN? EXTEND A DOCKING TUBE?
IT'LL BE TRICKY.
YES, BUT CAN YOU DO IT?
"NATURALLY."
CHU-CHU-CHU-CHU
VA-TUUM

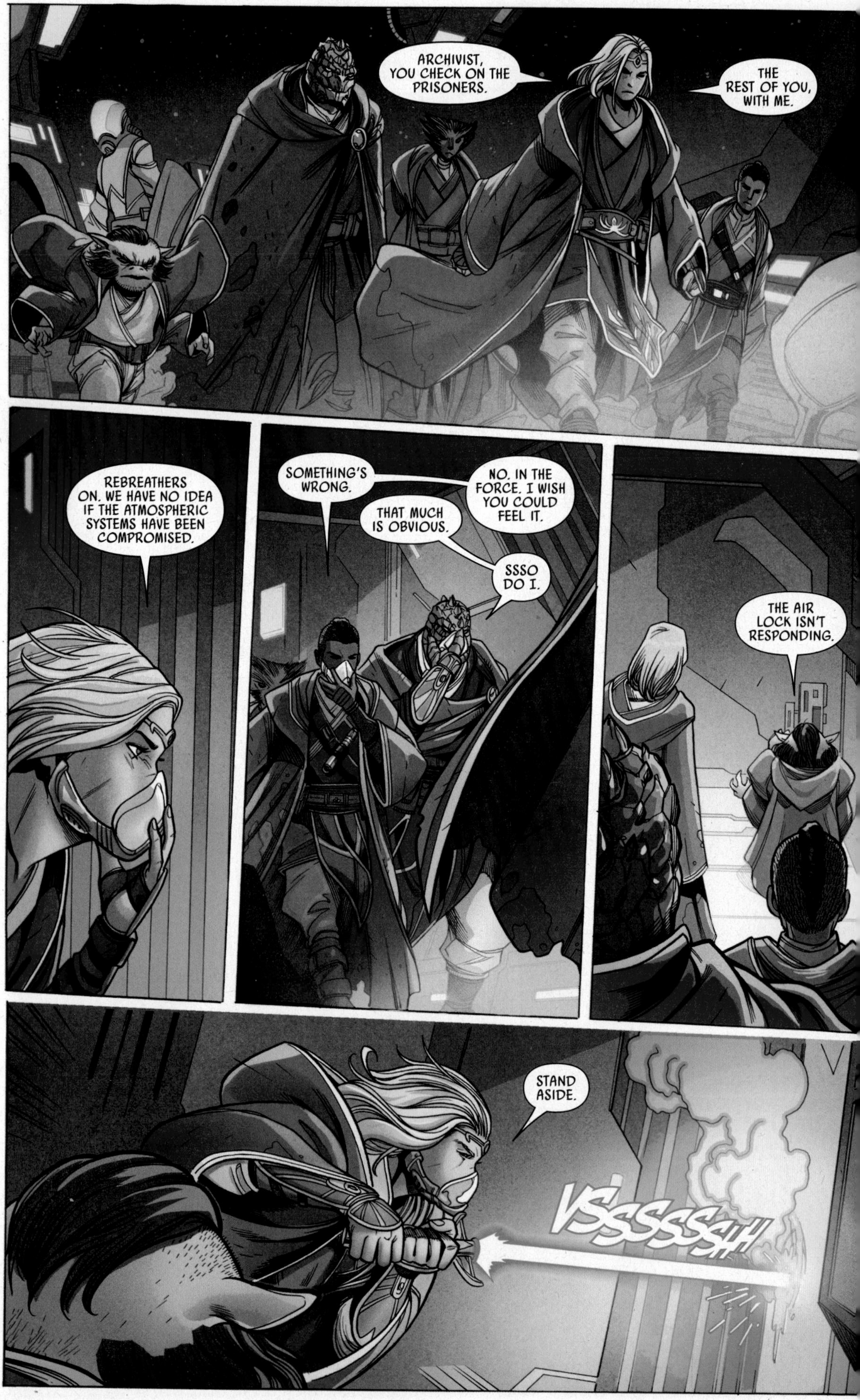
ARCHIVIST, YOU CHECK ON THE PRISONERS.
THE REST OF YOU, WITH ME.
REBREATHERS ON. WE HAVE NO IDEA IF THE ATMOSPHERIC SYSTEMS HAVE BEEN COMPROMISED.
SOMETHING'S WRONG.
THAT MUCH IS OBVIOUS.
NO. IN THE FORCE. I WISH YOU COULD FEEL IT.
SSSO DO I.
THE AIR LOCK ISN'T RESPONDING.
STAND ASIDE.
VSSSSSSH

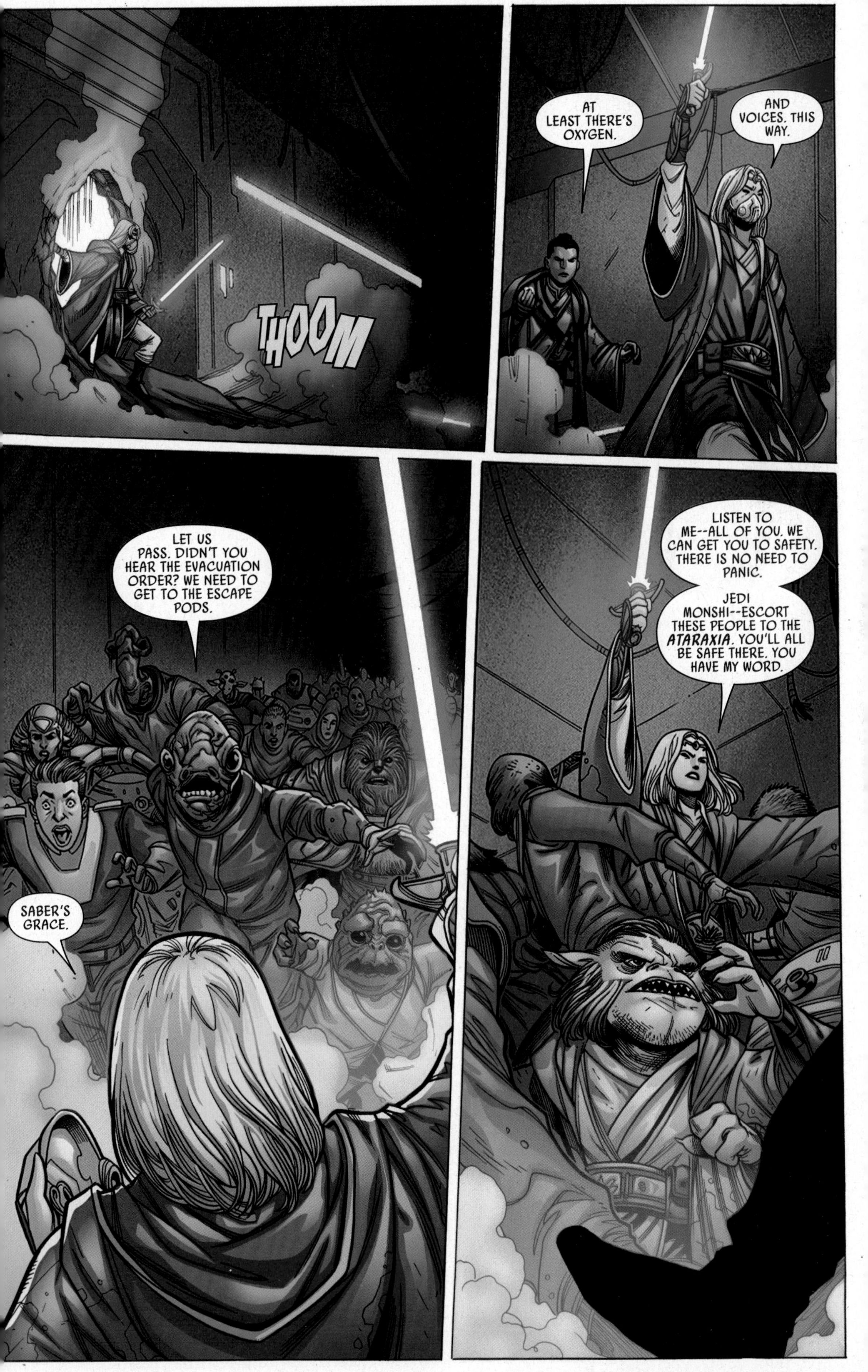
THOOM
AT LEAST THERE'S OXYGEN.
AND VOICES. THIS WAY.
LET US PASS. DIDN'T YOU HEAR THE EVACUATION ORDER? WE NEED TO GET TO THE ESCAPE PODS.
SABER'S GRACE.
LISTEN TO ME--ALL OF YOU. WE CAN GET YOU TO SAFETY. THERE IS NO NEED TO PANIC.
JEDI MONSHI--ESCORT THESE PEOPLE TO THE ATARAXIA. YOU'LL ALL BE SAFE THERE. YOU HAVE MY WORD.

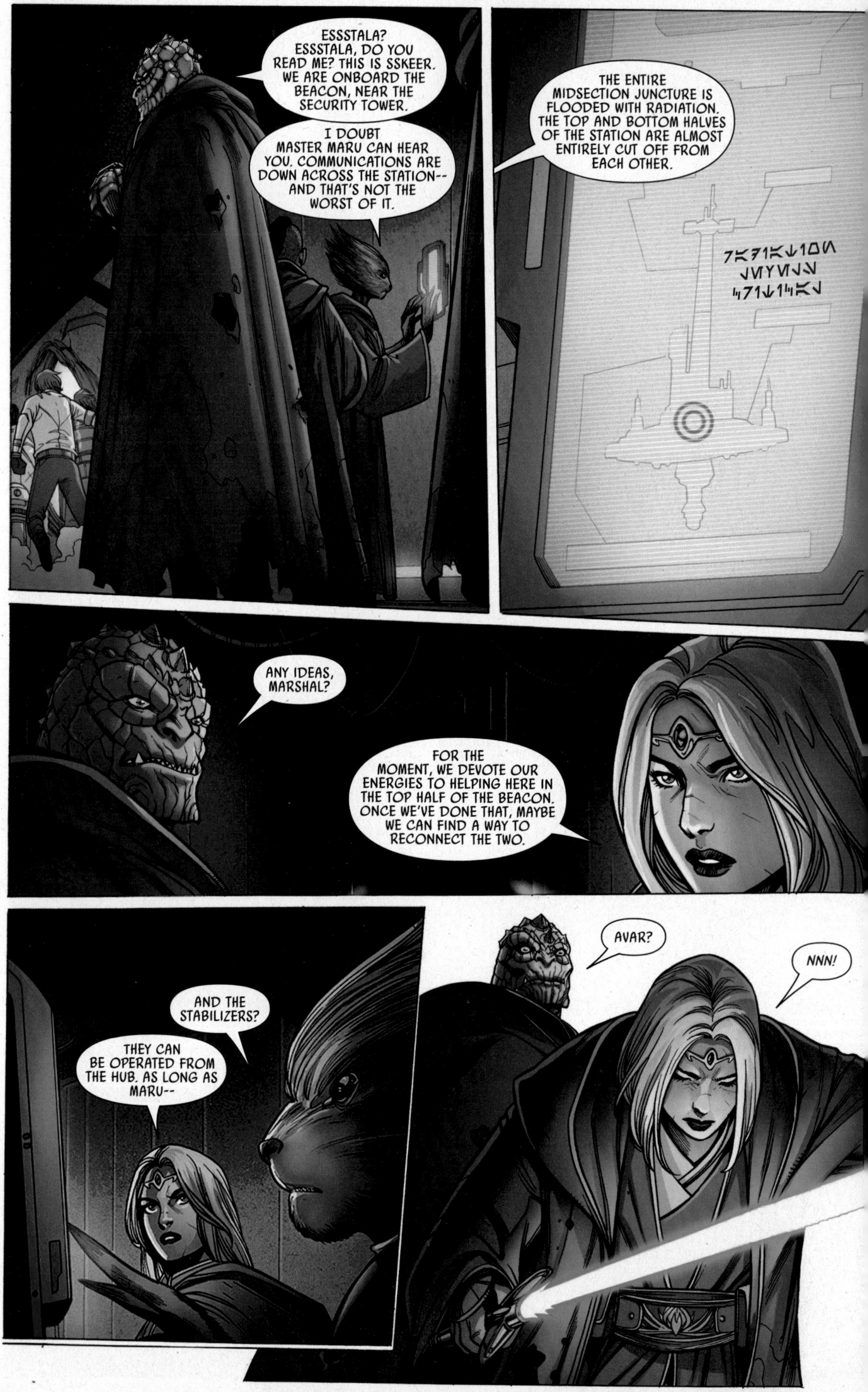
ESSSTALA? ESSSTALA, DO YOU READ ME? THIS IS SSKEER. WE ARE ONBOARD THE BEACON, NEAR THE SECURITY TOWER.
I DOUBT MASTER MARU CAN HEAR YOU. COMMUNICATIONS ARE DOWN ACROSS THE STATION-- AND THAT'S NOT THE WORST OF IT.
THE ENTIRE MIDSECTION JUNCTURE IS FLOODED WITH RADIATION. THE TOP AND BOTTOM HALVES OF THE STATION ARE ALMOST ENTIRELY CUT OFF FROM EACH OTHER.
ANY IDEAS, MARSHAL?
FOR THE MOMENT, WE DEVOTE OUR ENERGIES TO HELPING HERE IN THE TOP HALF OF THE BEACON. ONCE WE'VE DONE THAT, MAYBE WE CAN FIND A WAY TO RECONNECT THE TWO.
AND THE STABILIZERS?
THEY CAN BE OPERATED FROM THE HUB. AS LONG AS MARU--
AVAR?
NNN!

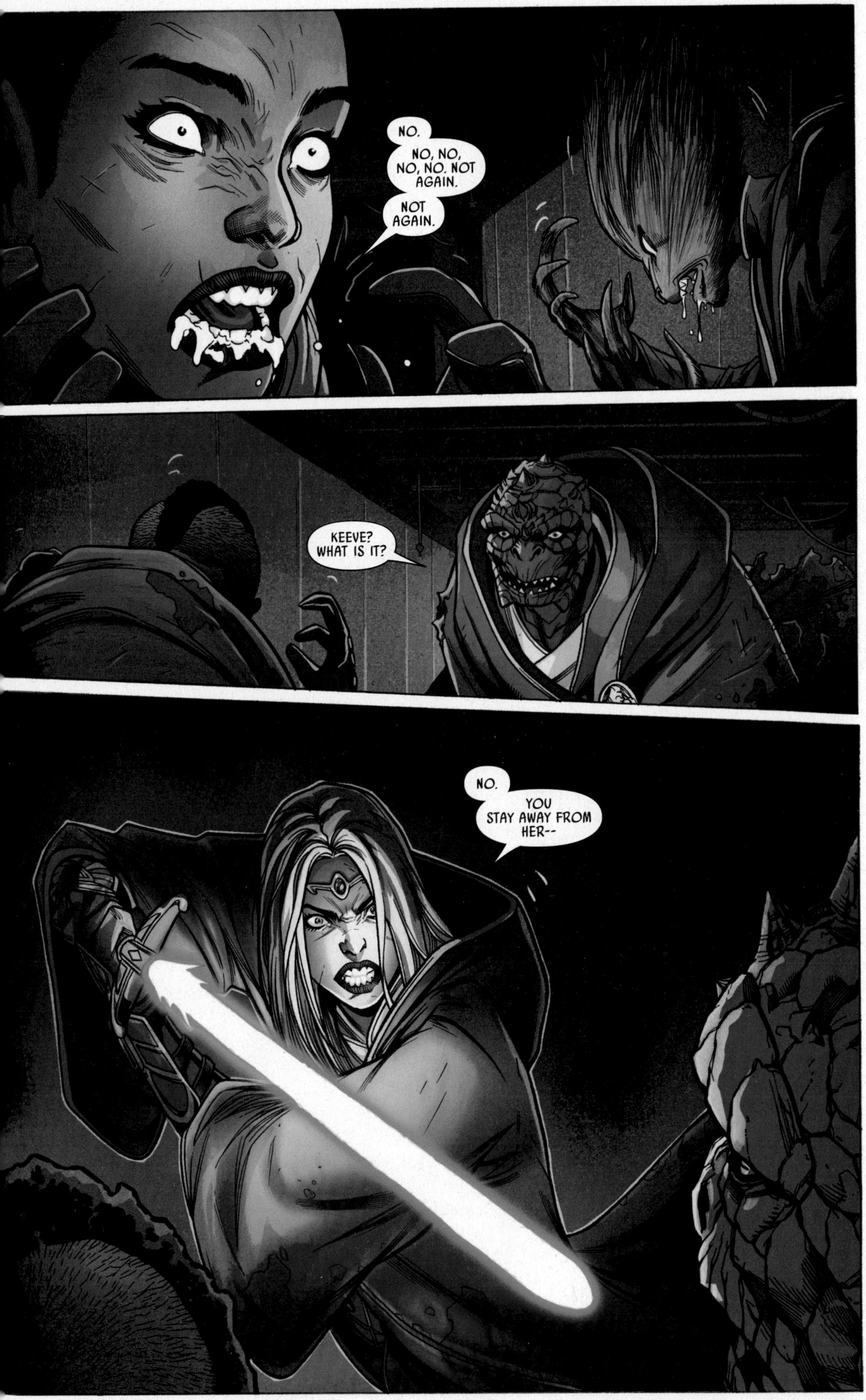
NO.
NO, NO, NO, NO. NOT AGAIN.
NOT AGAIN.
KEEVE? WHAT IS IT?
NO.
YOU STAY AWAY FROM HER--

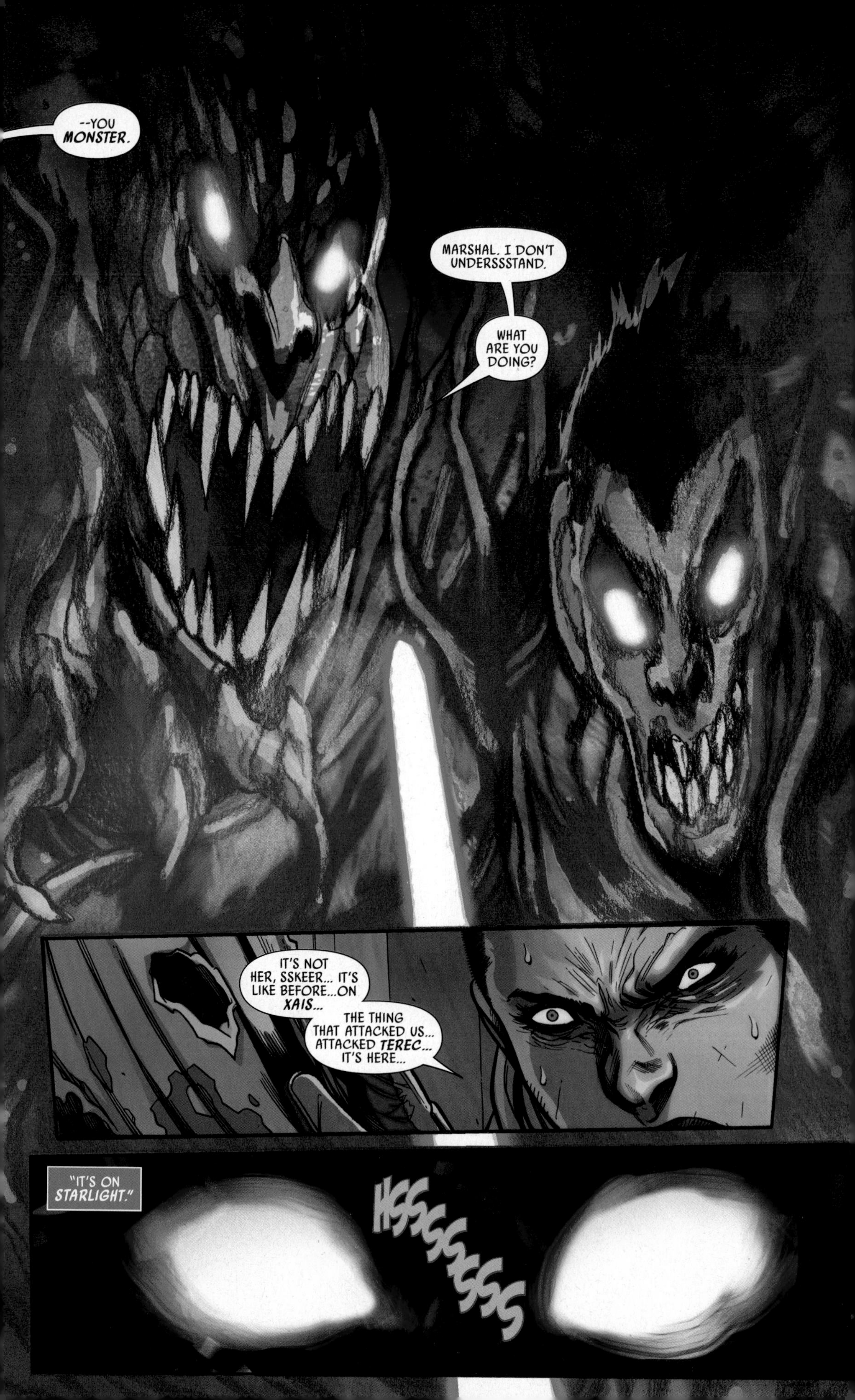
--YOU MONSTER.
MARSHAL. I DON'T UNDERSSSTAND.
WHAT ARE YOU DOING?
IT'S NOT HER, SSKEER... IT'S LIKE BEFORE...ON XAIS...
THE THING THAT ATTACKED US... ATTACKED TEREC... IT'S HERE...
"IT'S ON STARLIGHT."
HSSSSSSSS

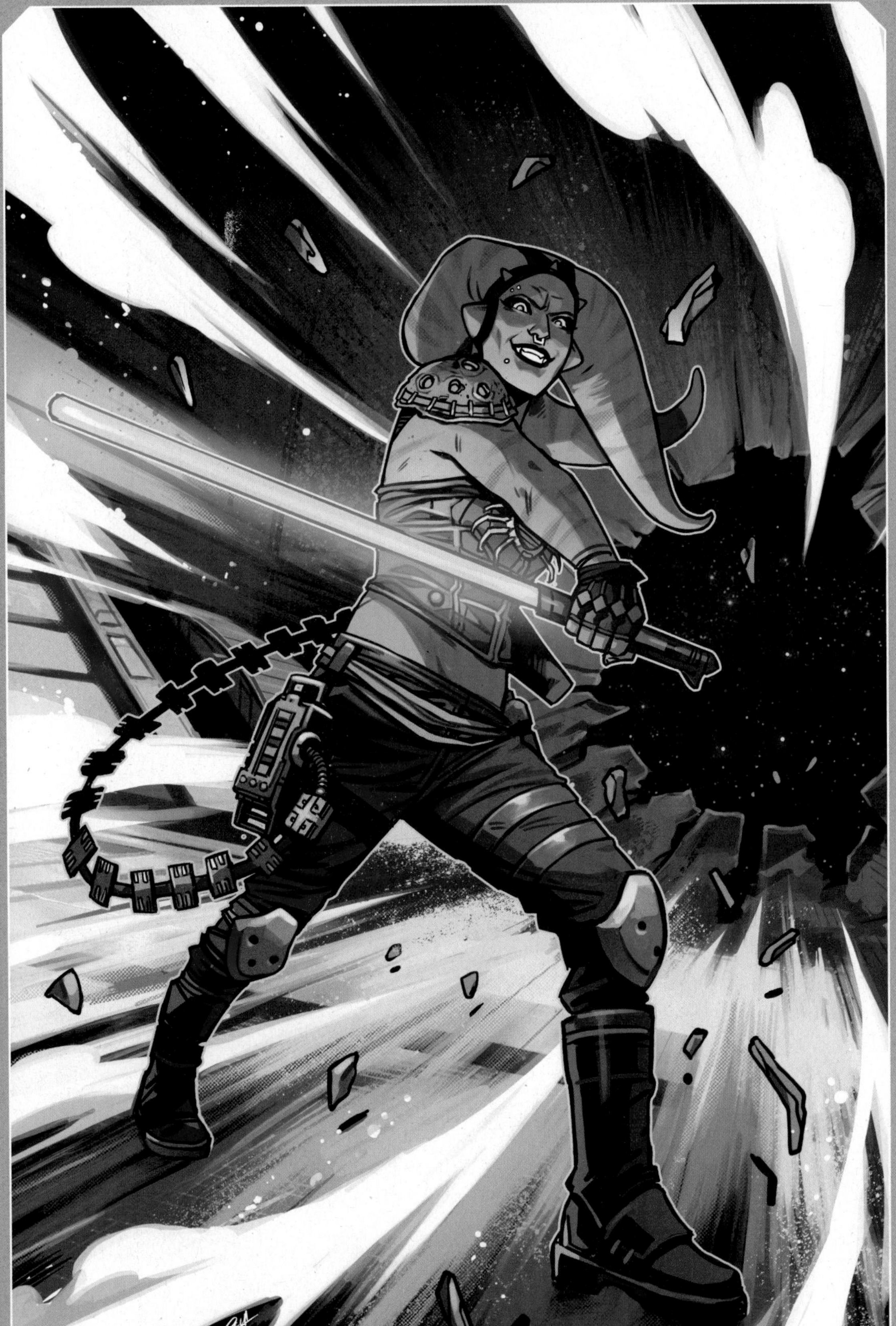

#14 Variant by
CASPAR WIJNGAARD

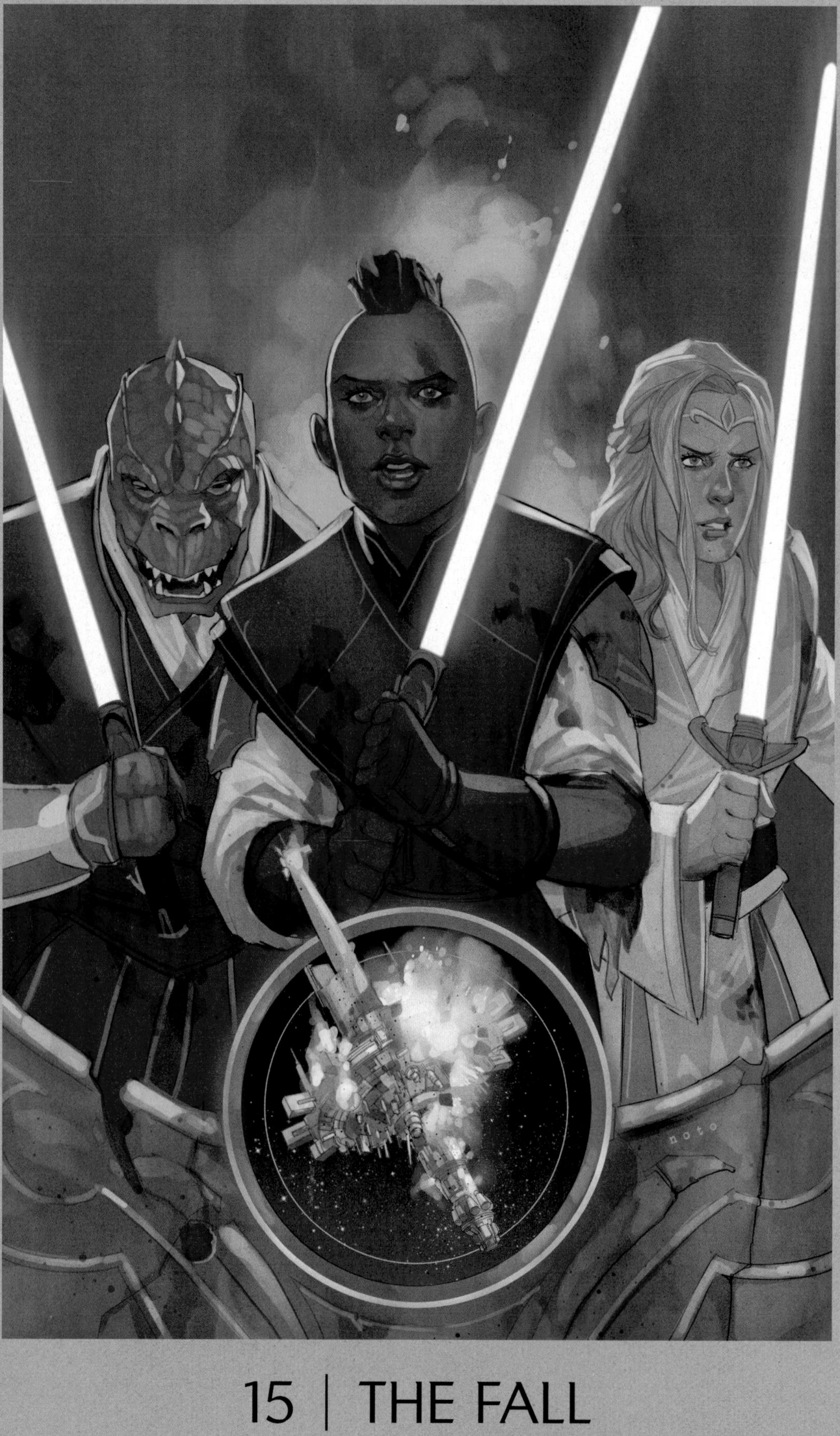

15 | THE FALL

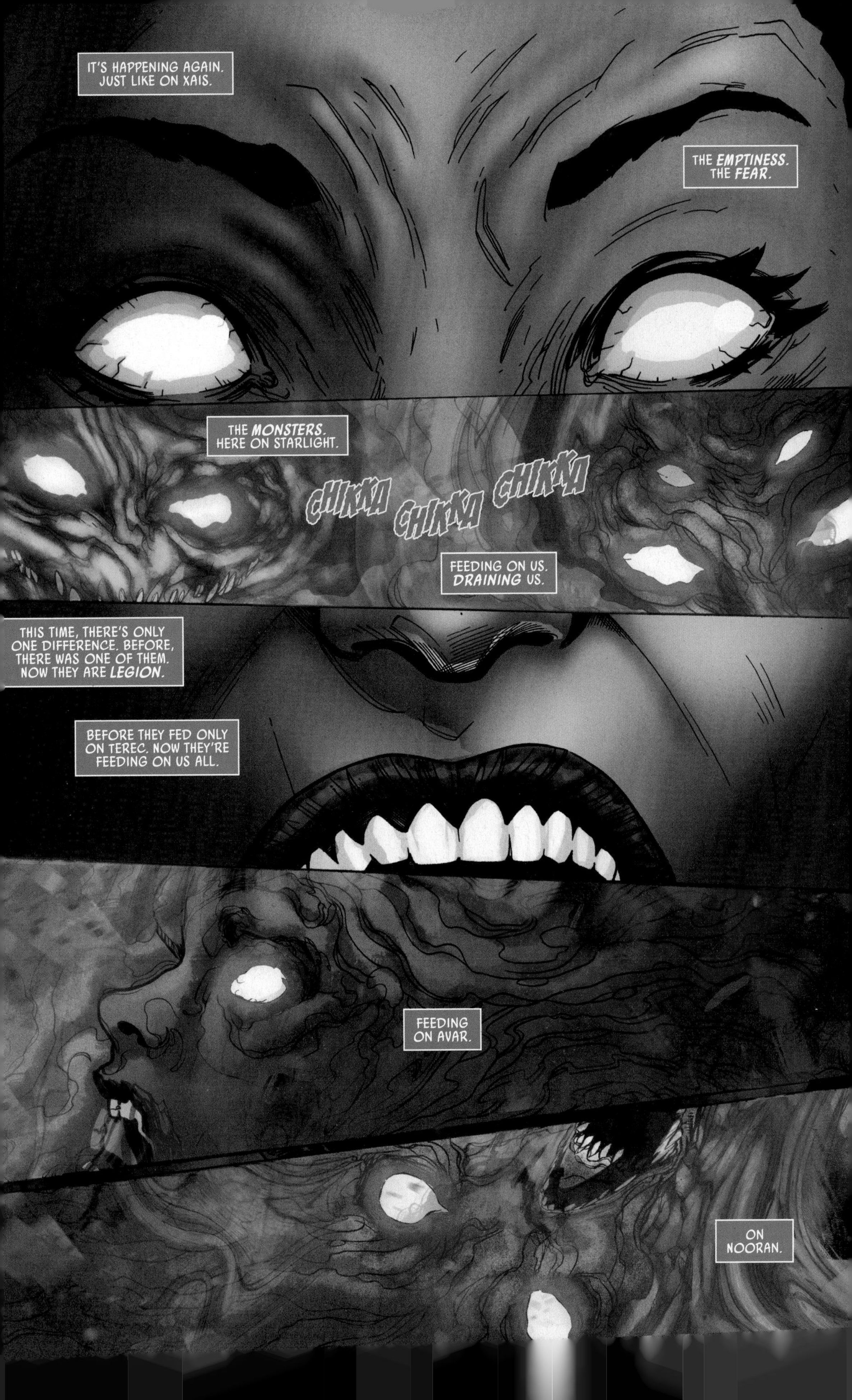
IT'S HAPPENING AGAIN. JUST LIKE ON XAIS.
THE EMPTINESS. THE FEAR.
THE MONSTERS. HERE ON STARLIGHT.
CHIKKA CHIKKA CHIKKA
FEEDING ON US. DRAINING US.
THIS TIME, THERE'S ONLY ONE DIFFERENCE. BEFORE, THERE WAS ONE OF THEM. NOW THEY ARE LEGION.
BEFORE THEY FED ONLY ON TEREC. NOW THEY'RE FEEDING ON US ALL.
FEEDING ON AVAR.
ON NOORAN.

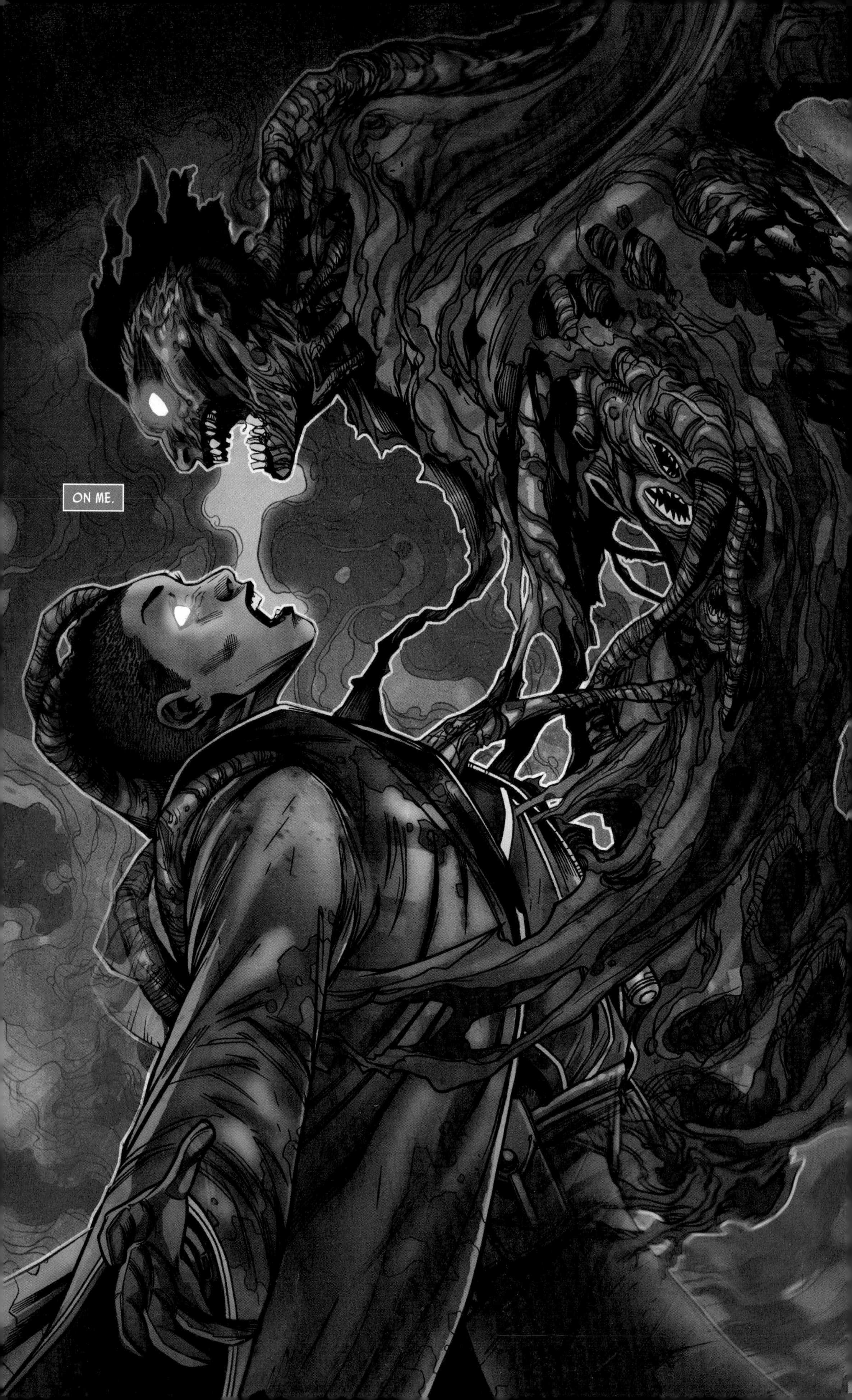
ON ME.

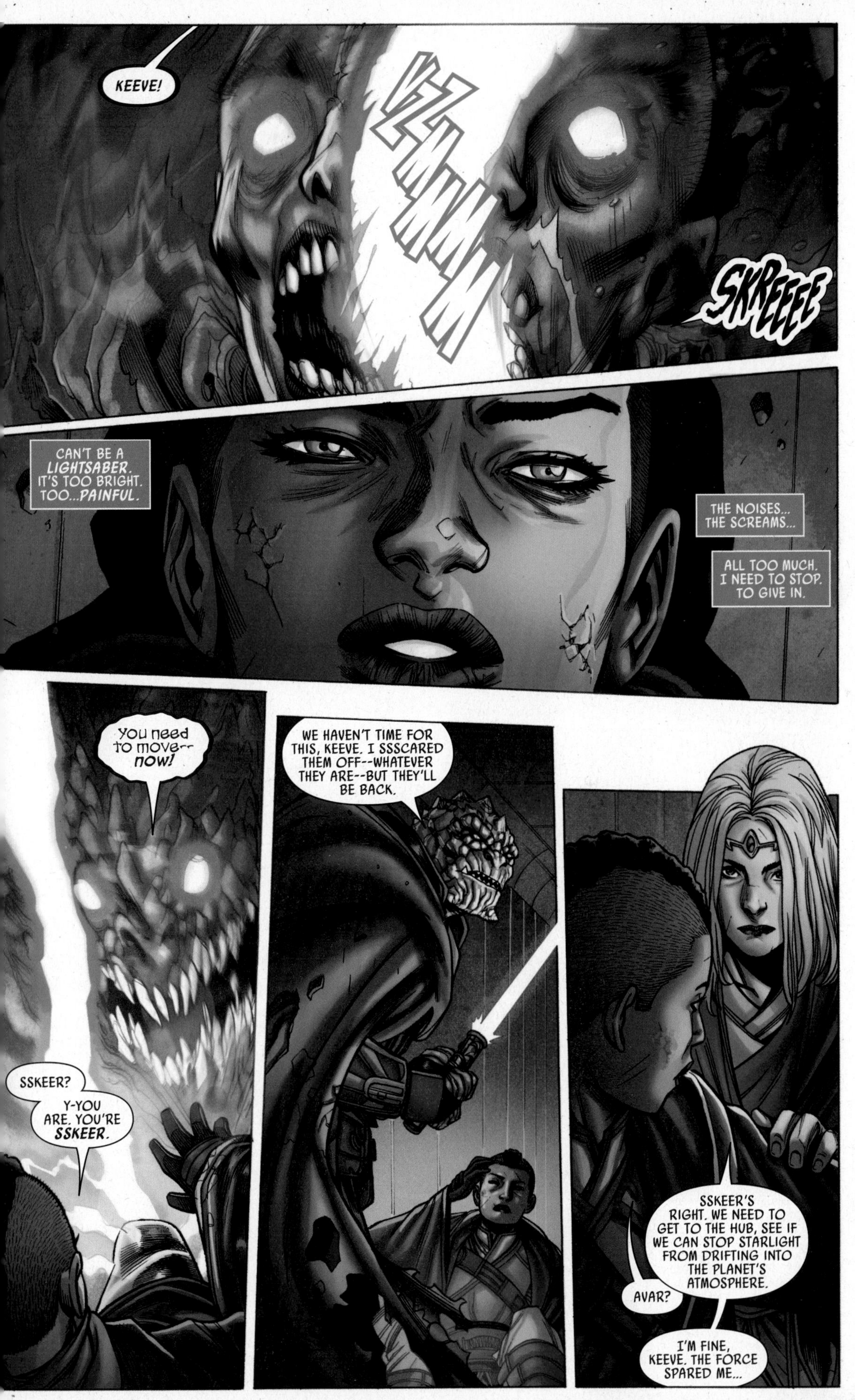
KEEVE!
VZZMMMM
SKREEEE
CAN'T BE A LIGHTSABER. IT'S TOO BRIGHT. TOO...PAINFUL.
THE NOISES... THE SCREAMS...
ALL TOO MUCH. I NEED TO STOP. TO GIVE IN.
You need to move-- NOW!
SSKEER?
Y-YOU ARE. YOU'RE SSKEER.
WE HAVEN'T TIME FOR THIS, KEEVE. I SSSCARED THEM OFF--WHATEVER THEY ARE--BUT THEY'LL BE BACK.
SSKEER'S RIGHT. WE NEED TO GET TO THE HUB, SEE IF WE CAN STOP STARLIGHT FROM DRIFTING INTO THE PLANET'S ATMOSPHERE.
AVAR?
I'M FINE, KEEVE. THE FORCE SPARED ME...

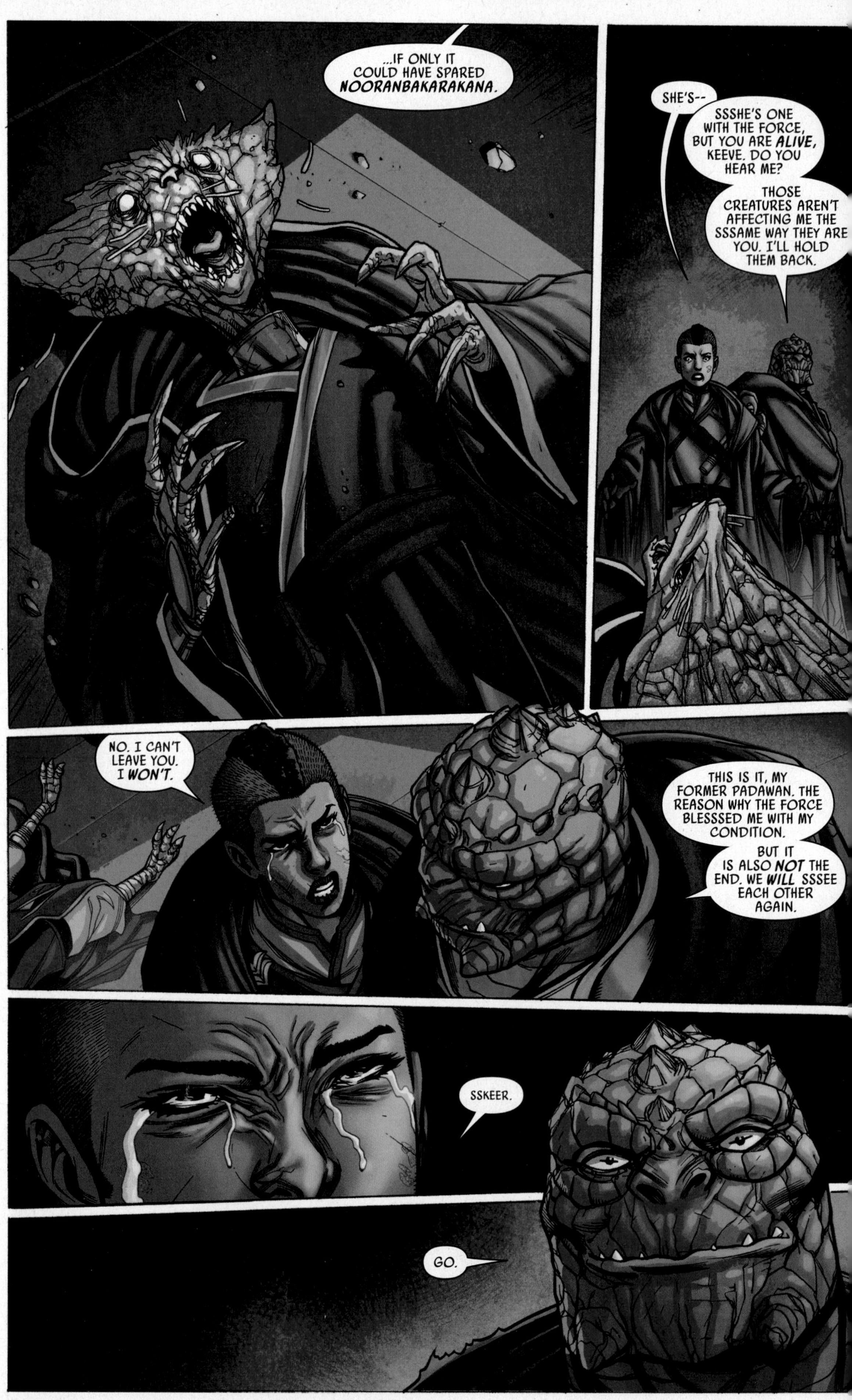
...IF ONLY IT COULD HAVE SPARED NOORANBAKARAKANA.
SHE'S--
SSSHE'S ONE WITH THE FORCE, BUT YOU ARE ALIVE, KEEVE. DO YOU HEAR ME?
THOSE CREATURES AREN'T AFFECTING ME THE SSSAME WAY THEY ARE YOU. I'LL HOLD THEM BACK.
NO. I CAN'T LEAVE YOU. I WON'T.
THIS IS IT, MY FORMER PADAWAN. THE REASON WHY THE FORCE BLESSSED ME WITH MY CONDITION.
BUT IT IS ALSO NOT THE END. WE WILL SSSEE EACH OTHER AGAIN.
SSKEER.
GO.

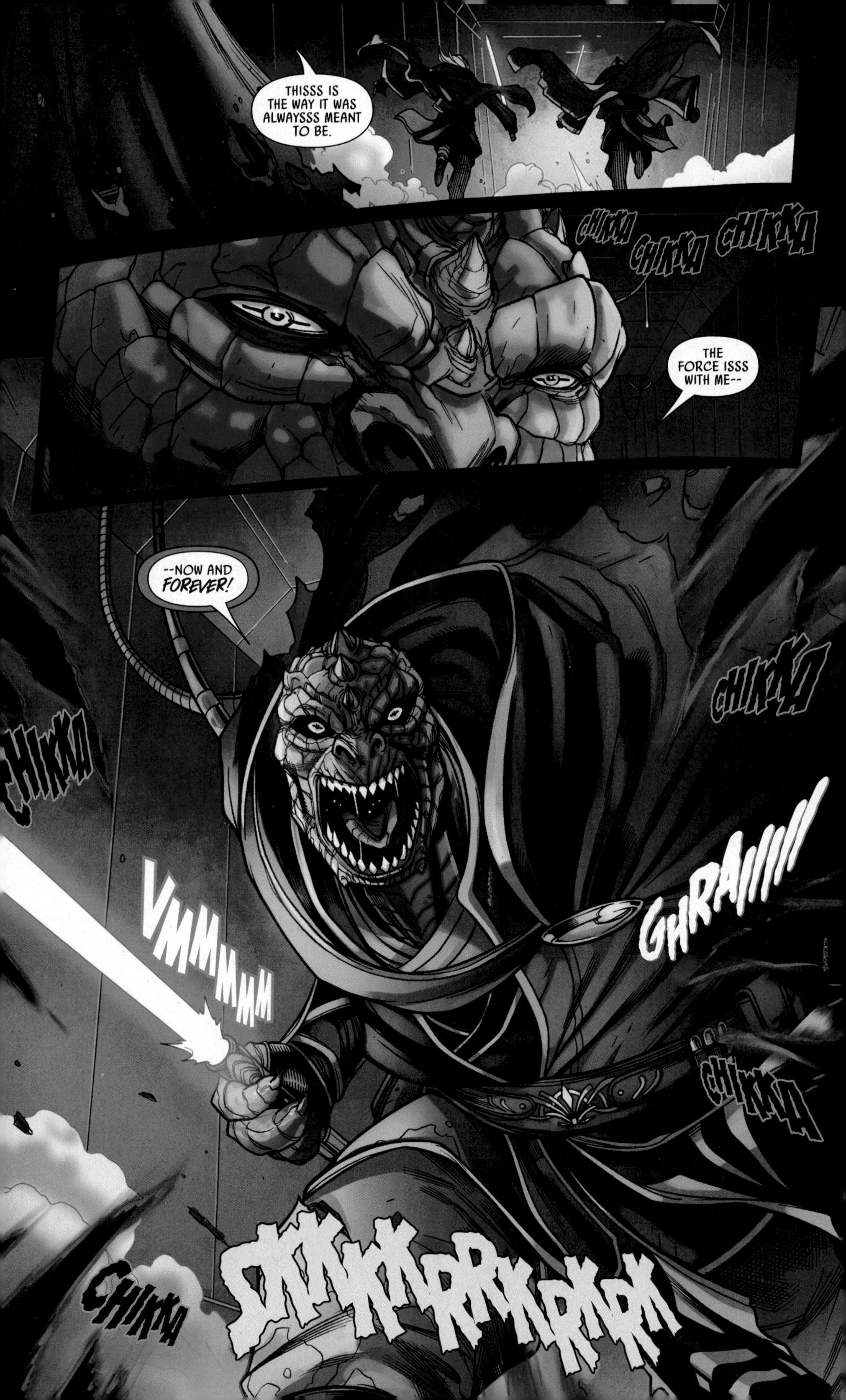
THISSS IS THE WAY IT WAS ALWAYSSS MEANT TO BE.
CHIKKA CHIKKA CHIKKA
THE FORCE ISSS WITH ME--
--NOW AND FOREVER!
CHIKKA
CHIKKA
VMMMMMM
GHRAIIIIII
CHIKKA
CHIKKA

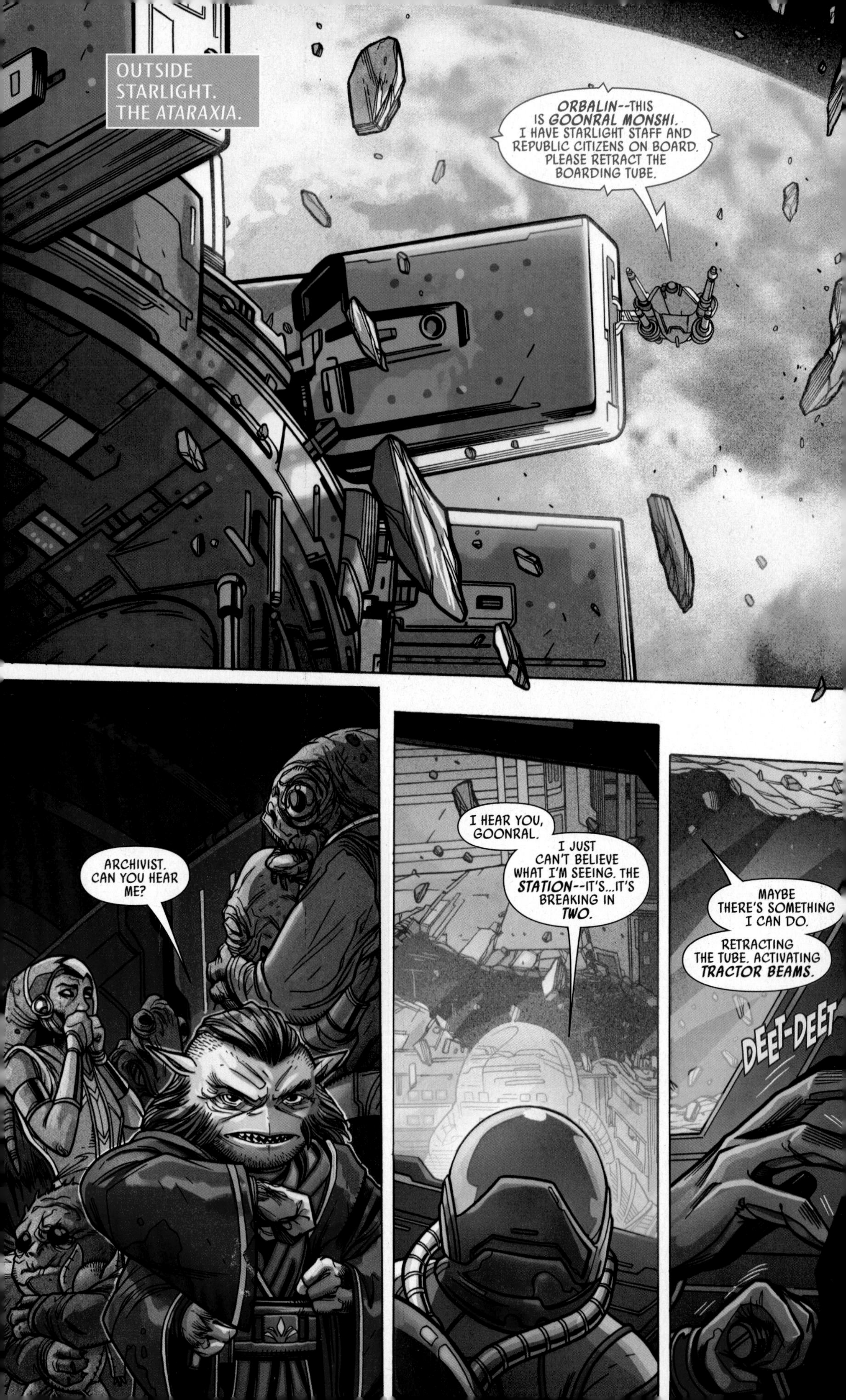
OUTSIDE STARLIGHT. THE ATARAXIA.
ORBALIN--THIS IS GOONRAL MONSHI. I HAVE STARLIGHT STAFF AND REPUBLIC CITIZENS ON BOARD. PLEASE RETRACT THE BOARDING TUBE.
ARCHIVIST. CAN YOU HEAR ME?
I HEAR YOU, GOONRAL.
I JUST CAN'T BELIEVE WHAT I'M SEEING. THE STATION--IT'S...IT'S BREAKING IN TWO.
MAYBE THERE'S SOMETHING I CAN DO.
RETRACTING THE TUBE. ACTIVATING TRACTOR BEAMS.
DEET-DEET

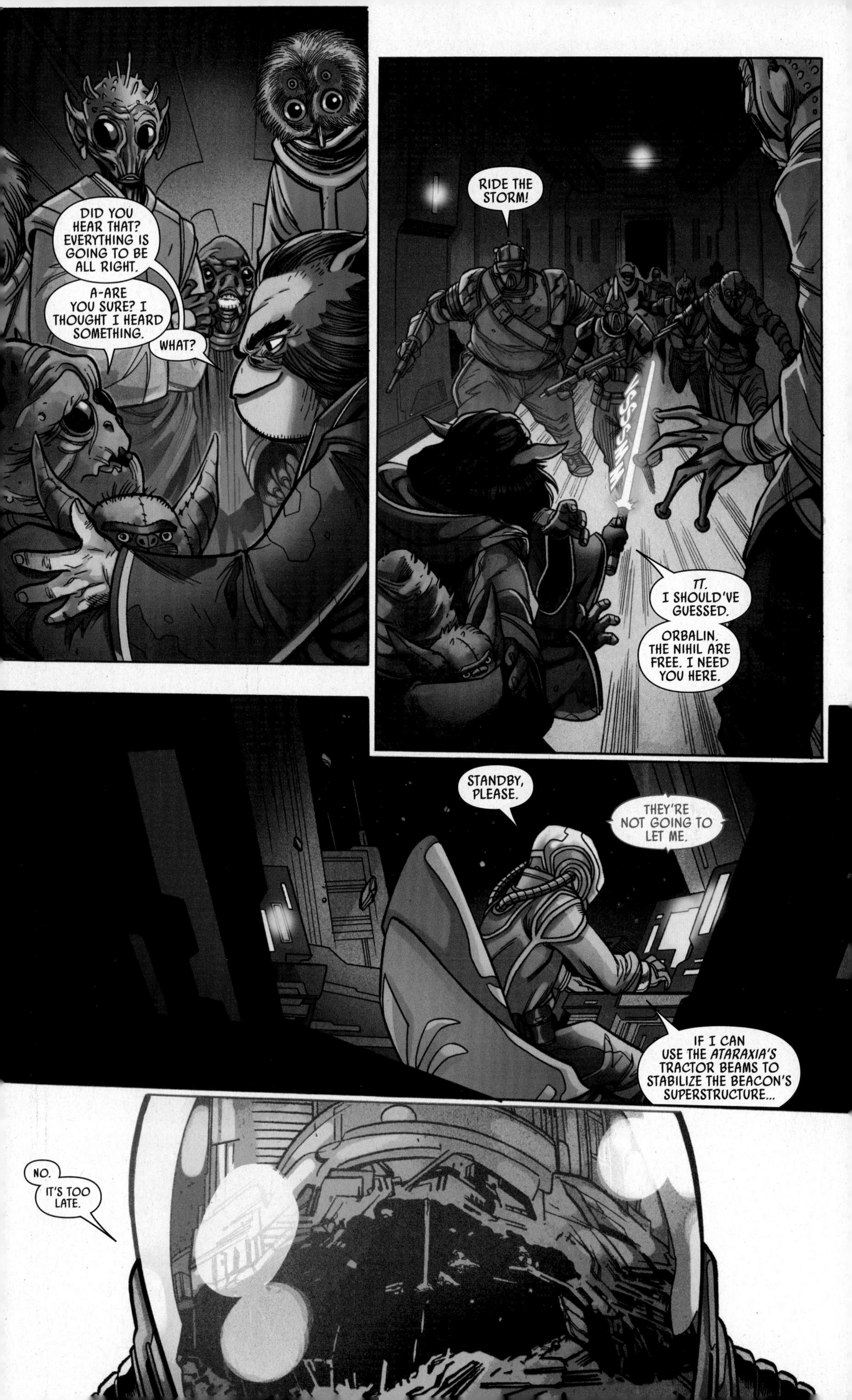
DID YOU HEAR THAT? EVERYTHING IS GOING TO BE ALL RIGHT.
A-ARE YOU SURE? I THOUGHT I HEARD SOMETHING.
WHAT?
RIDE THE STORM!
VSSSHM
TT. I SHOULD'VE GUESSED.
ORBALIN. THE NIHIL ARE FREE. I NEED YOU HERE.
STANDBY, PLEASE.
THEY'RE NOT GOING TO LET ME.
IF I CAN USE THE *ATARAXIA'S* TRACTOR BEAMS TO STABILIZE THE BEACON'S SUPERSTRUCTURE...
NO.
IT'S TOO LATE.

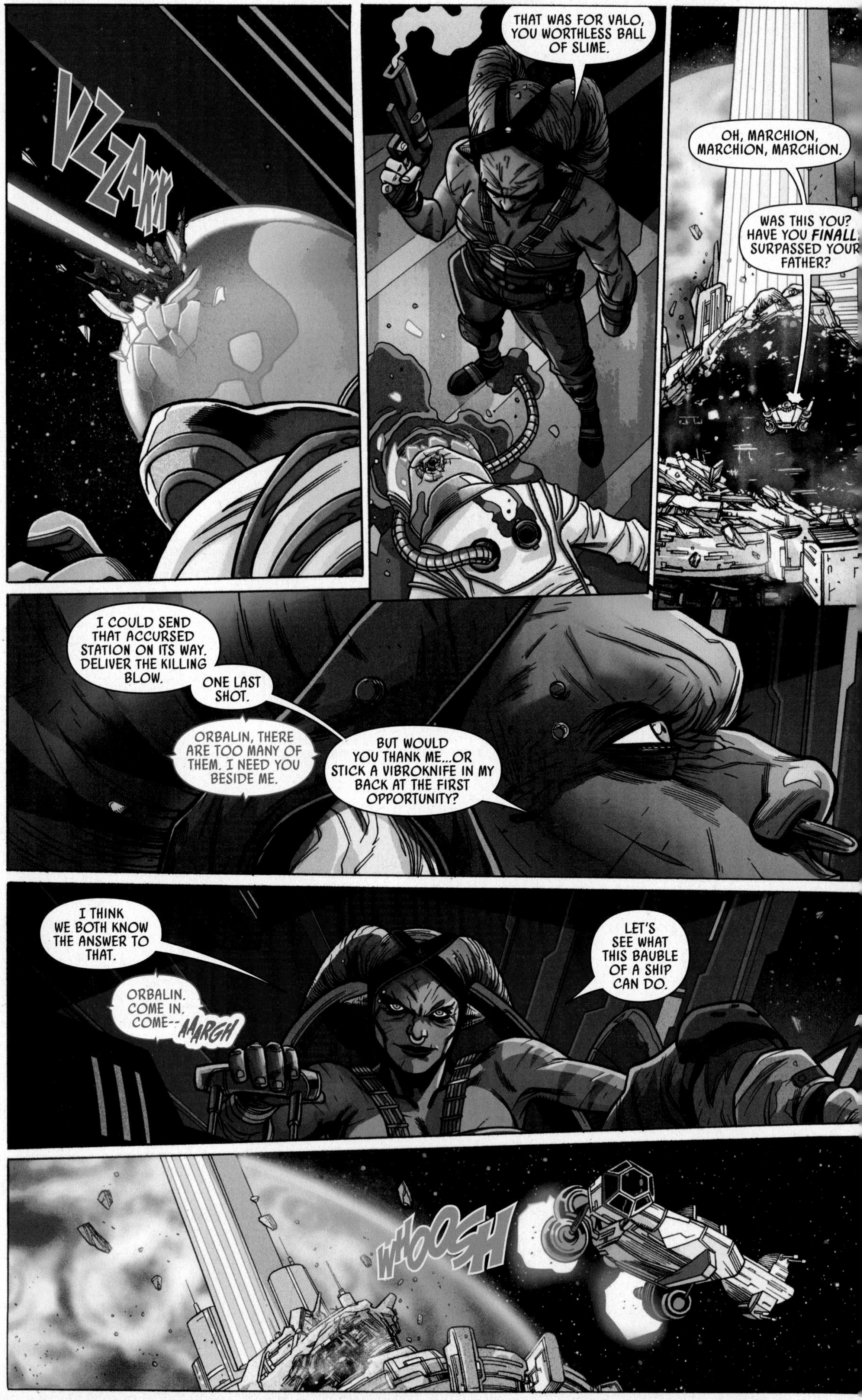
VZZAKK
THAT WAS FOR VALO, YOU WORTHLESS BALL OF SLIME.
OH, MARCHION, MARCHION, MARCHION.
WAS THIS YOU? HAVE YOU FINALLY SURPASSED YOUR FATHER?
I COULD SEND THAT ACCURSED STATION ON ITS WAY. DELIVER THE KILLING BLOW.
ONE LAST SHOT.
ORBALIN, THERE ARE TOO MANY OF THEM. I NEED YOU BESIDE ME.
BUT WOULD YOU THANK ME...OR STICK A VIBROKNIFE IN MY BACK AT THE FIRST OPPORTUNITY?
I THINK WE BOTH KNOW THE ANSWER TO THAT.
ORBALIN. COME IN. COME--AAARGH
LET'S SEE WHAT THIS BAUBLE OF A SHIP CAN DO.
WHOOSH

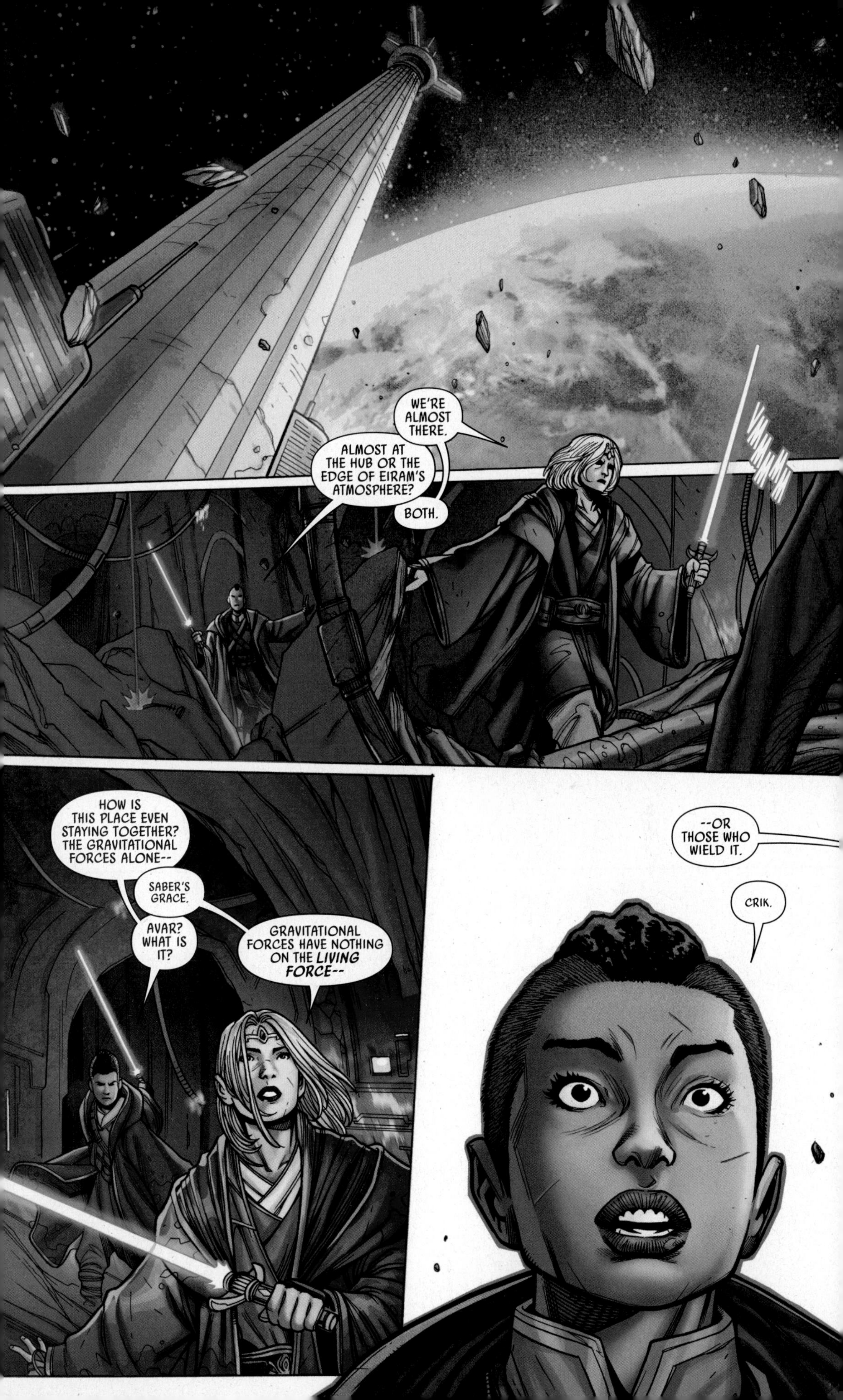
WE'RE ALMOST THERE.
ALMOST AT THE HUB OR THE EDGE OF EIRAM'S ATMOSPHERE?
BOTH.
VMMMM
HOW IS THIS PLACE EVEN STAYING TOGETHER? THE GRAVITATIONAL FORCES ALONE--
SABER'S GRACE.
AVAR? WHAT IS IT?
GRAVITATIONAL FORCES HAVE NOTHING ON THE *LIVING FORCE*--
--OR THOSE WHO WIELD IT.
CRIK.

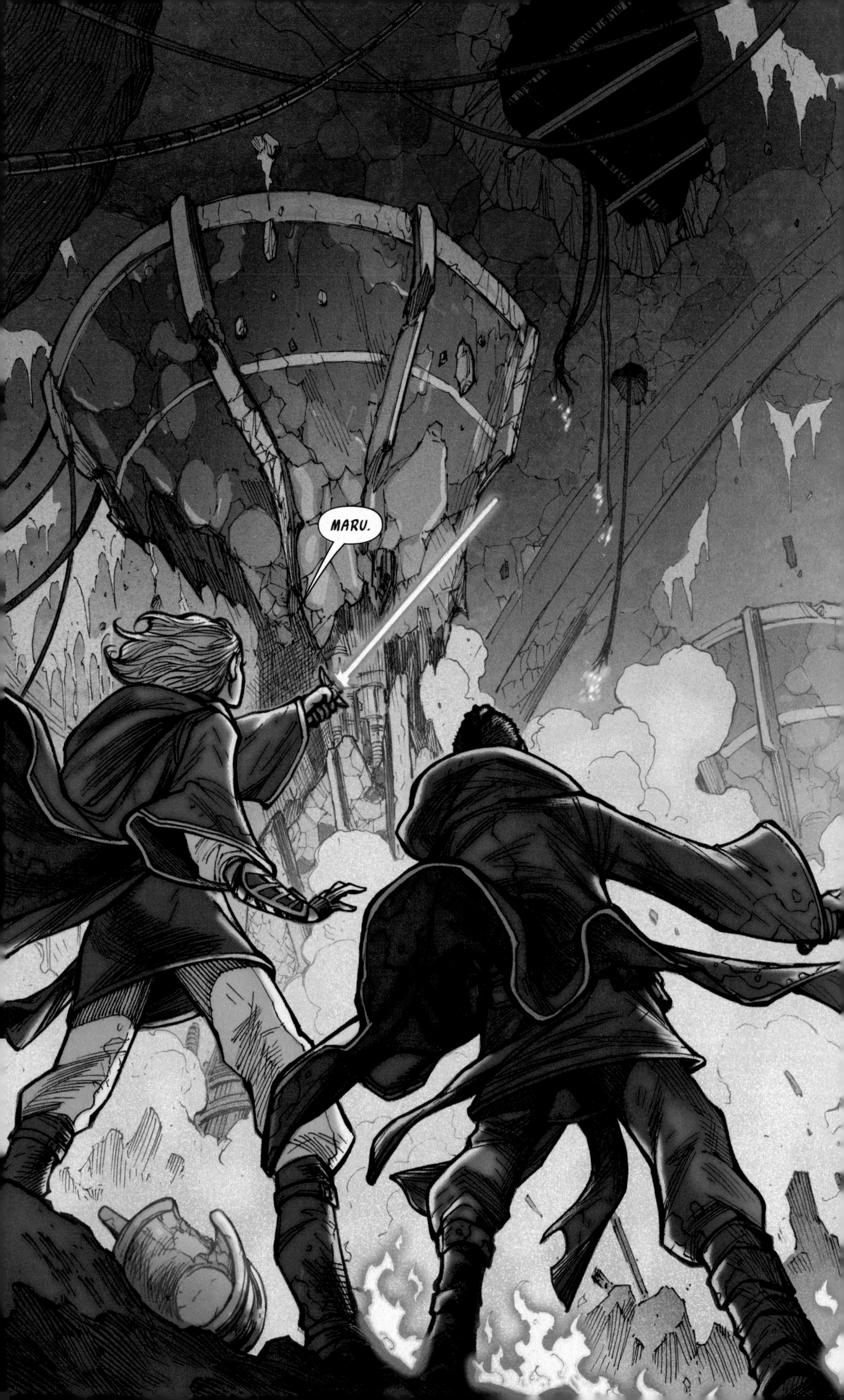
MARU.

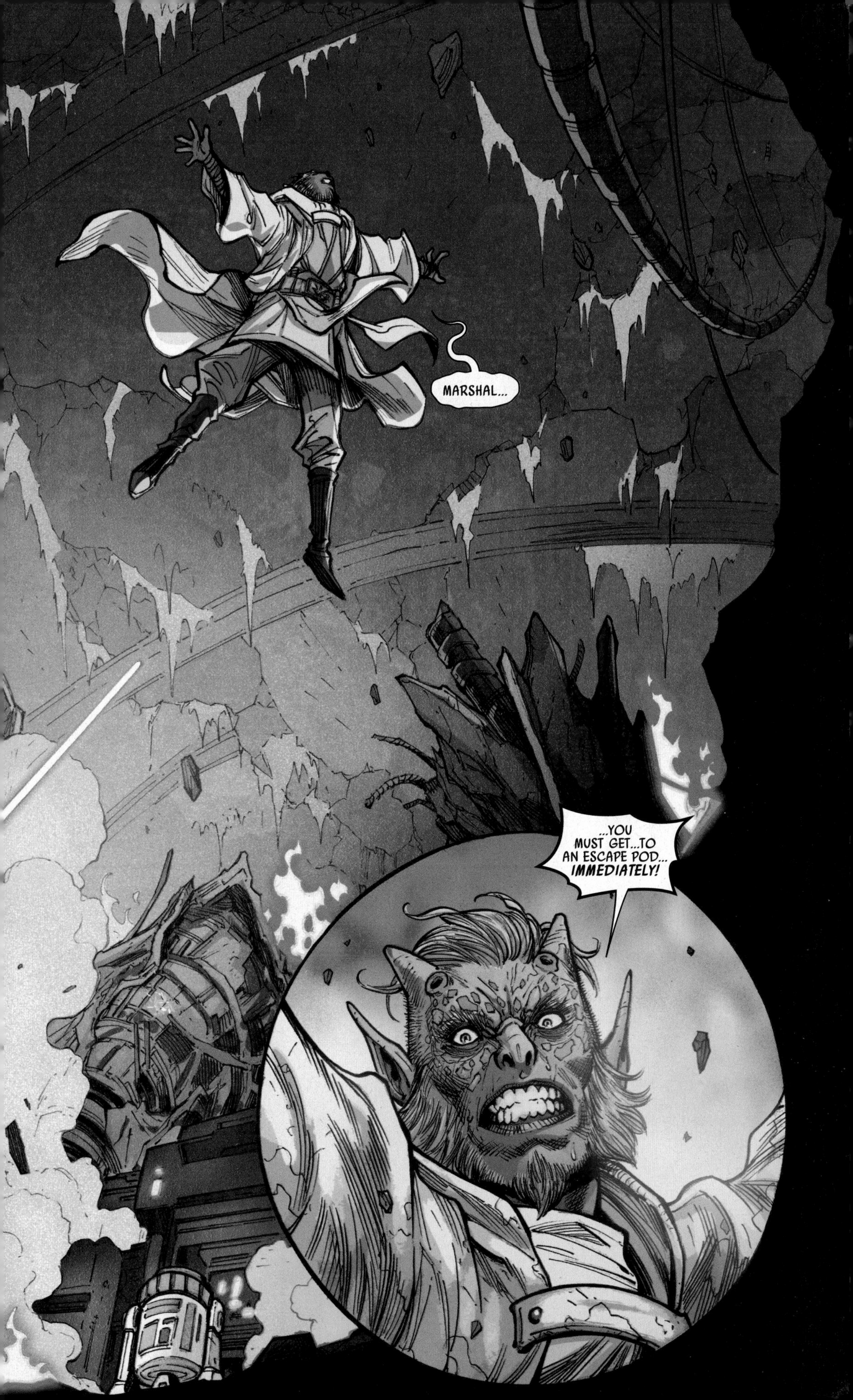
MARSHAL...
...YOU MUST GET...TO AN ESCAPE POD... IMMEDIATELY!

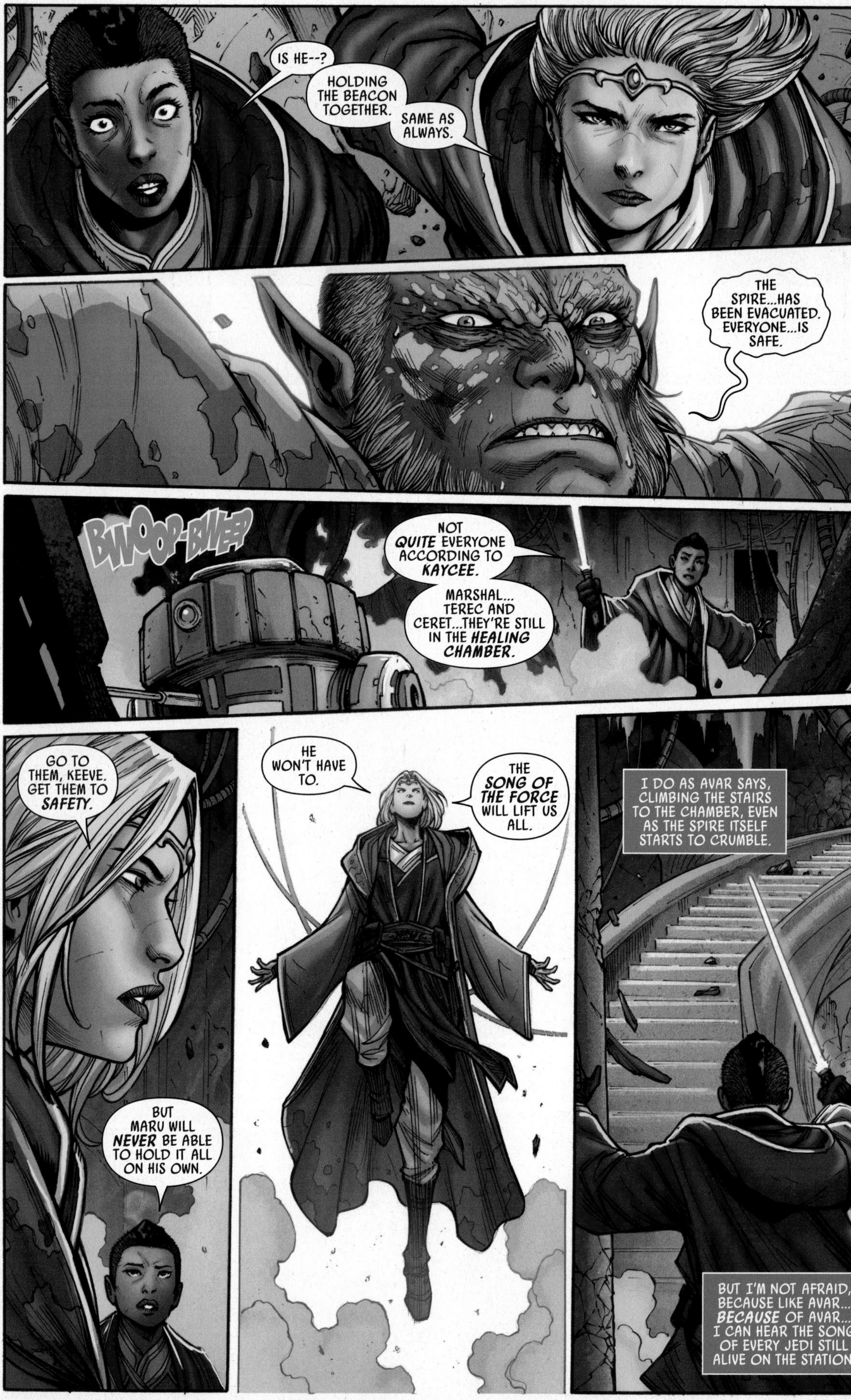
IS HE--?
HOLDING THE BEACON TOGETHER.
SAME AS ALWAYS.
THE SPIRE...HAS BEEN EVACUATED. EVERYONE...IS SAFE.
BWOOP-BWEEP
NOT QUITE EVERYONE ACCORDING TO KAYCEE.
MARSHAL... TEREC AND CERET...THEY'RE STILL IN THE HEALING CHAMBER.
GO TO THEM, KEEVE. GET THEM TO SAFETY.
BUT MARU WILL NEVER BE ABLE TO HOLD IT ALL ON HIS OWN.
HE WON'T HAVE TO.
THE SONG OF THE FORCE WILL LIFT US ALL.
I DO AS AVAR SAYS, CLIMBING THE STAIRS TO THE CHAMBER, EVEN AS THE SPIRE ITSELF STARTS TO CRUMBLE.
BUT I'M NOT AFRAID, BECAUSE LIKE AVAR... BECAUSE OF AVAR... I CAN HEAR THE SONG OF EVERY JEDI STILL ALIVE ON THE STATION.

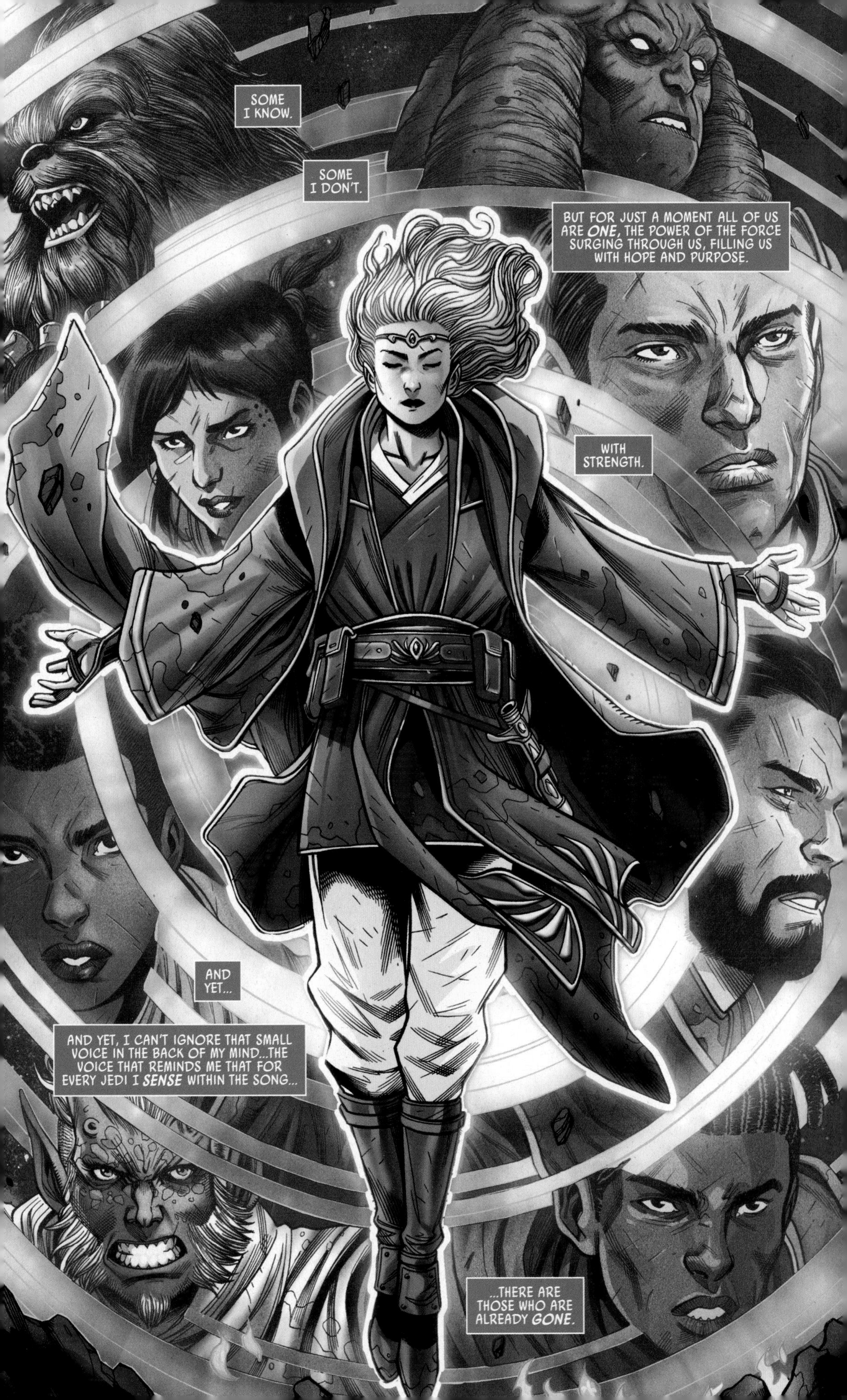
SOME I KNOW.
SOME I DON'T.
BUT FOR JUST A MOMENT ALL OF US ARE *ONE*, THE POWER OF THE FORCE SURGING THROUGH US, FILLING US WITH HOPE AND PURPOSE.
WITH STRENGTH.
AND YET...
AND YET, I CAN'T IGNORE THAT SMALL VOICE IN THE BACK OF MY MIND...THE VOICE THAT REMINDS ME THAT FOR EVERY JEDI I *SENSE* WITHIN THE SONG...
...THERE ARE THOSE WHO ARE ALREADY *GONE*.

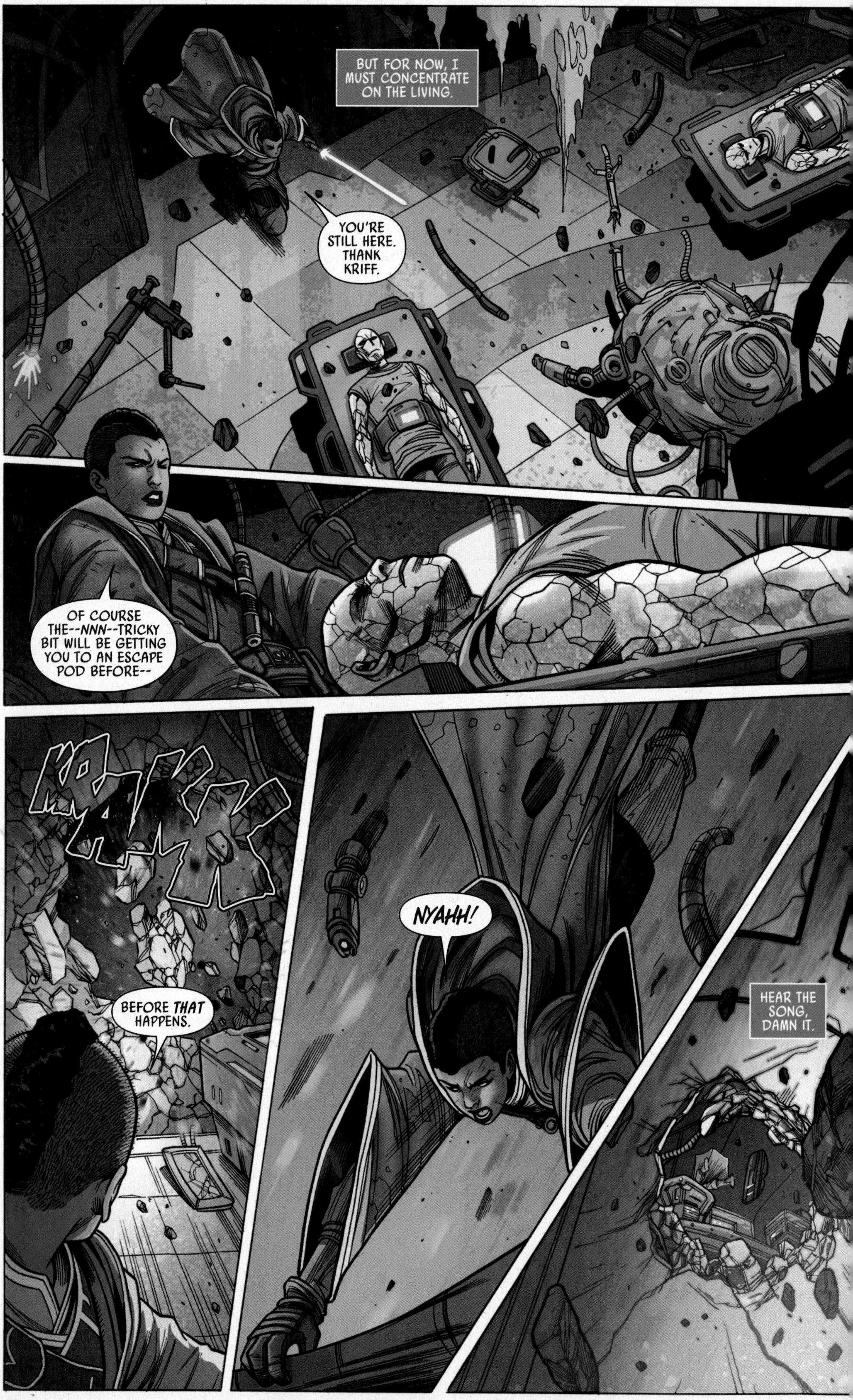
BUT FOR NOW, I MUST CONCENTRATE ON THE LIVING.
YOU'RE STILL HERE. THANK KRIFF.
OF COURSE THE--NNN--TRICKY BIT WILL BE GETTING YOU TO AN ESCAPE POD BEFORE--
BEFORE THAT HAPPENS.
NYAHH!
HEAR THE SONG, DAMN IT.

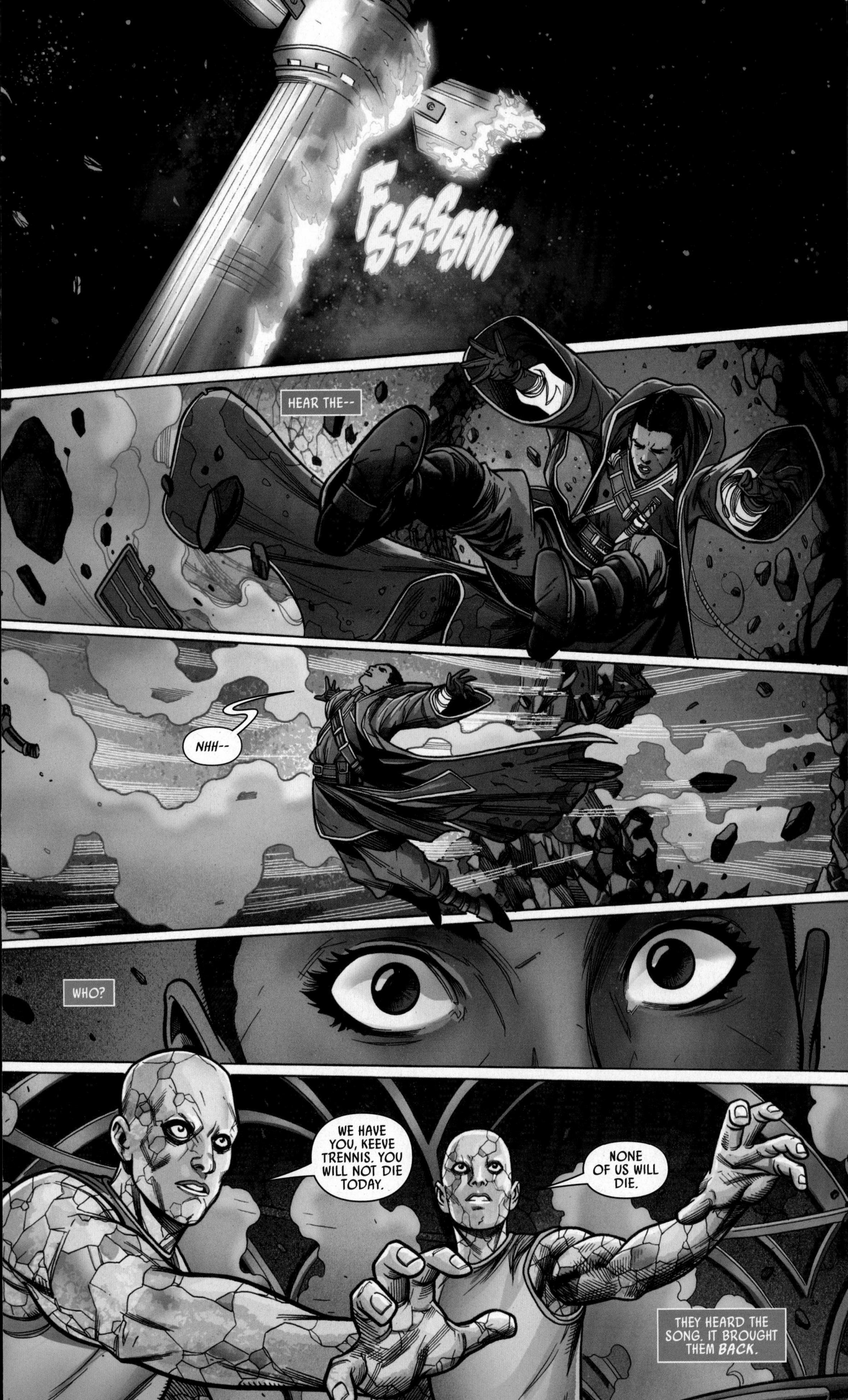
FSSSSNN
HEAR THE--
NHH--
WHO?
WE HAVE YOU, KEEVE TRENNIS. YOU WILL NOT DIE TODAY.
NONE OF US WILL DIE.
THEY HEARD THE SONG. IT BROUGHT THEM BACK.

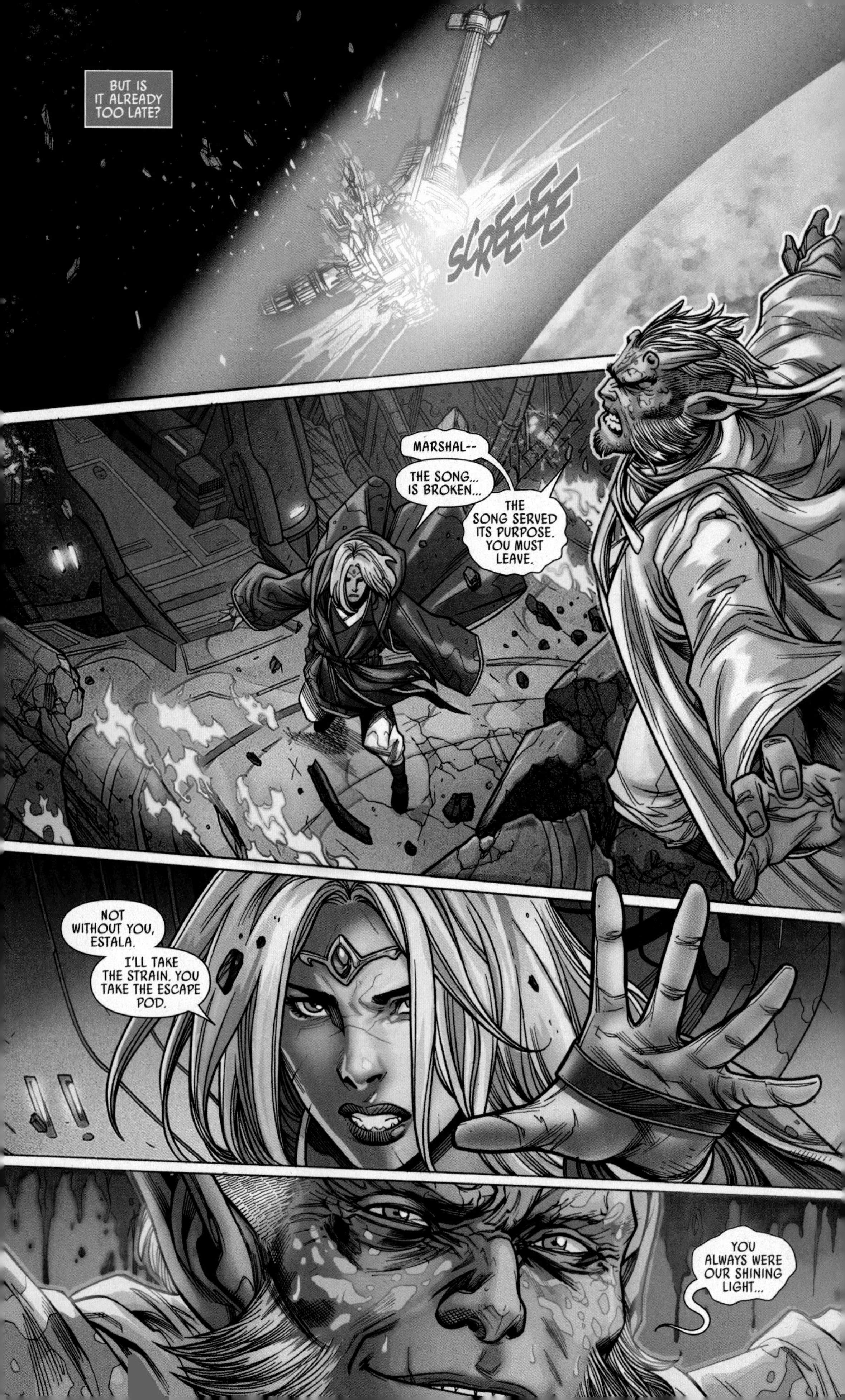

BUT IS IT ALREADY TOO LATE?
SCREEEEE
MARSHAL--
THE SONG... IS BROKEN...
THE SONG SERVED ITS PURPOSE. YOU MUST LEAVE.
NOT WITHOUT YOU, ESTALA.
I'LL TAKE THE STRAIN. YOU TAKE THE ESCAPE POD.
YOU ALWAYS WERE OUR SHINING LIGHT...

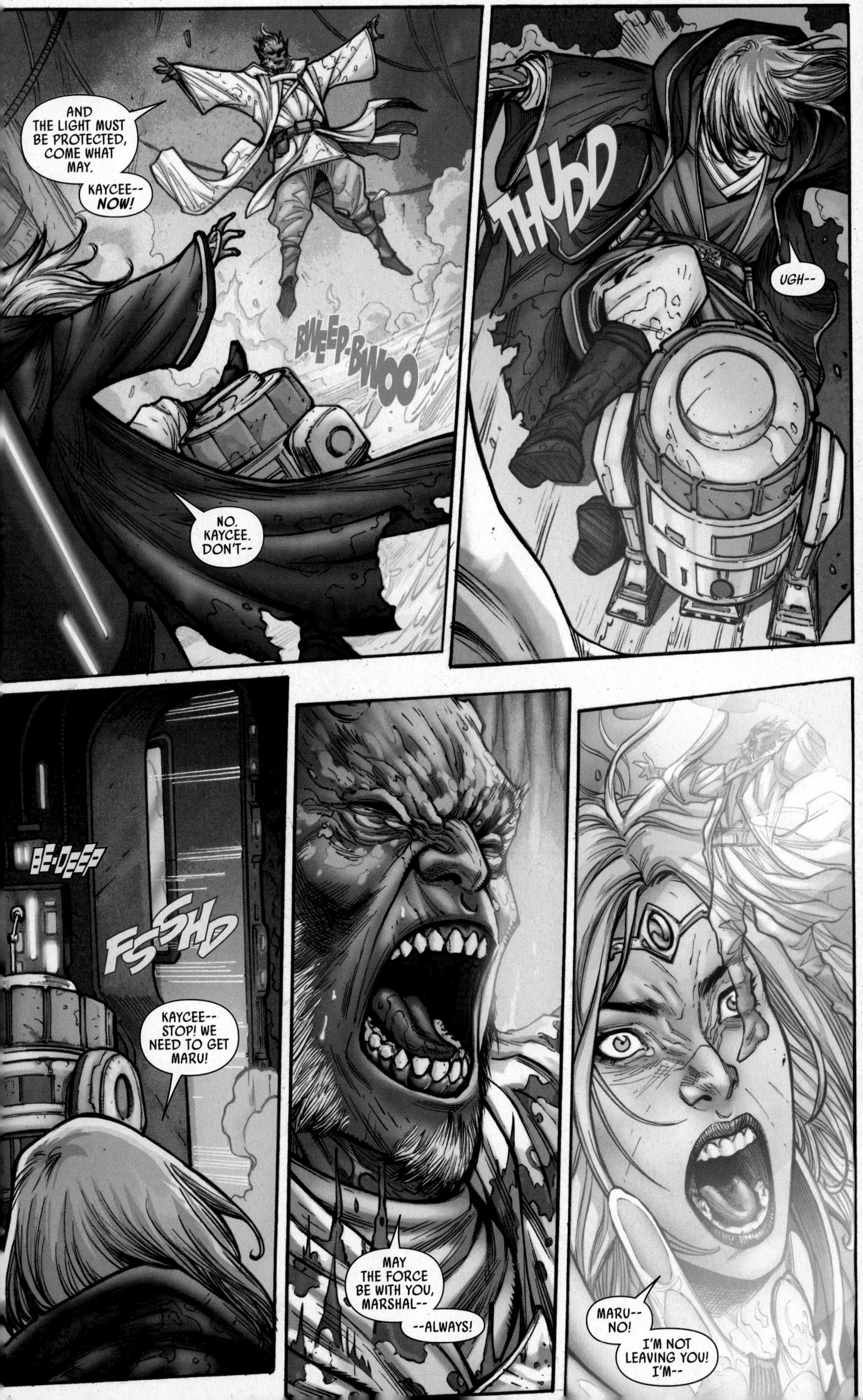
AND THE LIGHT MUST BE PROTECTED, COME WHAT MAY.
KAYCEE-- NOW!
BWEEP-BWOO
NO. KAYCEE. DON'T--
THUDD
UGH--
BE-DEEP
FSSHD
KAYCEE-- STOP! WE NEED TO GET MARU!
MAY THE FORCE BE WITH YOU, MARSHAL--
--ALWAYS!
MARU-- NO!
I'M NOT LEAVING YOU! I'M--

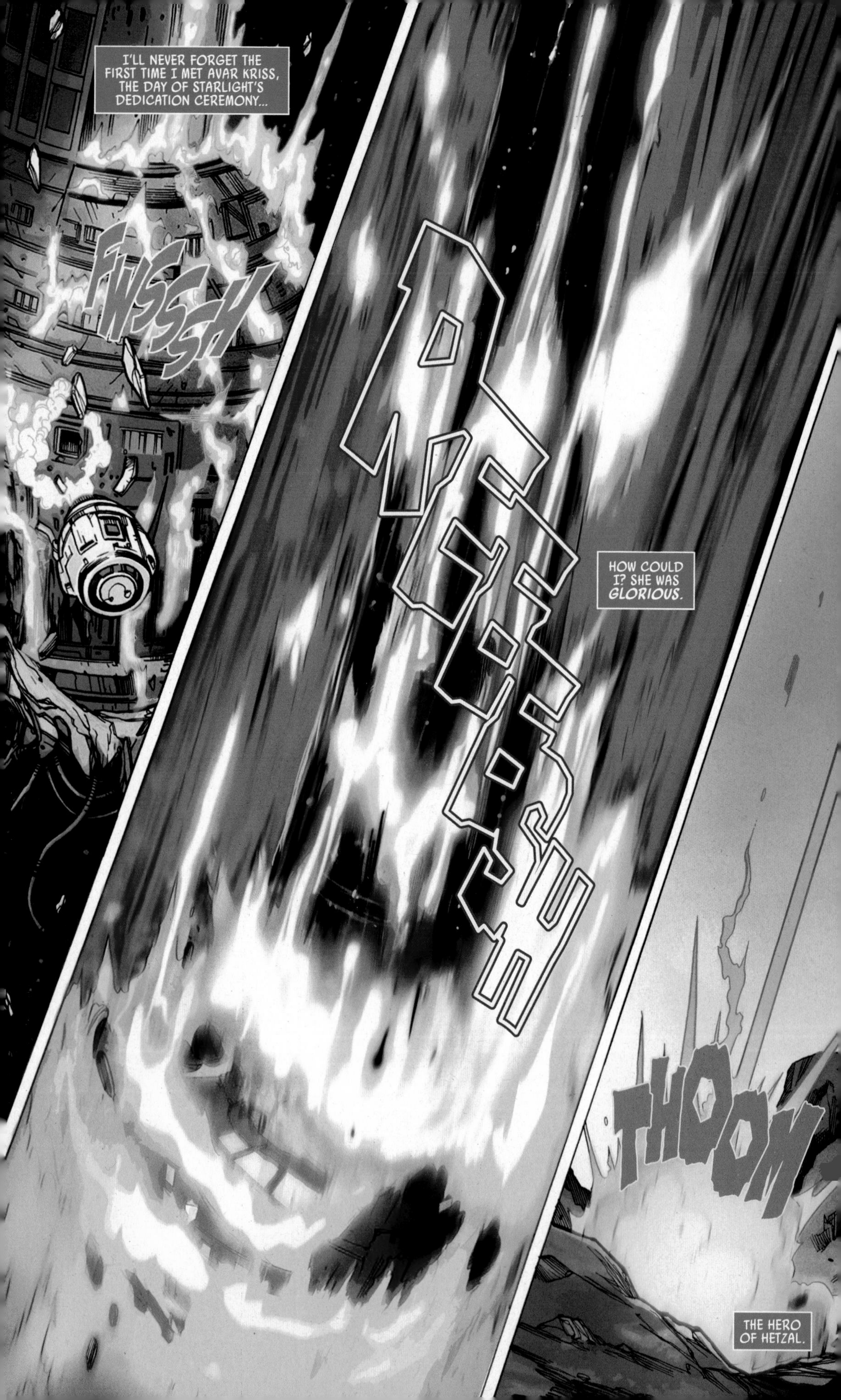
I'LL NEVER FORGET THE FIRST TIME I MET AVAR KRISS, THE DAY OF STARLIGHT'S DEDICATION CEREMONY...
FWSSSH
HOW COULD I? SHE WAS GLORIOUS.
THOOM
THE HERO OF HETZAL.

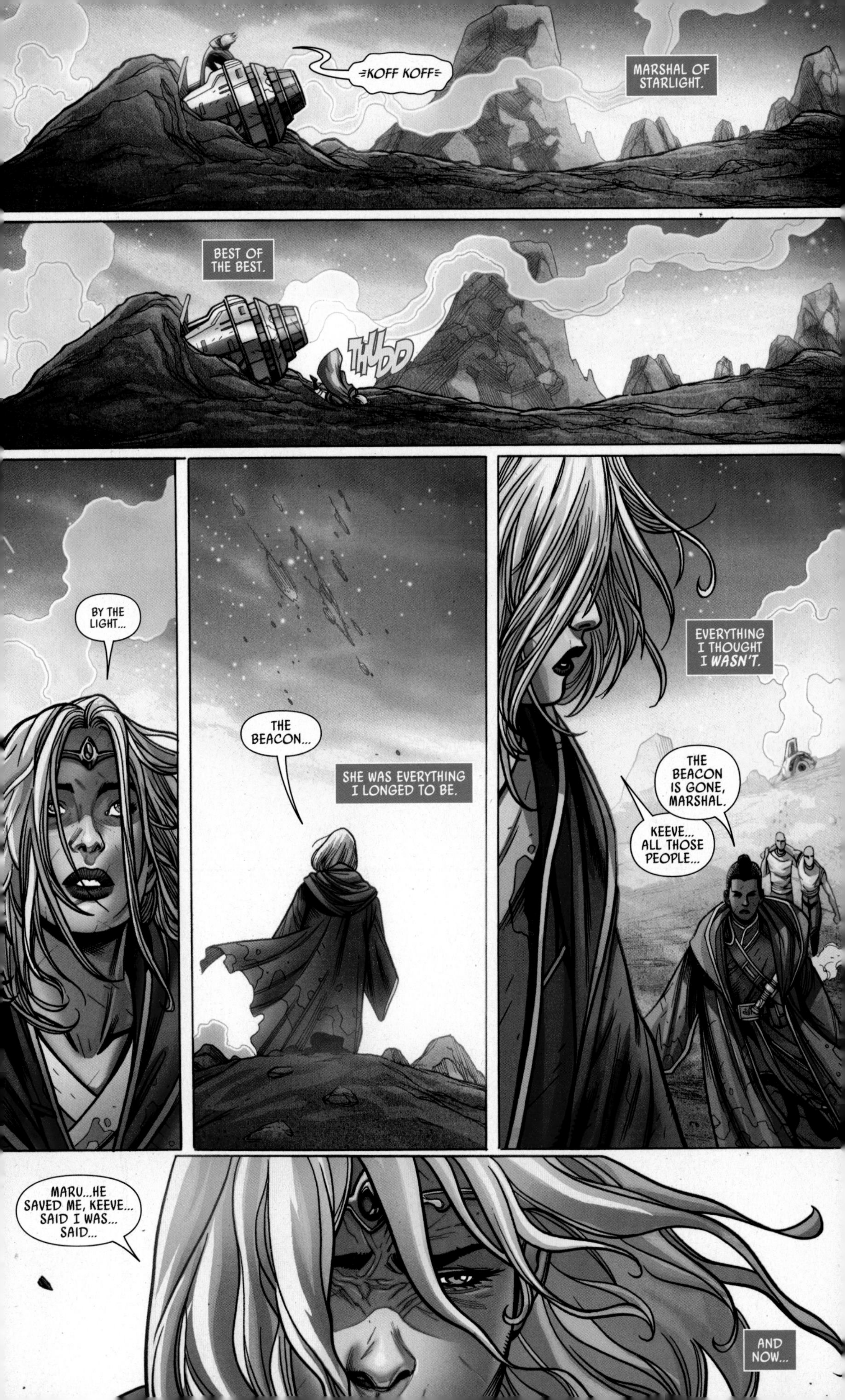

=KOFF KOFF=
MARSHAL OF STARLIGHT.
BEST OF THE BEST.
THUDD
BY THE LIGHT...
THE BEACON...
SHE WAS EVERYTHING I LONGED TO BE.
EVERYTHING I THOUGHT I WASN'T.
THE BEACON IS GONE, MARSHAL.
KEEVE... ALL THOSE PEOPLE...
MARU...HE SAVED ME, KEEVE... SAID I WAS... SAID...
AND NOW...

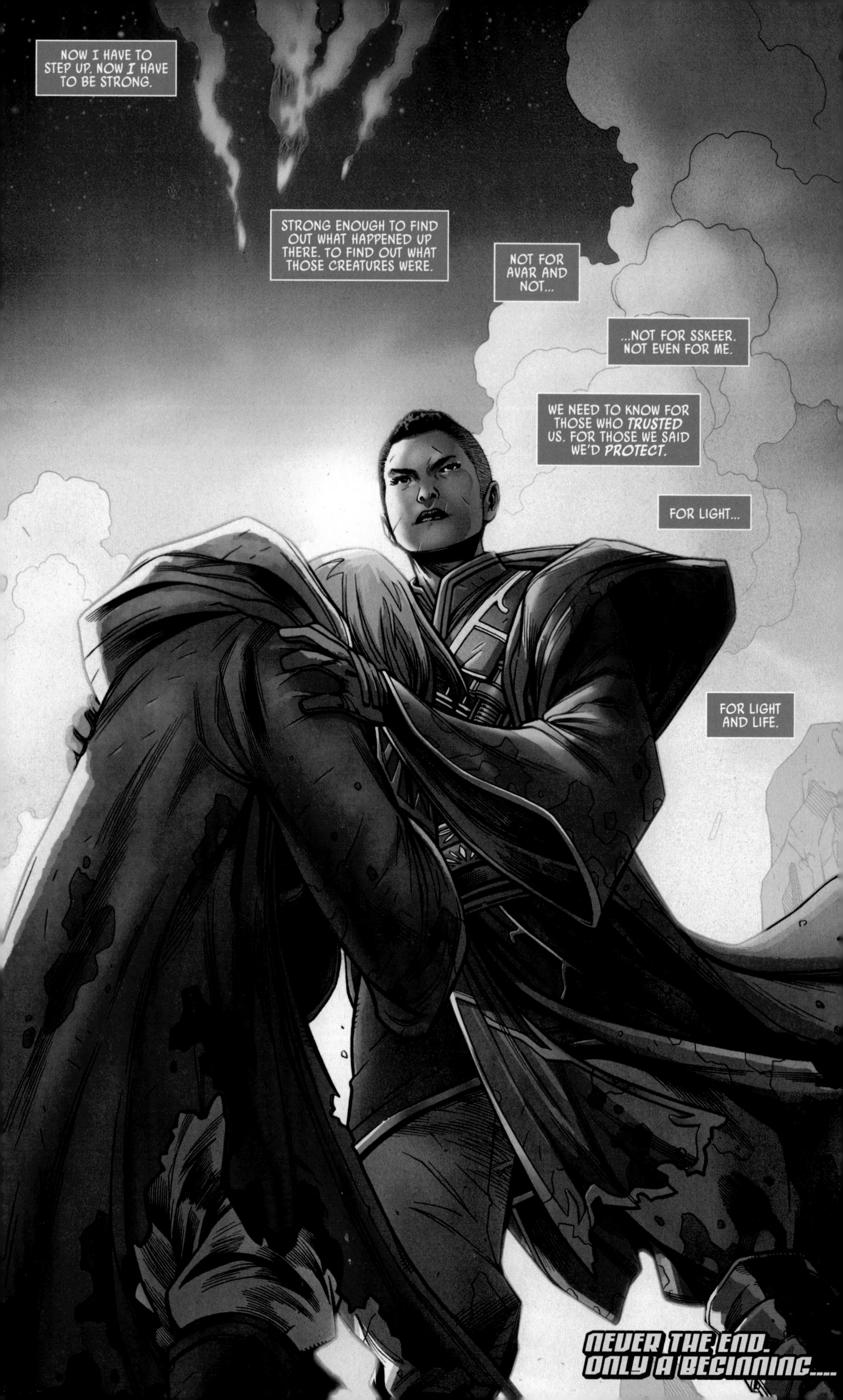
NOW I HAVE TO STEP UP. NOW *I* HAVE TO BE STRONG.
STRONG ENOUGH TO FIND OUT WHAT HAPPENED UP THERE. TO FIND OUT WHAT THOSE CREATURES WERE.
NOT FOR AVAR AND NOT...
...NOT FOR SSKEER. NOT EVEN FOR ME.
WE NEED TO KNOW FOR THOSE WHO *TRUSTED* US. FOR THOSE WE SAID WE'D *PROTECT.*
FOR LIGHT...
FOR LIGHT AND LIFE.
NEVER THE END. ONLY A BEGINNING....

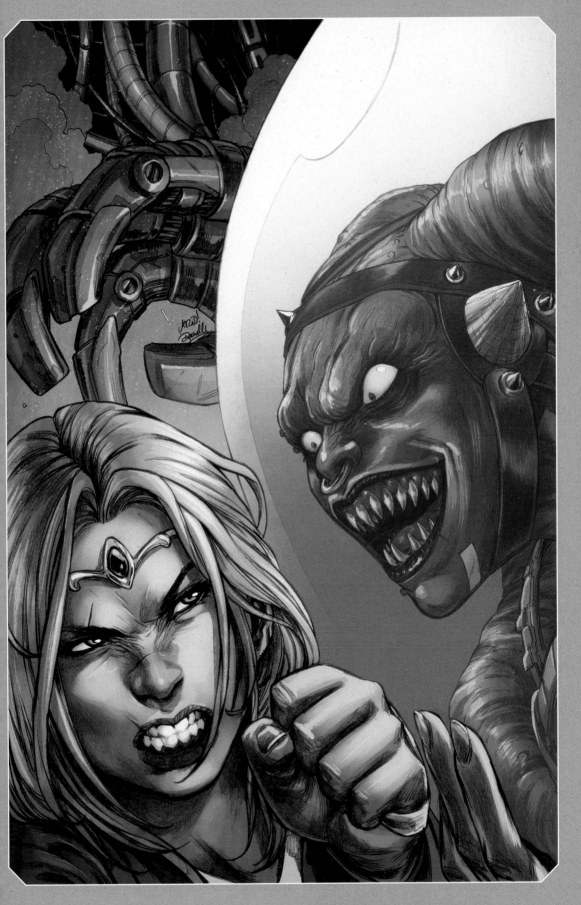

#15 Variant by
ARIO ANINDITO & **RACHELLE ROSENBERG**

EYE OF THE STORM 1

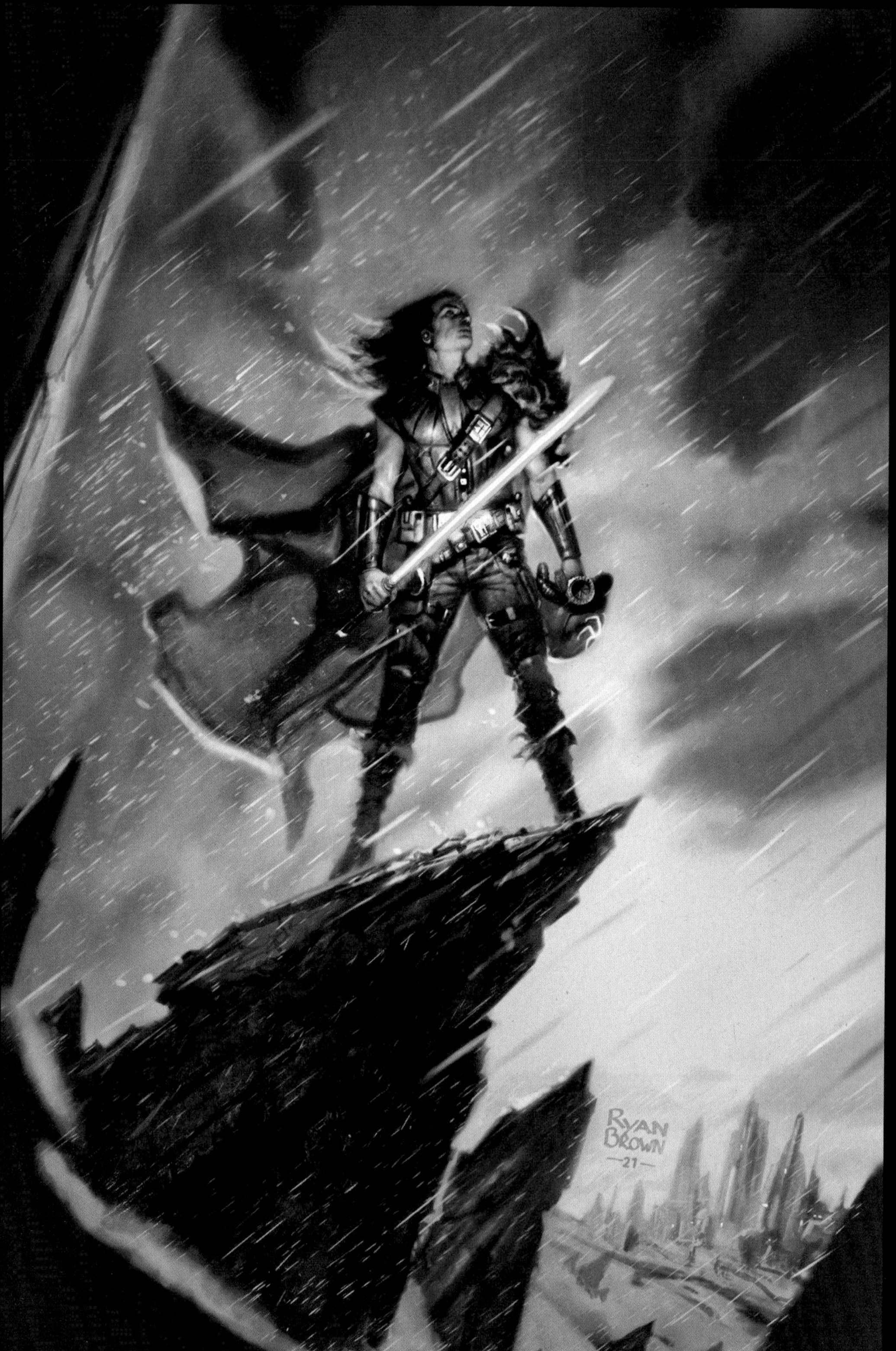
RYAN
BROWN
—21—

ACT I **RO**

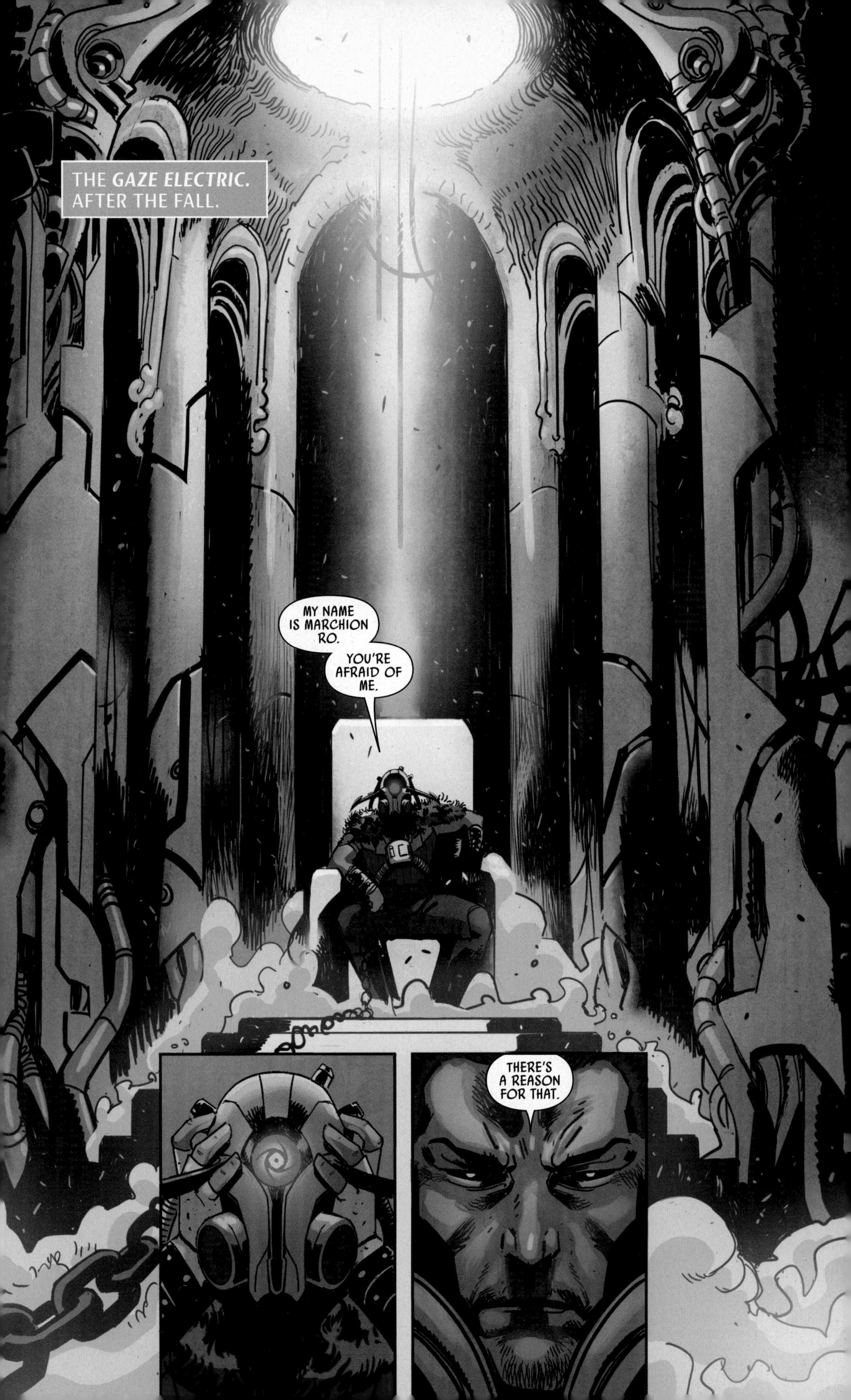
THE GAZE ELECTRIC. AFTER THE FALL.
MY NAME IS MARCHION RO.
YOU'RE AFRAID OF ME.
THERE'S A REASON FOR THAT.

SCENE I

THE TRUTH

In which a People learn Valuable Lessons
And are Greatly Changed by them;
In All Ways but One.

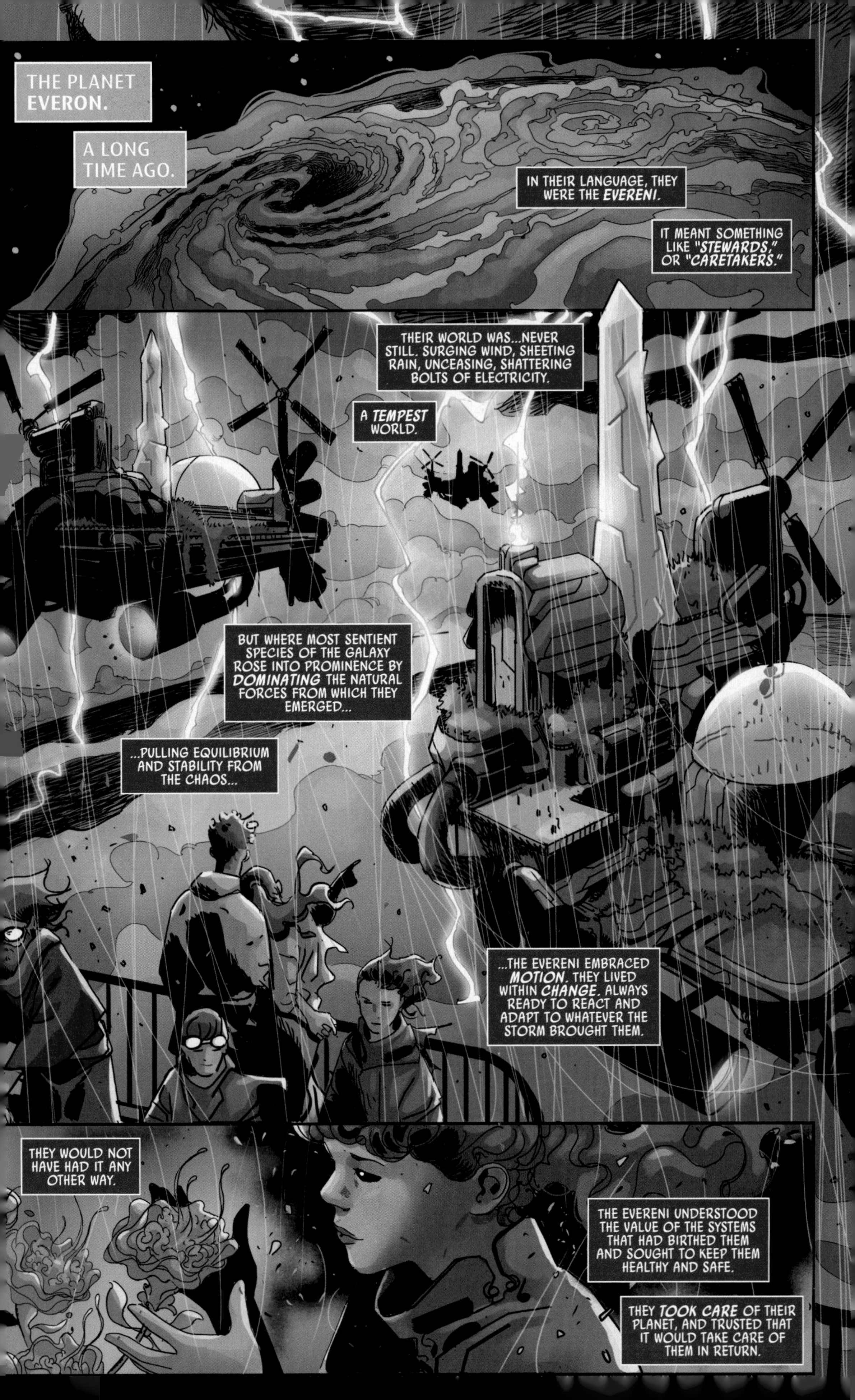
THE PLANET EVERON.
A LONG TIME AGO.
IN THEIR LANGUAGE, THEY WERE THE EVERENI.
IT MEANT SOMETHING LIKE "STEWARDS," OR "CARETAKERS."
THEIR WORLD WAS...NEVER STILL. SURGING WIND, SHEETING RAIN, UNCEASING, SHATTERING BOLTS OF ELECTRICITY.
A TEMPEST WORLD.
BUT WHERE MOST SENTIENT SPECIES OF THE GALAXY ROSE INTO PROMINENCE BY DOMINATING THE NATURAL FORCES FROM WHICH THEY EMERGED...
...PULLING EQUILIBRIUM AND STABILITY FROM THE CHAOS...
...THE EVERENI EMBRACED MOTION. THEY LIVED WITHIN CHANGE. ALWAYS READY TO REACT AND ADAPT TO WHATEVER THE STORM BROUGHT THEM.
THEY WOULD NOT HAVE HAD IT ANY OTHER WAY.
THE EVERENI UNDERSTOOD THE VALUE OF THE SYSTEMS THAT HAD BIRTHED THEM AND SOUGHT TO KEEP THEM HEALTHY AND SAFE.
THEY TOOK CARE OF THEIR PLANET, AND TRUSTED THAT IT WOULD TAKE CARE OF THEM IN RETURN.

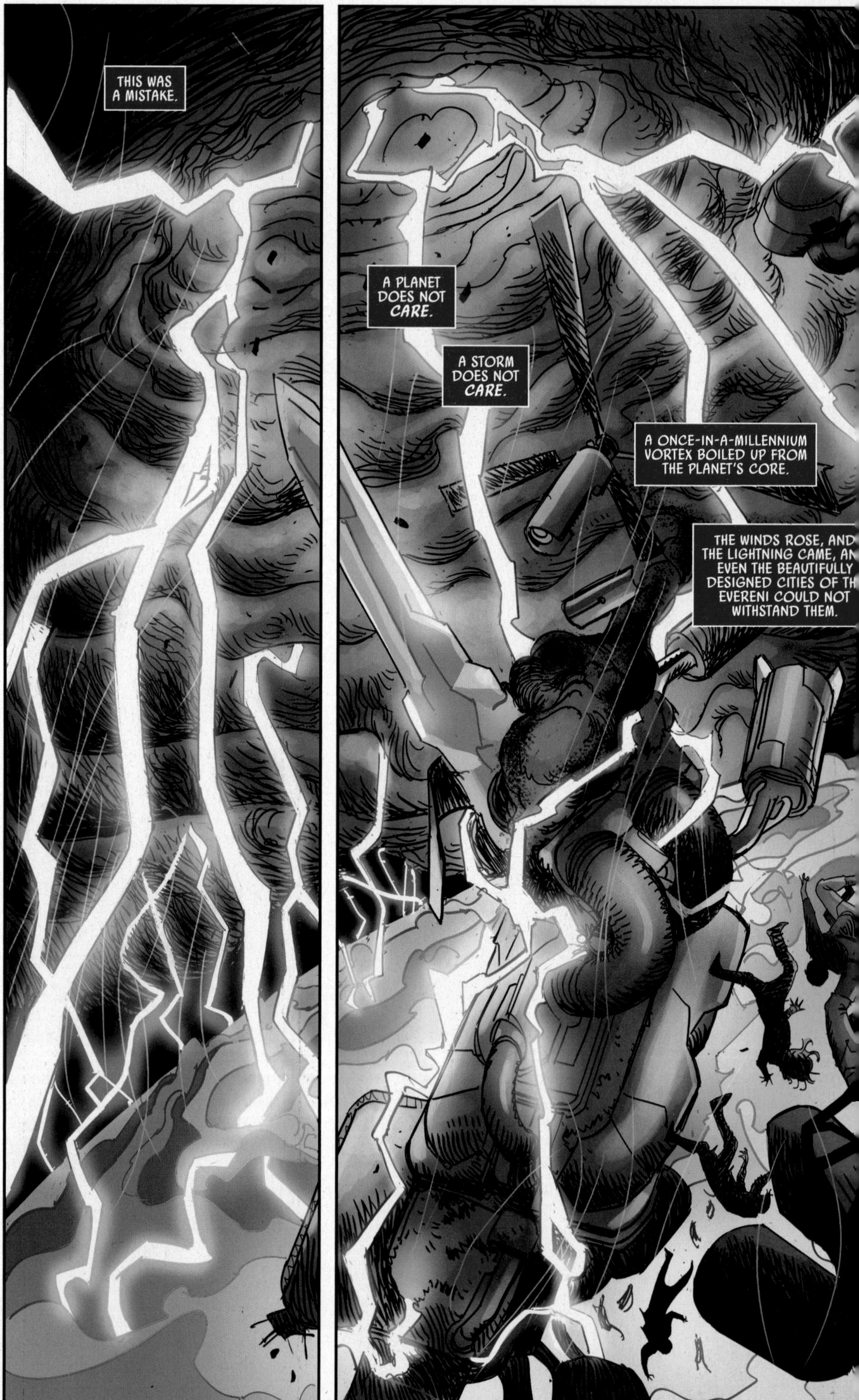

THIS WAS A MISTAKE.
A PLANET DOES NOT *CARE.*
A STORM DOES NOT *CARE.*
A ONCE-IN-A-MILLENNIUM VORTEX BOILED UP FROM THE PLANET'S CORE.
THE WINDS ROSE, AND THE LIGHTNING CAME, AN EVEN THE BEAUTIFULLY DESIGNED CITIES OF TH EVERENI COULD NOT WITHSTAND THEM.

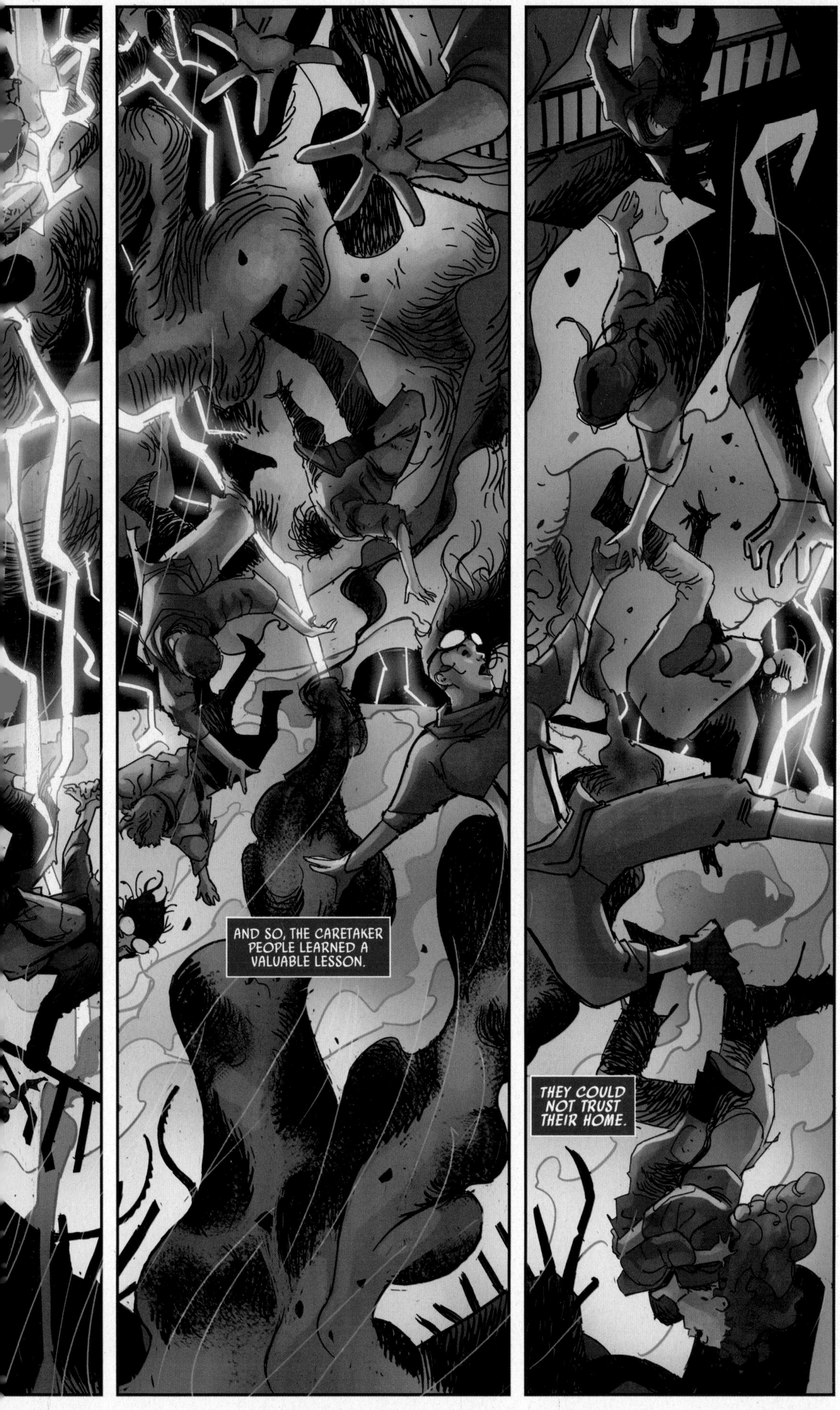
AND SO, THE CARETAKER PEOPLE LEARNED A VALUABLE LESSON.
THEY COULD NOT TRUST THEIR HOME.

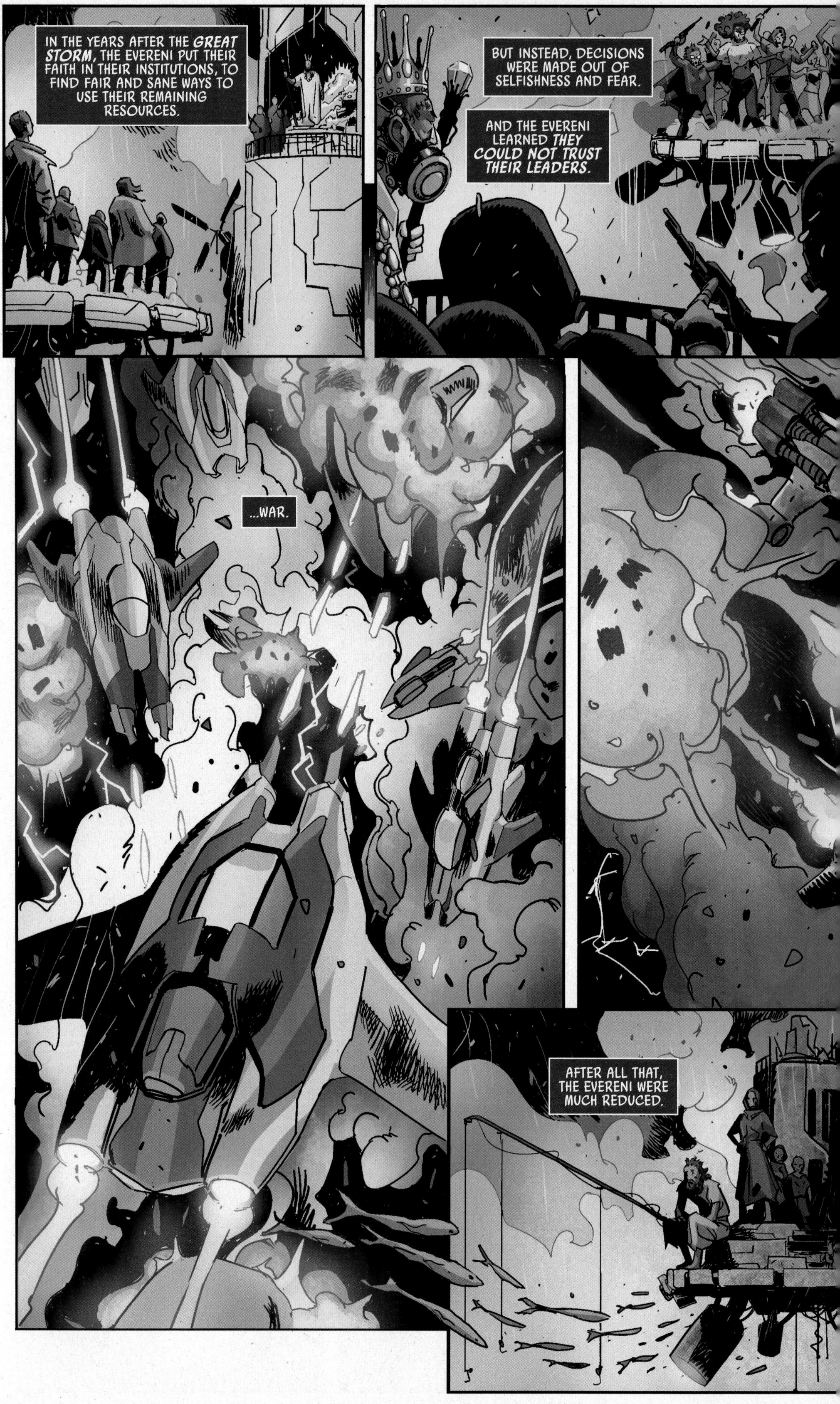
IN THE YEARS AFTER THE GREAT STORM, THE EVERENI PUT THEIR FAITH IN THEIR INSTITUTIONS, TO FIND FAIR AND SANE WAYS TO USE THEIR REMAINING RESOURCES.
BUT INSTEAD, DECISIONS WERE MADE OUT OF SELFISHNESS AND FEAR.
AND THE EVERENI LEARNED THEY COULD NOT TRUST THEIR LEADERS.
...WAR.
AFTER ALL THAT, THE EVERENI WERE MUCH REDUCED.

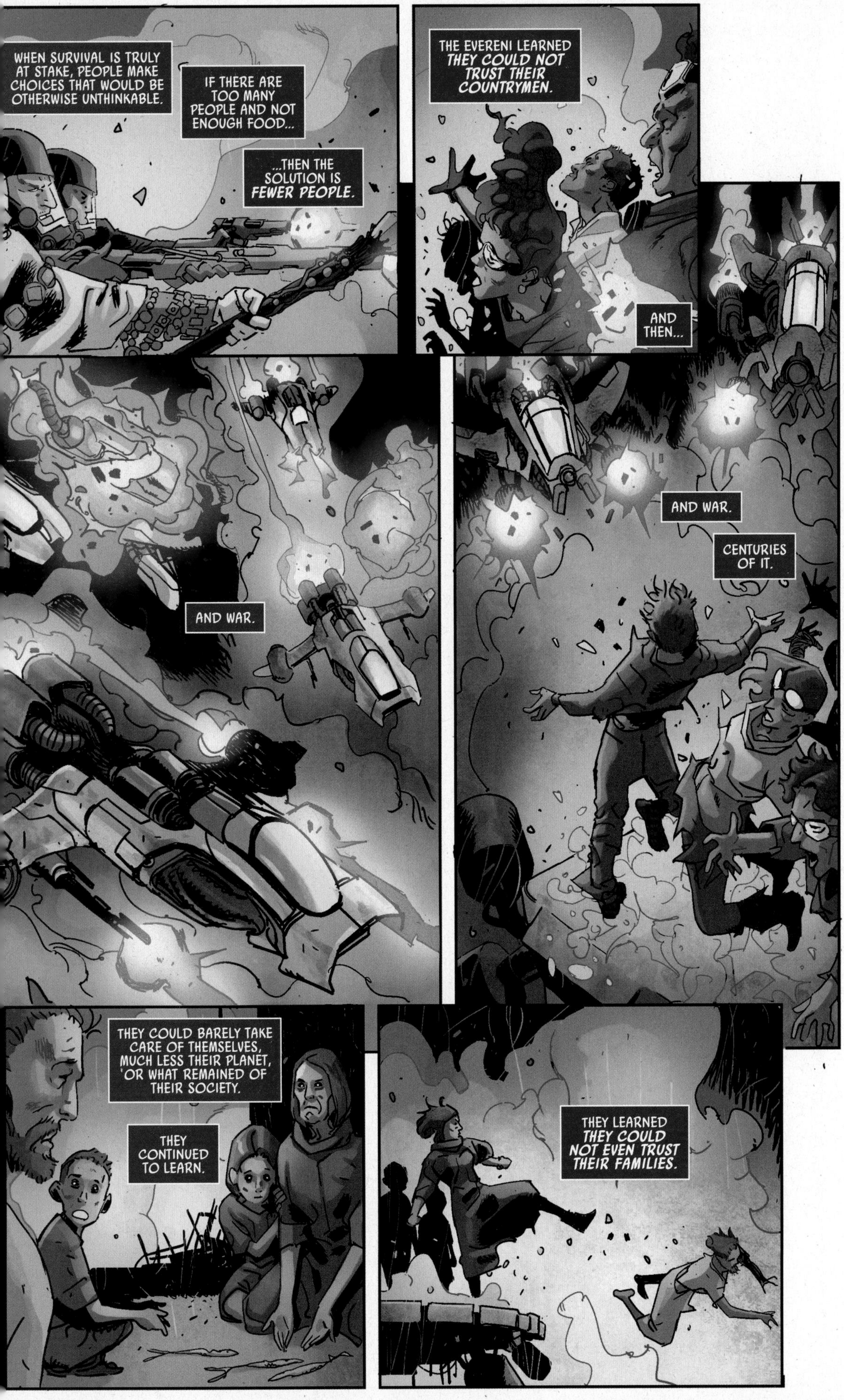
WHEN SURVIVAL IS TRULY AT STAKE, PEOPLE MAKE CHOICES THAT WOULD BE OTHERWISE UNTHINKABLE.
IF THERE ARE TOO MANY PEOPLE AND NOT ENOUGH FOOD...
...THEN THE SOLUTION IS FEWER PEOPLE.
THE EVERENI LEARNED THEY COULD NOT TRUST THEIR COUNTRYMEN.
AND THEN...
AND WAR.
AND WAR.
CENTURIES OF IT.
THEY COULD BARELY TAKE CARE OF THEMSELVES, MUCH LESS THEIR PLANET, 'OR WHAT REMAINED OF THEIR SOCIETY.
THEY CONTINUED TO LEARN.
THEY LEARNED THEY COULD NOT EVEN TRUST THEIR FAMILIES.

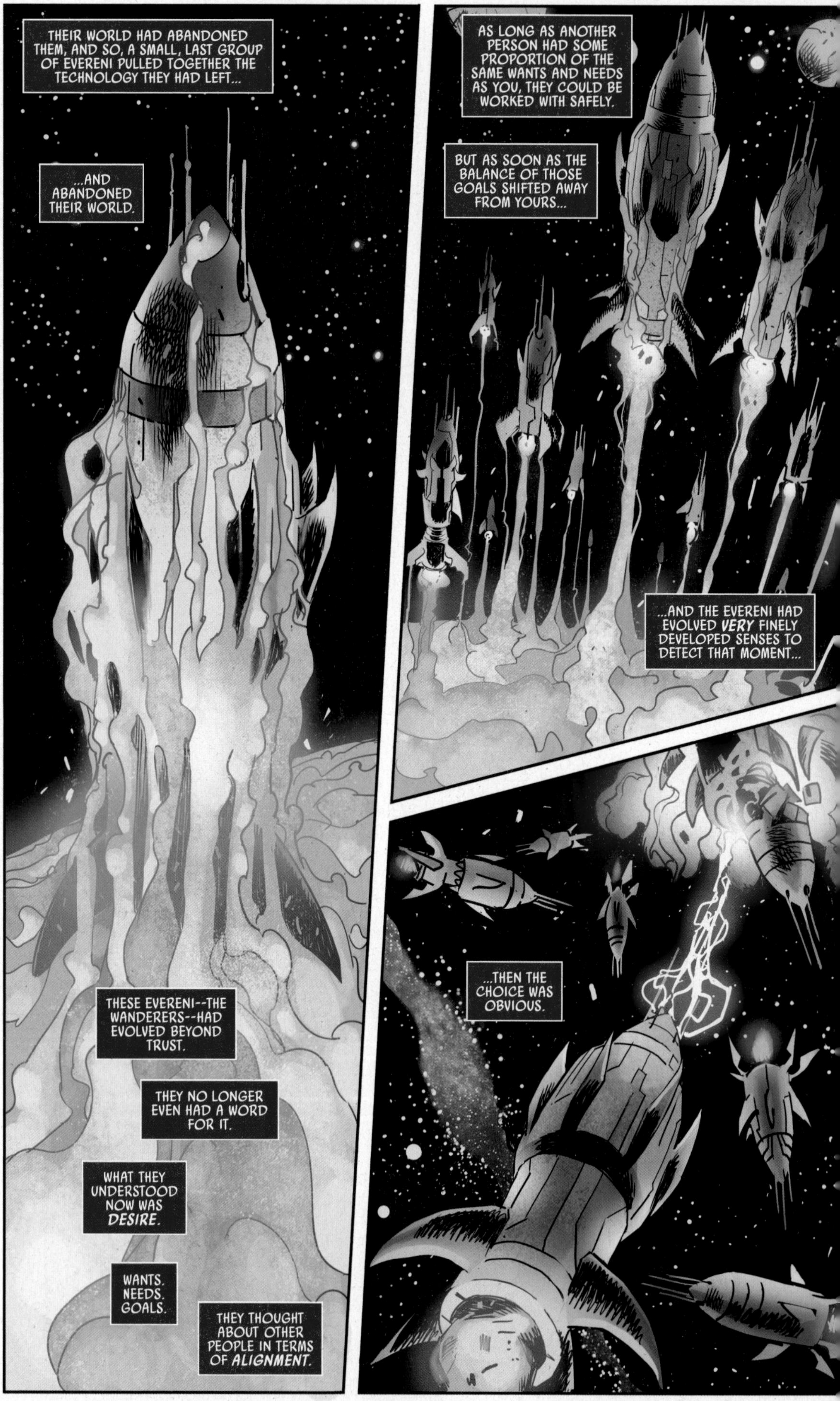
THEIR WORLD HAD ABANDONED THEM, AND SO, A SMALL, LAST GROUP OF EVERENI PULLED TOGETHER THE TECHNOLOGY THEY HAD LEFT...
...AND ABANDONED THEIR WORLD.
THESE EVERENI--THE WANDERERS--HAD EVOLVED BEYOND TRUST.
THEY NO LONGER EVEN HAD A WORD FOR IT.
WHAT THEY UNDERSTOOD NOW WAS DESIRE.
WANTS. NEEDS. GOALS.
THEY THOUGHT ABOUT OTHER PEOPLE IN TERMS OF ALIGNMENT.
AS LONG AS ANOTHER PERSON HAD SOME PROPORTION OF THE SAME WANTS AND NEEDS AS YOU, THEY COULD BE WORKED WITH SAFELY.
BUT AS SOON AS THE BALANCE OF THOSE GOALS SHIFTED AWAY FROM YOURS...
...AND THE EVERENI HAD EVOLVED VERY FINELY DEVELOPED SENSES TO DETECT THAT MOMENT...
...THEN THE CHOICE WAS OBVIOUS.

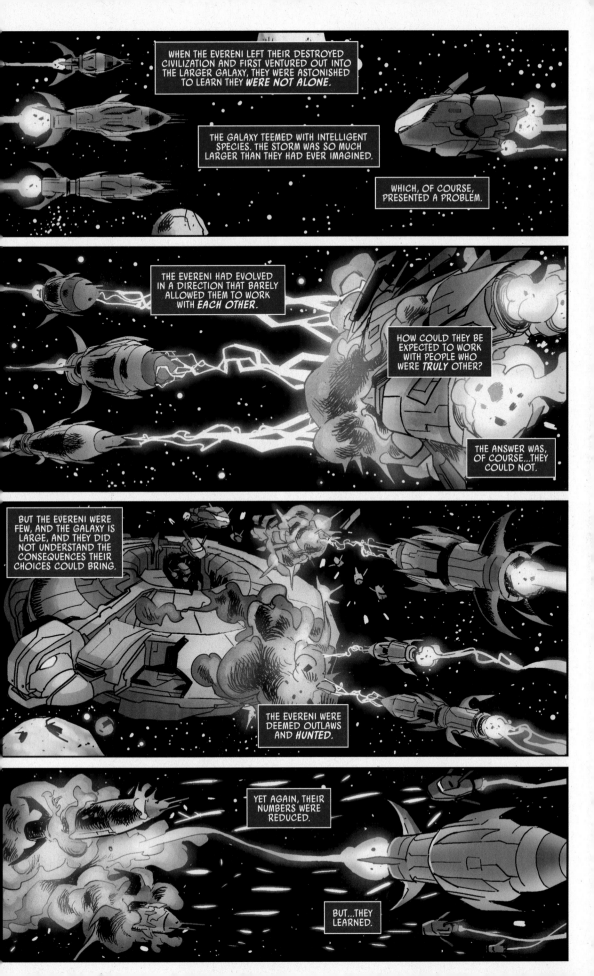

WHEN THE EVERENI LEFT THEIR DESTROYED CIVILIZATION AND FIRST VENTURED OUT INTO THE LARGER GALAXY, THEY WERE ASTONISHED TO LEARN THEY *WERE NOT ALONE.*

THE GALAXY TEEMED WITH INTELLIGENT SPECIES. THE STORM WAS SO MUCH LARGER THAN THEY HAD EVER IMAGINED.

WHICH, OF COURSE, PRESENTED A PROBLEM.

THE EVERENI HAD EVOLVED IN A DIRECTION THAT BARELY ALLOWED THEM TO WORK WITH *EACH OTHER.*

HOW COULD THEY BE EXPECTED TO WORK WITH PEOPLE WHO WERE *TRULY* OTHER?

THE ANSWER WAS, OF COURSE...THEY COULD NOT.

BUT THE EVERENI WERE FEW, AND THE GALAXY IS LARGE, AND THEY DID NOT UNDERSTAND THE CONSEQUENCES THEIR CHOICES COULD BRING.

THE EVERENI WERE DEEMED OUTLAWS AND *HUNTED.*

YET AGAIN, THEIR NUMBERS WERE REDUCED.

BUT...THEY LEARNED.

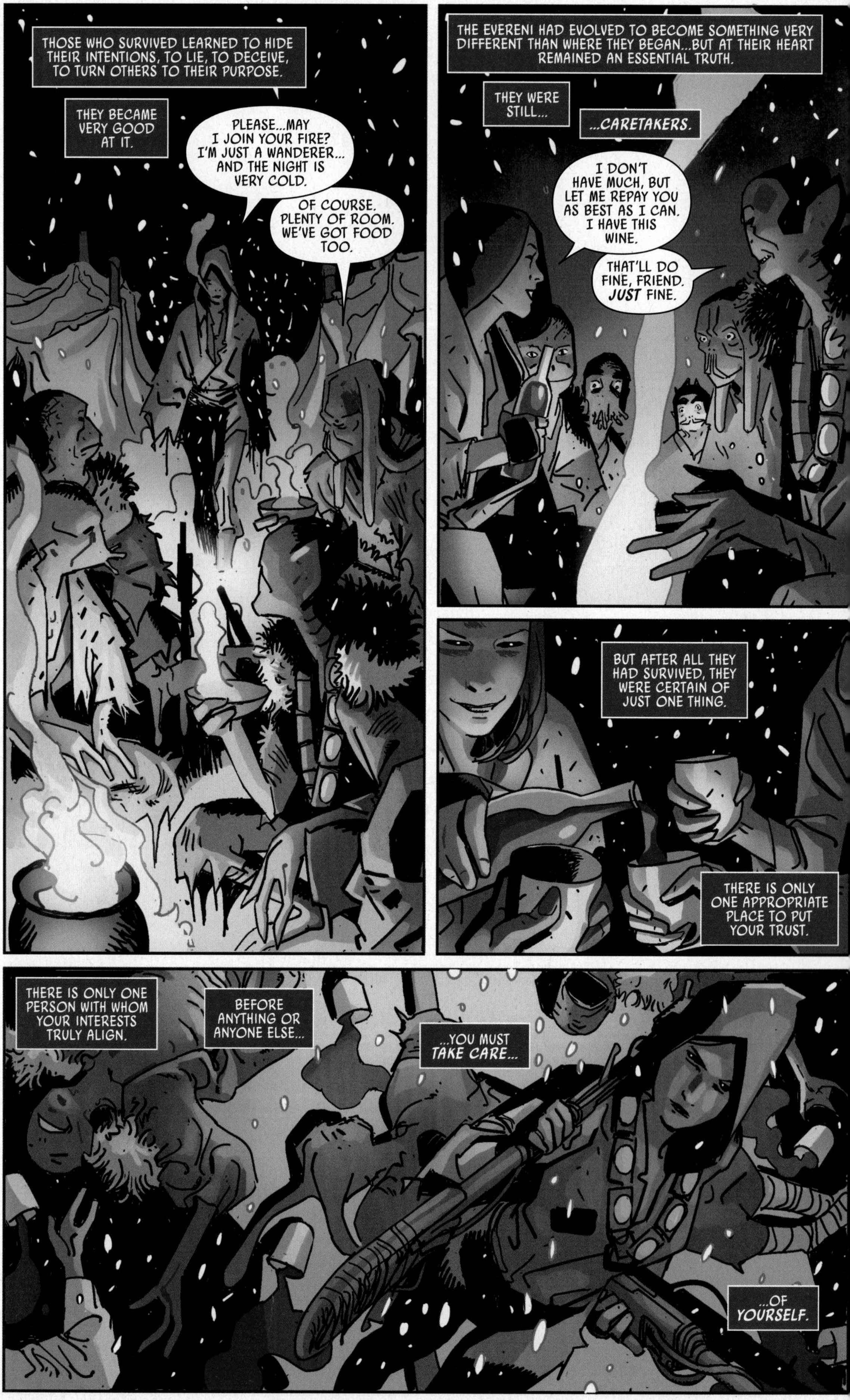
THOSE WHO SURVIVED LEARNED TO HIDE THEIR INTENTIONS, TO LIE, TO DECEIVE, TO TURN OTHERS TO THEIR PURPOSE.
THEY BECAME VERY GOOD AT IT.
PLEASE...MAY I JOIN YOUR FIRE? I'M JUST A WANDERER... AND THE NIGHT IS VERY COLD.
OF COURSE. PLENTY OF ROOM. WE'VE GOT FOOD TOO.
THE EVERENI HAD EVOLVED TO BECOME SOMETHING VERY DIFFERENT THAN WHERE THEY BEGAN...BUT AT THEIR HEART REMAINED AN ESSENTIAL TRUTH.
THEY WERE STILL...
...CARETAKERS.
I DON'T HAVE MUCH, BUT LET ME REPAY YOU AS BEST AS I CAN. I HAVE THIS WINE.
THAT'LL DO FINE, FRIEND. JUST FINE.
BUT AFTER ALL THEY HAD SURVIVED, THEY WERE CERTAIN OF JUST ONE THING.
THERE IS ONLY ONE APPROPRIATE PLACE TO PUT YOUR TRUST.
THERE IS ONLY ONE PERSON WITH WHOM YOUR INTERESTS TRULY ALIGN.
BEFORE ANYTHING OR ANYONE ELSE...
...YOU MUST TAKE CARE...
...OF YOURSELF.

THE LIE

In which a Small Family of Evereni Wanderers
In the Time of the High Republic
Finds Something they have Sought
For Generations.

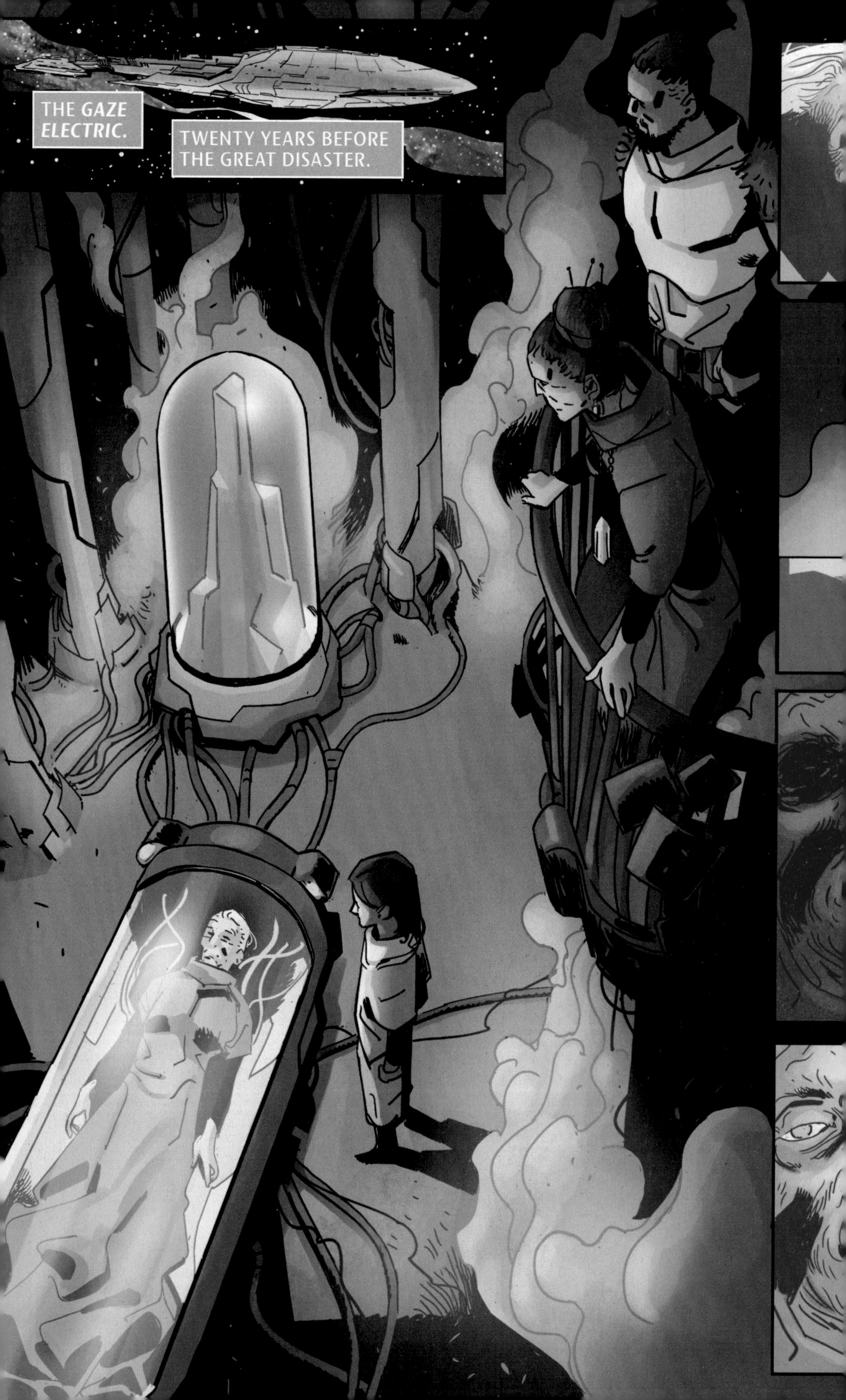
THE *GAZE ELECTRIC*.
TWENTY YEARS BEFORE THE GREAT DISASTER.

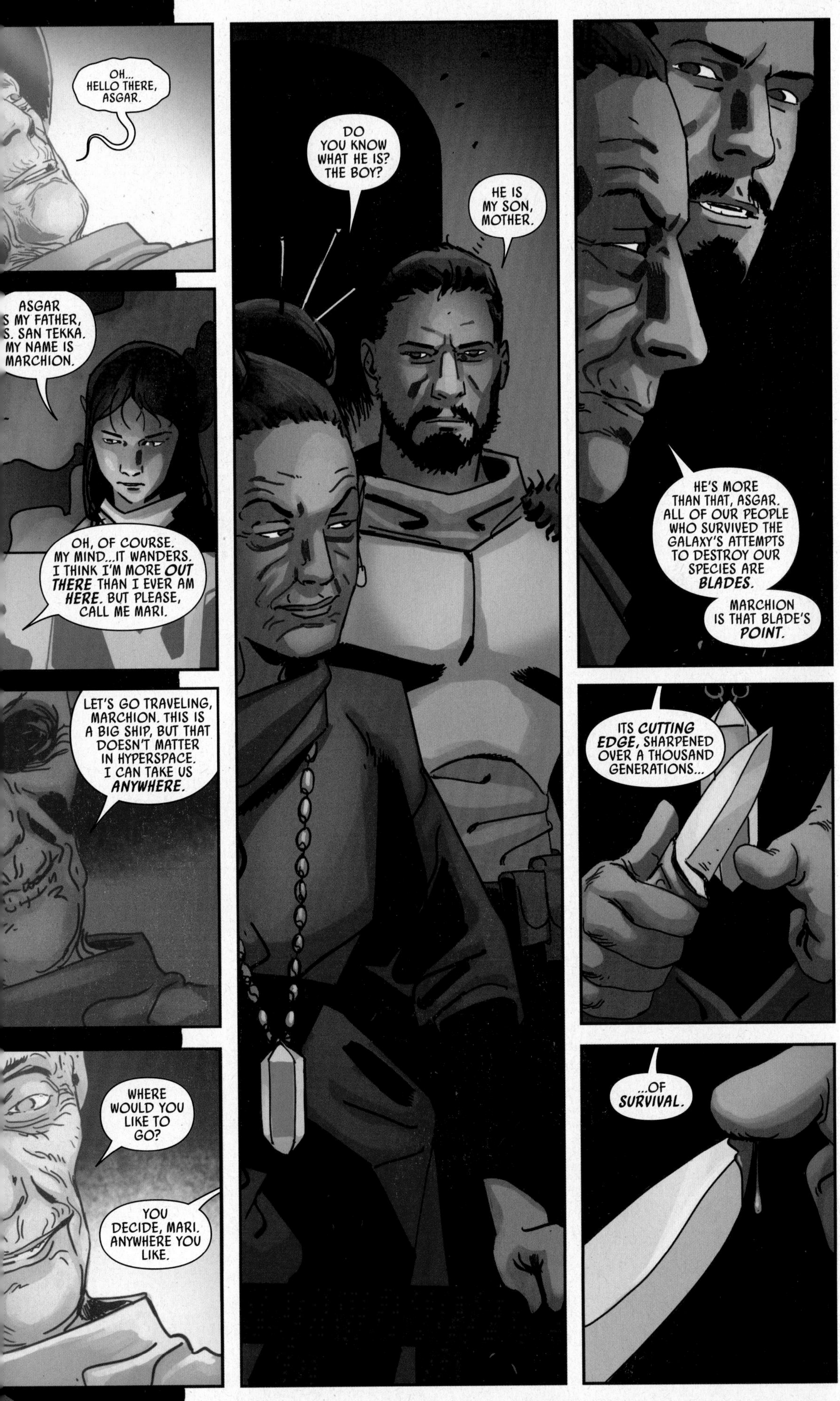
OH... HELLO THERE, ASGAR.
ASGAR IS MY FATHER, MS. SAN TEKKA. MY NAME IS MARCHION.
OH, OF COURSE. MY MIND...IT WANDERS. I THINK I'M MORE OUT THERE THAN I EVER AM HERE. BUT PLEASE, CALL ME MARI.
LET'S GO TRAVELING, MARCHION. THIS IS A BIG SHIP, BUT THAT DOESN'T MATTER IN HYPERSPACE. I CAN TAKE US ANYWHERE.
WHERE WOULD YOU LIKE TO GO?
YOU DECIDE, MARI. ANYWHERE YOU LIKE.
DO YOU KNOW WHAT HE IS? THE BOY?
HE IS MY SON, MOTHER.
HE'S MORE THAN THAT, ASGAR. ALL OF OUR PEOPLE WHO SURVIVED THE GALAXY'S ATTEMPTS TO DESTROY OUR SPECIES ARE BLADES.
MARCHION IS THAT BLADE'S POINT.
ITS CUTTING EDGE, SHARPENED OVER A THOUSAND GENERATIONS...
...OF SURVIVAL.

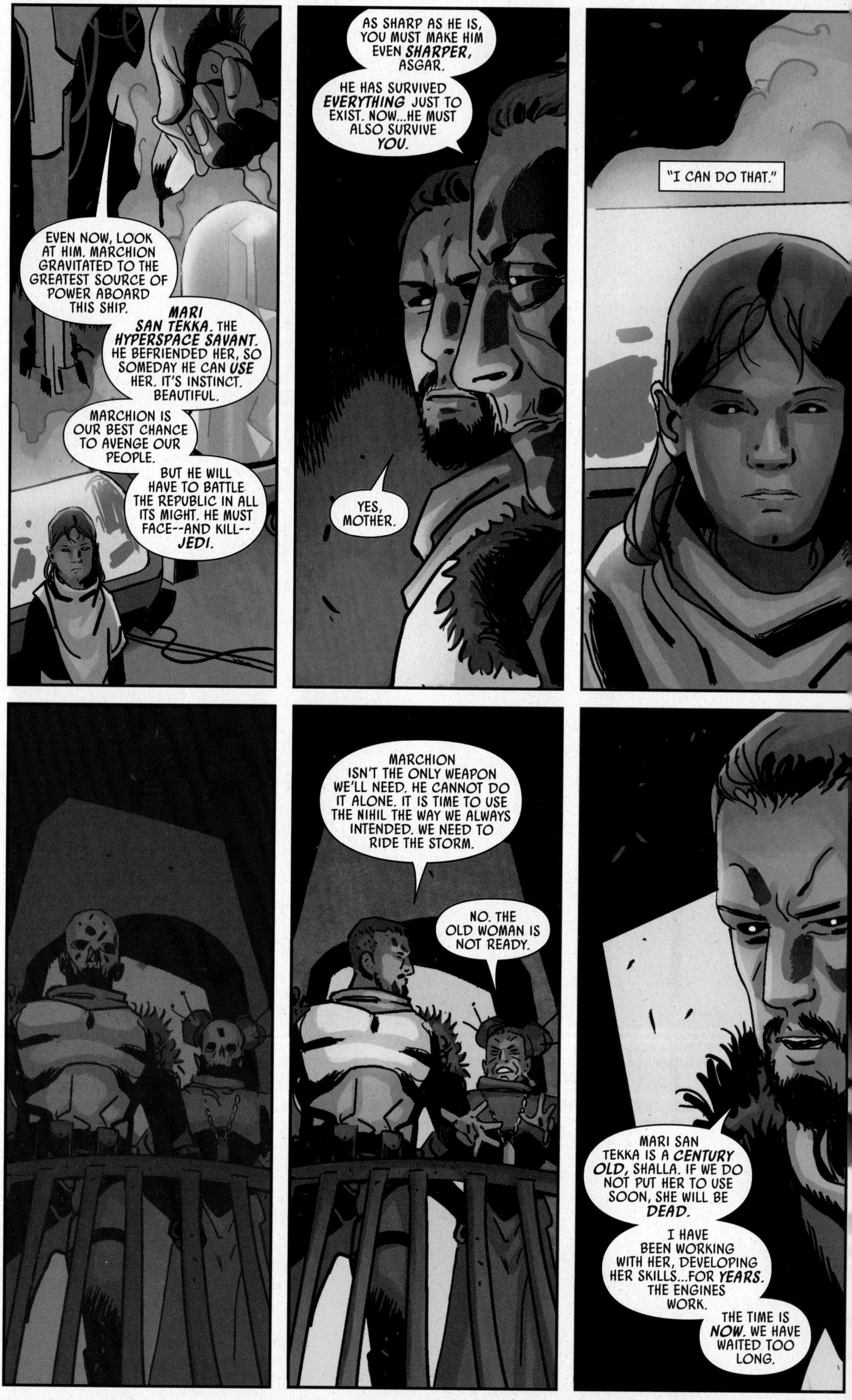

EVEN NOW, LOOK AT HIM. MARCHION GRAVITATED TO THE GREATEST SOURCE OF POWER ABOARD THIS SHIP.
MARI SAN TEKKA. THE HYPERSPACE SAVANT. HE BEFRIENDED HER, SO SOMEDAY HE CAN USE HER. IT'S INSTINCT. BEAUTIFUL.
MARCHION IS OUR BEST CHANCE TO AVENGE OUR PEOPLE.
BUT HE WILL HAVE TO BATTLE THE REPUBLIC IN ALL ITS MIGHT. HE MUST FACE--AND KILL--JEDI.
AS SHARP AS HE IS, YOU MUST MAKE HIM EVEN SHARPER, ASGAR.
HE HAS SURVIVED EVERYTHING JUST TO EXIST. NOW...HE MUST ALSO SURVIVE YOU.
YES, MOTHER.
"I CAN DO THAT."
MARCHION ISN'T THE ONLY WEAPON WE'LL NEED. HE CANNOT DO IT ALONE. IT IS TIME TO USE THE NIHIL THE WAY WE ALWAYS INTENDED. WE NEED TO RIDE THE STORM.
NO. THE OLD WOMAN IS NOT READY.
MARI SAN TEKKA IS A CENTURY OLD, SHALLA. IF WE DO NOT PUT HER TO USE SOON, SHE WILL BE DEAD.
I HAVE BEEN WORKING WITH HER, DEVELOPING HER SKILLS...FOR YEARS. THE ENGINES WORK.
THE TIME IS NOW. WE HAVE WAITED TOO LONG.

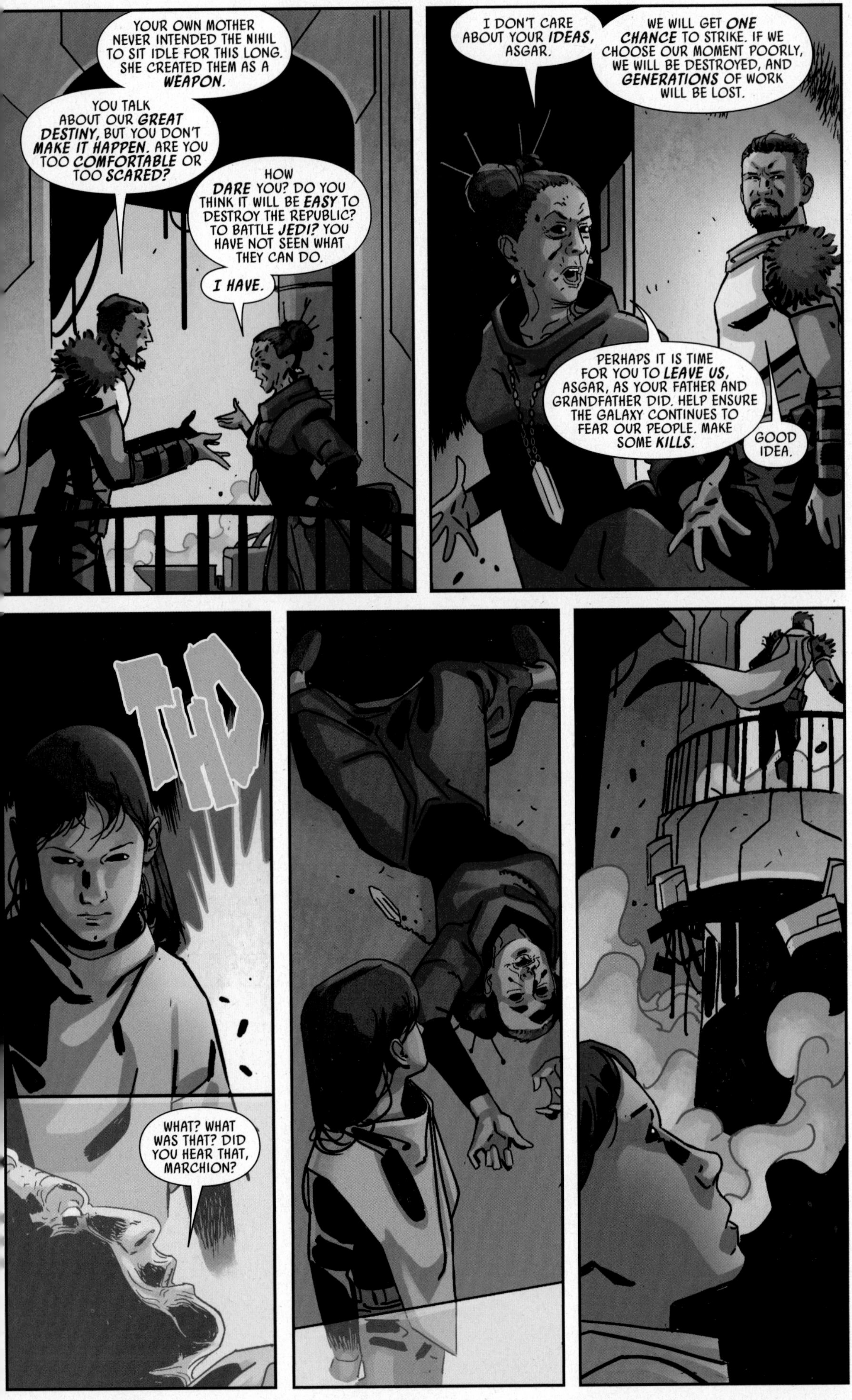
YOUR OWN MOTHER NEVER INTENDED THE NIHIL TO SIT IDLE FOR THIS LONG. SHE CREATED THEM AS A WEAPON.
YOU TALK ABOUT OUR GREAT DESTINY, BUT YOU DON'T MAKE IT HAPPEN. ARE YOU TOO COMFORTABLE OR TOO SCARED?
HOW DARE YOU? DO YOU THINK IT WILL BE EASY TO DESTROY THE REPUBLIC? TO BATTLE JEDI? YOU HAVE NOT SEEN WHAT THEY CAN DO.
I HAVE.
I DON'T CARE ABOUT YOUR IDEAS, ASGAR.
WE WILL GET ONE CHANCE TO STRIKE. IF WE CHOOSE OUR MOMENT POORLY, WE WILL BE DESTROYED, AND GENERATIONS OF WORK WILL BE LOST.
PERHAPS IT IS TIME FOR YOU TO LEAVE US, ASGAR, AS YOUR FATHER AND GRANDFATHER DID. HELP ENSURE THE GALAXY CONTINUES TO FEAR OUR PEOPLE. MAKE SOME KILLS.
GOOD IDEA.
THD
WHAT? WHAT WAS THAT? DID YOU HEAR THAT, MARCHION?

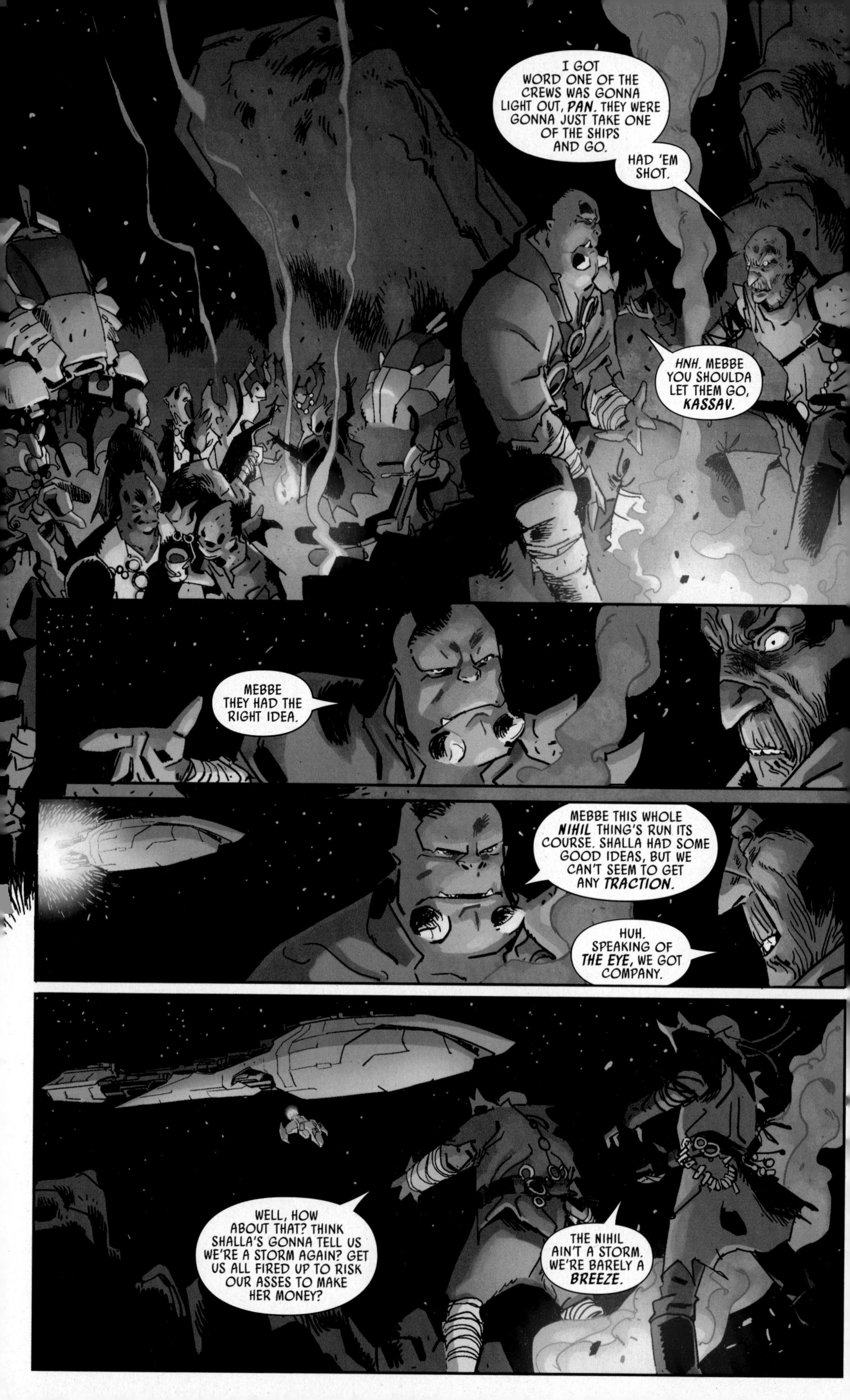
I GOT WORD ONE OF THE CREWS WAS GONNA LIGHT OUT, *PAN*. THEY WERE GONNA JUST TAKE ONE OF THE SHIPS AND GO.
HAD 'EM SHOT.
HNH. MEBBE YOU SHOULDA LET THEM GO, *KASSAV.*
MEBBE THEY HAD THE RIGHT IDEA.
MEBBE THIS WHOLE *NIHIL* THING'S RUN ITS COURSE. SHALLA HAD SOME GOOD IDEAS, BUT WE CAN'T SEEM TO GET ANY *TRACTION*.
HUH. SPEAKING OF *THE EYE*, WE GOT COMPANY.
WELL, HOW ABOUT THAT? THINK SHALLA'S GONNA TELL US WE'RE A STORM AGAIN? GET US ALL FIRED UP TO RISK OUR ASSES TO MAKE HER MONEY?
THE NIHIL AIN'T A STORM. WE'RE BARELY A *BREEZE*.

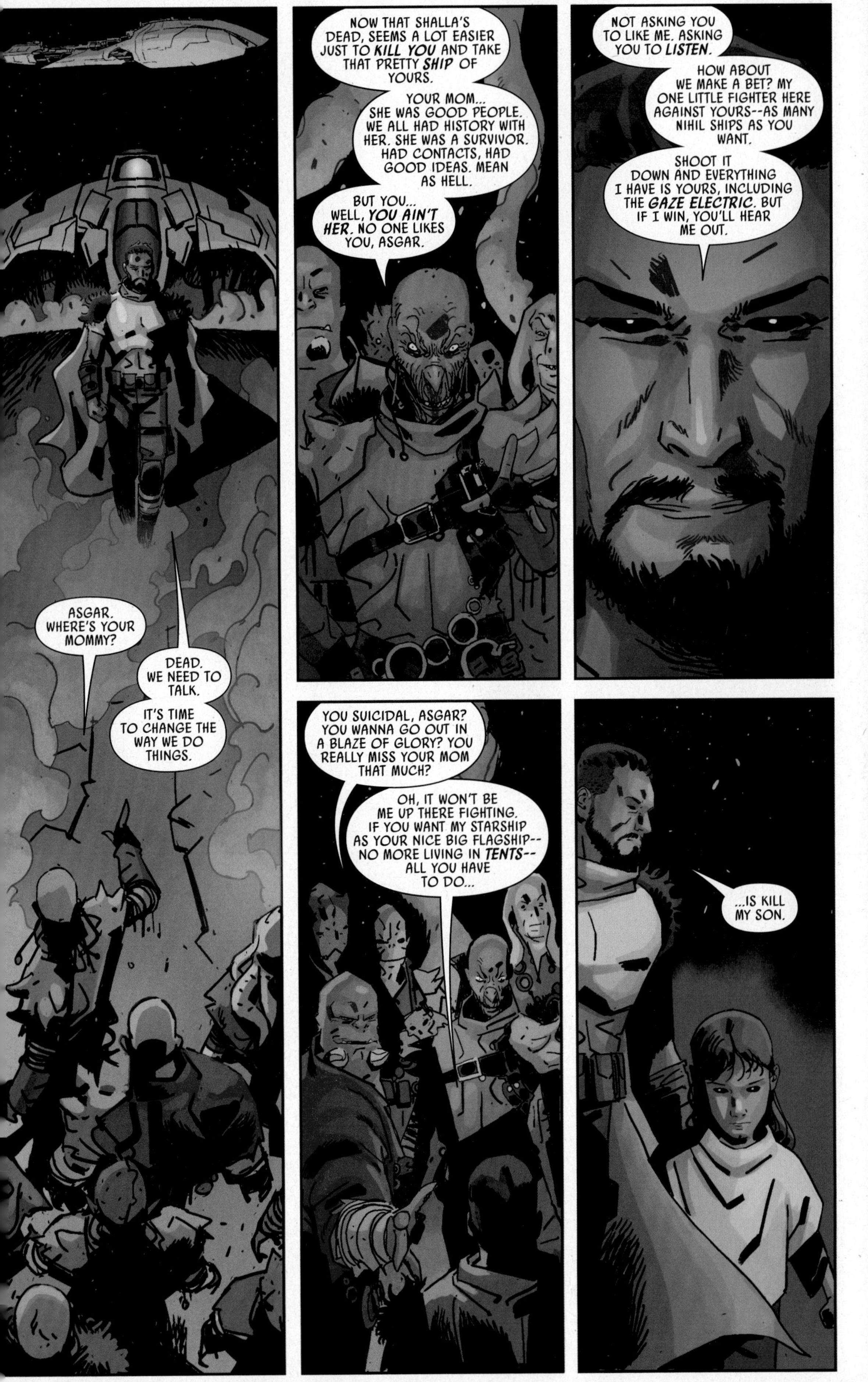
ASGAR. WHERE'S YOUR MOMMY?
DEAD. WE NEED TO TALK.
IT'S TIME TO CHANGE THE WAY WE DO THINGS.
NOW THAT SHALLA'S DEAD, SEEMS A LOT EASIER JUST TO KILL YOU AND TAKE THAT PRETTY SHIP OF YOURS.
YOUR MOM... SHE WAS GOOD PEOPLE. WE ALL HAD HISTORY WITH HER. SHE WAS A SURVIVOR. HAD CONTACTS, HAD GOOD IDEAS. MEAN AS HELL.
BUT YOU... WELL, YOU AIN'T HER. NO ONE LIKES YOU, ASGAR.
NOT ASKING YOU TO LIKE ME. ASKING YOU TO LISTEN.
HOW ABOUT WE MAKE A BET? MY ONE LITTLE FIGHTER HERE AGAINST YOURS--AS MANY NIHIL SHIPS AS YOU WANT.
SHOOT IT DOWN AND EVERYTHING I HAVE IS YOURS, INCLUDING THE GAZE ELECTRIC. BUT IF I WIN, YOU'LL HEAR ME OUT.
YOU SUICIDAL, ASGAR? YOU WANNA GO OUT IN A BLAZE OF GLORY? YOU REALLY MISS YOUR MOM THAT MUCH?
OH, IT WON'T BE ME UP THERE FIGHTING. IF YOU WANT MY STARSHIP AS YOUR NICE BIG FLAGSHIP-- NO MORE LIVING IN TENTS-- ALL YOU HAVE TO DO...
...IS KILL MY SON.

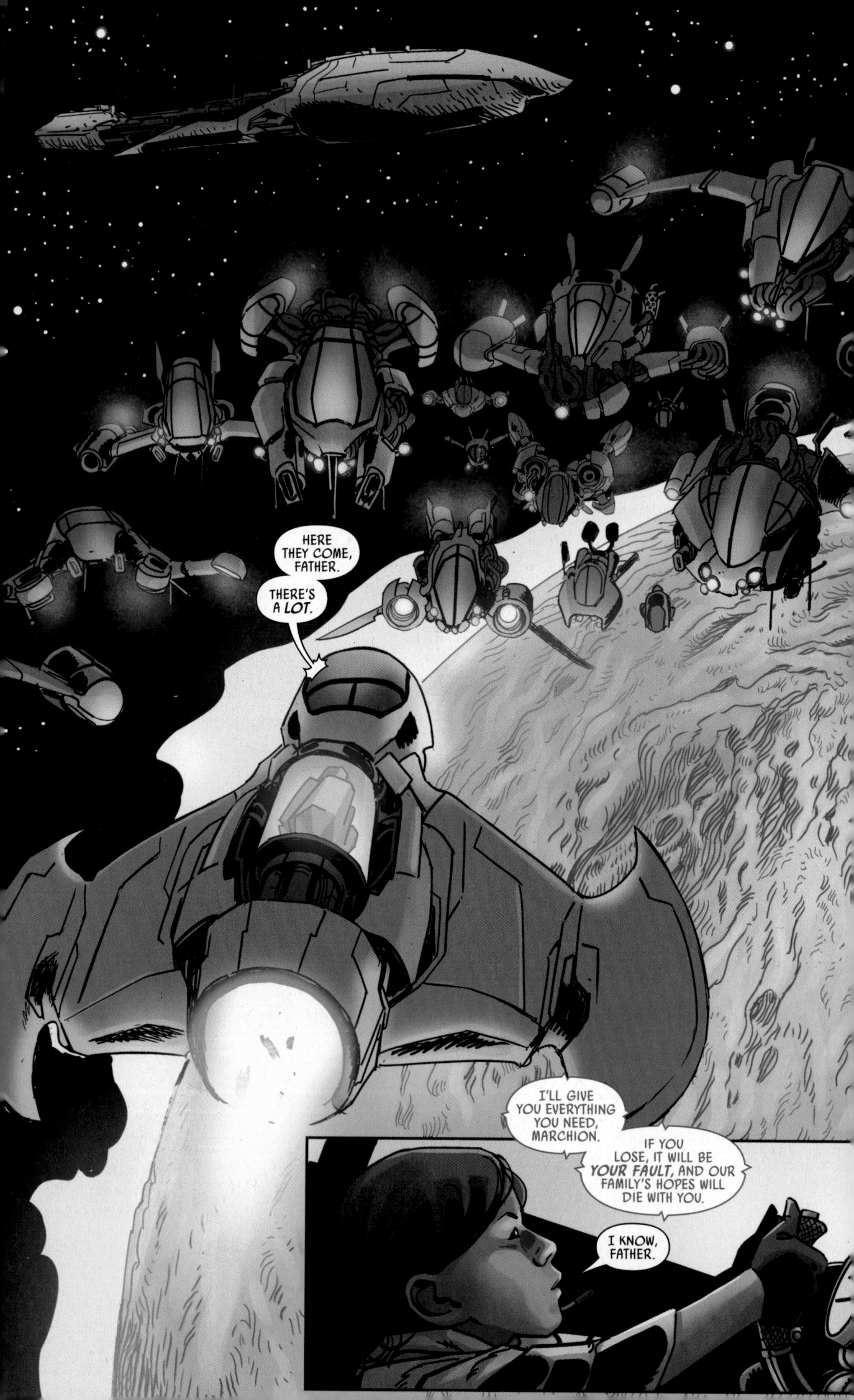
HERE THEY COME, FATHER.
THERE'S A *LOT*.
I'LL GIVE YOU EVERYTHING YOU NEED, MARCHION.
IF YOU LOSE, IT WILL BE ***YOUR FAULT,*** AND OUR FAMILY'S HOPES WILL DIE WITH YOU.
I KNOW, FATHER.

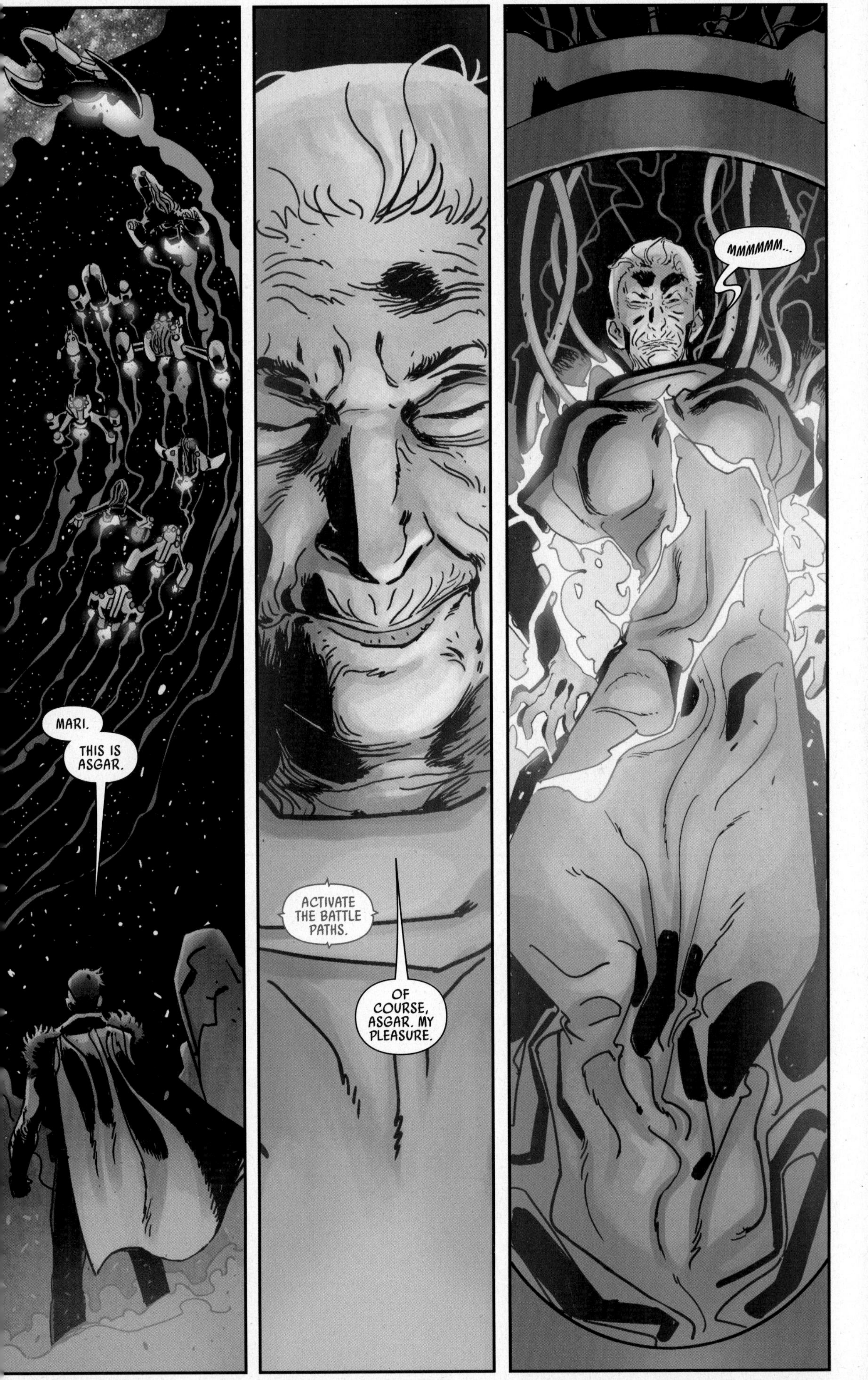
MARI.
THIS IS ASGAR.
ACTIVATE THE BATTLE PATHS.
OF COURSE, ASGAR. MY PLEASURE.
MMMMMM...

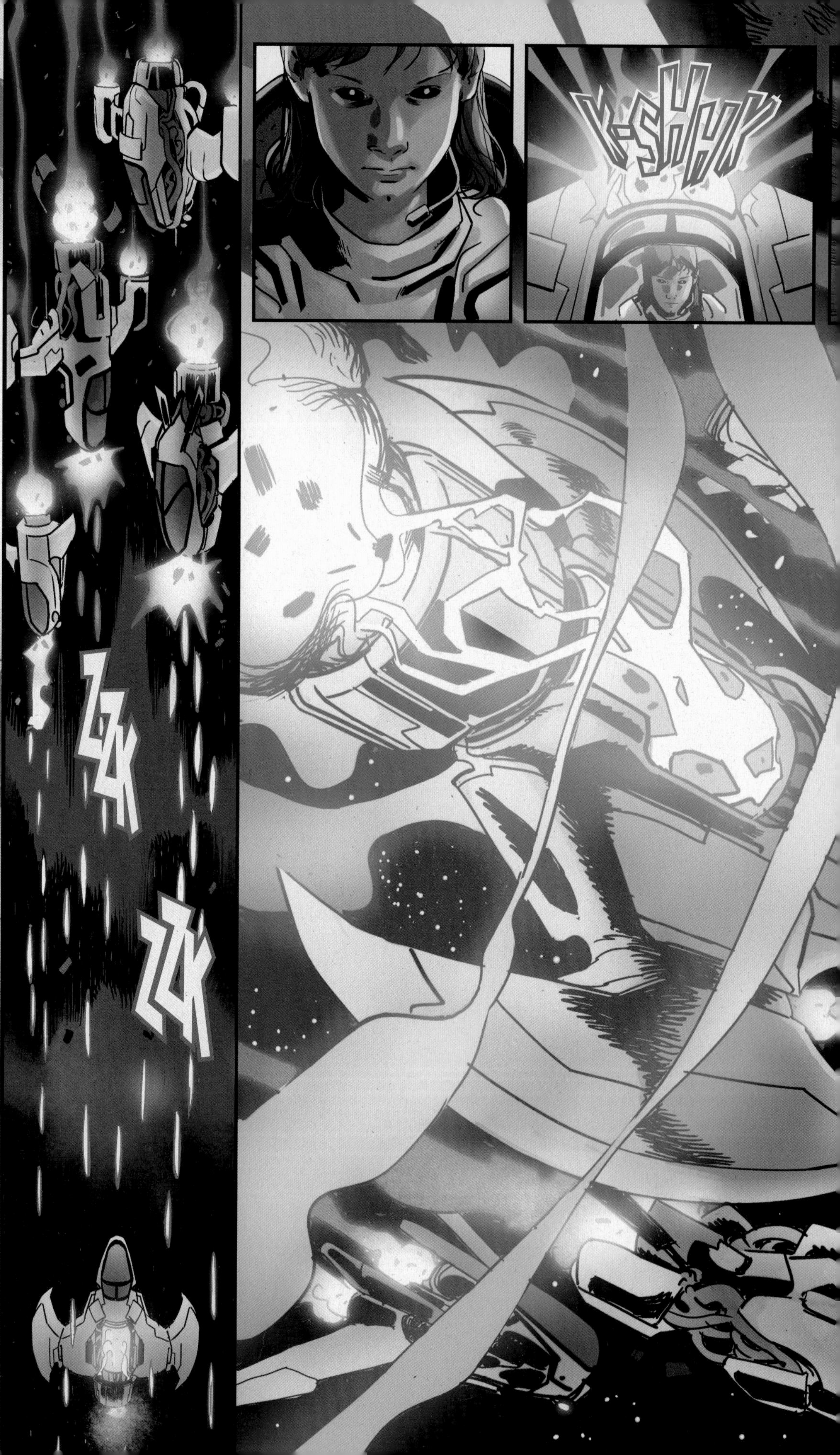
ZZK
ZZK
K-SHCHK

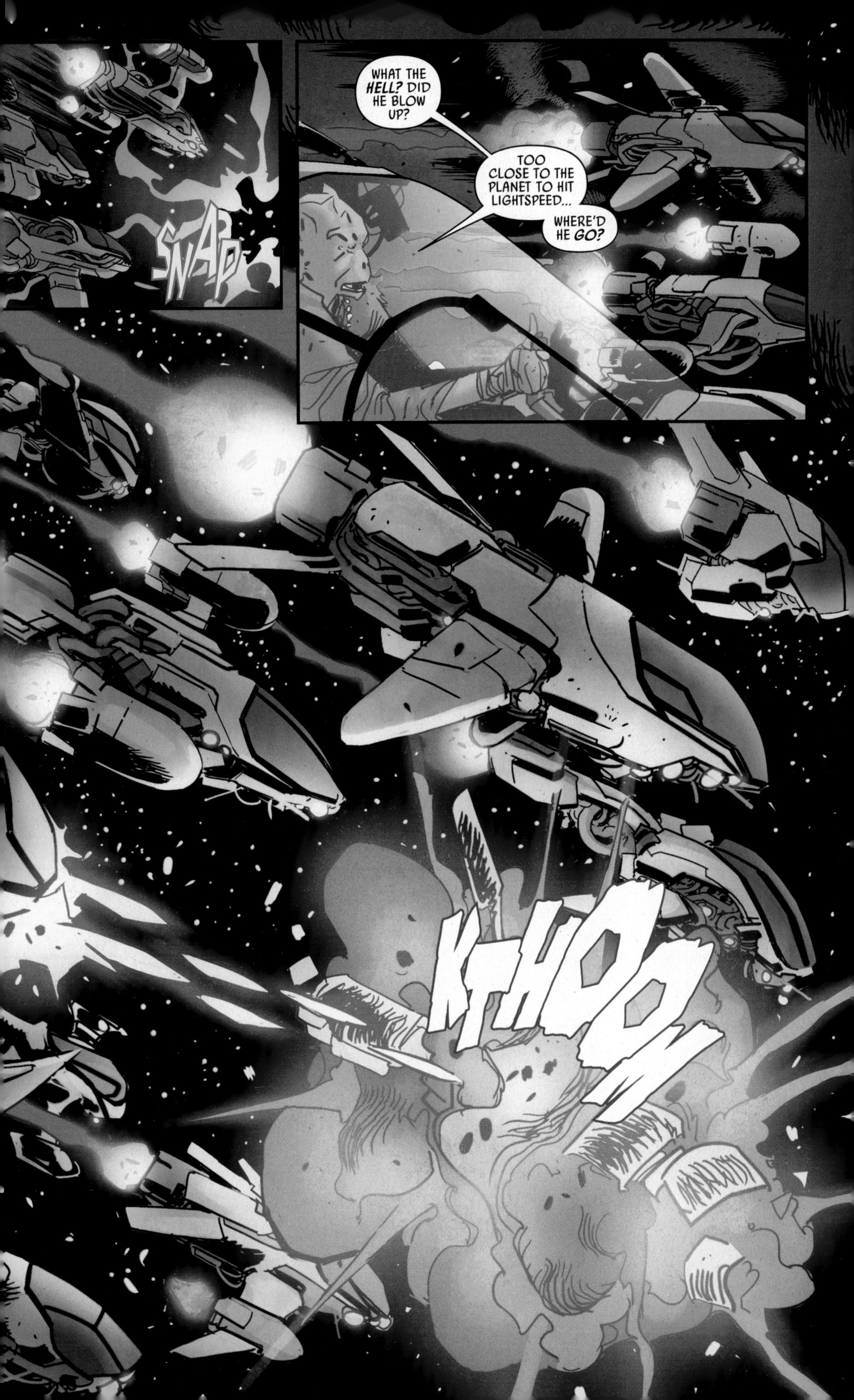
SNAP
WHAT THE HELL? DID HE BLOW UP?
TOO CLOSE TO THE PLANET TO HIT LIGHTSPEED...
WHERE'D HE GO?
KTHOOM

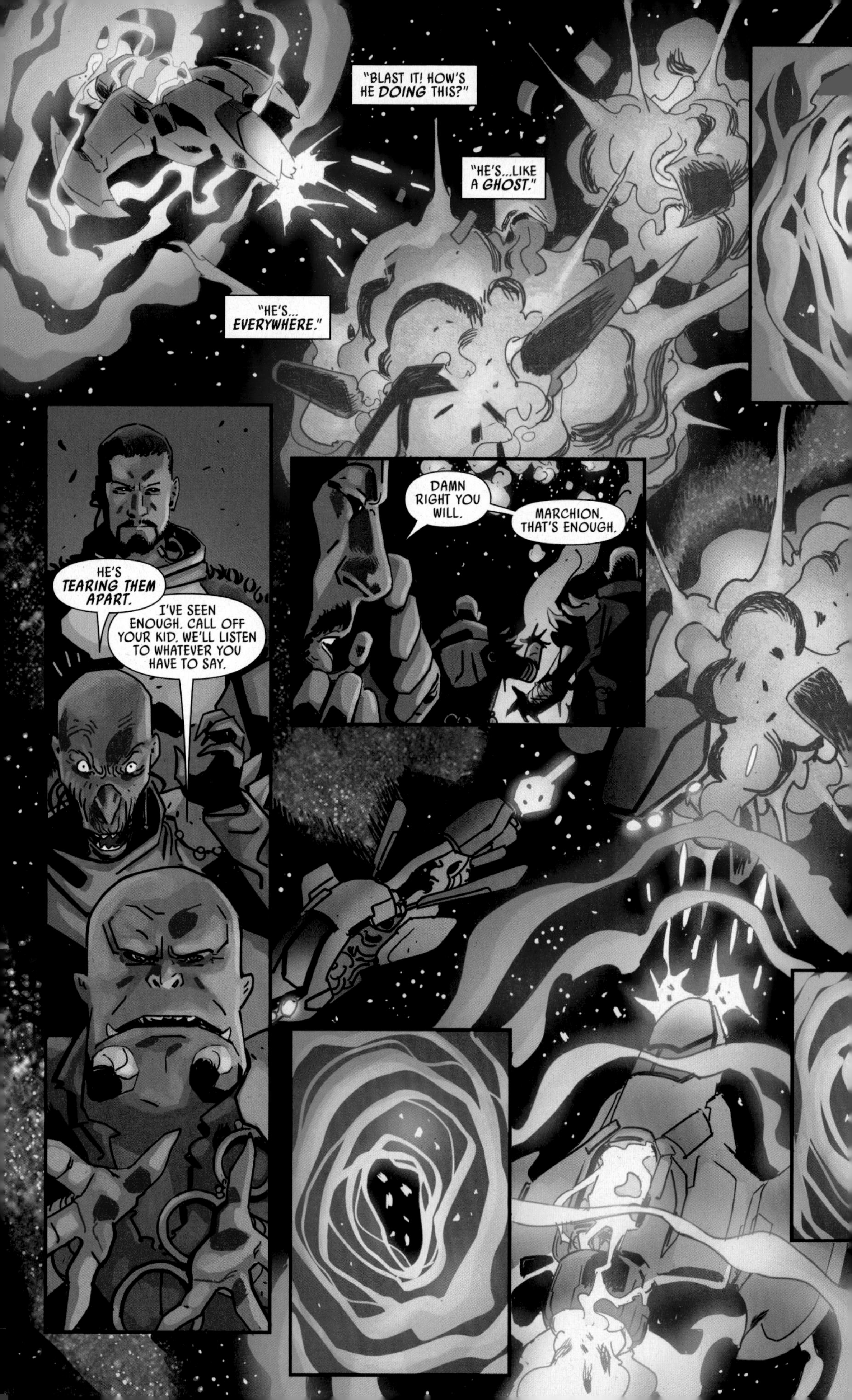
"BLAST IT! HOW'S HE *DOING* THIS?"
"HE'S...LIKE A *GHOST*."
"HE'S... *EVERYWHERE*."
HE'S *TEARING THEM APART*.
I'VE SEEN ENOUGH. CALL OFF YOUR KID. WE'LL LISTEN TO WHATEVER YOU HAVE TO SAY.
DAMN RIGHT YOU WILL.
MARCHION. THAT'S ENOUGH.

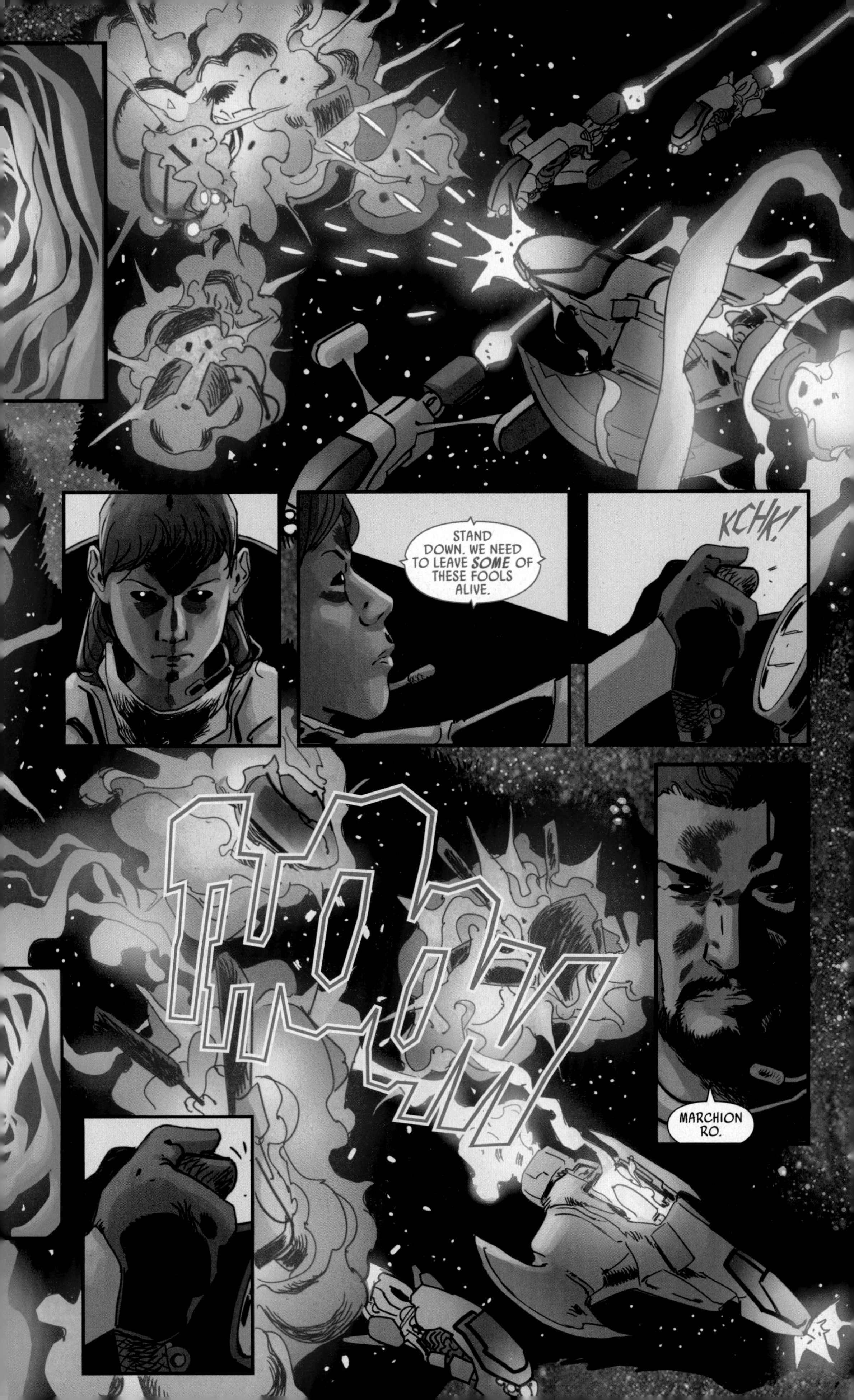
STAND DOWN. WE NEED TO LEAVE SOME OF THESE FOOLS ALIVE.
KCHK!
MARCHION RO.

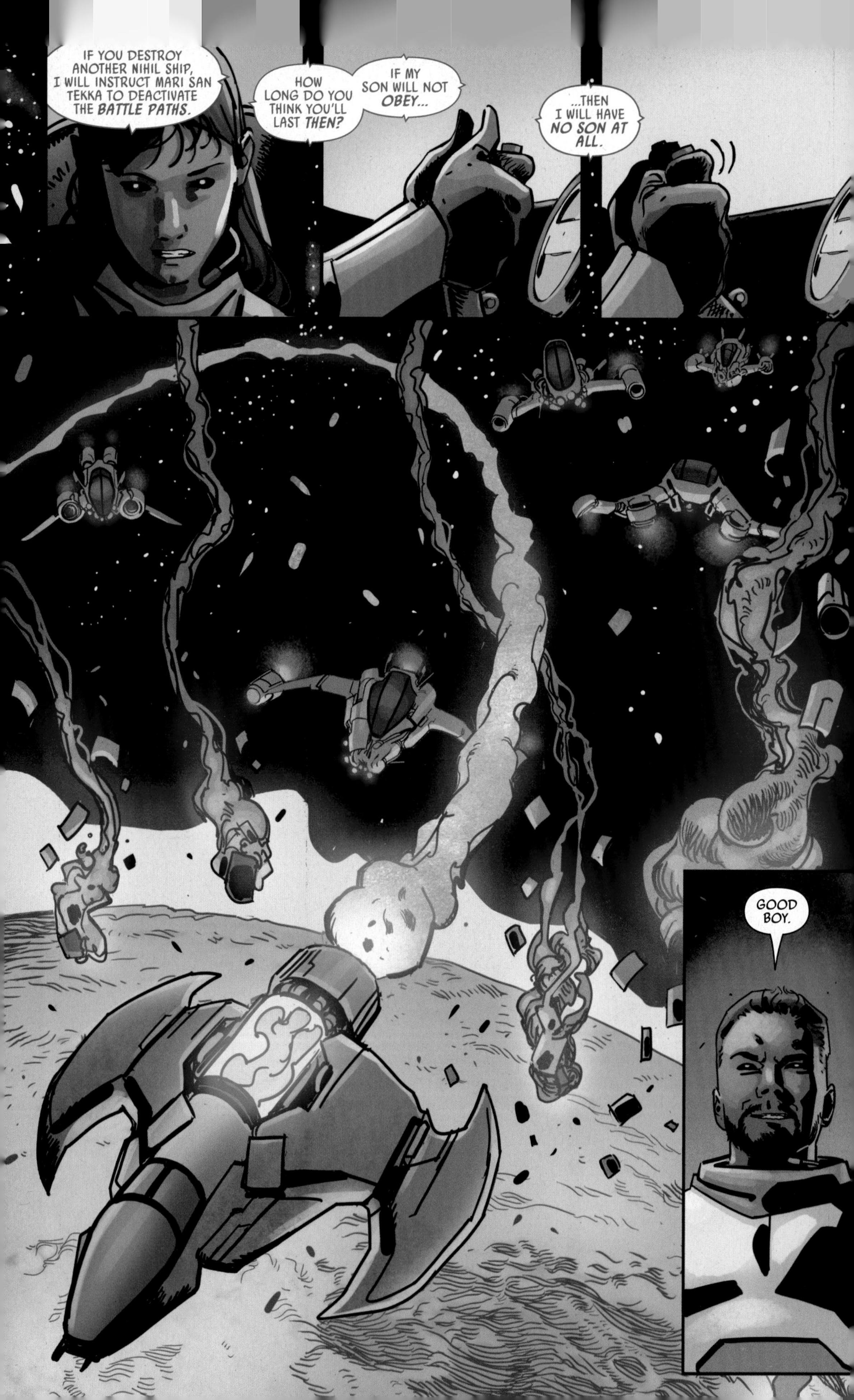
IF YOU DESTROY ANOTHER NIHIL SHIP, I WILL INSTRUCT MARI SAN TEKKA TO DEACTIVATE THE BATTLE PATHS.
HOW LONG DO YOU THINK YOU'LL LAST THEN?
IF MY SON WILL NOT OBEY...
...THEN I WILL HAVE NO SON AT ALL.
GOOD BOY.

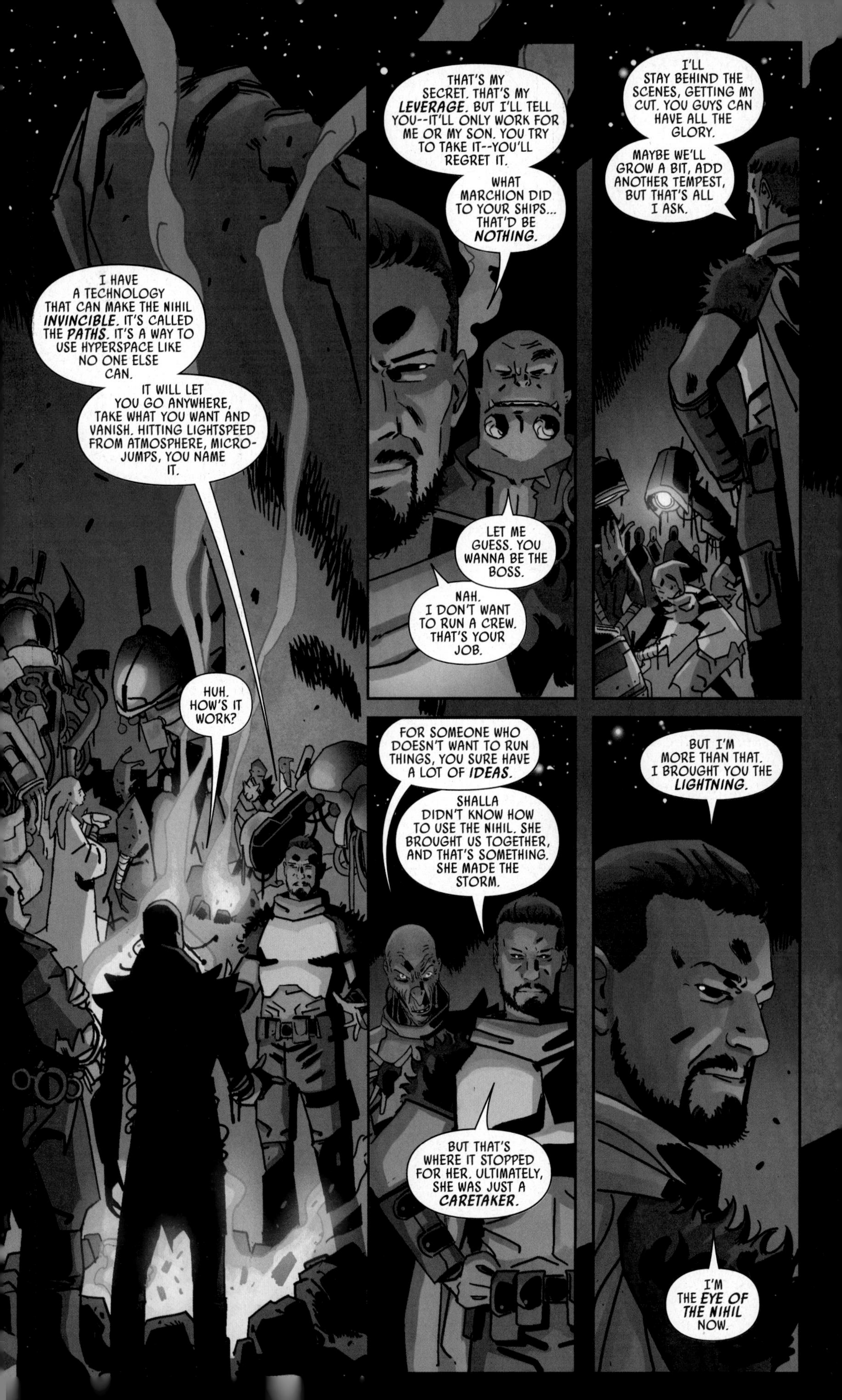
I HAVE A TECHNOLOGY THAT CAN MAKE THE NIHIL INVINCIBLE. IT'S CALLED THE PATHS. IT'S A WAY TO USE HYPERSPACE LIKE NO ONE ELSE CAN.
IT WILL LET YOU GO ANYWHERE, TAKE WHAT YOU WANT AND VANISH. HITTING LIGHTSPEED FROM ATMOSPHERE, MICRO-JUMPS, YOU NAME IT.
HUH. HOW'S IT WORK?
THAT'S MY SECRET. THAT'S MY LEVERAGE. BUT I'LL TELL YOU--IT'LL ONLY WORK FOR ME OR MY SON. YOU TRY TO TAKE IT--YOU'LL REGRET IT.
WHAT MARCHION DID TO YOUR SHIPS... THAT'D BE NOTHING.
LET ME GUESS. YOU WANNA BE THE BOSS.
NAH. I DON'T WANT TO RUN A CREW. THAT'S YOUR JOB.
I'LL STAY BEHIND THE SCENES, GETTING MY CUT. YOU GUYS CAN HAVE ALL THE GLORY.
MAYBE WE'LL GROW A BIT, ADD ANOTHER TEMPEST, BUT THAT'S ALL I ASK.
FOR SOMEONE WHO DOESN'T WANT TO RUN THINGS, YOU SURE HAVE A LOT OF IDEAS.
SHALLA DIDN'T KNOW HOW TO USE THE NIHIL. SHE BROUGHT US TOGETHER, AND THAT'S SOMETHING. SHE MADE THE STORM.
BUT THAT'S WHERE IT STOPPED FOR HER. ULTIMATELY, SHE WAS JUST A CARETAKER.
BUT I'M MORE THAN THAT. I BROUGHT YOU THE LIGHTNING.
I'M THE EYE OF THE NIHIL NOW.

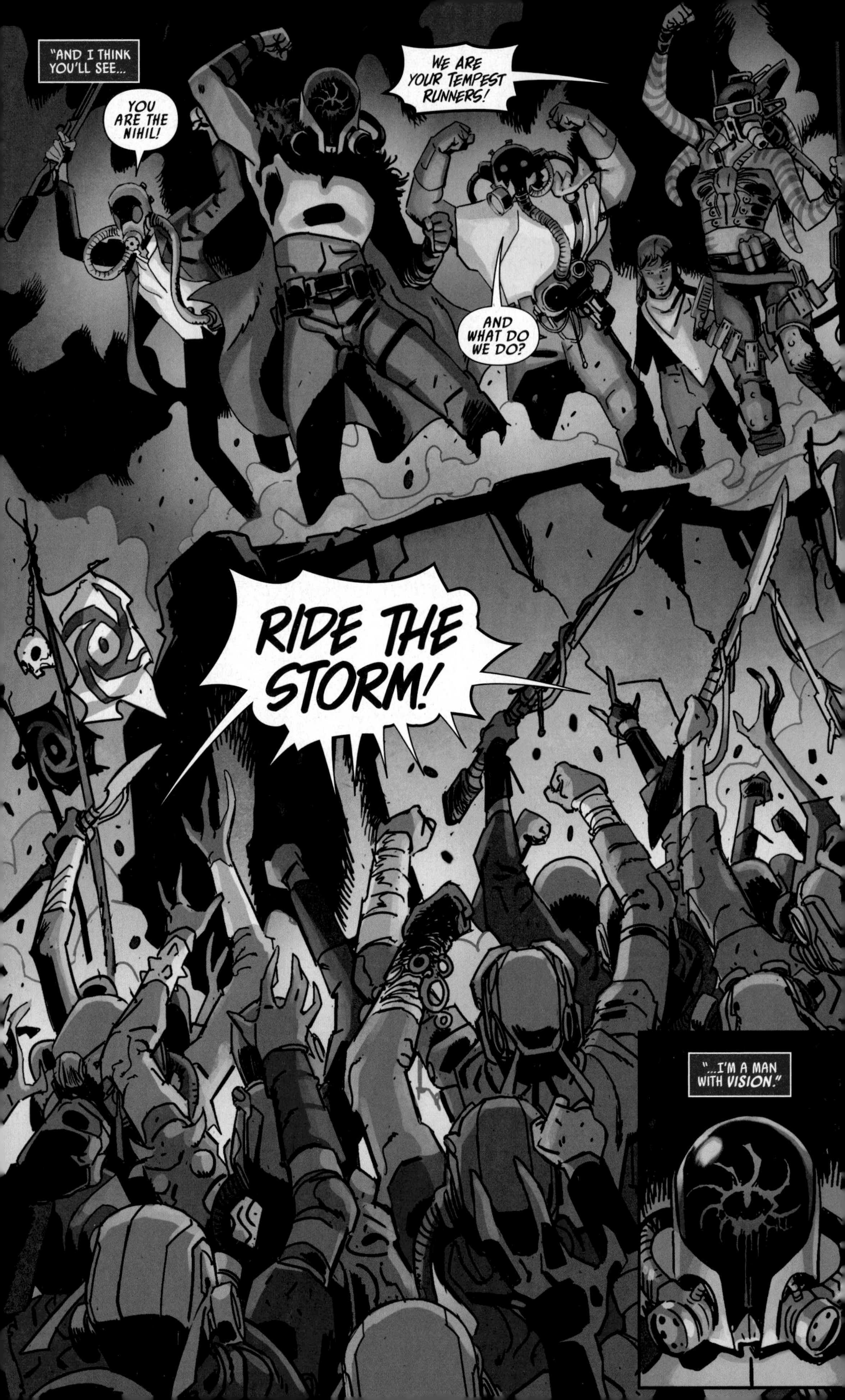

"AND I THINK YOU'LL SEE...
YOU ARE THE NIHIL!
WE ARE YOUR TEMPEST RUNNERS!
AND WHAT DO WE DO?
RIDE THE STORM!
"...I'M A MAN WITH VISION."

SCENE III

THE KILL

In which, Through the Power of the Paths,
The Nihil have become much more than they were.
An Eye Closes,
And an Eye Opens.

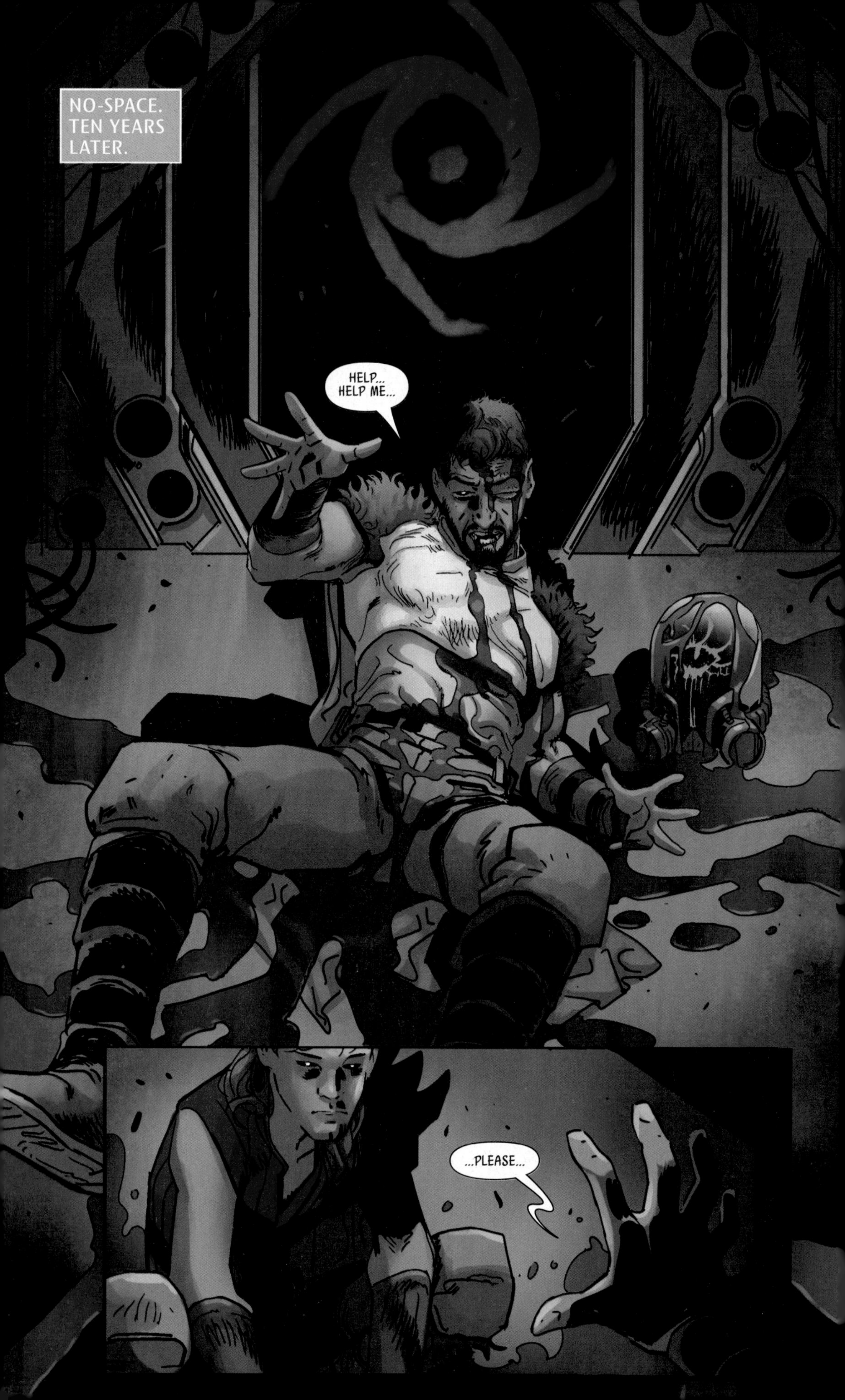
NO-SPACE. TEN YEARS LATER.
HELP... HELP ME...
...PLEASE...

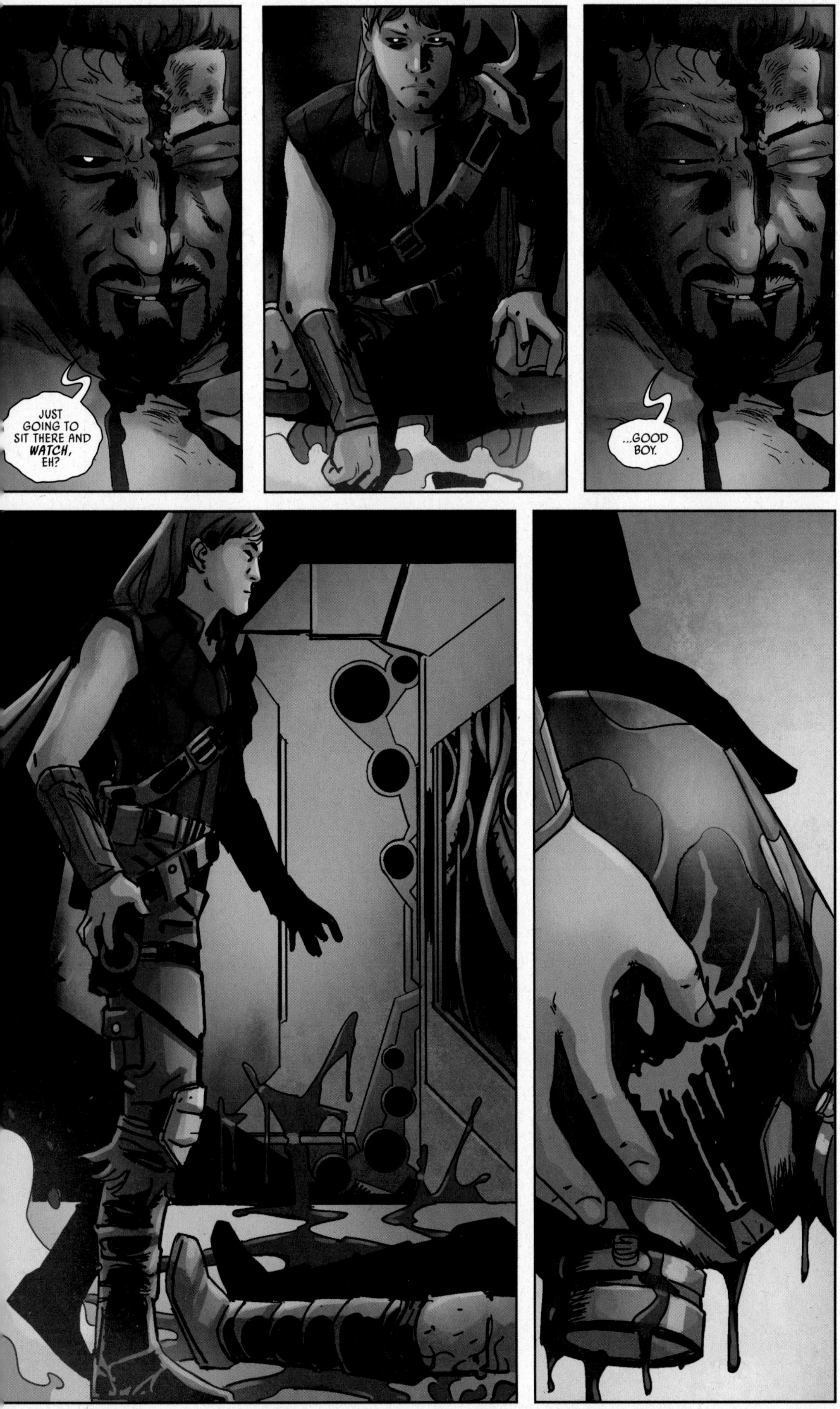
JUST GOING TO SIT THERE AND WATCH, EH?
...GOOD BOY.

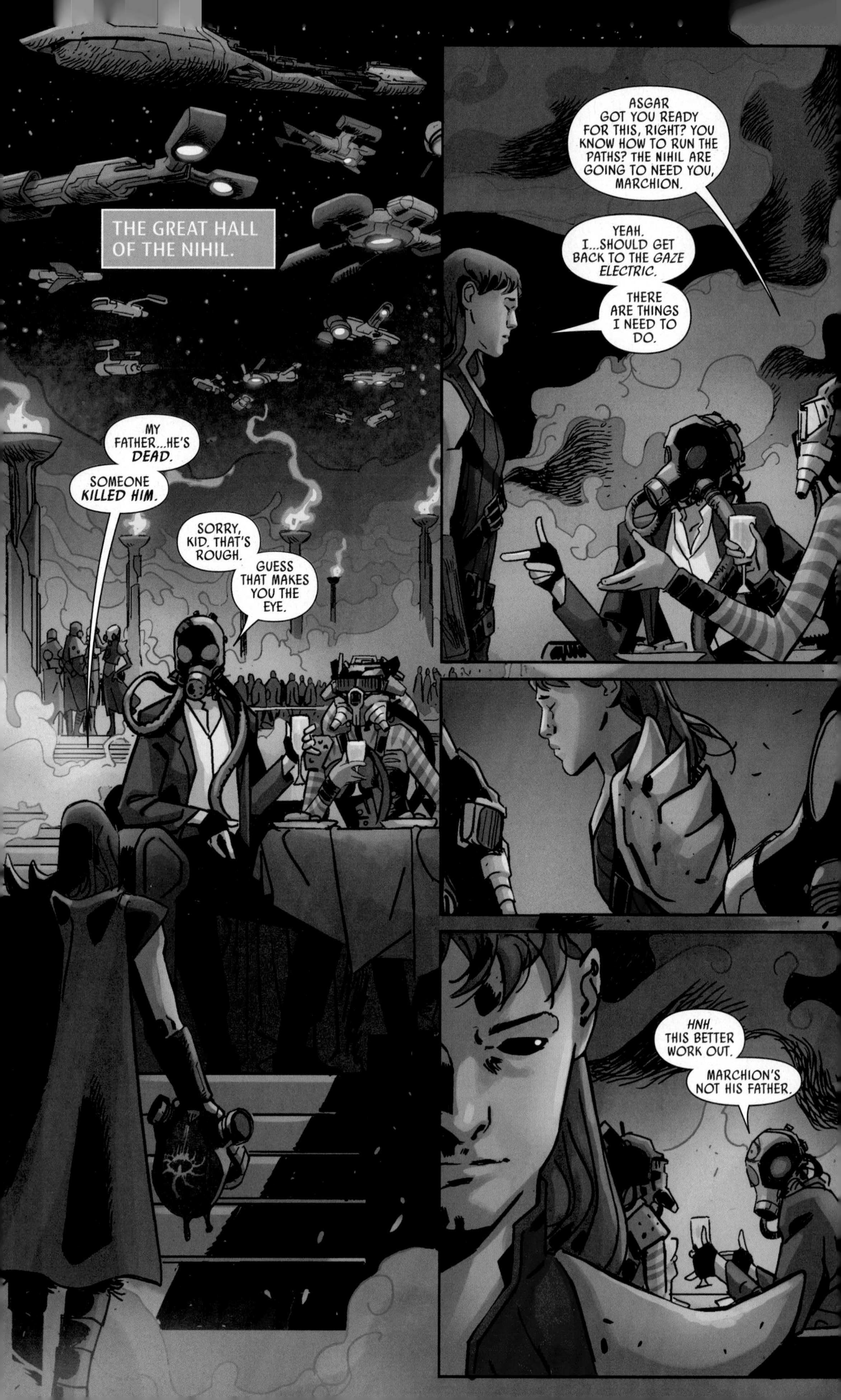
THE GREAT HALL OF THE NIHIL.
MY FATHER...HE'S DEAD.
SOMEONE KILLED HIM.
SORRY, KID. THAT'S ROUGH.
GUESS THAT MAKES YOU THE EYE.
ASGAR GOT YOU READY FOR THIS, RIGHT? YOU KNOW HOW TO RUN THE PATHS? THE NIHIL ARE GOING TO NEED YOU, MARCHION.
YEAH. I...SHOULD GET BACK TO THE GAZE ELECTRIC.
THERE ARE THINGS I NEED TO DO.
HNH. THIS BETTER WORK OUT.
MARCHION'S NOT HIS FATHER.

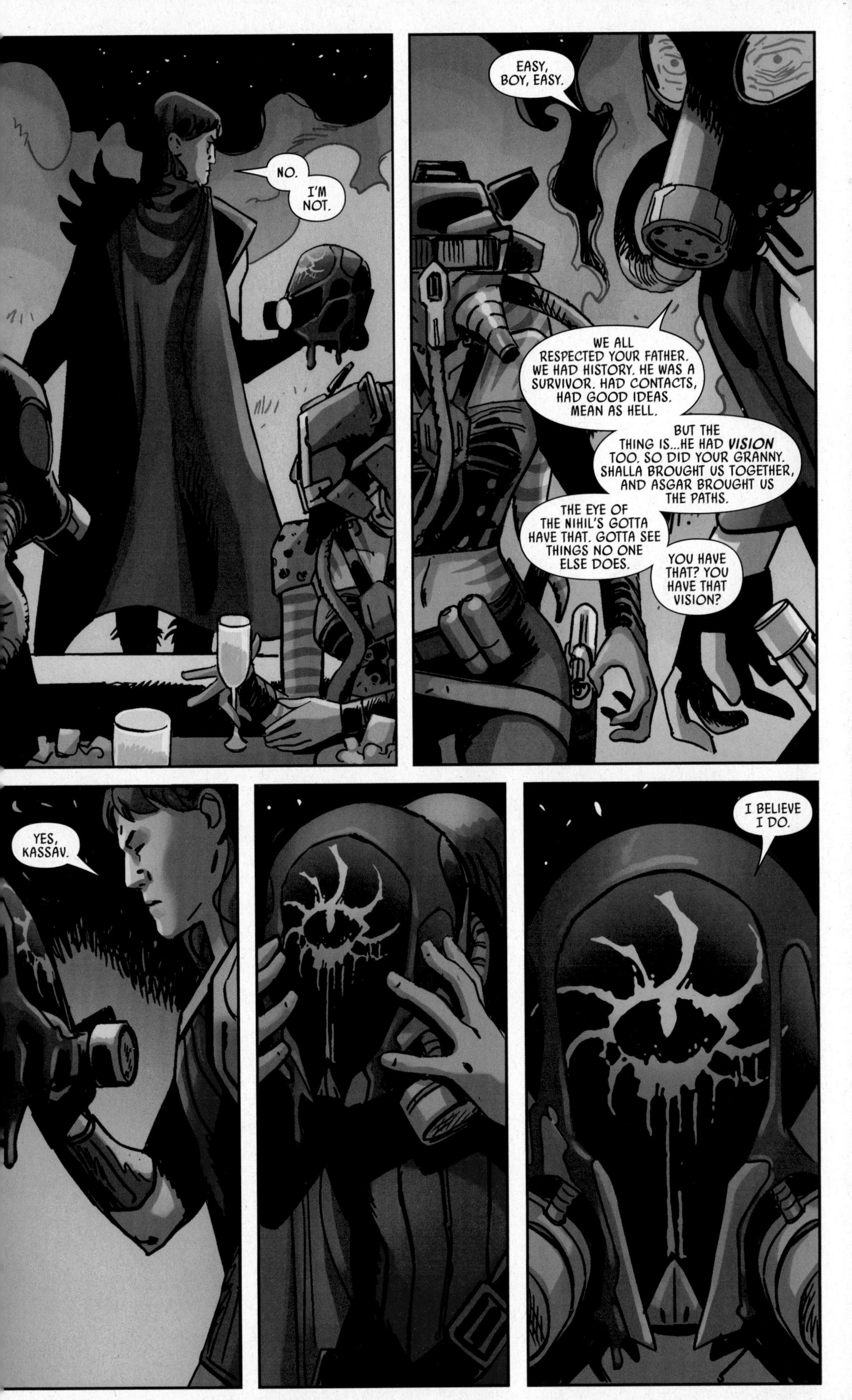
NO.
I'M NOT.
EASY, BOY, EASY.
WE ALL RESPECTED YOUR FATHER. WE HAD HISTORY. HE WAS A SURVIVOR. HAD CONTACTS, HAD GOOD IDEAS. MEAN AS HELL.
BUT THE THING IS...HE HAD VISION TOO. SO DID YOUR GRANNY. SHALLA BROUGHT US TOGETHER, AND ASGAR BROUGHT US THE PATHS.
THE EYE OF THE NIHIL'S GOTTA HAVE THAT. GOTTA SEE THINGS NO ONE ELSE DOES.
YOU HAVE THAT? YOU HAVE THAT VISION?
YES, KASSAV.
I BELIEVE I DO.

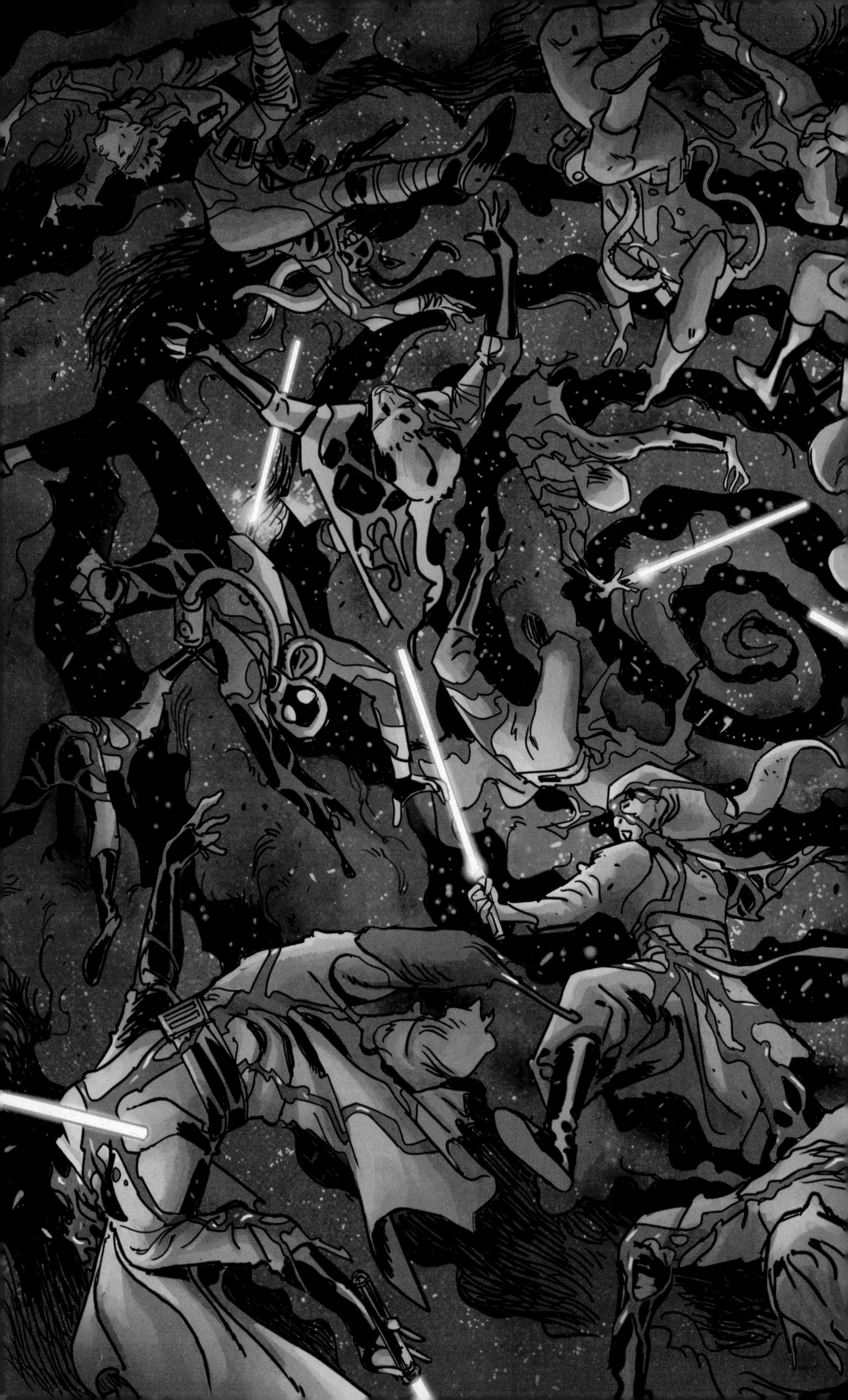

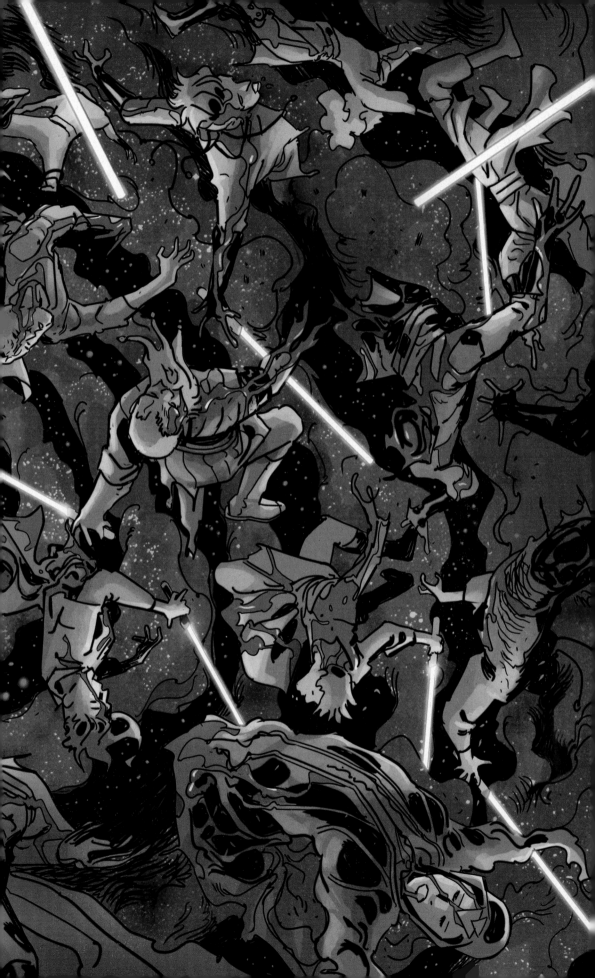

EYE OF THE STORM 2

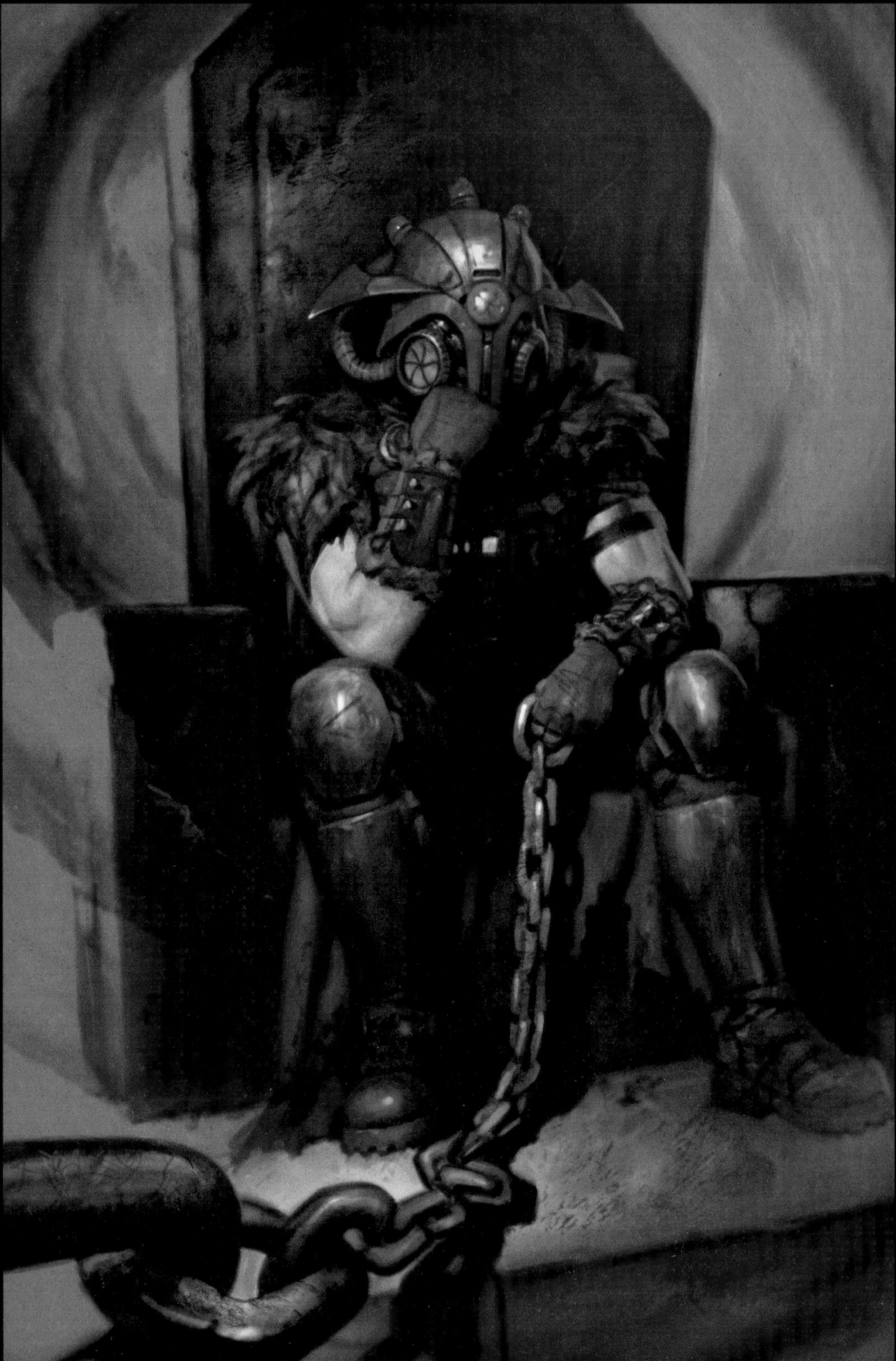

ACT II **MARCHION**

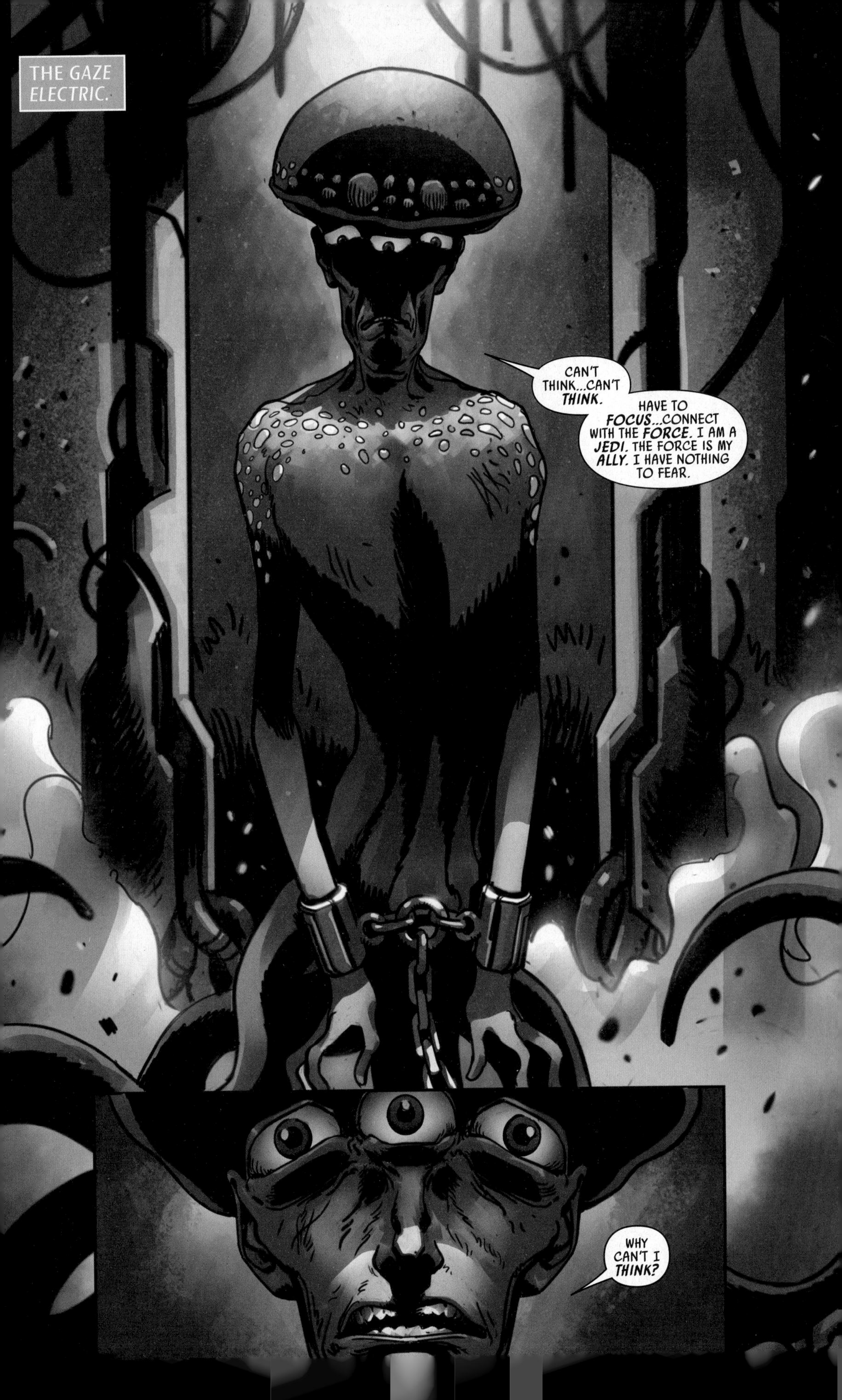
THE GAZE ELECTRIC.
CAN'T THINK...CAN'T THINK.
HAVE TO FOCUS...CONNECT WITH THE FORCE. I AM A JEDI. THE FORCE IS MY ALLY. I HAVE NOTHING TO FEAR.
WHY CAN'T I THINK?

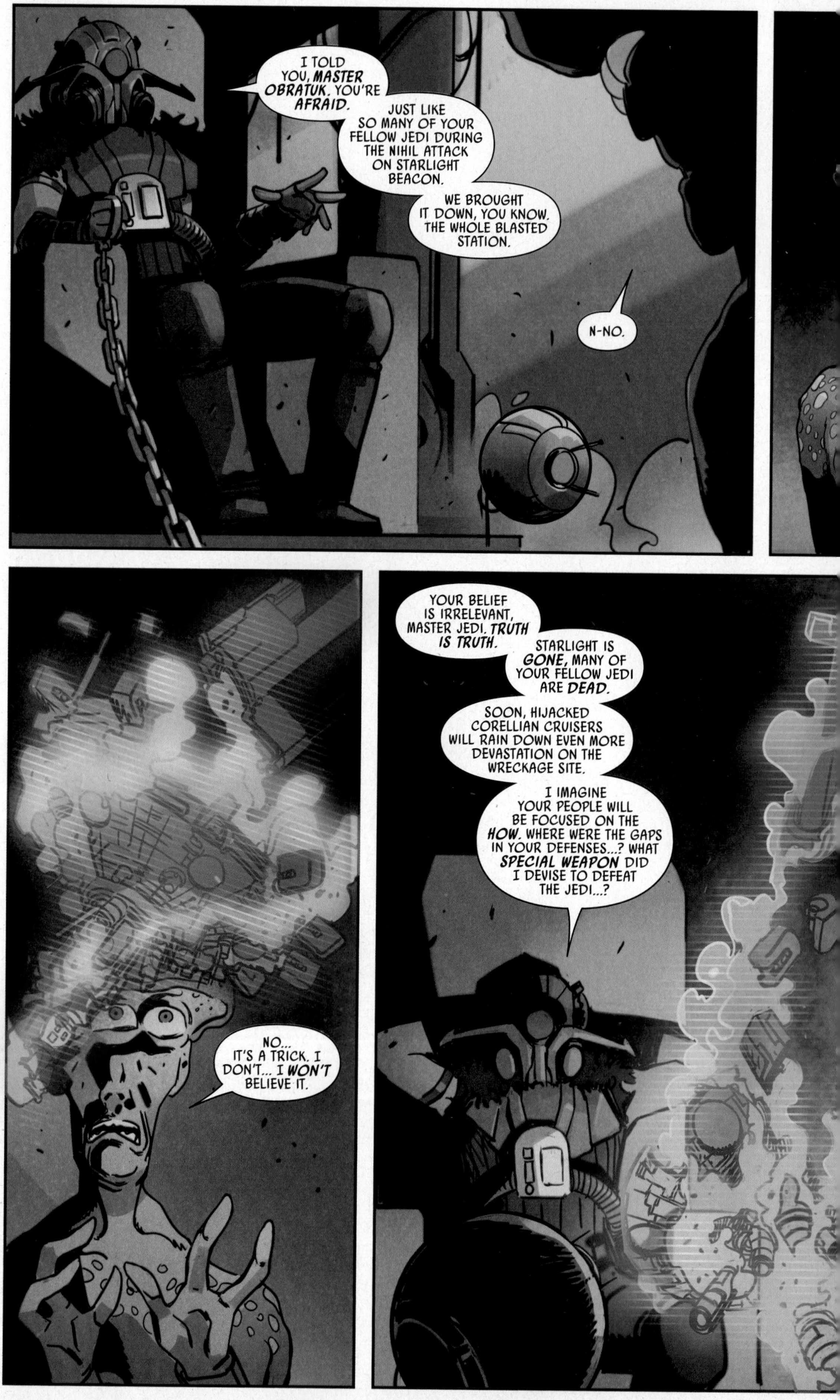
I TOLD YOU, MASTER OBRATUK. YOU'RE AFRAID.
JUST LIKE SO MANY OF YOUR FELLOW JEDI DURING THE NIHIL ATTACK ON STARLIGHT BEACON.
WE BROUGHT IT DOWN, YOU KNOW. THE WHOLE BLASTED STATION.
N-NO.
NO... IT'S A TRICK. I DON'T... I WON'T BELIEVE IT.
YOUR BELIEF IS IRRELEVANT, MASTER JEDI. TRUTH IS TRUTH.
STARLIGHT IS GONE, MANY OF YOUR FELLOW JEDI ARE DEAD.
SOON, HIJACKED CORELLIAN CRUISERS WILL RAIN DOWN EVEN MORE DEVASTATION ON THE WRECKAGE SITE.
I IMAGINE YOUR PEOPLE WILL BE FOCUSED ON THE HOW. WHERE WERE THE GAPS IN YOUR DEFENSES...? WHAT SPECIAL WEAPON DID I DEVISE TO DEFEAT THE JEDI...?

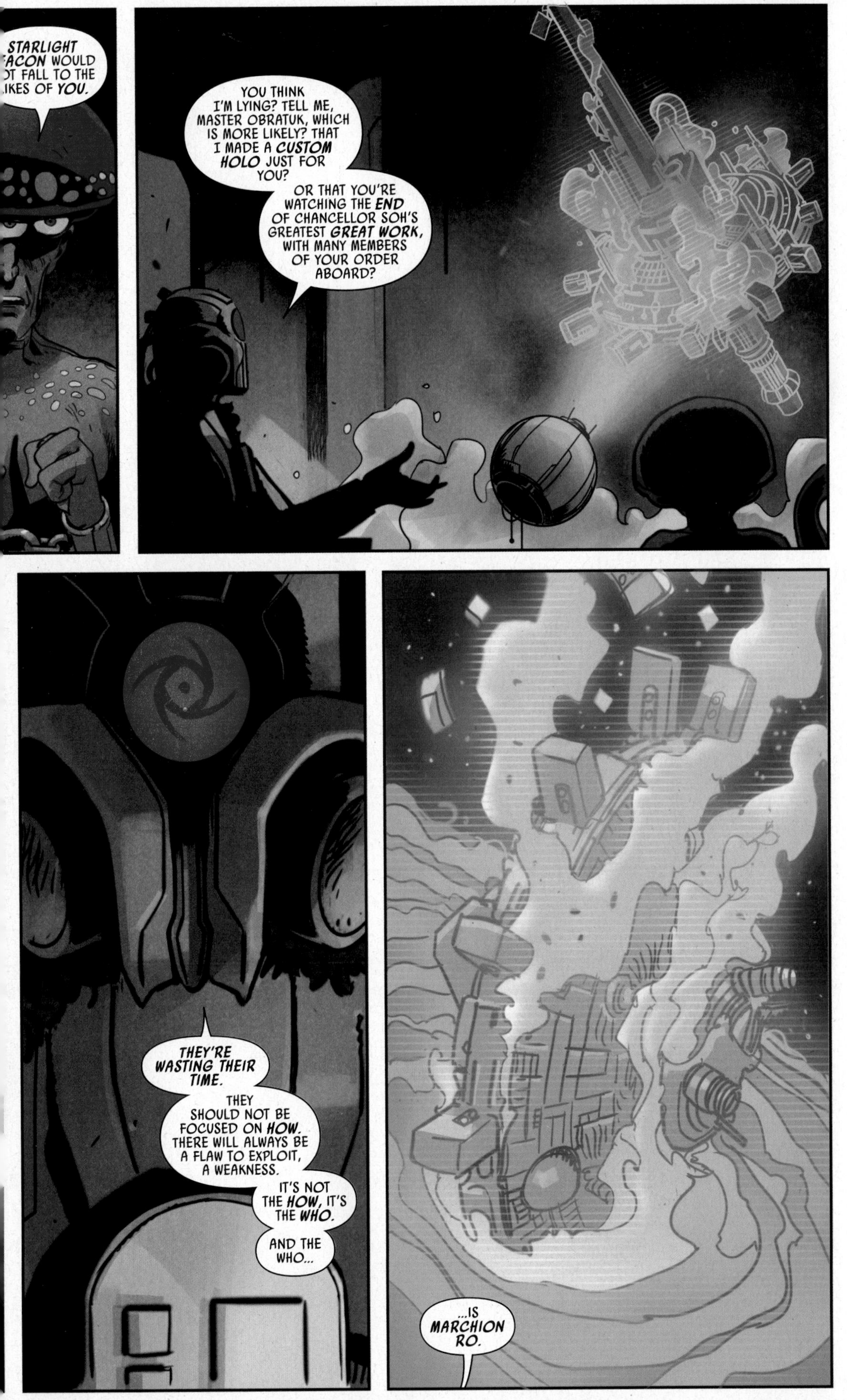
STARLIGHT
ACON WOULD
T FALL TO THE
IKES OF YOU.
YOU THINK I'M LYING? TELL ME, MASTER OBRATUK, WHICH IS MORE LIKELY? THAT I MADE A CUSTOM HOLO JUST FOR YOU?
OR THAT YOU'RE WATCHING THE END OF CHANCELLOR SOH'S GREATEST GREAT WORK, WITH MANY MEMBERS OF YOUR ORDER ABOARD?
THEY'RE WASTING THEIR TIME.
THEY SHOULD NOT BE FOCUSED ON HOW. THERE WILL ALWAYS BE A FLAW TO EXPLOIT, A WEAKNESS.
IT'S NOT THE HOW, IT'S THE WHO.
AND THE WHO...
...IS MARCHION RO.

THE WRECKAGE

In which a Group of Powerful People
Realize the Depth of their Failure,
and Questions are Asked.

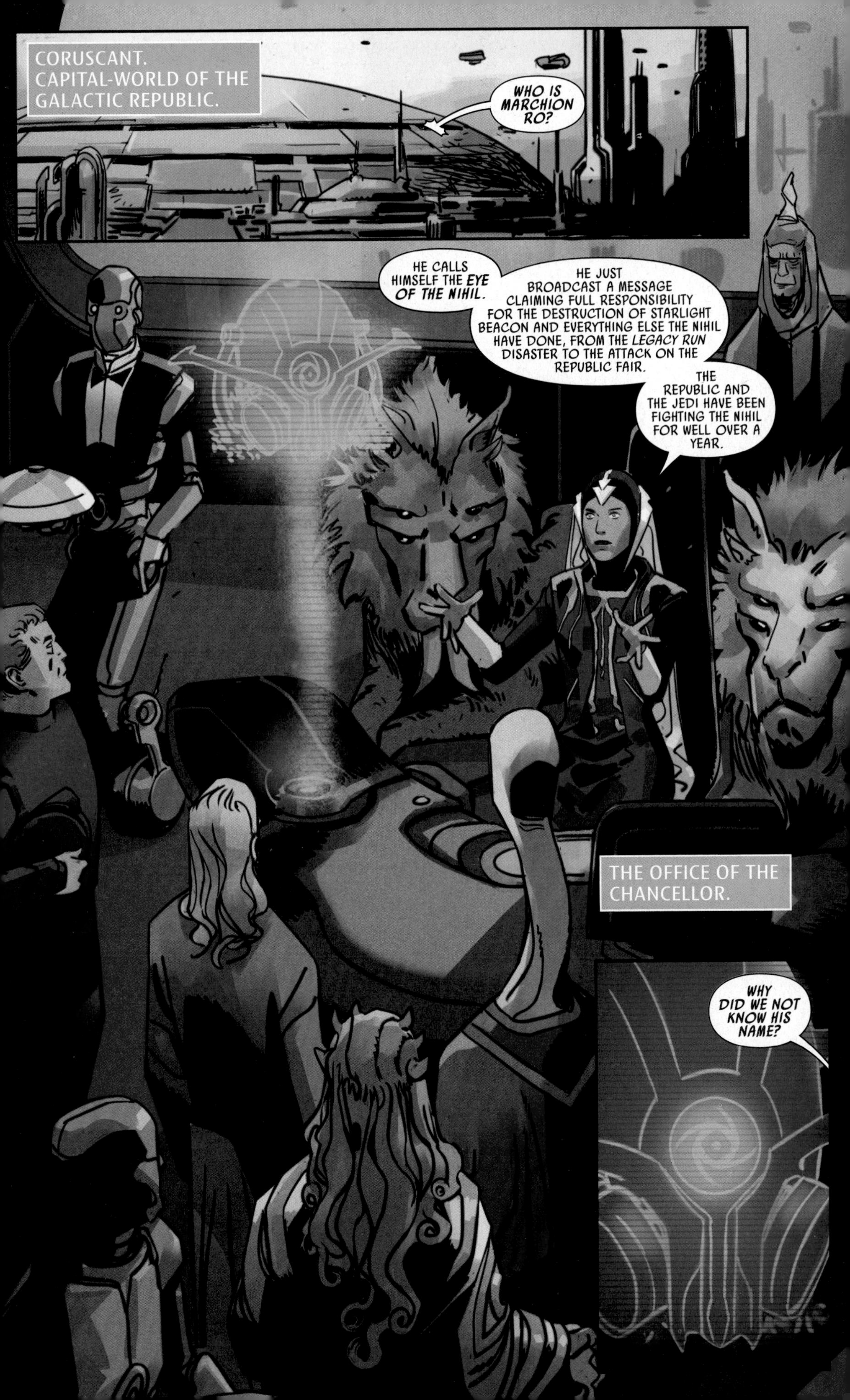
CORUSCANT. CAPITAL-WORLD OF THE GALACTIC REPUBLIC.
WHO IS MARCHION RO?
HE CALLS HIMSELF THE *EYE OF THE NIHIL.*
HE JUST BROADCAST A MESSAGE CLAIMING FULL RESPONSIBILITY FOR THE DESTRUCTION OF STARLIGHT BEACON AND EVERYTHING ELSE THE NIHIL HAVE DONE, FROM THE *LEGACY RUN* DISASTER TO THE ATTACK ON THE REPUBLIC FAIR.
THE REPUBLIC AND THE JEDI HAVE BEEN FIGHTING THE NIHIL FOR WELL OVER A YEAR.
THE OFFICE OF THE CHANCELLOR.
WHY DID WE NOT KNOW HIS NAME?

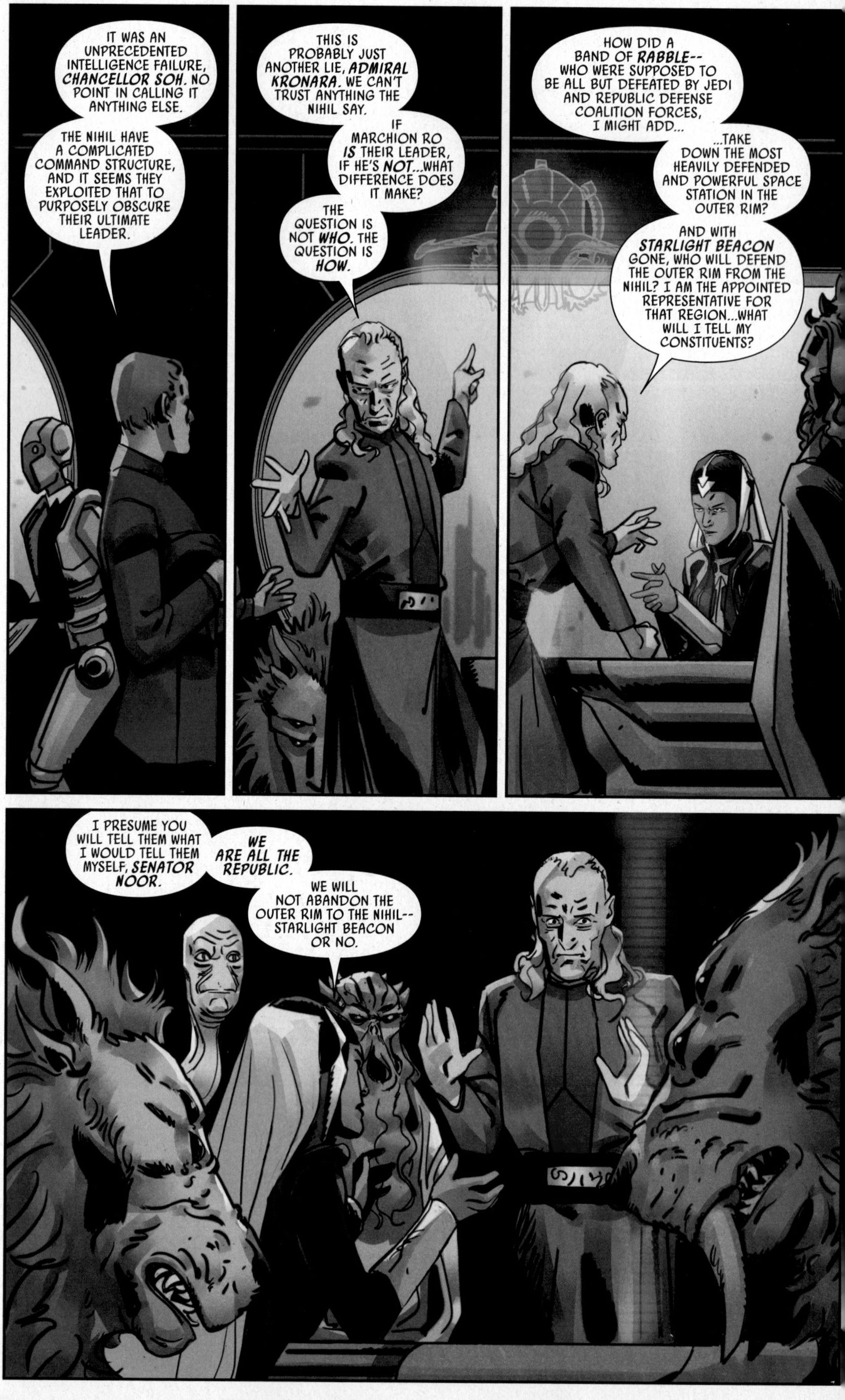
IT WAS AN UNPRECEDENTED INTELLIGENCE FAILURE, CHANCELLOR SOH. NO POINT IN CALLING IT ANYTHING ELSE.
THE NIHIL HAVE A COMPLICATED COMMAND STRUCTURE, AND IT SEEMS THEY EXPLOITED THAT TO PURPOSELY OBSCURE THEIR ULTIMATE LEADER.
THIS IS PROBABLY JUST ANOTHER LIE, ADMIRAL KRONARA. WE CAN'T TRUST ANYTHING THE NIHIL SAY.
IF MARCHION RO IS THEIR LEADER, IF HE'S NOT...WHAT DIFFERENCE DOES IT MAKE?
THE QUESTION IS NOT WHO. THE QUESTION IS HOW.
HOW DID A BAND OF RABBLE-- WHO WERE SUPPOSED TO BE ALL BUT DEFEATED BY JEDI AND REPUBLIC DEFENSE COALITION FORCES, I MIGHT ADD...
...TAKE DOWN THE MOST HEAVILY DEFENDED AND POWERFUL SPACE STATION IN THE OUTER RIM?
AND WITH STARLIGHT BEACON GONE, WHO WILL DEFEND THE OUTER RIM FROM THE NIHIL? I AM THE APPOINTED REPRESENTATIVE FOR THAT REGION...WHAT WILL I TELL MY CONSTITUENTS?
I PRESUME YOU WILL TELL THEM WHAT I WOULD TELL THEM MYSELF, SENATOR NOOR.
WE ARE ALL THE REPUBLIC.
WE WILL NOT ABANDON THE OUTER RIM TO THE NIHIL-- STARLIGHT BEACON OR NO.

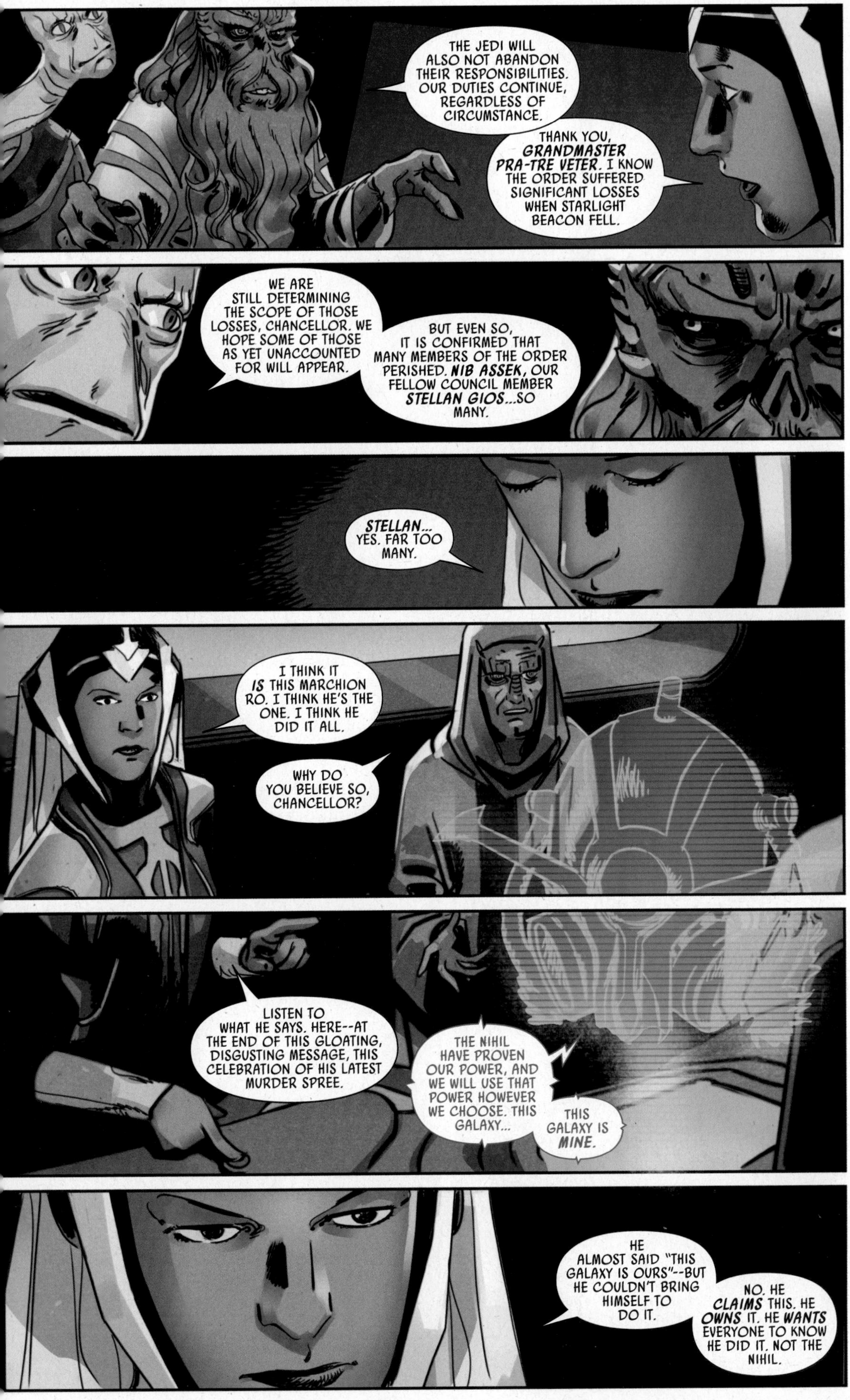
THE JEDI WILL ALSO NOT ABANDON THEIR RESPONSIBILITIES. OUR DUTIES CONTINUE, REGARDLESS OF CIRCUMSTANCE.
THANK YOU, GRANDMASTER PRA-TRE VETER. I KNOW THE ORDER SUFFERED SIGNIFICANT LOSSES WHEN STARLIGHT BEACON FELL.
WE ARE STILL DETERMINING THE SCOPE OF THOSE LOSSES, CHANCELLOR. WE HOPE SOME OF THOSE AS YET UNACCOUNTED FOR WILL APPEAR.
BUT EVEN SO, IT IS CONFIRMED THAT MANY MEMBERS OF THE ORDER PERISHED. NIB ASSEK, OUR FELLOW COUNCIL MEMBER STELLAN GIOS...SO MANY.
STELLAN... YES. FAR TOO MANY.
I THINK IT IS THIS MARCHION RO. I THINK HE'S THE ONE. I THINK HE DID IT ALL.
WHY DO YOU BELIEVE SO, CHANCELLOR?
LISTEN TO WHAT HE SAYS. HERE--AT THE END OF THIS GLOATING, DISGUSTING MESSAGE, THIS CELEBRATION OF HIS LATEST MURDER SPREE.
THE NIHIL HAVE PROVEN OUR POWER, AND WE WILL USE THAT POWER HOWEVER WE CHOOSE. THIS GALAXY...
THIS GALAXY IS MINE.
HE ALMOST SAID "THIS GALAXY IS OURS"--BUT HE COULDN'T BRING HIMSELF TO DO IT.
NO. HE CLAIMS THIS. HE OWNS IT. HE WANTS EVERYONE TO KNOW HE DID IT. NOT THE NIHIL.

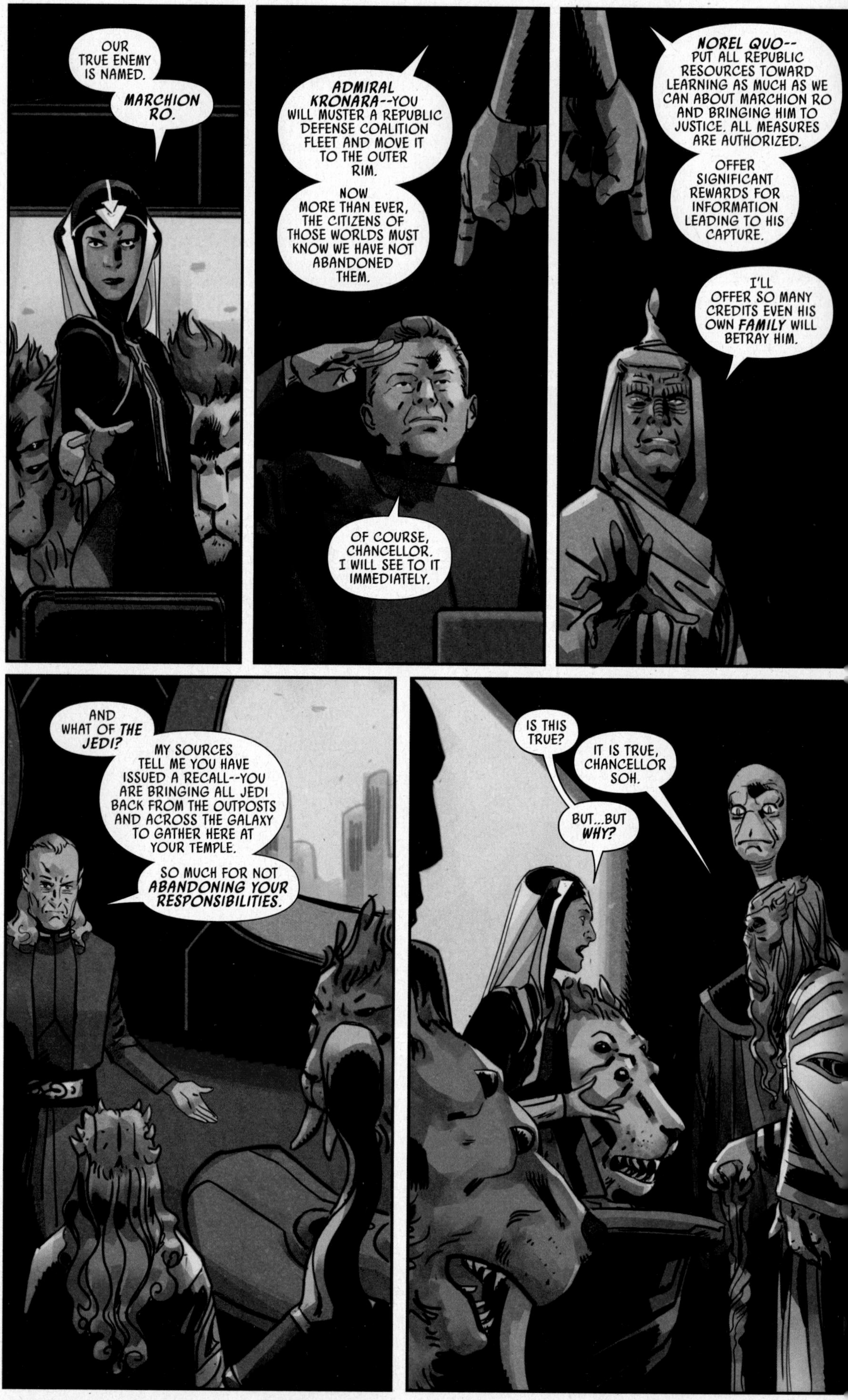
OUR TRUE ENEMY IS NAMED.
MARCHION RO.
ADMIRAL KRONARA--YOU WILL MUSTER A REPUBLIC DEFENSE COALITION FLEET AND MOVE IT TO THE OUTER RIM.
NOW MORE THAN EVER, THE CITIZENS OF THOSE WORLDS MUST KNOW WE HAVE NOT ABANDONED THEM.
OF COURSE, CHANCELLOR. I WILL SEE TO IT IMMEDIATELY.
NOREL QUO--PUT ALL REPUBLIC RESOURCES TOWARD LEARNING AS MUCH AS WE CAN ABOUT MARCHION RO AND BRINGING HIM TO JUSTICE. ALL MEASURES ARE AUTHORIZED.
OFFER SIGNIFICANT REWARDS FOR INFORMATION LEADING TO HIS CAPTURE.
I'LL OFFER SO MANY CREDITS EVEN HIS OWN FAMILY WILL BETRAY HIM.
AND WHAT OF THE JEDI?
MY SOURCES TELL ME YOU HAVE ISSUED A RECALL--YOU ARE BRINGING ALL JEDI BACK FROM THE OUTPOSTS AND ACROSS THE GALAXY TO GATHER HERE AT YOUR TEMPLE.
SO MUCH FOR NOT ABANDONING YOUR RESPONSIBILITIES.
IS THIS TRUE?
IT IS TRUE, CHANCELLOR SOH.
BUT...BUT WHY?

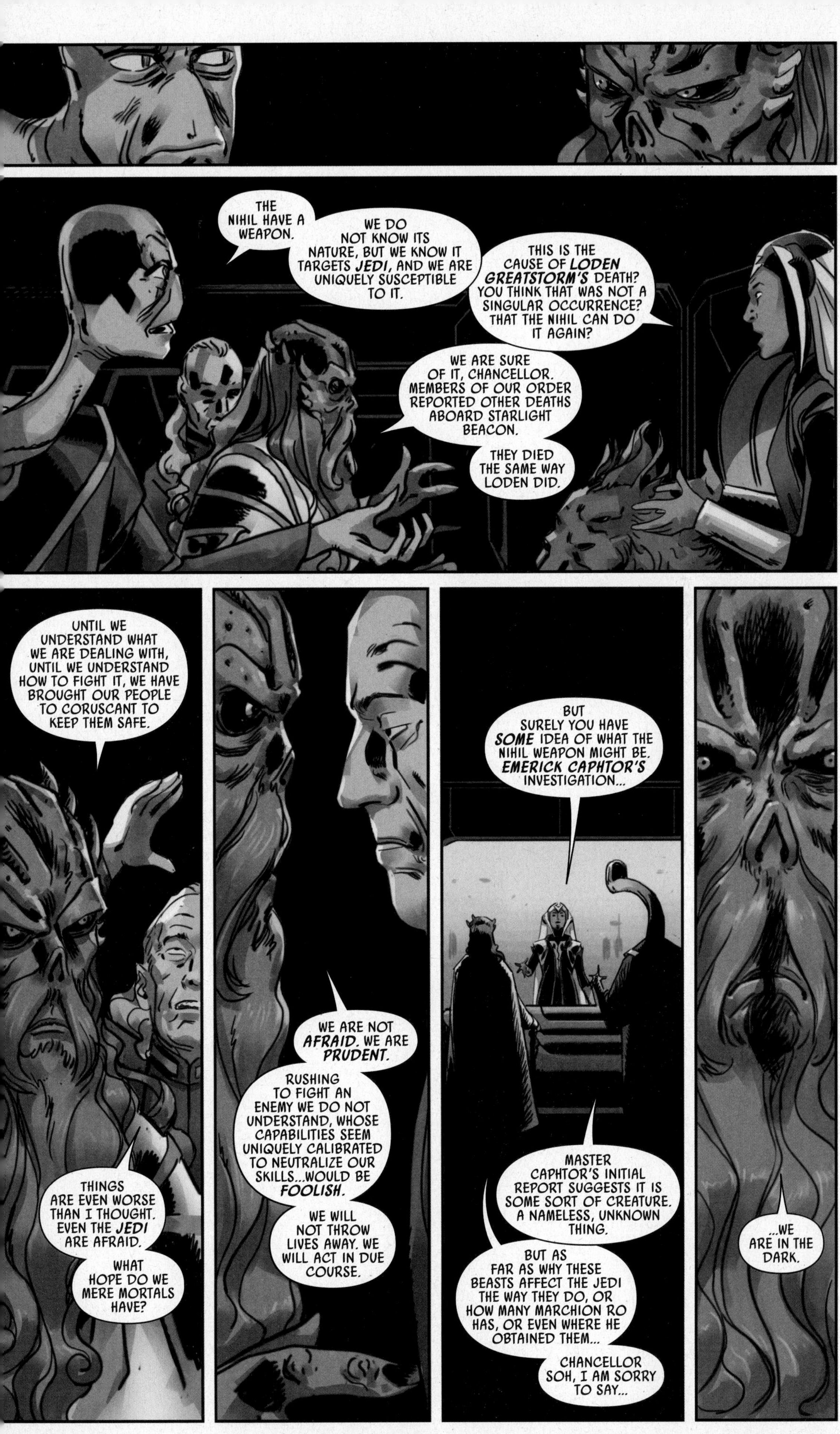
THE NIHIL HAVE A WEAPON.
WE DO NOT KNOW ITS NATURE, BUT WE KNOW IT TARGETS *JEDI*, AND WE ARE UNIQUELY SUSCEPTIBLE TO IT.
THIS IS THE CAUSE OF **LODEN GREATSTORM'S** DEATH? YOU THINK THAT WAS NOT A SINGULAR OCCURRENCE? THAT THE NIHIL CAN DO IT AGAIN?
WE ARE SURE OF IT, CHANCELLOR. MEMBERS OF OUR ORDER REPORTED OTHER DEATHS ABOARD STARLIGHT BEACON.
THEY DIED THE SAME WAY LODEN DID.
UNTIL WE UNDERSTAND WHAT WE ARE DEALING WITH, UNTIL WE UNDERSTAND HOW TO FIGHT IT, WE HAVE BROUGHT OUR PEOPLE TO CORUSCANT TO KEEP THEM SAFE.
THINGS ARE EVEN WORSE THAN I THOUGHT. EVEN THE *JEDI* ARE AFRAID.
WHAT HOPE DO WE MERE MORTALS HAVE?
WE ARE NOT *AFRAID*. WE ARE *PRUDENT*.
RUSHING TO FIGHT AN ENEMY WE DO NOT UNDERSTAND, WHOSE CAPABILITIES SEEM UNIQUELY CALIBRATED TO NEUTRALIZE OUR SKILLS...WOULD BE *FOOLISH*.
WE WILL NOT THROW LIVES AWAY. WE WILL ACT IN DUE COURSE.
BUT SURELY YOU HAVE **SOME** IDEA OF WHAT THE NIHIL WEAPON MIGHT BE. **EMERICK CAPHTOR'S** INVESTIGATION...
MASTER CAPHTOR'S INITIAL REPORT SUGGESTS IT IS SOME SORT OF CREATURE. A NAMELESS, UNKNOWN THING.
BUT AS FAR AS WHY THESE BEASTS AFFECT THE JEDI THE WAY THEY DO, OR HOW MANY MARCHION RO HAS, OR EVEN WHERE HE OBTAINED THEM...
CHANCELLOR SOH, I AM SORRY TO SAY...
...WE ARE IN THE DARK.

SCENE II

THE HUNT

In which the Source of Marchion Ro's
Weapon against the Jedi is Revealed,
While its Name and Nature
Remain Obscured.

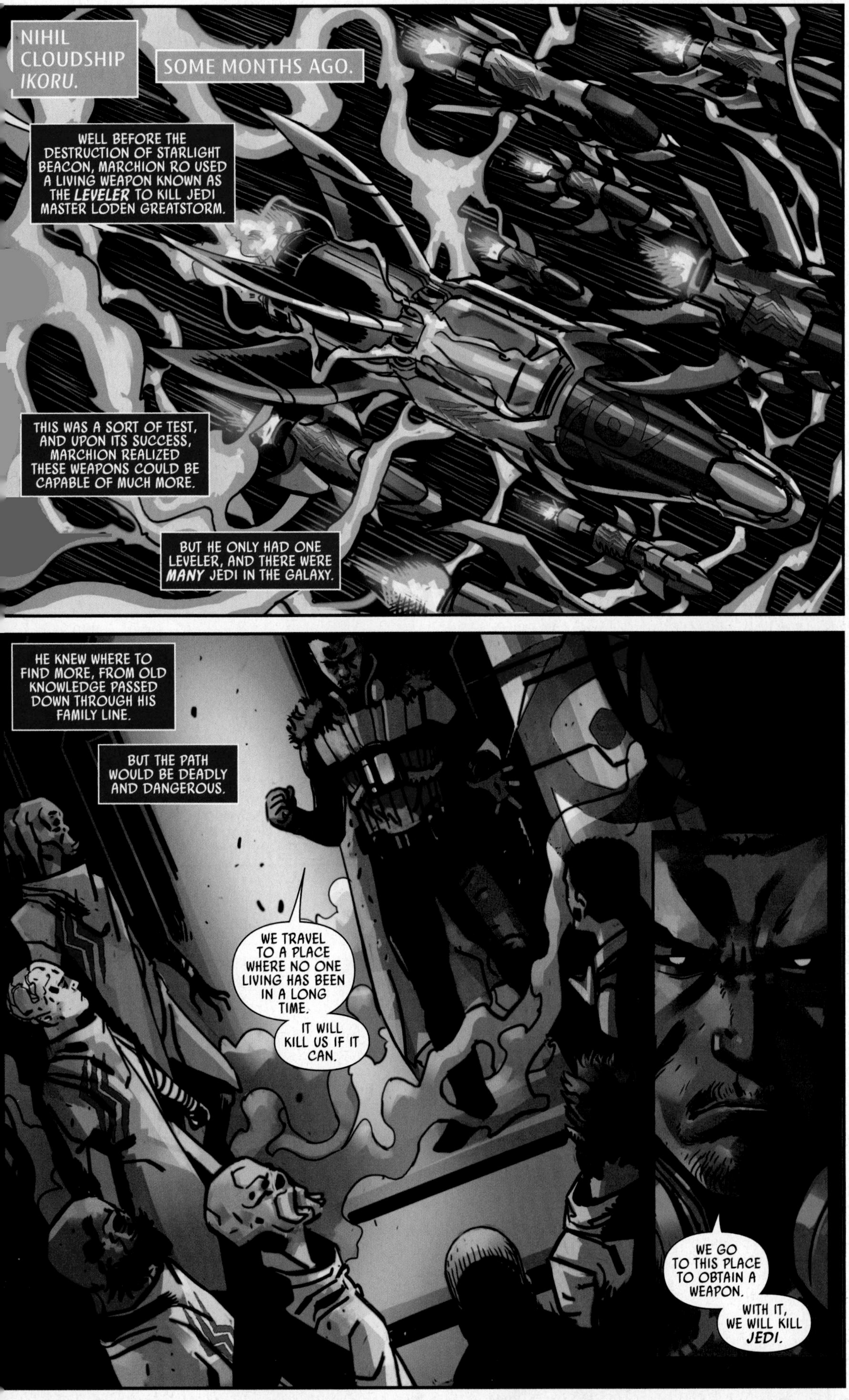
NIHIL CLOUDSHIP *IKORU*.
SOME MONTHS AGO.
WELL BEFORE THE DESTRUCTION OF STARLIGHT BEACON, MARCHION RO USED A LIVING WEAPON KNOWN AS THE *LEVELER* TO KILL JEDI MASTER LODEN GREATSTORM.
THIS WAS A SORT OF TEST, AND UPON ITS SUCCESS, MARCHION REALIZED THESE WEAPONS COULD BE CAPABLE OF MUCH MORE.
BUT HE ONLY HAD ONE LEVELER, AND THERE WERE *MANY* JEDI IN THE GALAXY.
HE KNEW WHERE TO FIND MORE, FROM OLD KNOWLEDGE PASSED DOWN THROUGH HIS FAMILY LINE.
BUT THE PATH WOULD BE DEADLY AND DANGEROUS.
WE TRAVEL TO A PLACE WHERE NO ONE LIVING HAS BEEN IN A LONG TIME.
IT WILL KILL US IF IT CAN.
WE GO TO THIS PLACE TO OBTAIN A WEAPON.
WITH IT, WE WILL KILL *JEDI*.

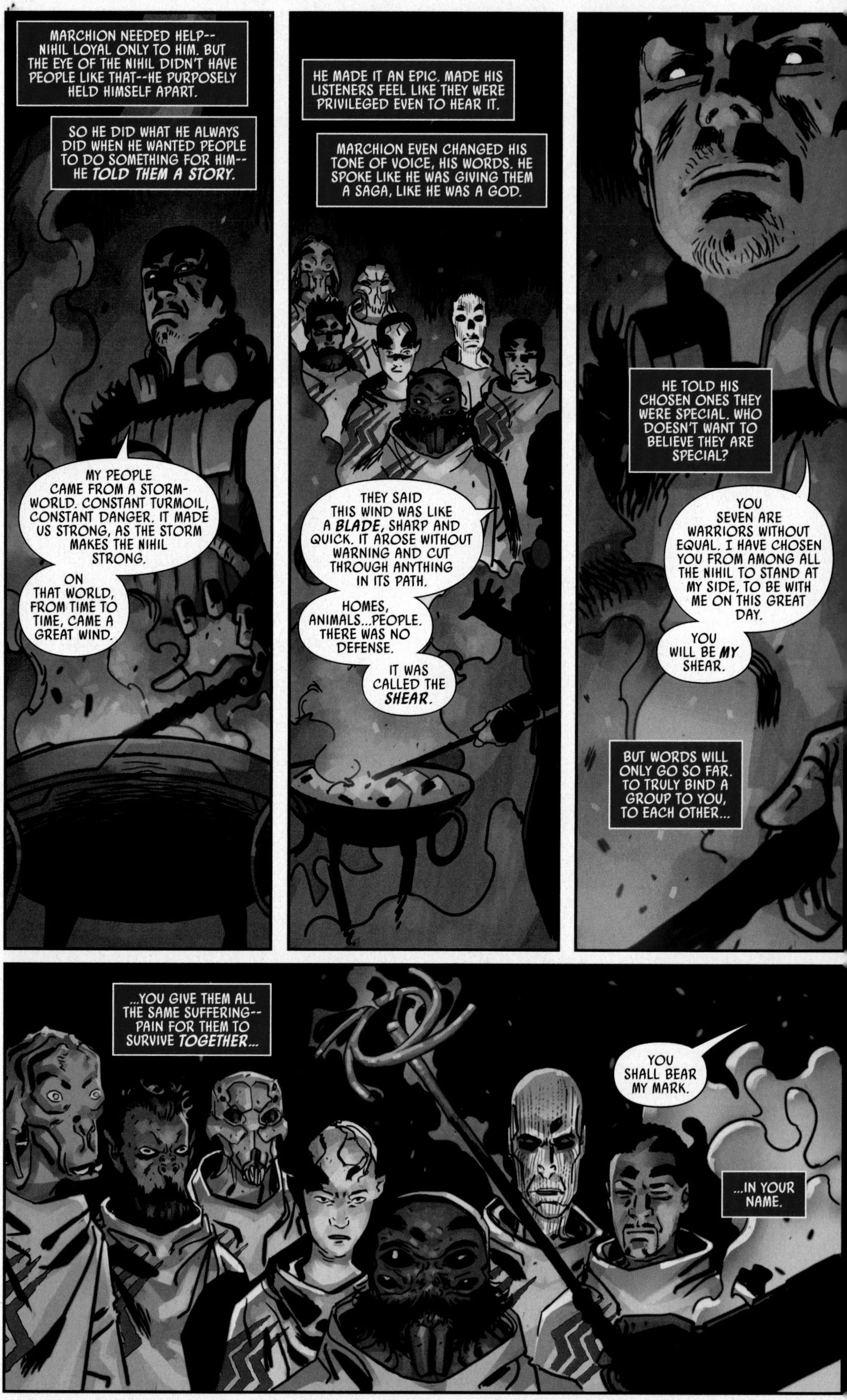
MARCHION NEEDED HELP--NIHIL LOYAL ONLY TO HIM. BUT THE EYE OF THE NIHIL DIDN'T HAVE PEOPLE LIKE THAT--HE PURPOSELY HELD HIMSELF APART.
SO HE DID WHAT HE ALWAYS DID WHEN HE WANTED PEOPLE TO DO SOMETHING FOR HIM--HE *TOLD THEM A STORY.*
MY PEOPLE CAME FROM A STORM-WORLD. CONSTANT TURMOIL, CONSTANT DANGER. IT MADE US STRONG, AS THE STORM MAKES THE NIHIL STRONG.
ON THAT WORLD, FROM TIME TO TIME, CAME A GREAT WIND.
HE MADE IT AN EPIC. MADE HIS LISTENERS FEEL LIKE THEY WERE PRIVILEGED EVEN TO HEAR IT.
MARCHION EVEN CHANGED HIS TONE OF VOICE, HIS WORDS. HE SPOKE LIKE HE WAS GIVING THEM A SAGA, LIKE HE WAS A GOD.
THEY SAID THIS WIND WAS LIKE A *BLADE*, SHARP AND QUICK. IT AROSE WITHOUT WARNING AND CUT THROUGH ANYTHING IN ITS PATH.
HOMES, ANIMALS...PEOPLE. THERE WAS NO DEFENSE.
IT WAS CALLED THE *SHEAR*.
HE TOLD HIS CHOSEN ONES THEY WERE SPECIAL. WHO DOESN'T WANT TO BELIEVE THEY ARE SPECIAL?
YOU SEVEN ARE WARRIORS WITHOUT EQUAL. I HAVE CHOSEN YOU FROM AMONG ALL THE NIHIL TO STAND AT MY SIDE, TO BE WITH ME ON THIS GREAT DAY.
YOU WILL BE *MY* SHEAR.
BUT WORDS WILL ONLY GO SO FAR. TO TRULY BIND A GROUP TO YOU, TO EACH OTHER...
...YOU GIVE THEM ALL THE SAME SUFFERING--PAIN FOR THEM TO SURVIVE *TOGETHER*...
YOU SHALL BEAR MY MARK.
...IN YOUR NAME.

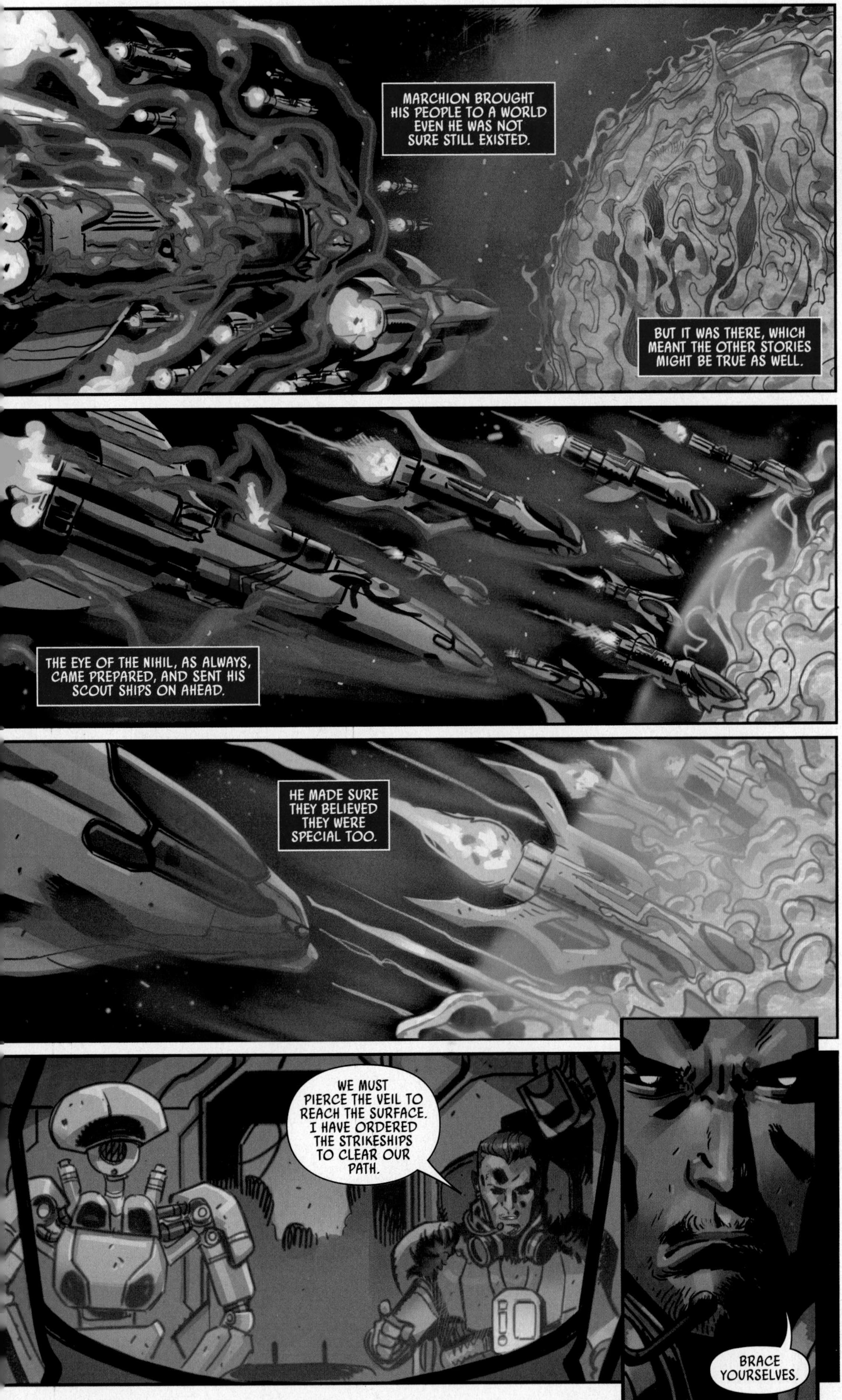
MARCHION BROUGHT HIS PEOPLE TO A WORLD EVEN HE WAS NOT SURE STILL EXISTED.
BUT IT WAS THERE, WHICH MEANT THE OTHER STORIES MIGHT BE TRUE AS WELL.
THE EYE OF THE NIHIL, AS ALWAYS, CAME PREPARED, AND SENT HIS SCOUT SHIPS ON AHEAD.
HE MADE SURE THEY BELIEVED THEY WERE SPECIAL TOO.
WE MUST PIERCE THE VEIL TO REACH THE SURFACE. I HAVE ORDERED THE STRIKESHIPS TO CLEAR OUR PATH.
BRACE YOURSELVES.

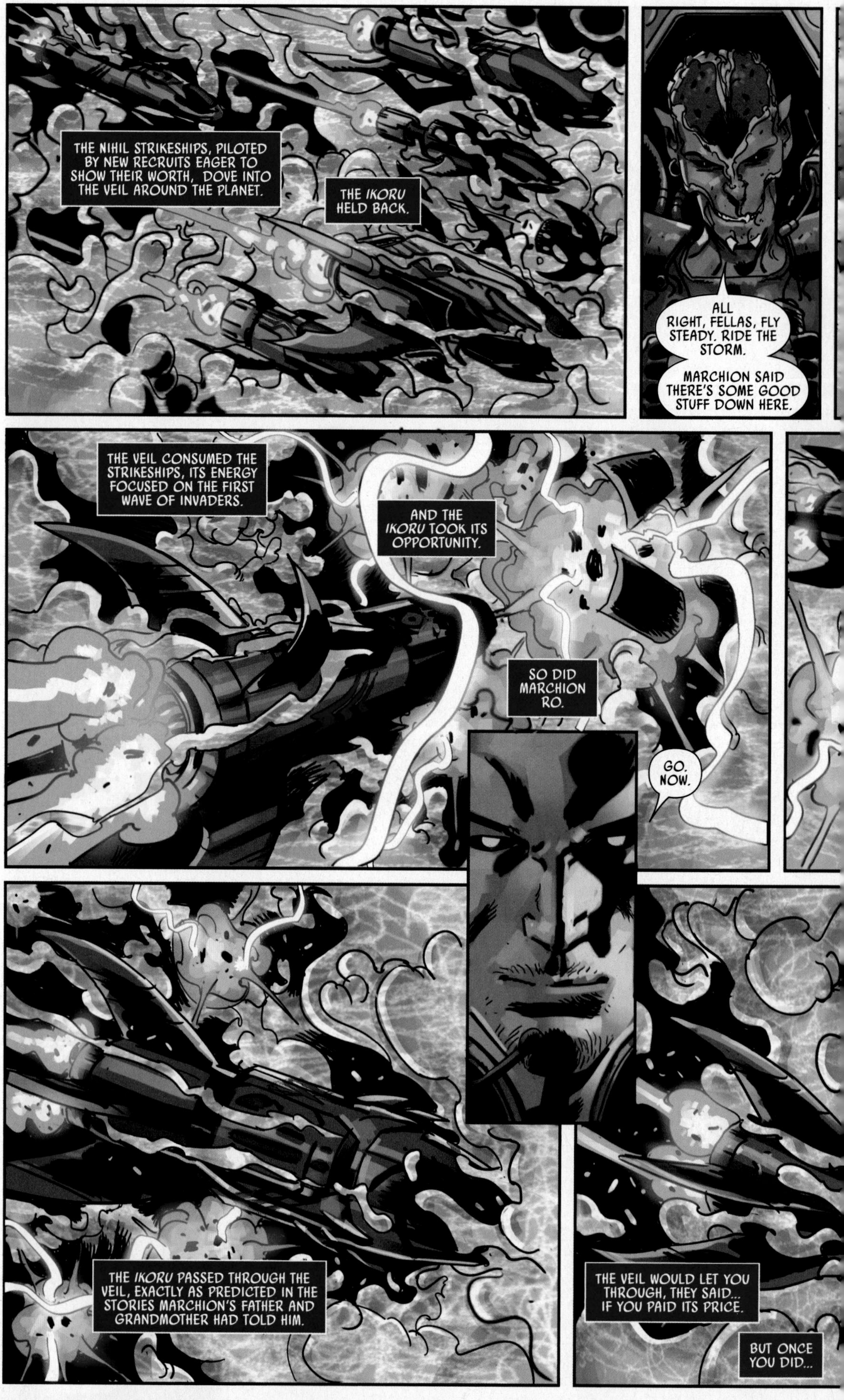
THE NIHIL STRIKESHIPS, PILOTED BY NEW RECRUITS EAGER TO SHOW THEIR WORTH, DOVE INTO THE VEIL AROUND THE PLANET.
THE *IKORU* HELD BACK.
ALL RIGHT, FELLAS, FLY STEADY. RIDE THE STORM.
MARCHION SAID THERE'S SOME GOOD STUFF DOWN HERE.
THE VEIL CONSUMED THE STRIKESHIPS, ITS ENERGY FOCUSED ON THE FIRST WAVE OF INVADERS.
AND THE *IKORU* TOOK ITS OPPORTUNITY.
SO DID MARCHION RO.
GO. NOW.
THE *IKORU* PASSED THROUGH THE VEIL, EXACTLY AS PREDICTED IN THE STORIES MARCHION'S FATHER AND GRANDMOTHER HAD TOLD HIM.
THE VEIL WOULD LET YOU THROUGH, THEY SAID... IF YOU PAID ITS PRICE.
BUT ONCE YOU DID...

THE VEIL WAS LIKE NOTHING ANY OF THEM HAD EVER SEEN.

NOT AN *ATMOSPHERE*, SO MUCH AS AN *IMMUNE SYSTEM*.

NNNARRRGH!

THE NIHIL WERE *FOREIGN BODIES*.

ALIEN.

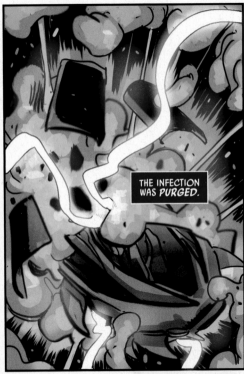

THE INFECTION WAS *PURGED*.

THE GREAT CLOUDSHIP FLEW PAST THE SMALLER NIHIL VESSELS. THE STRIKESHIP PILOTS CALLED OUT FOR AID.

AIIIEEE!

THE SHE'AR HEARD THEM SCREAMING AS THEY DIED.

...OH, WHAT RICHES. WHAT TREASURE.

AND ALL OF IT...

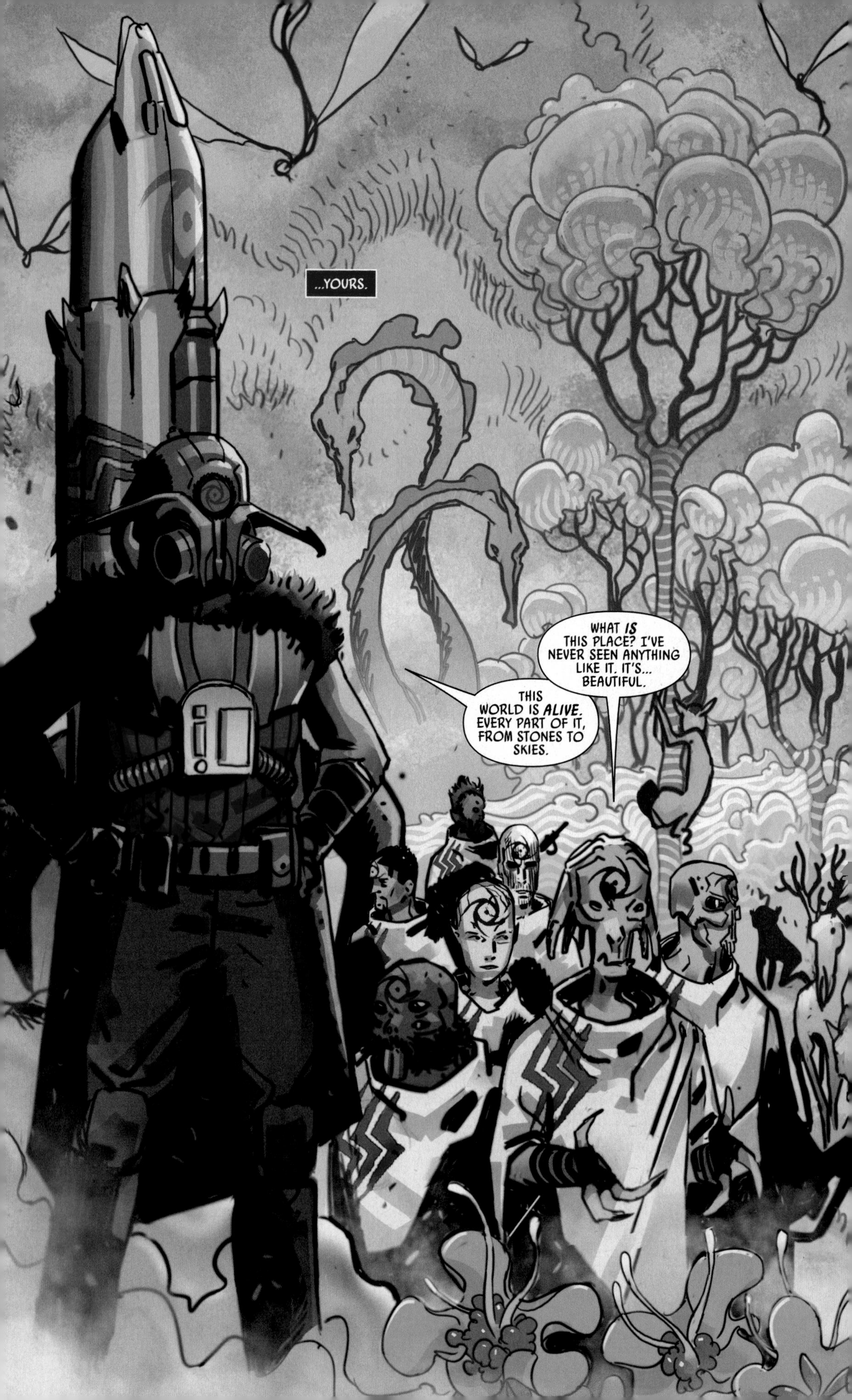
...YOURS.
WHAT IS THIS PLACE? I'VE NEVER SEEN ANYTHING LIKE IT. IT'S... BEAUTIFUL.
THIS WORLD IS ALIVE. EVERY PART OF IT, FROM STONES TO SKIES.

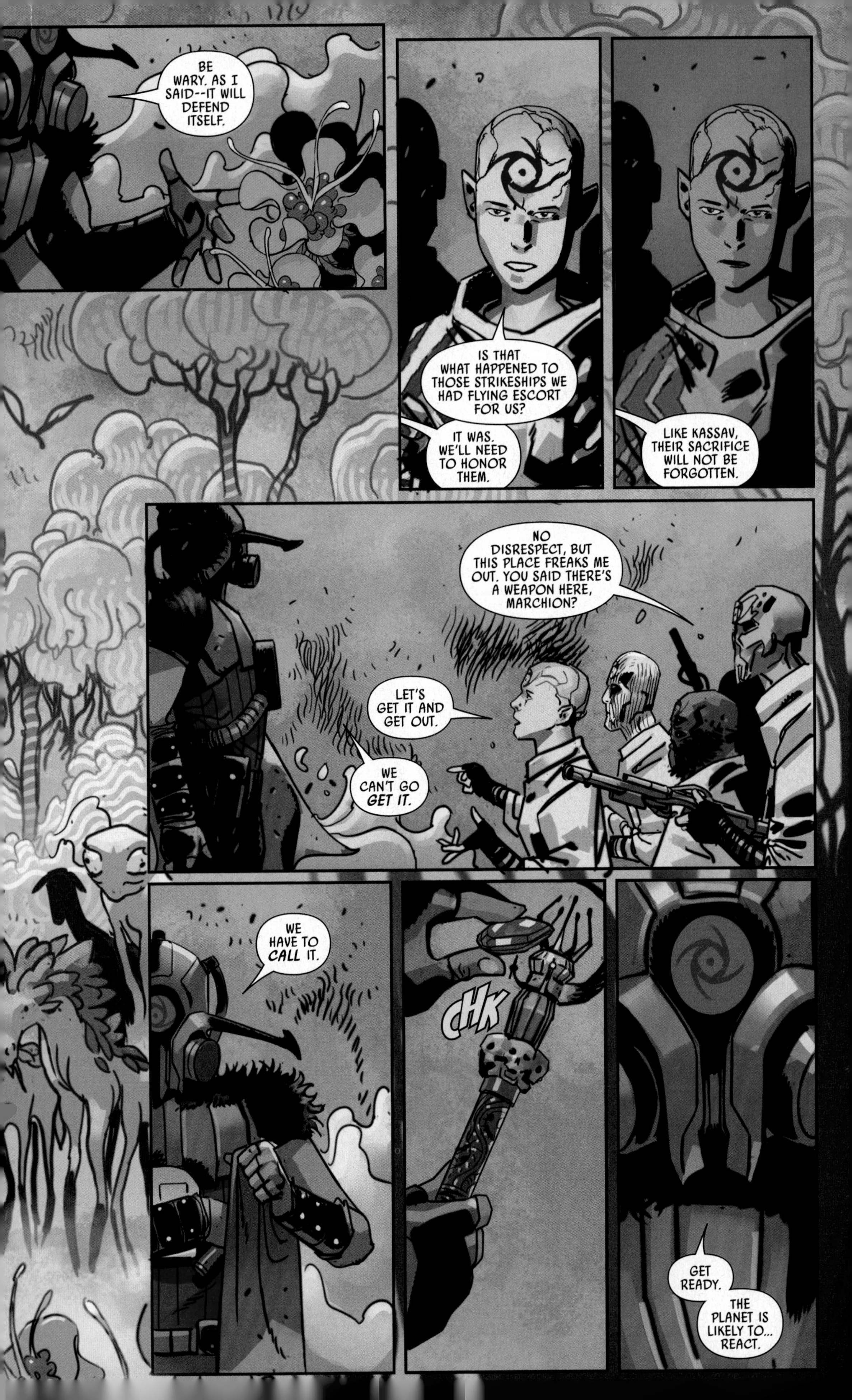
BE WARY. AS I SAID--IT WILL DEFEND ITSELF.
IS THAT WHAT HAPPENED TO THOSE STRIKESHIPS WE HAD FLYING ESCORT FOR US?
IT WAS. WE'LL NEED TO HONOR THEM.
LIKE KASSAV, THEIR SACRIFICE WILL NOT BE FORGOTTEN.
NO DISRESPECT, BUT THIS PLACE FREAKS ME OUT. YOU SAID THERE'S A WEAPON HERE, MARCHION?
LET'S GET IT AND GET OUT.
WE CAN'T GO GET IT.
WE HAVE TO CALL IT.
CHK
GET READY.
THE PLANET IS LIKELY TO... REACT.

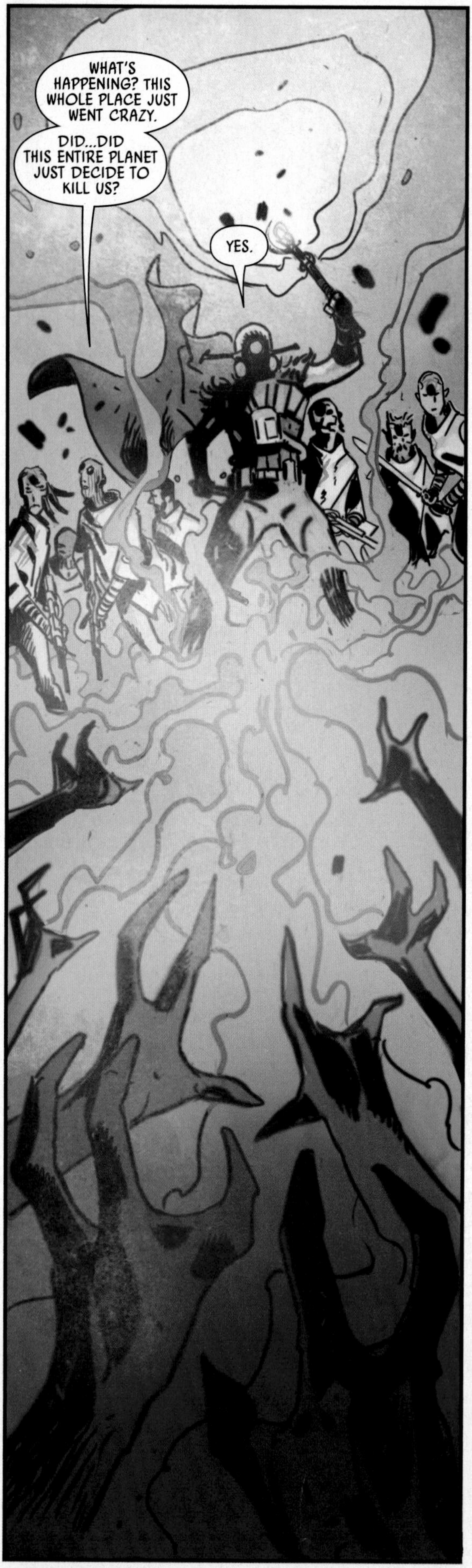
WHAT'S HAPPENING? THIS WHOLE PLACE JUST WENT CRAZY.
DID...DID THIS ENTIRE PLANET JUST DECIDE TO KILL US?
YES.

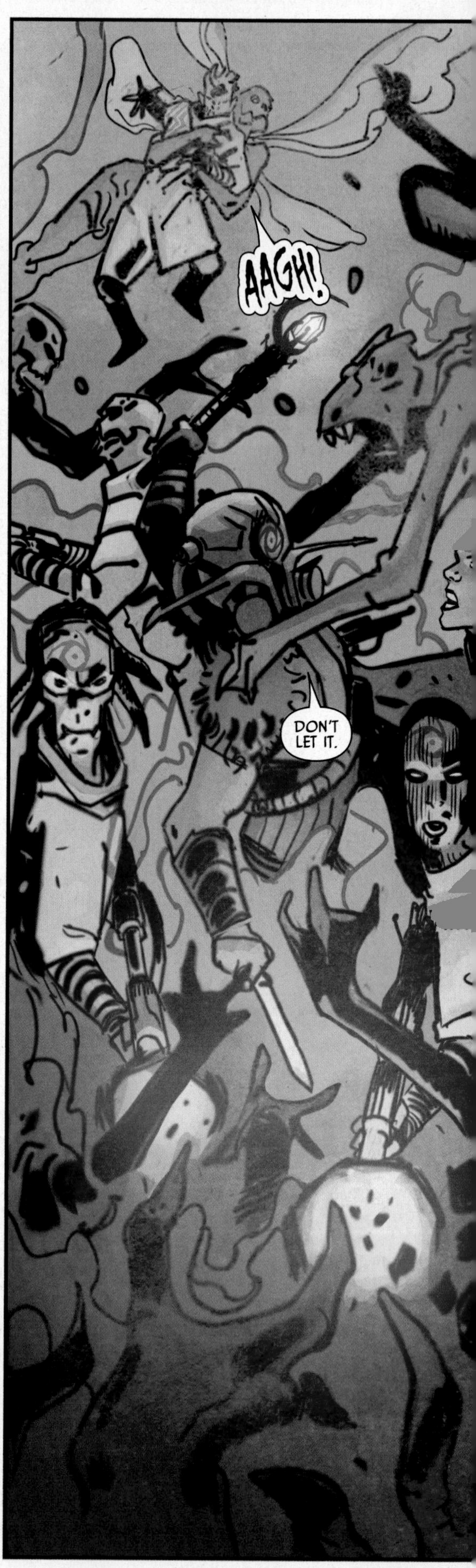
AAGH!
DON'T LET IT.

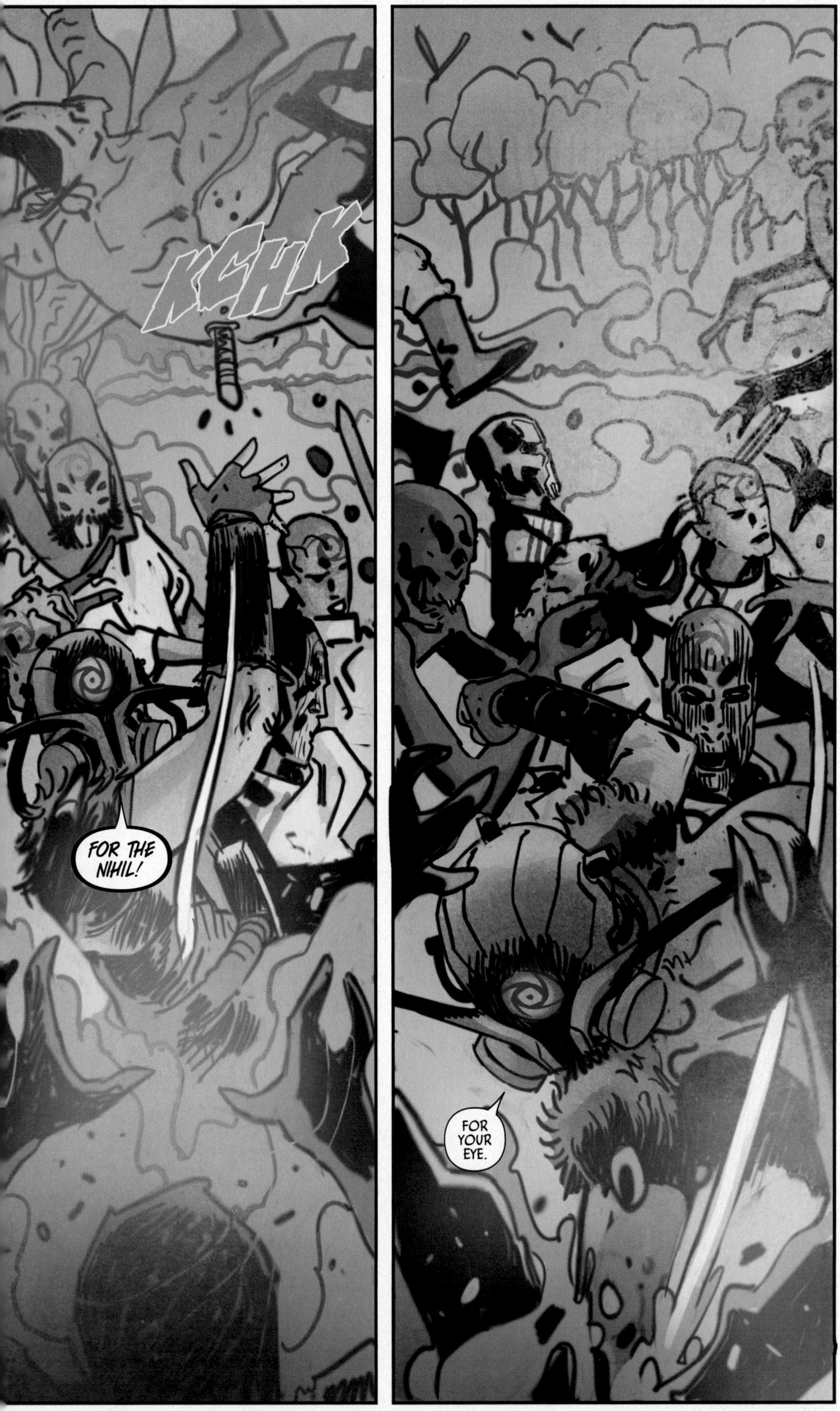
KCHK
FOR THE NIHIL!
FOR YOUR EYE.

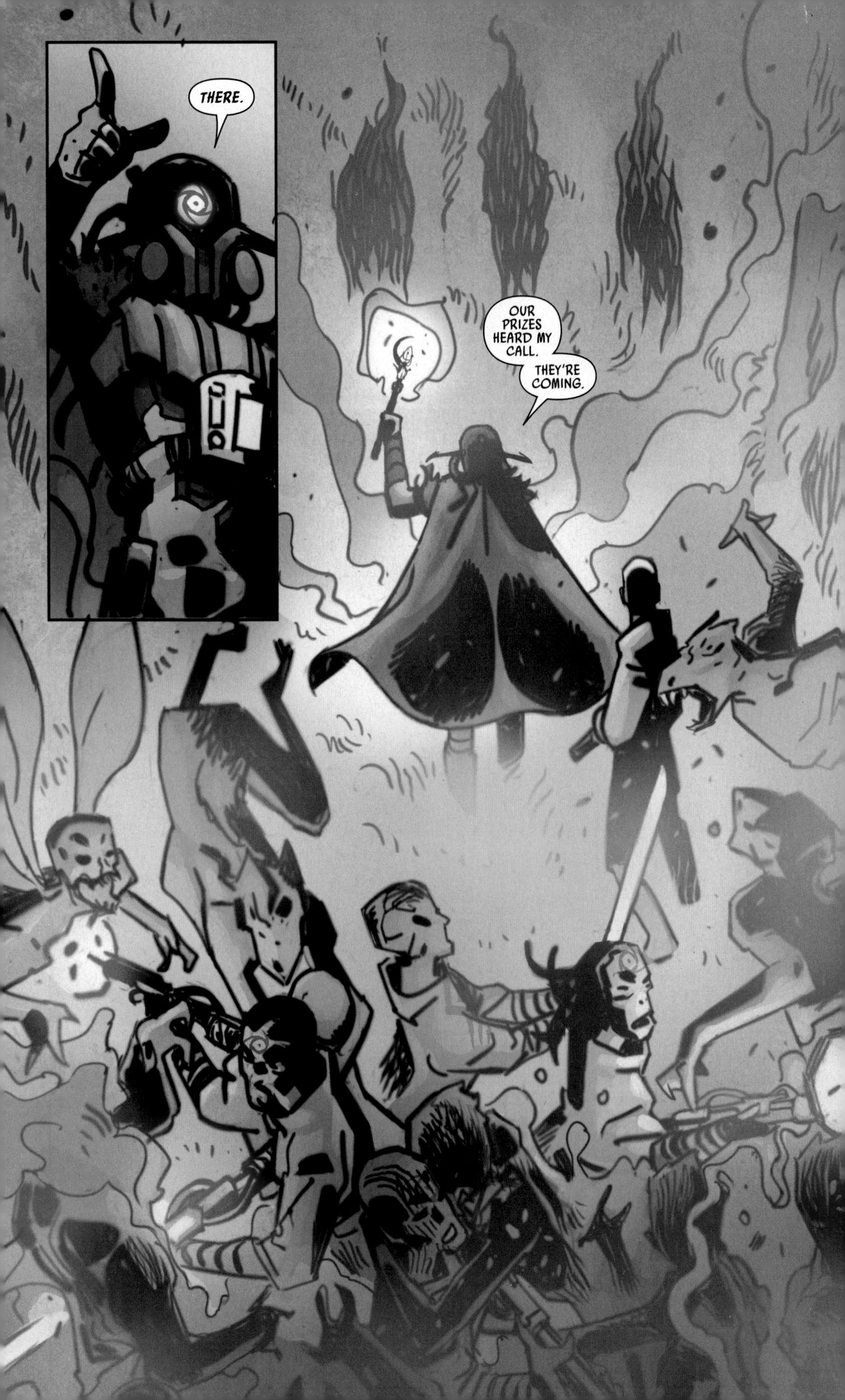
THERE.
OUR PRIZES HEARD MY CALL.
THEY'RE COMING.

WHAT DO WE DO? ARE WE SUPPOSED TO KILL THESE THINGS TOO?

NO.

THEY ARE PRECIOUS TO ME.

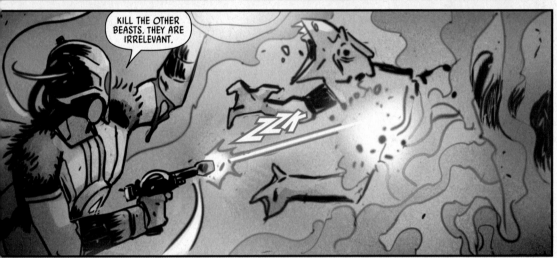

KILL THE OTHER BEASTS. THEY ARE IRRELEVANT.

ZZK

BUT THESE... FOR OUR PURPOSES...

...THEY ARE THE MOST VALUABLE CREATURES IN THE GALAXY.

GET THE RESTRAINTS.

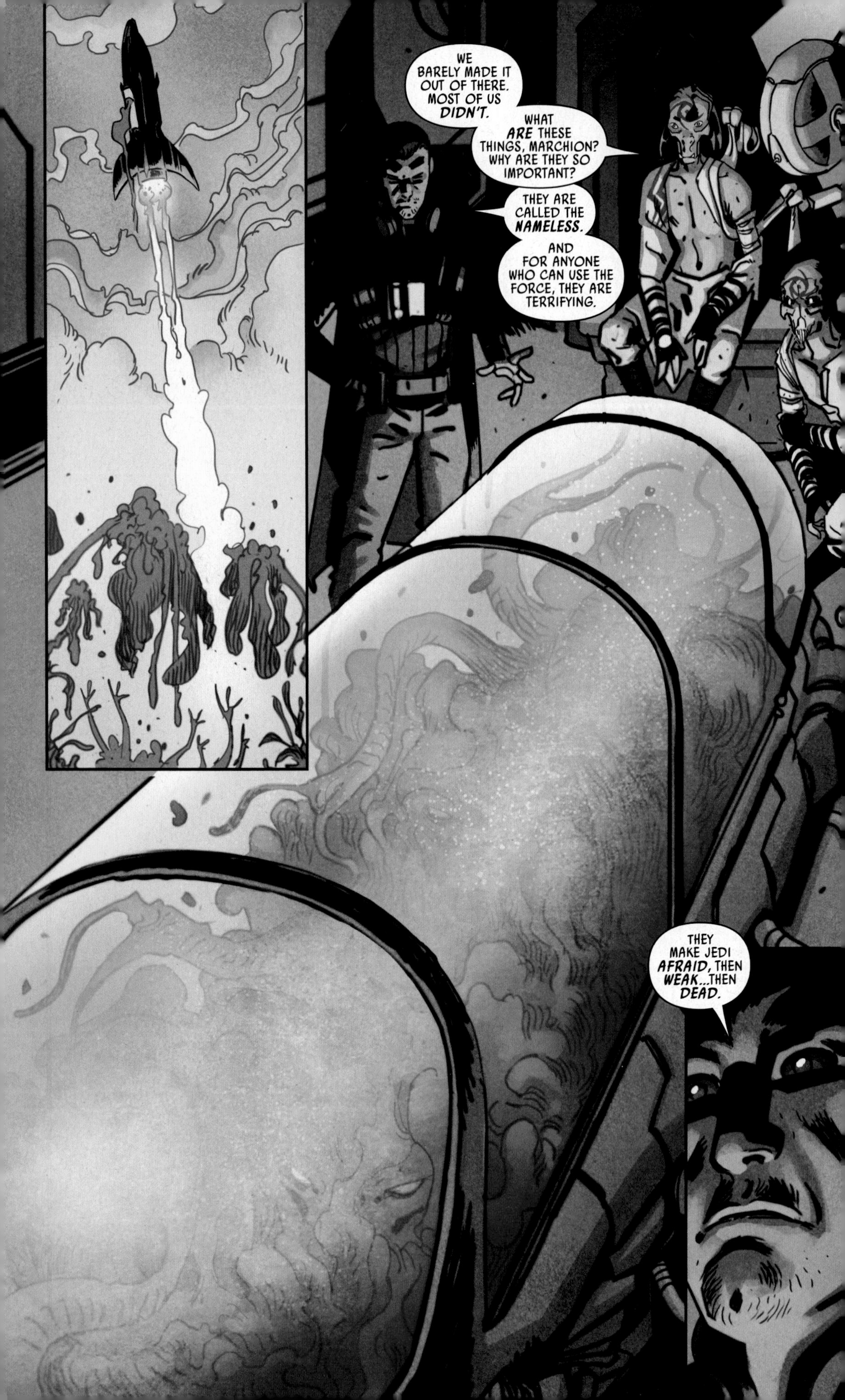
WE BARELY MADE IT OUT OF THERE. MOST OF US *DIDN'T.*
WHAT *ARE* THESE THINGS, MARCHION? WHY ARE THEY SO IMPORTANT?
THEY ARE CALLED THE *NAMELESS.*
AND FOR ANYONE WHO CAN USE THE FORCE, THEY ARE TERRIFYING.
THEY MAKE JEDI *AFRAID,* THEN *WEAK*...THEN *DEAD.*

I WILL USE THE NAMELESS TO KILL JEDI.

MANY JEDI.

"THE ONES WHO ARE LEFT WON'T BE ABLE TO ACT, BECAUSE THEY DON'T KNOW HOW TO FIGHT THESE THINGS.

"THE JEDI RELY ON THE FORCE TO WIN THEIR BATTLES--BUT THAT IS WHAT MAKES THEM WEAK AGAINST THE NAMELESS."

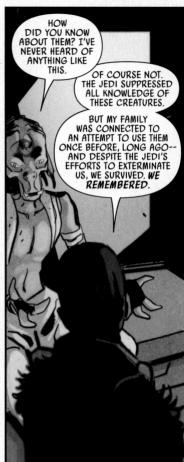

HOW DID YOU KNOW ABOUT THEM? I'VE NEVER HEARD OF ANYTHING LIKE THIS.

OF COURSE NOT. THE JEDI SUPPRESSED ALL KNOWLEDGE OF THESE CREATURES.

BUT MY FAMILY WAS CONNECTED TO AN ATTEMPT TO USE THEM ONCE BEFORE, LONG AGO-- AND DESPITE THE JEDI'S EFFORTS TO EXTERMINATE US, WE SURVIVED. *WE REMEMBERED.*

THE JEDI ARE *DONE.* THEY DON'T KNOW THAT YET.

BUT SOON, THE REALITY OF THEIR SITUATION WILL BE PRESENTED TO THEM IN THE CLEAREST POSSIBLE TERMS.

AND... THEN WHAT?

AND *THEN WHAT?*

YOU PICKED US TO FIGHT FOR YOU, GAVE US A NAME. A LOT OF US JUST DIED FOR YOU. MAYBE THAT WAS THE IDEA ALL ALONG.

THAT'S FINE. THAT'S THE GAME. THAT'S THE NIHIL. YOU'VE GOT MY LOYALTY, MARCHION RO.

BUT IT WOULD BE NICE TO THINK THERE'S A PLAN TO ALL OF THIS. NOT JUST... *ESCALATION.*

TRYING TO DESTROY THE JEDI, BRING DOWN THE REPUBLIC...

...THE NIHIL STARTED OUT AS RAIDERS. WHY ARE WE GOING *SO HARD?*

WHY ARE WE *DOING* ALL OF THIS?

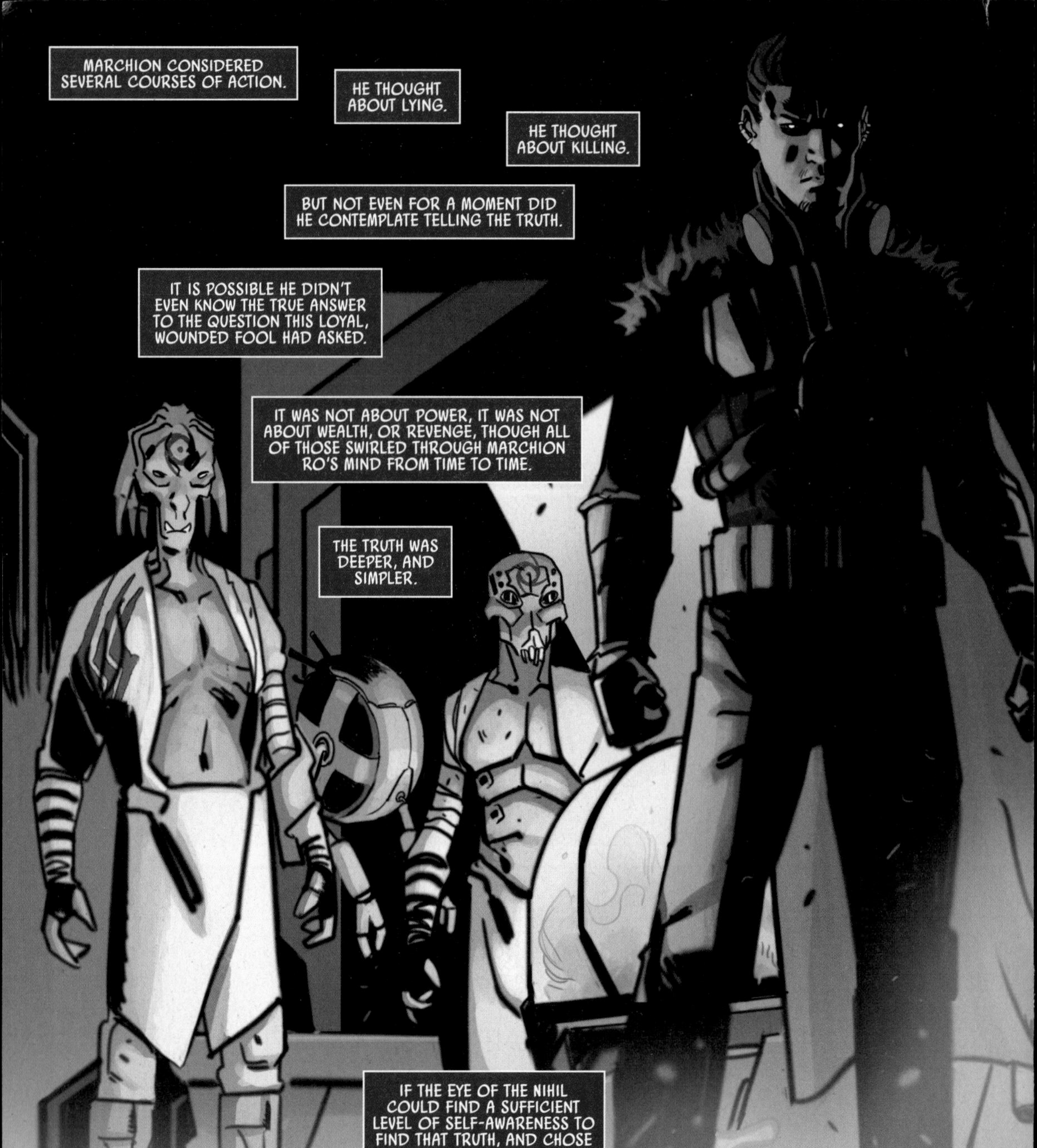
MARCHION CONSIDERED SEVERAL COURSES OF ACTION.
HE THOUGHT ABOUT LYING.
HE THOUGHT ABOUT KILLING.
BUT NOT EVEN FOR A MOMENT DID HE CONTEMPLATE TELLING THE TRUTH.
IT IS POSSIBLE HE DIDN'T EVEN KNOW THE TRUE ANSWER TO THE QUESTION THIS LOYAL, WOUNDED FOOL HAD ASKED.
IT WAS NOT ABOUT POWER, IT WAS NOT ABOUT WEALTH, OR REVENGE, THOUGH ALL OF THOSE SWIRLED THROUGH MARCHION RO'S MIND FROM TIME TO TIME.
THE TRUTH WAS DEEPER, AND SIMPLER.
IF THE EYE OF THE NIHIL COULD FIND A SUFFICIENT LEVEL OF SELF-AWARENESS TO FIND THAT TRUTH, AND CHOSE TO RESPOND HONESTLY, THIS IS WHAT HE WOULD SAY...
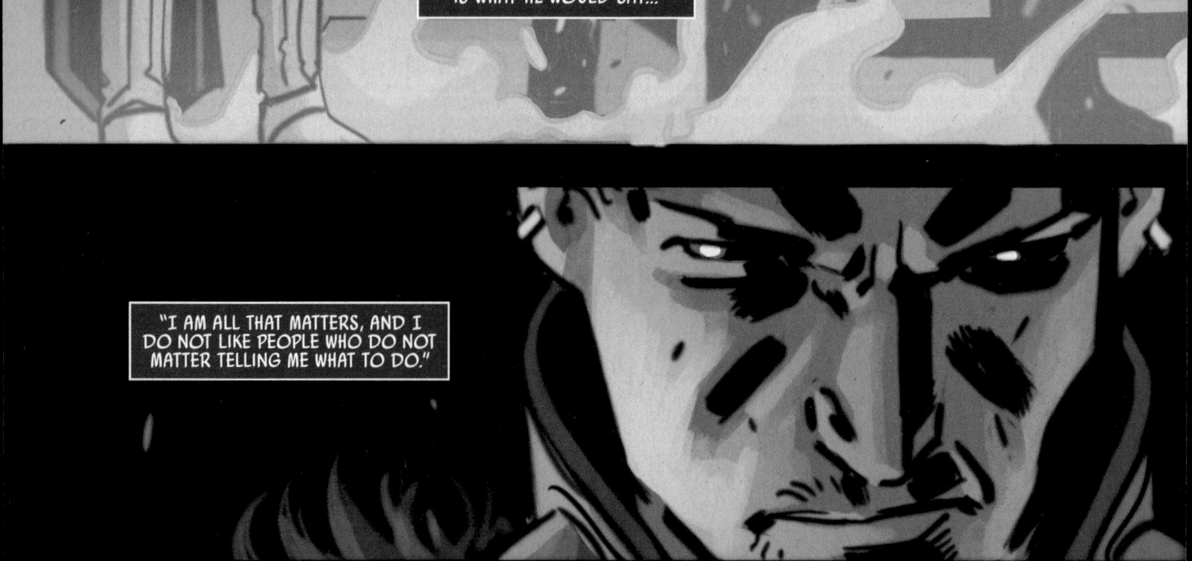
"I AM ALL THAT MATTERS, AND I DO NOT LIKE PEOPLE WHO DO NOT MATTER TELLING ME WHAT TO DO."

SCENE III

THE TRIUMPH

In which No One
Tells Marchion Ro
What to Do.

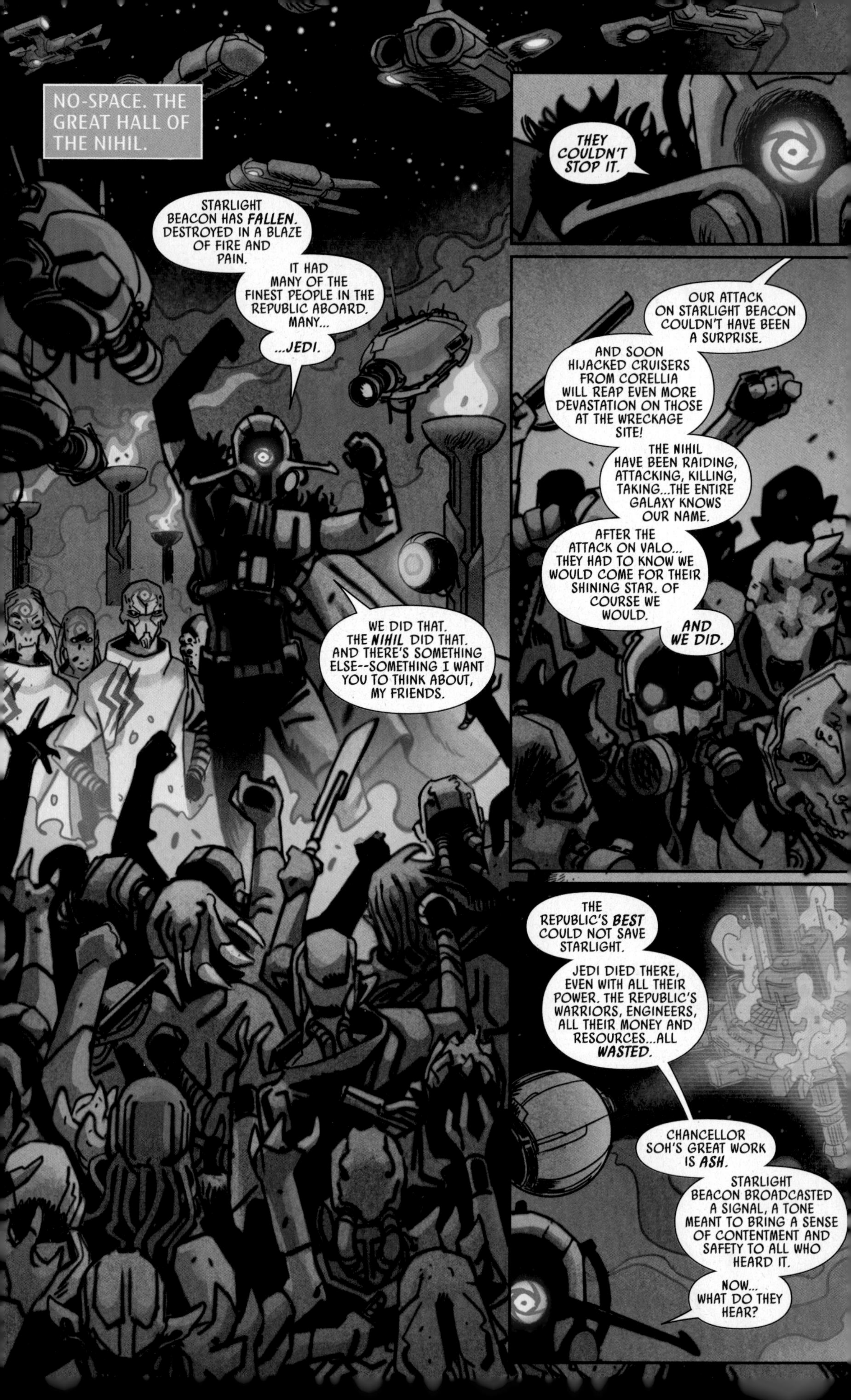
NO-SPACE. THE GREAT HALL OF THE NIHIL.
STARLIGHT BEACON HAS FALLEN. DESTROYED IN A BLAZE OF FIRE AND PAIN.
IT HAD MANY OF THE FINEST PEOPLE IN THE REPUBLIC ABOARD. MANY...
...JEDI.
WE DID THAT. THE NIHIL DID THAT. AND THERE'S SOMETHING ELSE--SOMETHING I WANT YOU TO THINK ABOUT, MY FRIENDS.
THEY COULDN'T STOP IT.
OUR ATTACK ON STARLIGHT BEACON COULDN'T HAVE BEEN A SURPRISE.
AND SOON HIJACKED CRUISERS FROM CORELLIA WILL REAP EVEN MORE DEVASTATION ON THOSE AT THE WRECKAGE SITE!
THE NIHIL HAVE BEEN RAIDING, ATTACKING, KILLING, TAKING...THE ENTIRE GALAXY KNOWS OUR NAME.
AFTER THE ATTACK ON VALO... THEY HAD TO KNOW WE WOULD COME FOR THEIR SHINING STAR. OF COURSE WE WOULD.
AND WE DID.
THE REPUBLIC'S BEST COULD NOT SAVE STARLIGHT.
JEDI DIED THERE, EVEN WITH ALL THEIR POWER. THE REPUBLIC'S WARRIORS, ENGINEERS, ALL THEIR MONEY AND RESOURCES...ALL WASTED.
CHANCELLOR SOH'S GREAT WORK IS ASH.
STARLIGHT BEACON BROADCASTED A SIGNAL, A TONE MEANT TO BRING A SENSE OF CONTENTMENT AND SAFETY TO ALL WHO HEARD IT.
NOW... WHAT DO THEY HEAR?

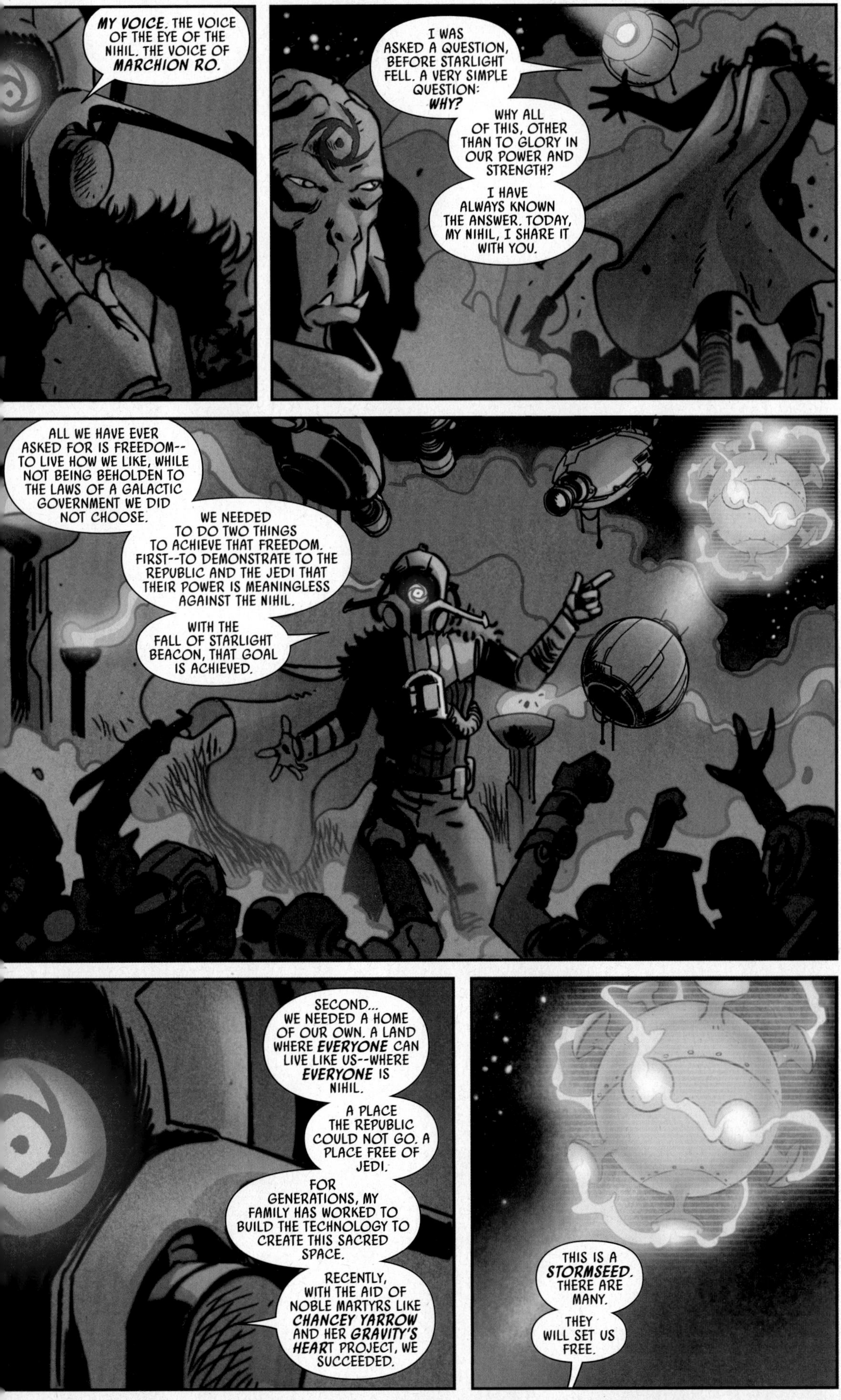
MY VOICE. THE VOICE OF THE EYE OF THE NIHIL. THE VOICE OF MARCHION RO.
I WAS ASKED A QUESTION, BEFORE STARLIGHT FELL. A VERY SIMPLE QUESTION: WHY?
WHY ALL OF THIS, OTHER THAN TO GLORY IN OUR POWER AND STRENGTH?
I HAVE ALWAYS KNOWN THE ANSWER. TODAY, MY NIHIL, I SHARE IT WITH YOU.
ALL WE HAVE EVER ASKED FOR IS FREEDOM--TO LIVE HOW WE LIKE, WHILE NOT BEING BEHOLDEN TO THE LAWS OF A GALACTIC GOVERNMENT WE DID NOT CHOOSE.
WE NEEDED TO DO TWO THINGS TO ACHIEVE THAT FREEDOM. FIRST--TO DEMONSTRATE TO THE REPUBLIC AND THE JEDI THAT THEIR POWER IS MEANINGLESS AGAINST THE NIHIL.
WITH THE FALL OF STARLIGHT BEACON, THAT GOAL IS ACHIEVED.
SECOND... WE NEEDED A HOME OF OUR OWN. A LAND WHERE EVERYONE CAN LIVE LIKE US--WHERE EVERYONE IS NIHIL.
A PLACE THE REPUBLIC COULD NOT GO. A PLACE FREE OF JEDI.
FOR GENERATIONS, MY FAMILY HAS WORKED TO BUILD THE TECHNOLOGY TO CREATE THIS SACRED SPACE.
RECENTLY, WITH THE AID OF NOBLE MARTYRS LIKE CHANCEY YARROW AND HER GRAVITY'S HEART PROJECT, WE SUCCEEDED.
THIS IS A STORMSEED. THERE ARE MANY.
THEY WILL SET US FREE.

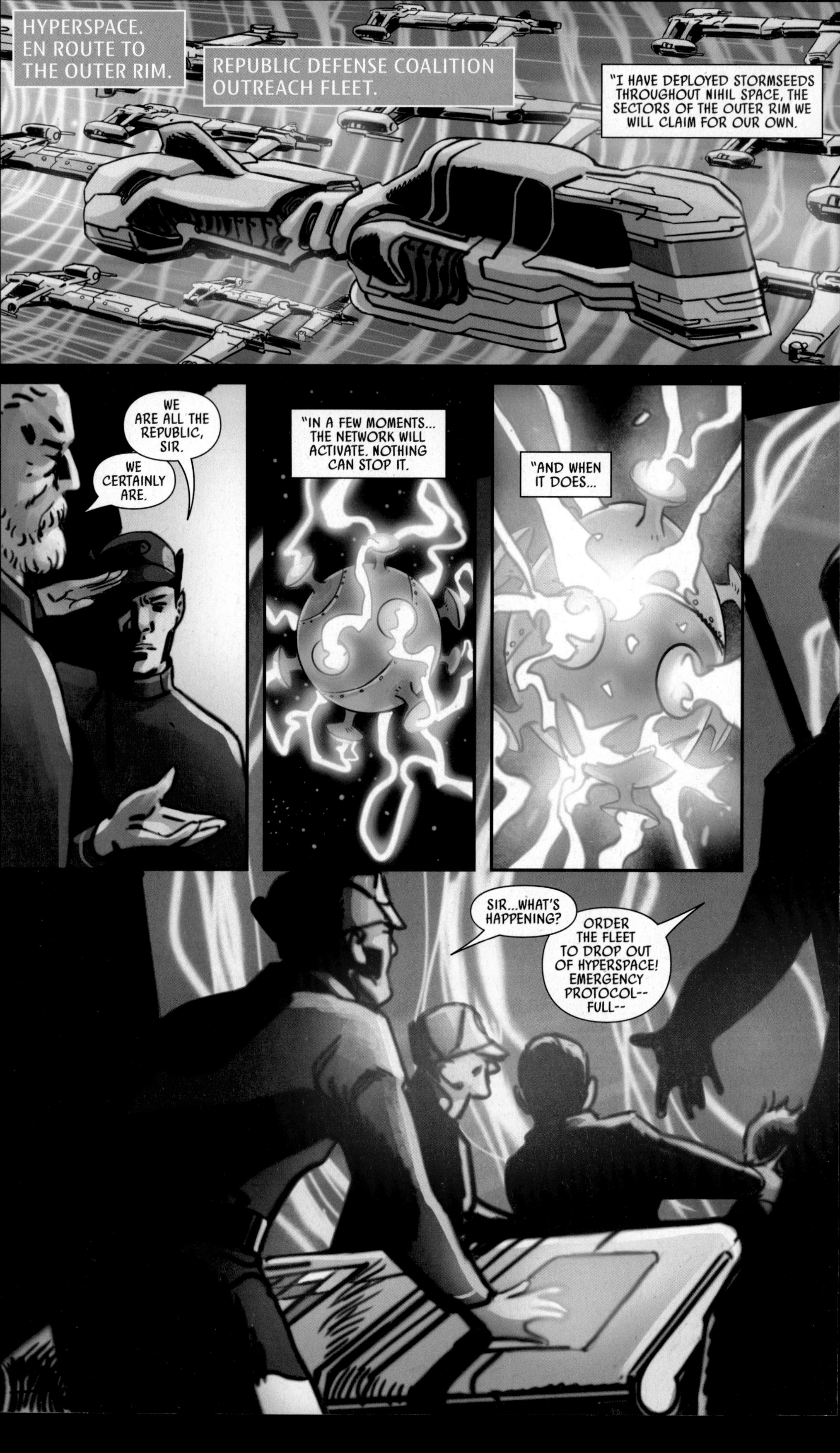
HYPERSPACE. EN ROUTE TO THE OUTER RIM.
REPUBLIC DEFENSE COALITION OUTREACH FLEET.
"I HAVE DEPLOYED STORMSEEDS THROUGHOUT NIHIL SPACE, THE SECTORS OF THE OUTER RIM WE WILL CLAIM FOR OUR OWN.
WE ARE ALL THE REPUBLIC, SIR.
WE CERTAINLY ARE.
"IN A FEW MOMENTS... THE NETWORK WILL ACTIVATE. NOTHING CAN STOP IT.
"AND WHEN IT DOES...
SIR...WHAT'S HAPPENING?
ORDER THE FLEET TO DROP OUT OF HYPERSPACE! EMERGENCY PROTOCOL-- FULL--

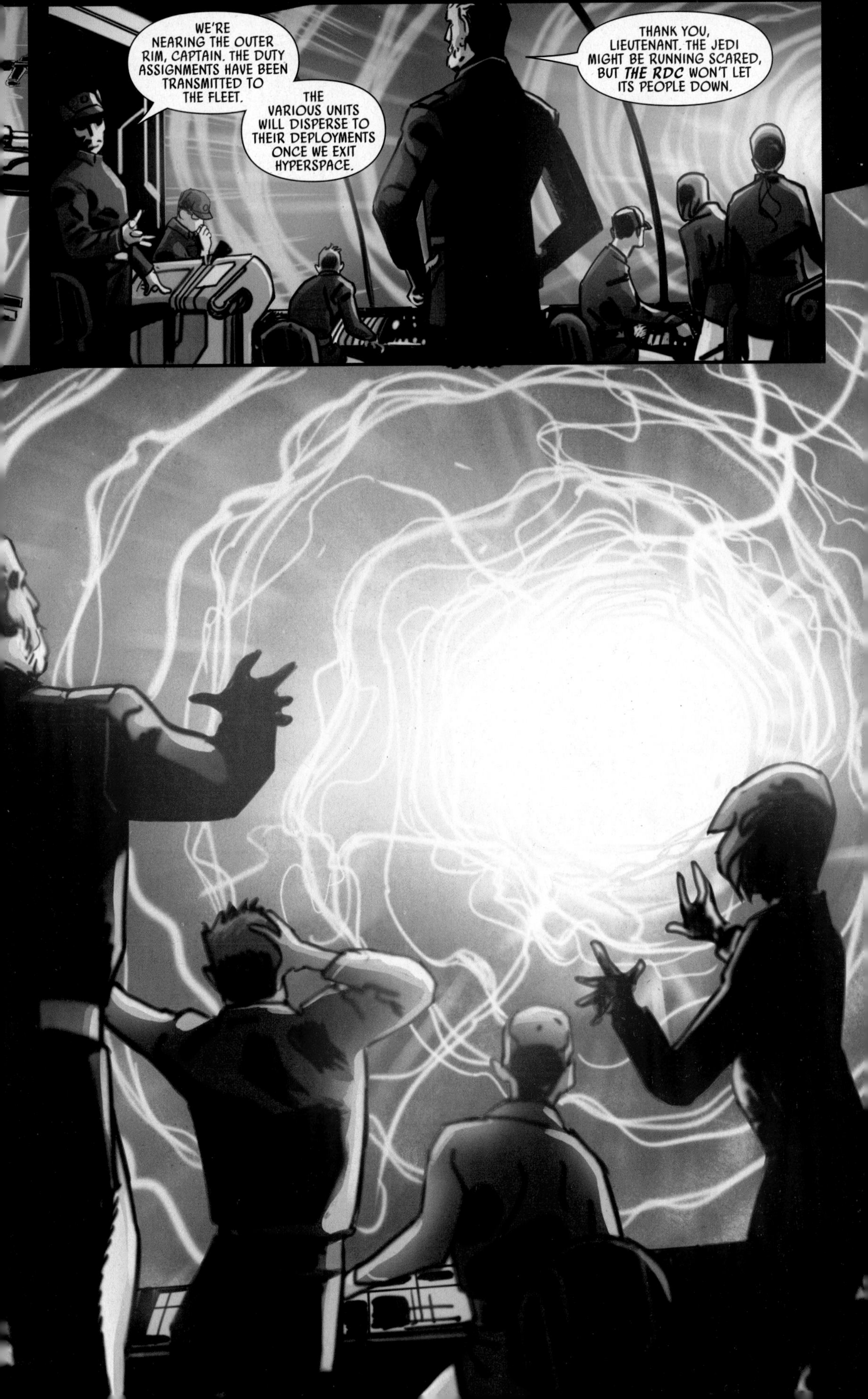
WE'RE NEARING THE OUTER RIM, CAPTAIN. THE DUTY ASSIGNMENTS HAVE BEEN TRANSMITTED TO THE FLEET.
THE VARIOUS UNITS WILL DISPERSE TO THEIR DEPLOYMENTS ONCE WE EXIT HYPERSPACE.
THANK YOU, LIEUTENANT. THE JEDI MIGHT BE RUNNING SCARED, BUT *THE RDC* WON'T LET ITS PEOPLE DOWN.

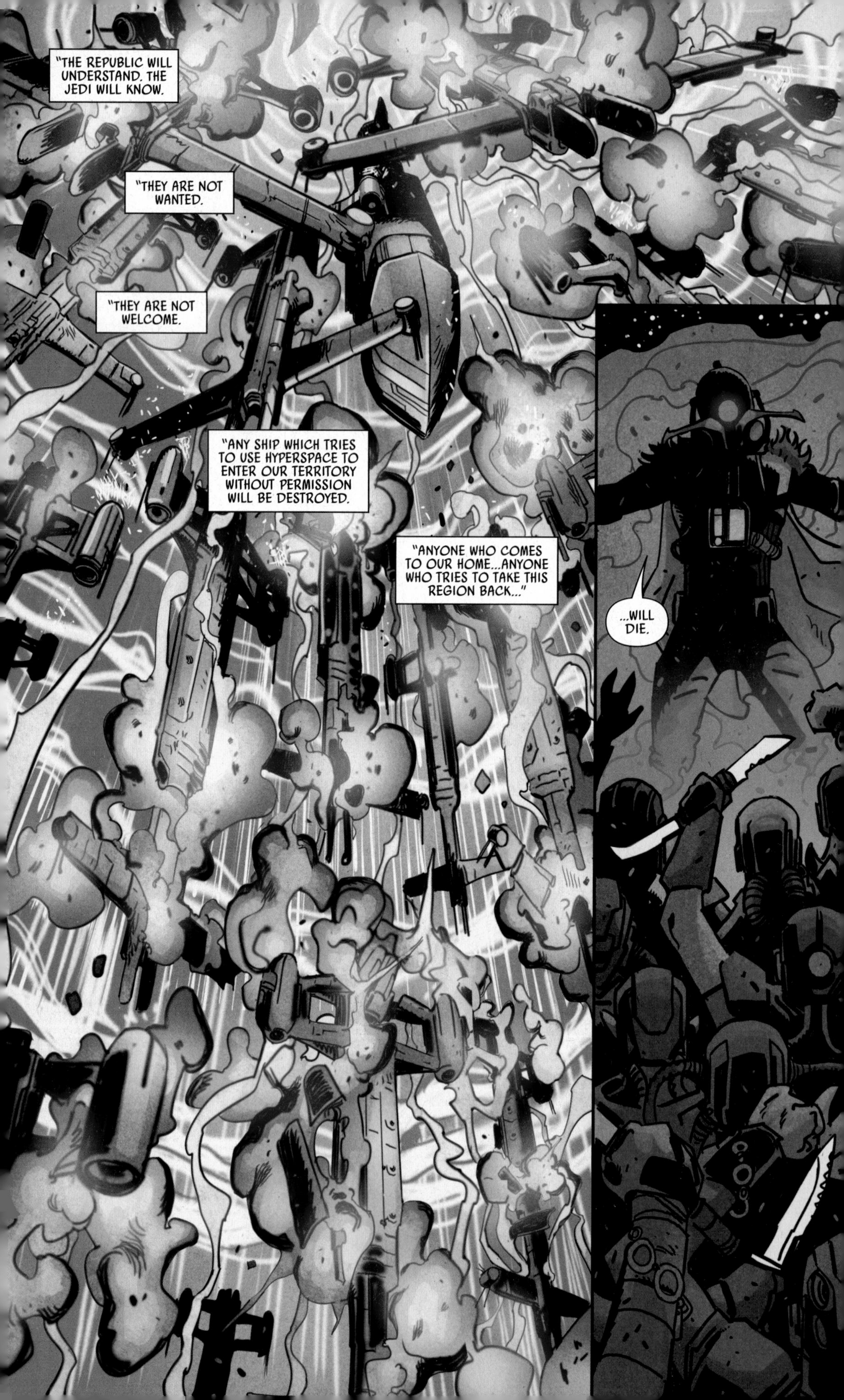
"THE REPUBLIC WILL UNDERSTAND. THE JEDI WILL KNOW.
"THEY ARE NOT WANTED.
"THEY ARE NOT WELCOME.
"ANY SHIP WHICH TRIES TO USE HYPERSPACE TO ENTER OUR TERRITORY WITHOUT PERMISSION WILL BE DESTROYED.
"ANYONE WHO COMES TO OUR HOME...ANYONE WHO TRIES TO TAKE THIS REGION BACK..."
...WILL DIE.

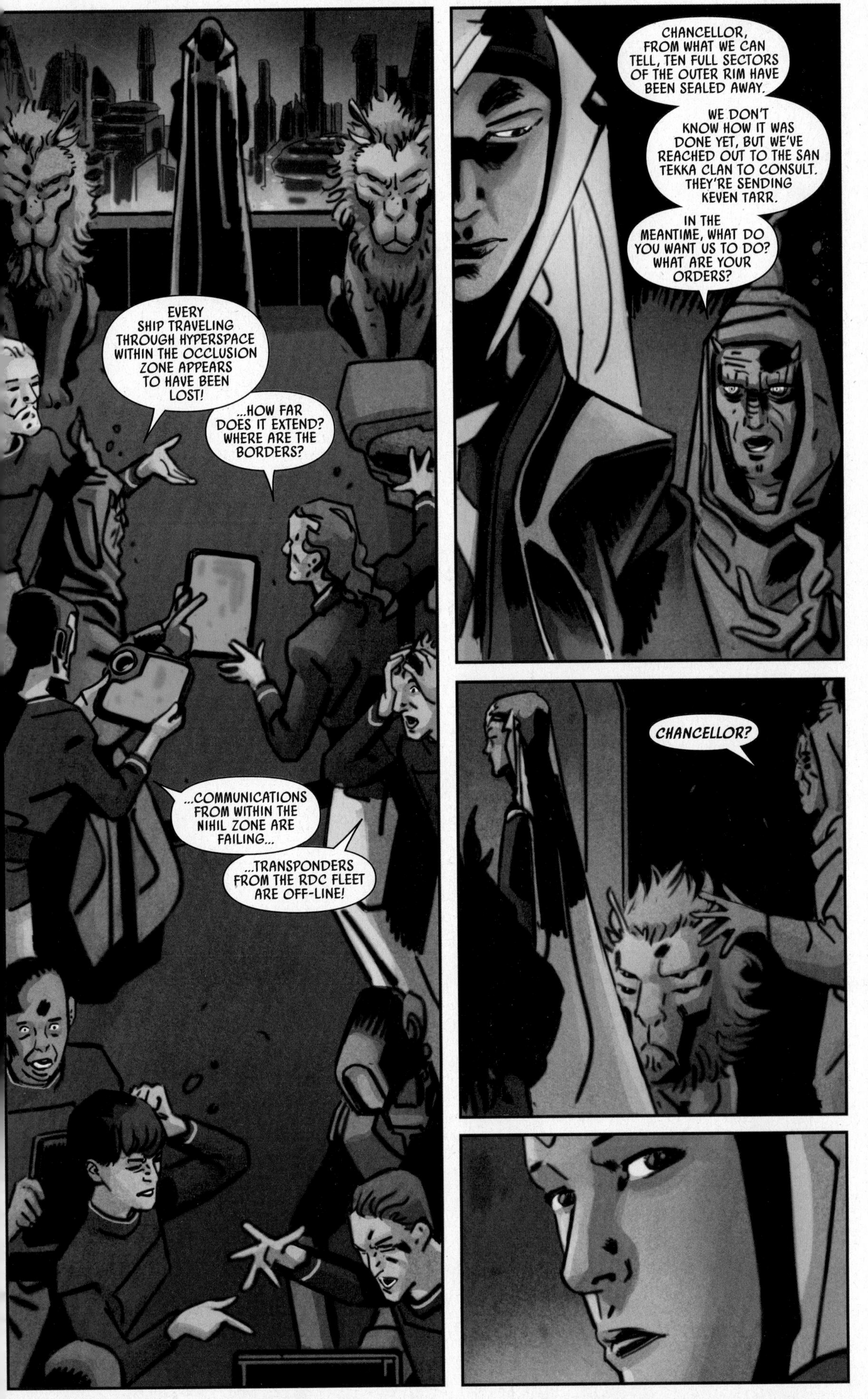
EVERY SHIP TRAVELING THROUGH HYPERSPACE WITHIN THE OCCLUSION ZONE APPEARS TO HAVE BEEN LOST!
...HOW FAR DOES IT EXTEND? WHERE ARE THE BORDERS?
...COMMUNICATIONS FROM WITHIN THE NIHIL ZONE ARE FAILING...
...TRANSPONDERS FROM THE RDC FLEET ARE OFF-LINE!
CHANCELLOR, FROM WHAT WE CAN TELL, TEN FULL SECTORS OF THE OUTER RIM HAVE BEEN SEALED AWAY.
WE DON'T KNOW HOW IT WAS DONE YET, BUT WE'VE REACHED OUT TO THE SAN TEKKA CLAN TO CONSULT. THEY'RE SENDING KEVEN TARR.
IN THE MEANTIME, WHAT DO YOU WANT US TO DO? WHAT ARE YOUR ORDERS?
CHANCELLOR?

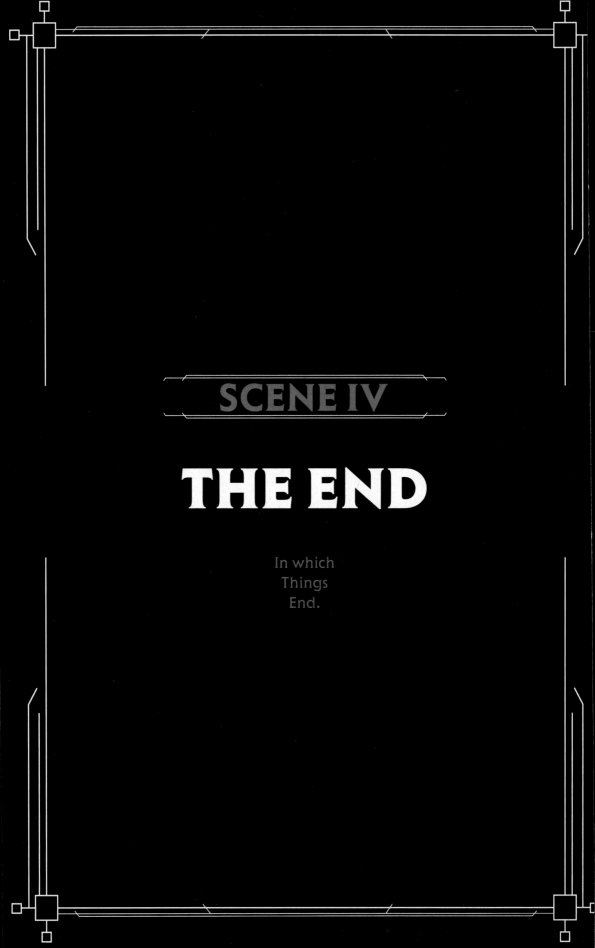

SCENE IV

THE END

In which
Things
End.

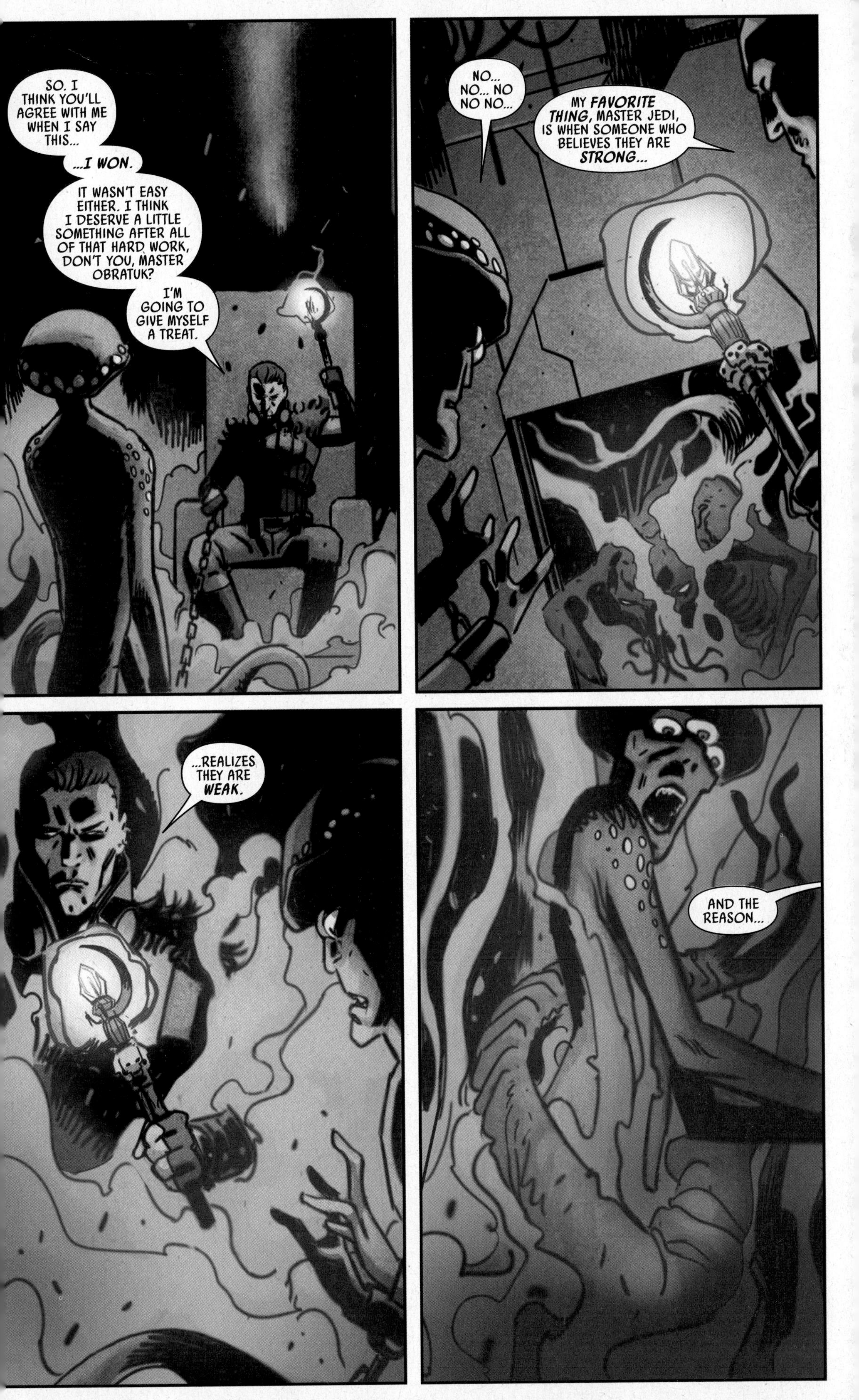
SO. I THINK YOU'LL AGREE WITH ME WHEN I SAY THIS...
...I WON.
IT WASN'T EASY EITHER. I THINK I DESERVE A LITTLE SOMETHING AFTER ALL OF THAT HARD WORK, DON'T YOU, MASTER OBRATUK?
I'M GOING TO GIVE MYSELF A TREAT.
NO... NO... NO NO NO...
MY FAVORITE THING, MASTER JEDI, IS WHEN SOMEONE WHO BELIEVES THEY ARE STRONG...
...REALIZES THEY ARE WEAK.
AND THE REASON...

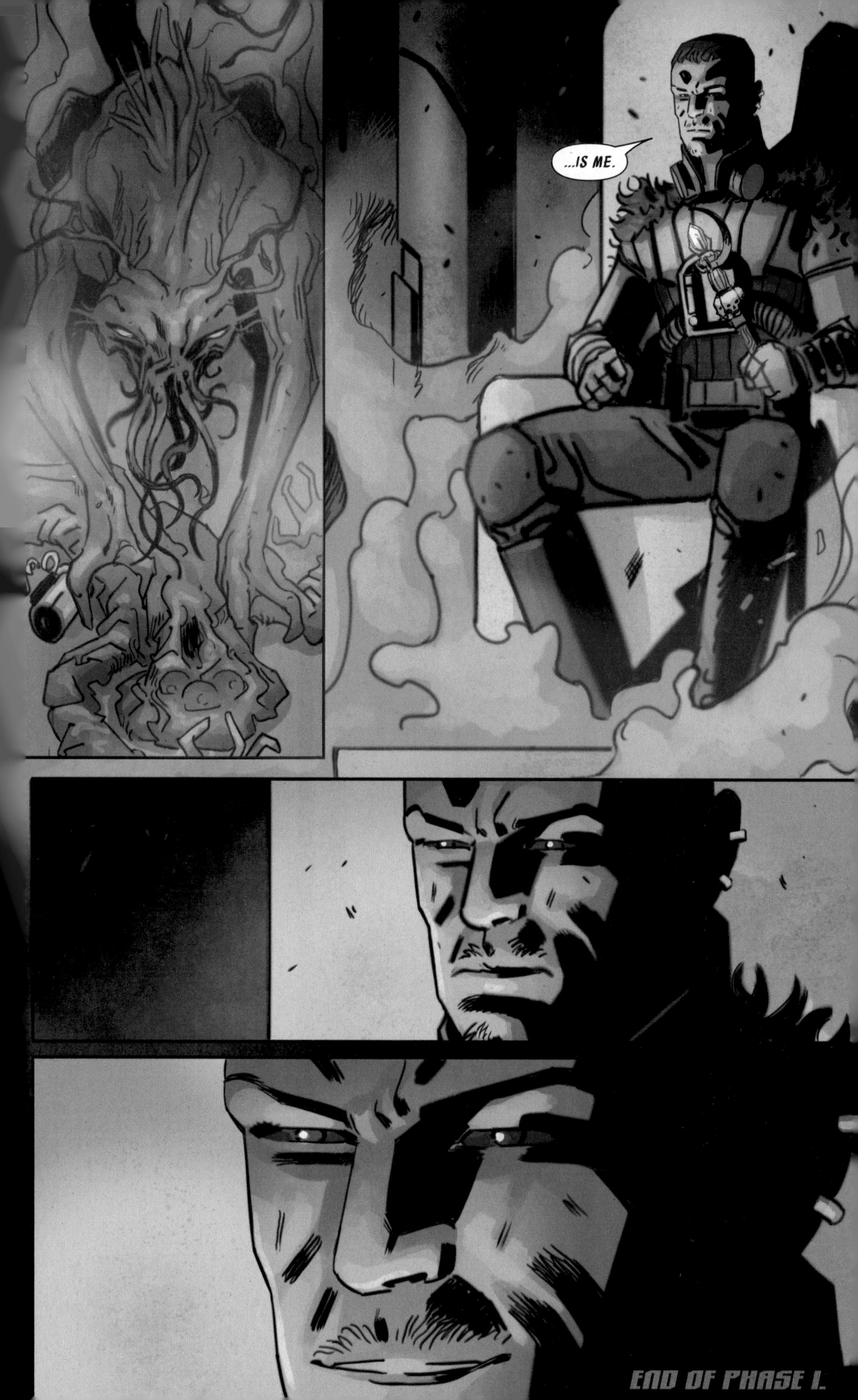
...IS ME.
END OF PHASE I.

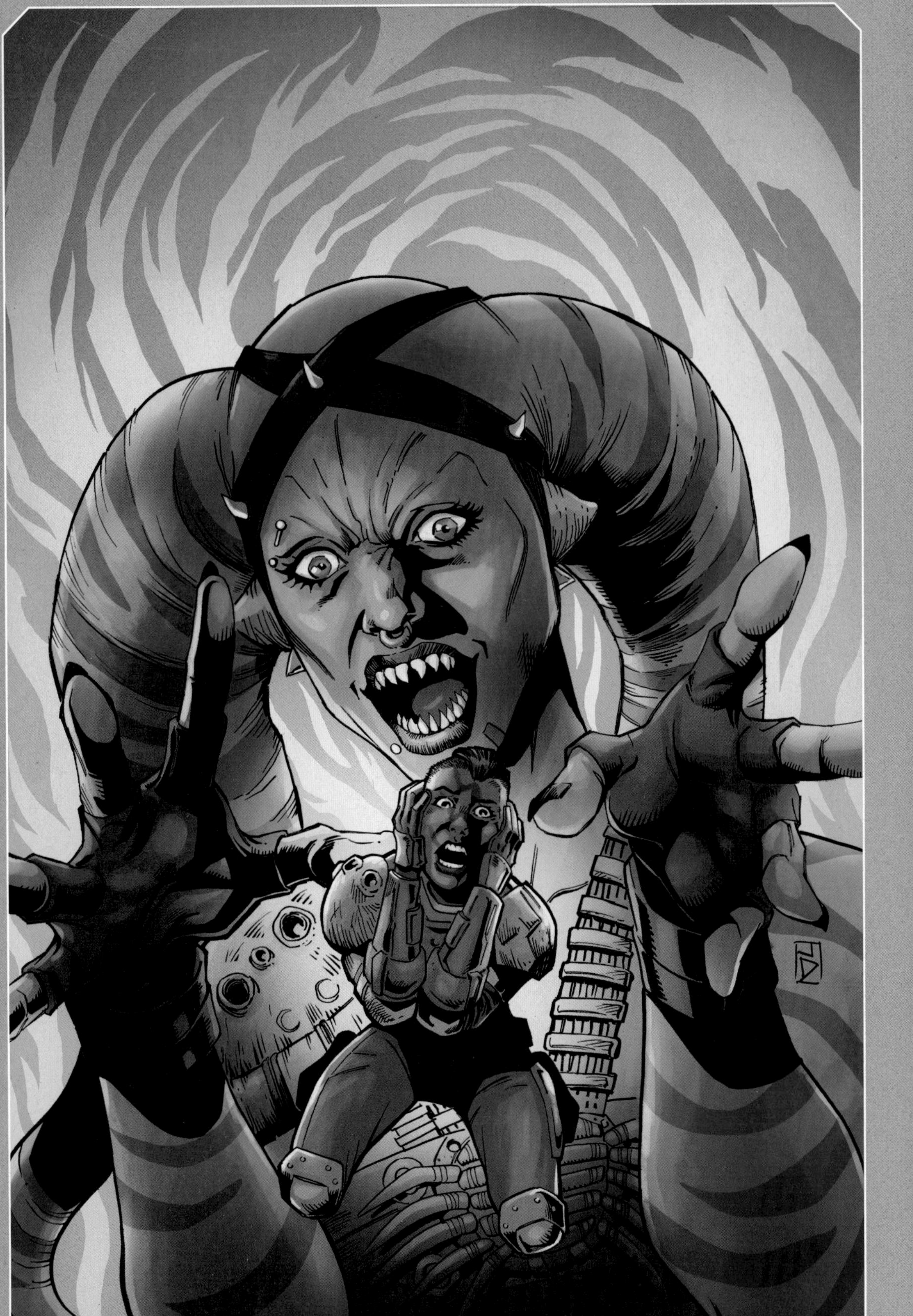

#11 Variant by
JAN DUURSEMA & ANNALISA LEONI

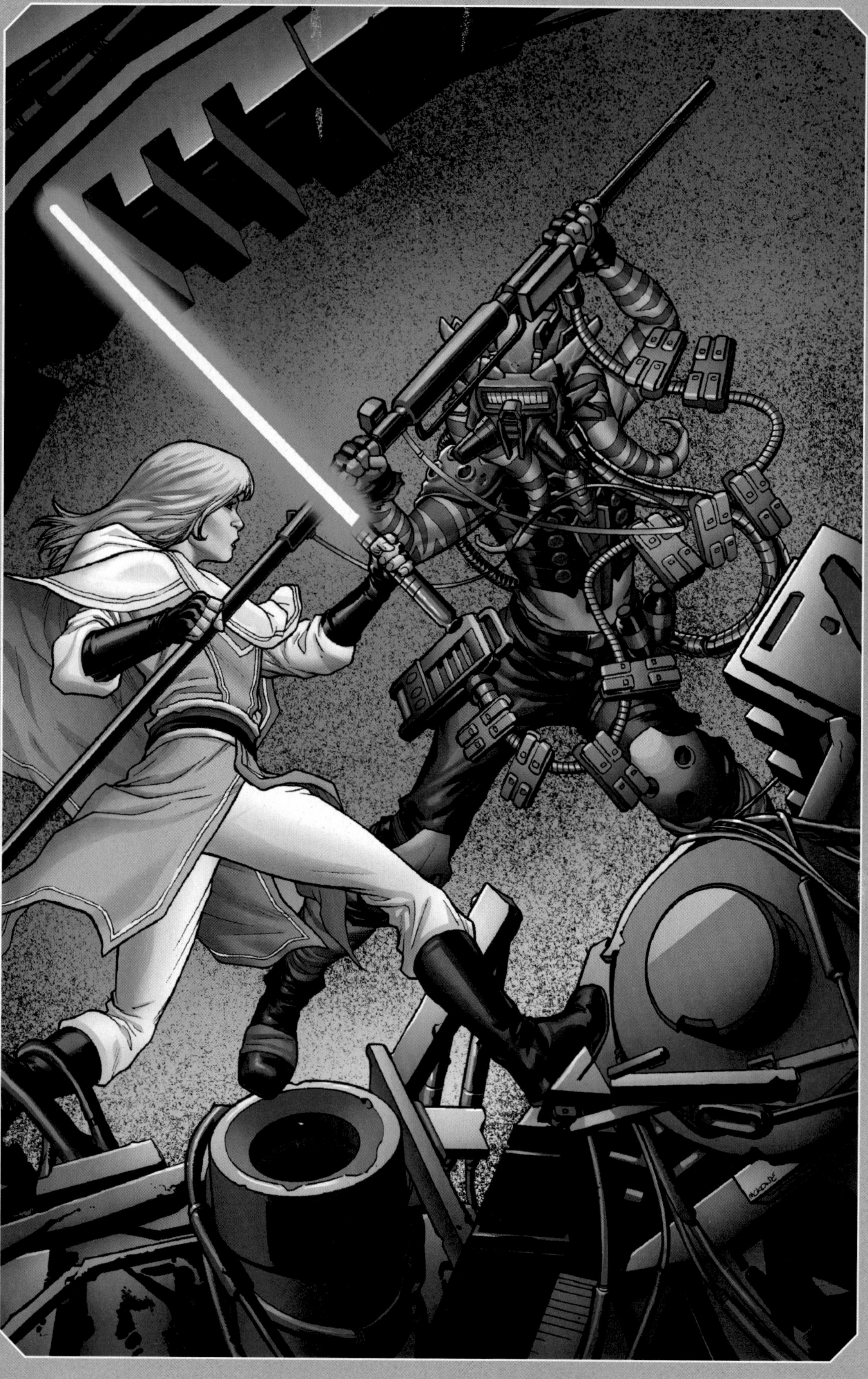

#12 Variant by
MIKE McKONE & GURU-eFX

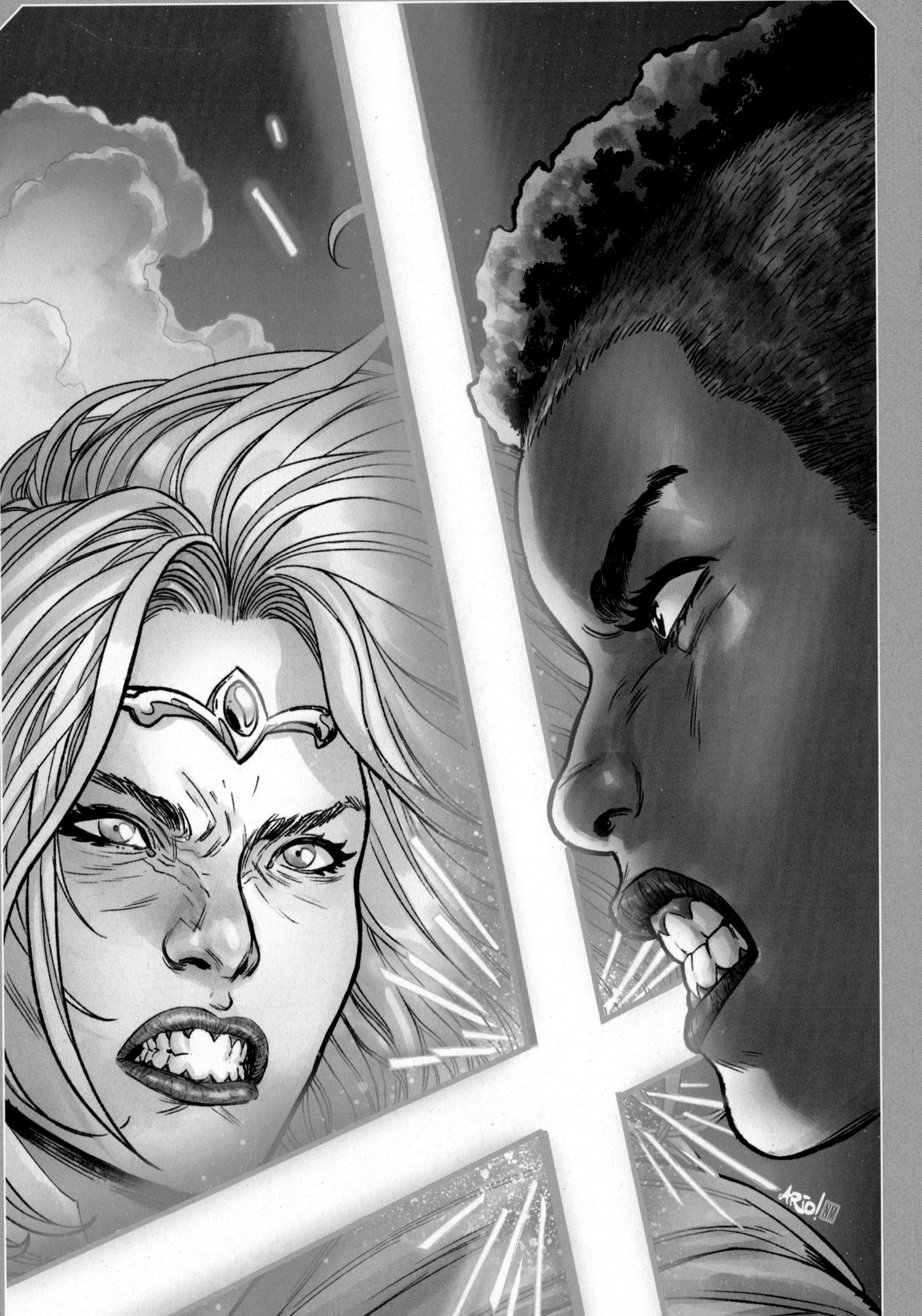

#13 Variant by
ARIO ANINDITO & RACHELLE ROSENBERG

#14 Variant by
MIKE McKONE &
GURU-eFX

#15 Variant by
PASQUAL FERRY &
MATT HOLLINGSWORTH

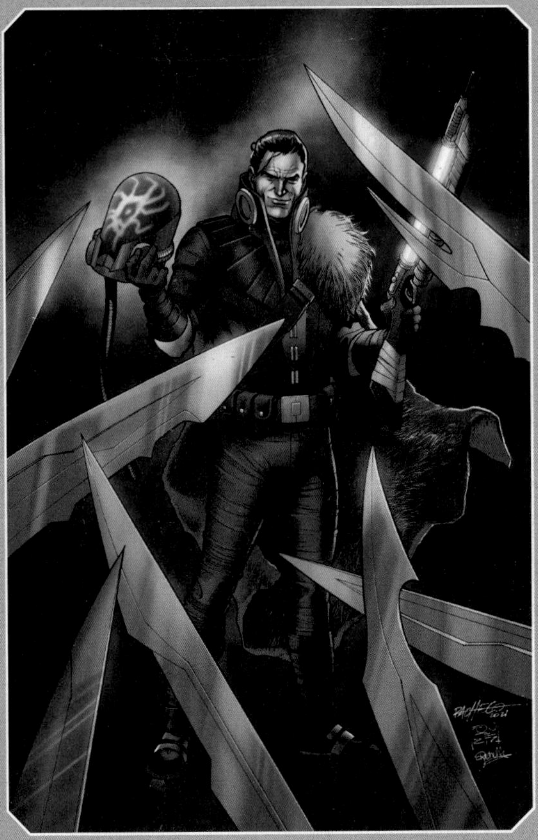

Eye of the Storm #1 Variant by
CARLOS PACHECO

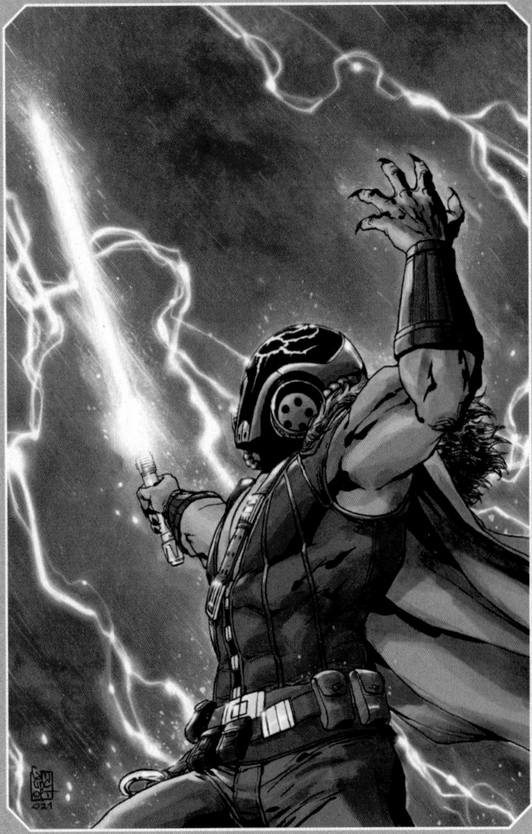

Eye of the Storm #1 Variant by
GIUSEPPE CAMUNCOLI

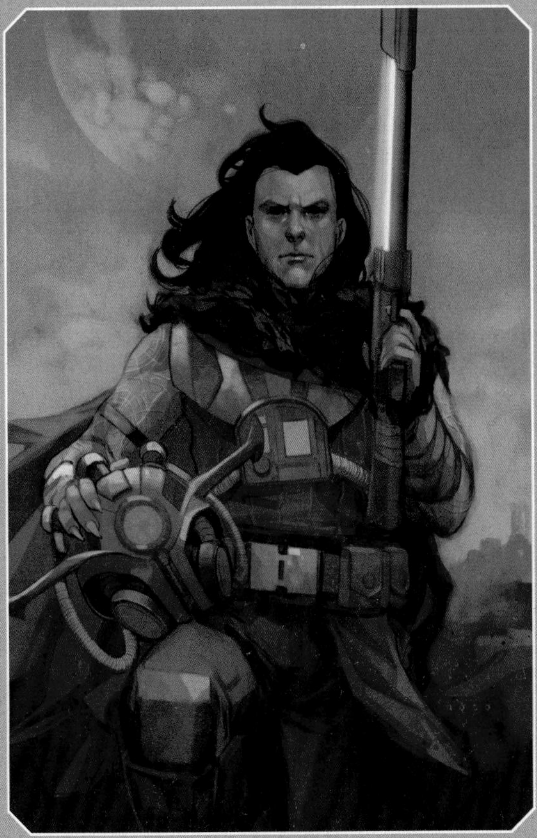

Eye of the Storm #2 Variant by
PHIL NOTO

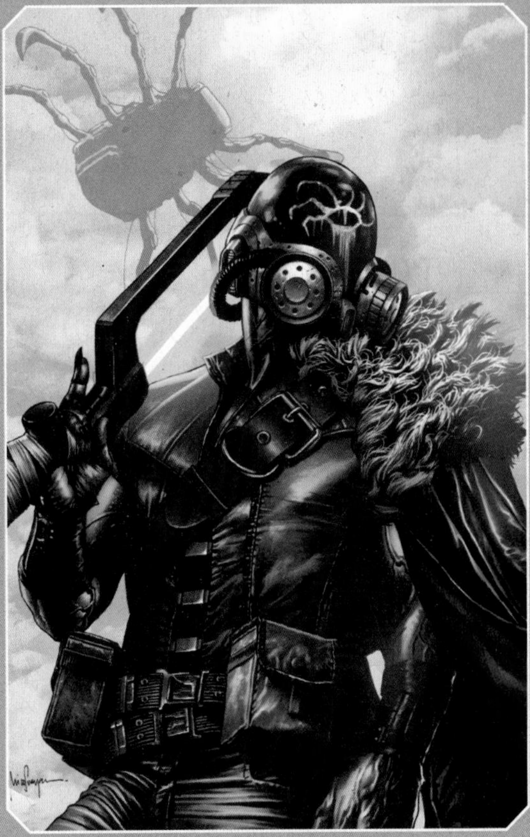

Eye of the Storm #2 Variant by
MICO SUAYAN

WANT TO KNOW THE BEST WAY TO EXPLORE THE MARVEL *STAR WARS* UNIVERSE?

THIS GUIDE WILL SHOW YOU WHERE TO BEGIN!

FOLLOW THE ADVENTURES OF LUKE, HAN AND LEIA IN THESE

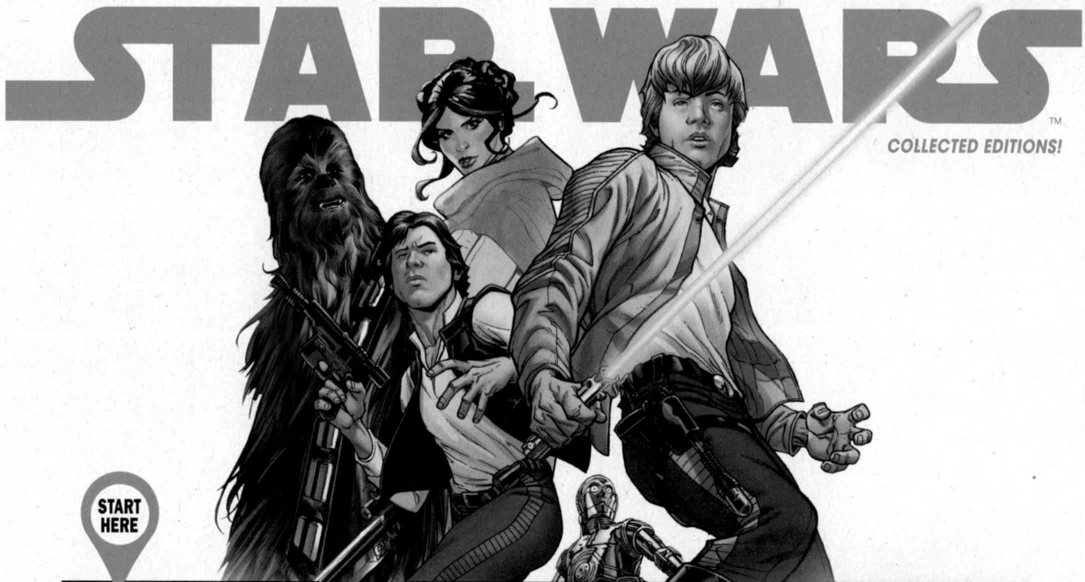

STAR WARS™
COLLECTED EDITIONS!

START HERE

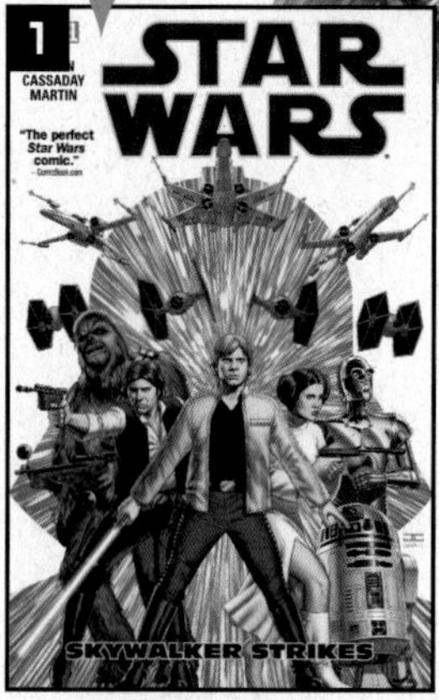

1
CASSADAY
MARTIN
STAR WARS
"The perfect Star Wars comic."
SKYWALKER STRIKES

Star Wars Vol. 1:
Skywalker Strikes

ISBN 978-0-7851-9213-8

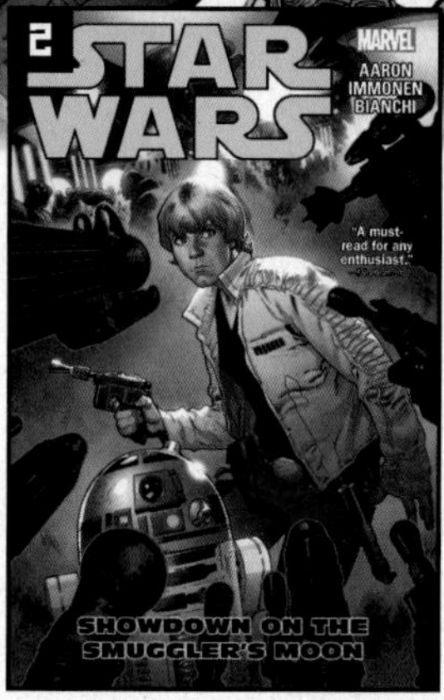

2
STAR WARS
MARVEL
AARON
IMMONEN
BIANCHI
"A must-read for any enthusiast."
SHOWDOWN ON THE SMUGGLER'S MOON

Star Wars Vol. 2:
Showdown on the Smuggler's Moon

ISBN 978-0-7851-9214-5

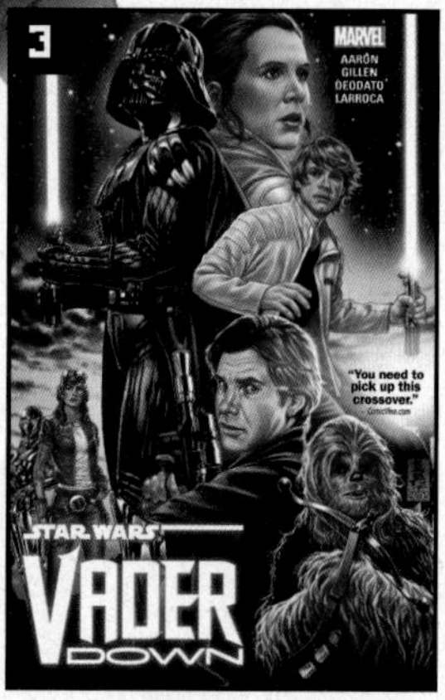

3
MARVEL
AARON
GILLEN
DEODATO
LARROCA
"You need to pick up this crossover."
STAR WARS
VADER DOWN

Star Wars:
Vader Down

ISBN 978-0-7851-9789-8

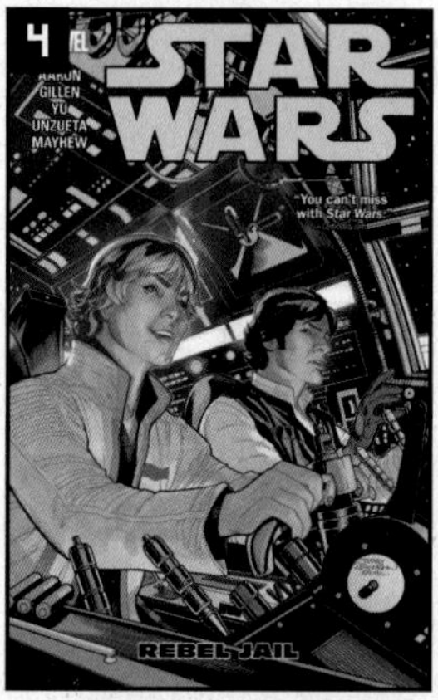

4
GILLEN
YU
UNZUETA
MAYHEW
STAR WARS
"You can't miss with Star Wars."
REBEL JAIL

Star Wars Vol. 3:
Rebel Jail

ISBN 978-0-7851-9983-0

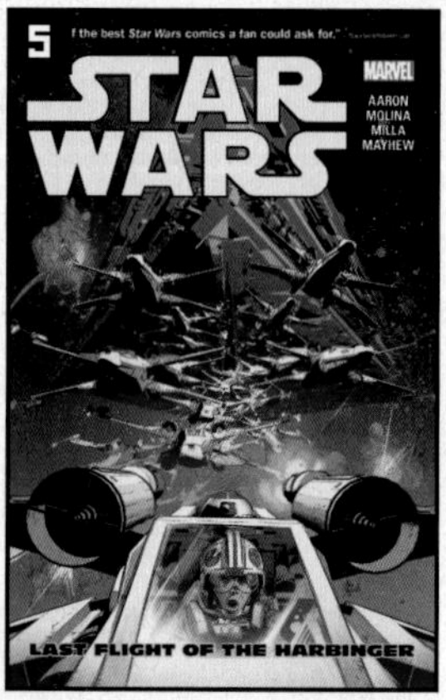

5
STAR WARS
MARVEL
AARON
MOLINA
MILLA
MAYHEW
LAST FLIGHT OF THE HARBINGER

Star Wars Vol. 4:
Last Flight of the Harbinger

ISBN 978-0-7851-9984-7

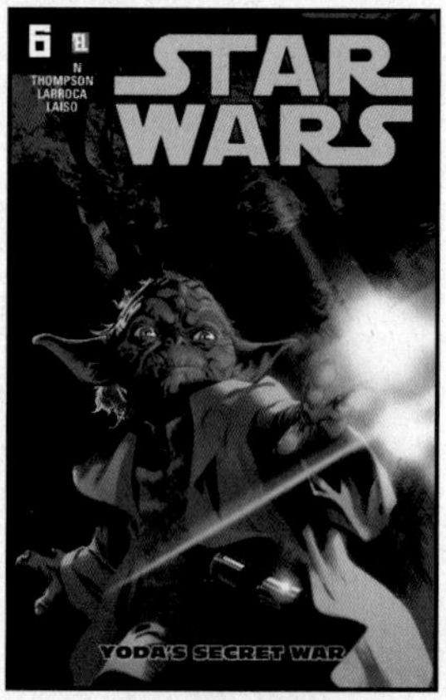

6
THOMPSON
LARROCA
LAISO
STAR WARS
YODA'S SECRET WAR

Star Wars Vol. 5:
Yoda's Secret War

ISBN 978-1-302-90265-0

7
STAR WARS
SCREAMING CITADEL
AARON
CHECCHETTO
LARROCA
BROCCARDO

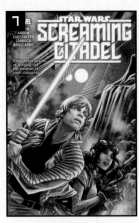

Star Wars:
The Screaming Citadel
ISBN 978-1-302-90678-8

8
STAR WARS
LATOUR
LARROCA
WALSH
OUT AMONG THE STARS

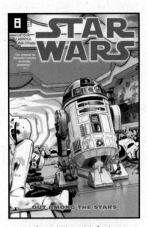

Star Wars Vol. 6:
Out Among the Stars
ISBN 978-1-302-90553-8

9
STAR WARS
LARROCA
GURU-eFX
THE ASHES OF JEDHA

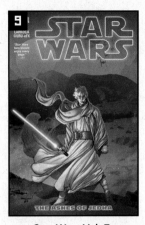

Star Wars Vol. 7:
The Ashes of Jedha
ISBN 978-1-302-91052-5

10
STAR WARS
MUTINY AT MON CALA

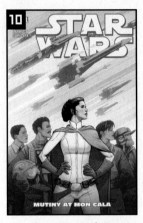

Star Wars Vol. 8:
Mutiny at Mon Cala
ISBN 978-1-302-91053-2

11
STAR WARS
MARVEL
GILLEN
LARROCA
GURU-eFX
HOPE DIES

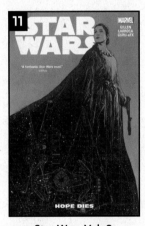

Star Wars Vol. 9:
Hope Dies
ISBN 978-1-302-91054-9

12
STAR WARS
THE ESCAPE

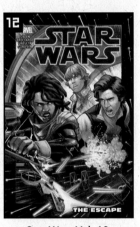

Star Wars Vol. 10:
The Escape
ISBN 978-1-302-91449-3

13
GILLEN • BROCCARDO • UNZUETA • GURU-eFX
STAR WARS
THE SCOURGING OF SHU-TORUN

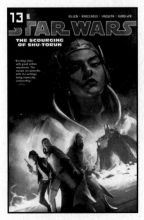

Star Wars Vol. 11:
The Scourging of Shu-Torun
ISBN 978-1-302-91450-9

14
STAR WARS
REBELS AND ROGUES

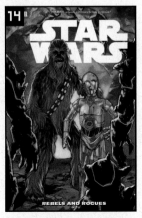

Star Wars Vol. 12:
Rebels and Rogues
ISBN 978-1-302-91451-6

15
PAK
MARVEL
NOTO
STAR WARS
ROGUES AND REBELS

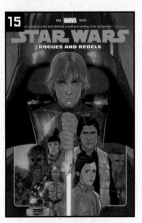

Star Wars Vol. 13:
Rogues and Rebels
ISBN 978-1-302-91450-9

STAR WARS
THE HIGH REPUBLIC

Centuries before the Skywalker saga, a new adventure begins....

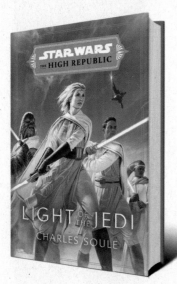

Books, Comics, ebooks, and Audiobooks Available Now!

Visit StarWars.com/TheHighRepublic for the latest news